High School Equivalency Test Pr...

SOCIAL STUDIES

Student Edition

PAXEN

PAXEN

Melbourne, Florida
www.paxen.com

Acknowledgments

For each of the selections and images listed below, grateful acknowledgment is made for permission to excerpt and/or reprint original or copyrighted material, as follows:

Text

150 Used with permission of Columbia Encyclopedia. **169** From United Nations, General Assembly, Official *Records: Eighth Session,* Supplement No. 16 (A/2505 and A/2505/Add.1 "Report of the United Nations Commission on the Racial Situation in the Union of South Africa," Annex V (New York: 1952), pp. 139–140. **172** From *Chicago Tribune,* October 17, 2004 © Chicago Tribune. **173** From *The New York Times,* October 17, 2004 © The New York Times. All rights reserved. Used by permission and protected by the Copyright Laws of the United States.

Images

(cover) Daniel Aguilera/Getty Images. **v** iStockphoto. **vi** iStockphoto. **x** Jamie Carroll/iStockphoto. **82 (left)** Used with the permission of the Franklin Delano Roosevelt Library. **82 (right)** Used with the permission of the Franklin Delano Roosevelt Library. **83 (right)** Used with permission of the University of Minnesota Libraries. **84 (left)** Used with permission of the University of Minnesota Libraries. **84 (right)** A 1930 Herblock Cartoon, © The Herb Block Foundation. **93** A 1966 Herblock Cartoon, © The Herb Block Foundation. **127** A 1999 Herblock Cartoon, © The Herb Block Foundation. **148** Copyright by Bill Mauldin (1963). Courtesy of the Bill Mauldin Estate LLC. **154** OLIPHANT © UNIVERSAL UCLICK. Reprinted with permission. All rights reserved. **162** Used with permission of David J. Frent/Political Americana. **167** Copyright by Bill Mauldin (1958). Courtesy of the Bill Mauldin Estate LLC. **168** A 1938 Herblock Cartoon, © The Herb Block Foundation. **170** Copyright by Bill Mauldin (1962). Courtesy of the Bill Mauldin Estate LLC. **184** A 1999 Herblock Cartoon, © The Herb Block Foundation. **185** Copyright by Bill Mauldin (1962). Courtesy of the Bill Mauldin Estate LLC.

ISBN: 978-1-934350-61-4

1 2 3 4 5 6 7 8 9 10   1689   20 19 18 17 16 15 14   Printed in the U.S.A.

4500508872

High School Equivalency Test Preparation

Table of Contents

About High School Equivalency Tests

Simply by turning to this page, you've made a decision that will change your life for the better. Each year, thousands of people just like you decide to pursue a high school equivalency certificate. Like you, they left school for one reason or another. And now, just like them, you've decided to continue your education by studying for and taking the high school equivalency tests.

However, these tests are no easy task. The tests, five in all, are spread across the subject areas of Language Arts/Reading, Language Arts/Writing, Mathematics, Science, and Social Studies. Preparation for the tests can involve extensive study and review. The payoff, however, is significant: more and better career options, higher earnings, and the sense of achievement that comes with a high school equivalency certificate. Employers and colleges and universities accept the certificate as they would a high school diploma. On average, certificate recipients earn $10,000 more per year than do employees without a high school diploma or an equivalency certificate.

High school equivalency tests are designed to mirror a high school curriculum. Although you will not need to know all of the information typically taught in high school, you will need to answer a variety of questions in specific subject areas. In Language Arts/Writing, you will need to write an essay.

In all cases, you will need to effectively read and follow directions, correctly interpret questions, and critically examine answer options. The table below details the five subject areas. Since different states have different requirements for the number of tests you may take in a single day, you will need to check with your local adult education center for requirements in your state or territory.

SUBJECT AREA TEST	CONTENT AREAS
Language Arts/Reading	Literary Texts Informational Texts
Language Arts/Writing (Editing)	Organization of Ideas Language Facility Writing Conventions
Language Arts/Writing (Essay)	Development and Organization of Ideas Language Facility Writing Conventions
Mathematics	Numbers and Operations on Numbers Data Analysis/Probability/Statistics Measurement/Geometry Algebraic Concepts
Science	Life Science Earth/Space Science Physical Science
Social Studies	History Civics/Government Economics Geography

Three of the subject-area tests—Language Arts/Reading, Science, and Social Studies—will require you to answer questions by interpreting passages. The Science and Social Studies tests also require you to interpret tables, charts, graphs, diagrams, timelines, political cartoons, and other visuals. In Language Arts/Reading, you also will need to answer questions based on workplace and consumer texts. The Mathematics Test will require you to use basic computation, analysis, and reasoning skills to solve a variety of word problems, many of them involving graphics. On most tests, questions will be multiple-choice with four answer options. An example follows:

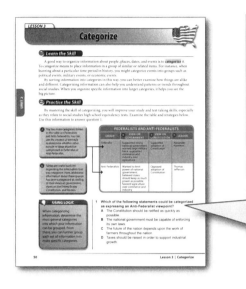

Which of the following statements could be categorized as expressing an Anti-Federalist viewpoint?

A   The Constitution should be ratified as quickly as possible.

B   The national government must be capable of enforcing its own laws.

C   The future of the nation depends upon the work of farmers throughout the nation.

D   Taxes should be raised in order to support industrial growth.

On the Mathematics Test, you will have four or five answer options for each multiple-choice question.

As the table on page iv indicates, the Language Arts/Writing Test contains two parts, one for editing and the other for essay. In the editing portion of Language Arts/Writing, you will be asked to identify and correct common errors in various passages and texts while also deciding on the most effective organization of a text. In the essay portion, you will write an essay that analyzes texts or provides an explanation or an opinion on a single topic of general knowledge.

So now that you understand the task at hand—and the benefits of a high school equivalency certificate—you must prepare for the tests. In the pages that follow, you will find a recipe of sorts that, if followed, will help guide you toward successful completion of your certificate. So turn the page. The next chapter of your life begins right now.

About *High School Equivalency Test Preparation*

Along with choosing to pursue your high school equivalency certificate, you've made another smart decision by selecting this program as your main study and preparation tool. Simply by purchasing *High School Equivalency Test Preparation,* you've joined an elite club with thousands of members, all with a common goal—earning their high school equivalency certificates. In this case, membership most definitely has its privileges.

For more than 70 years, high school equivalency tests have offered a second chance to people who need it most. To date, 17 million Americans like you have studied for and earned high school equivalency certificates and, in so doing, jump-started their lives and careers. Benefits abound for certificate holders: Recent studies have shown that people with certificates earn more money, enjoy better health, and exhibit greater interest in and understanding of the world around them than do those without.

In addition, many certificate recipients plan to further their educations, which will provide them with more and better options. As if to underscore the point, the U.S. government's Division of Occupational Employment Projections estimates that through 2022, about 3.1 million new jobs will require a bachelor's degree for entry.

Your pathway to the future—a *brighter* future—begins now, on this page, with *High School Equivalency Test Preparation.* Unlike other programs, which take months to teach through a content-based approach, *High School Equivalency Test Preparation* gets to the heart of the tests—and quickly—by emphasizing *concepts.* At their core, the majority of the tests are reading-comprehension exams. Students must be able to read and interpret excerpts, passages, and various visuals— tables, charts, graphs, timelines, and so on—and then answer questions based upon them.

High School Equivalency Test Preparation shows you the way. By emphasizing key reading and thinking concepts, *High School Equivalency Test Preparation* equips learners like you with the skills and strategies you'll need to correctly interpret and answer questions on the tests. Five-page lessons in each student book provide focused and efficient instruction, while callout boxes, sample exercises, and test-taking and other thinking strategies aid in understanding complex concepts.

Unlike other high school equivalency test preparation materials, which were designed *for* the classroom, these materials were designed *from* the classroom, using proven educational theory and cutting-cdgc classroom philosophy. For learners who have long had the deck stacked against them, the odds are finally in their favor. And yours.

HIGH SCHOOL EQUIVALENCY TESTS— FAST FACTS

- About 800,000 people take high school equivalency exams each year.
- Workers with a high school equivalency certificate earn an average of $10,000 a year more than people without a high school diploma or its equivalent.
- Over 3,000,000 students drop out of high school each year.
- Over 85% of Americans have a high school diploma or its equivalent.
- High school dropouts are not eligible for 90% of U.S. jobs.

About *High School Equivalency Test Preparation: Social Studies*

Some people who have taken a social studies high school equivalency test have been surprised by how difficult it was. While the social studies test assesses your ability to understand and interpret subject-specific text or graphics, it also requires some basic geographical and historical knowledge. On pages x–xiii, you will learn to use logic and reasoning to help you assess information and graphics on the test. You will answer questions organized across four main content areas: Geography, History, U.S. Government/Civics, and Economics. Material in *High School Equivalency Test Preparation: Social Studies* has been organized with these content areas in mind.

High School Equivalency Test Preparation: Social Studies helps deconstruct the different elements of the test by helping people like you build and develop key reading and thinking skills. A combination of targeted strategies, informational call-outs and sample questions, key geographic terms, assorted tips and hints (including Test-Taking Tips, Using Logic, and Making Assumptions), and many test-like questions help to clearly focus your efforts in needed areas, all with an eye toward the end goal: Success on high school equivalency tests. As on the science test, the social studies test uses the thinking skills of *comprehension, analysis, application,* and *evaluation.*

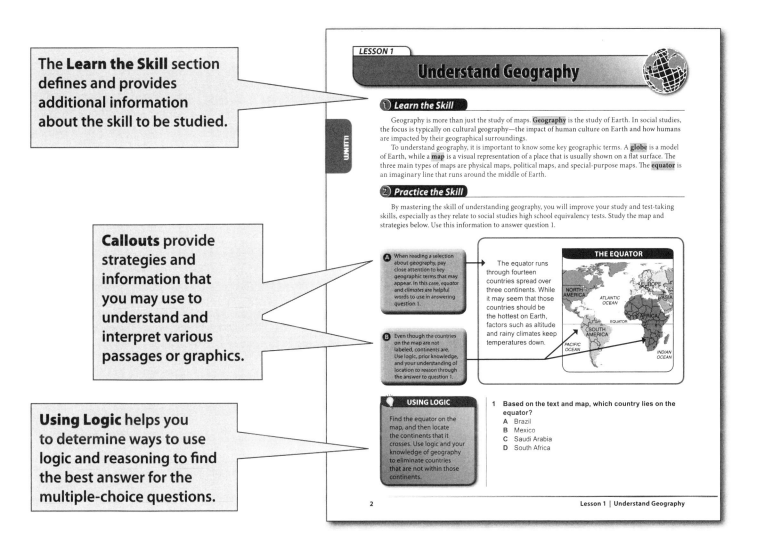

The **Learn the Skill** section defines and provides additional information about the skill to be studied.

Callouts provide strategies and information that you may use to understand and interpret various passages or graphics.

Using Logic helps you to determine ways to use logic and reasoning to find the best answer for the multiple-choice questions.

Test-Taking Tips

High school equivalency tests include questions across the five subject-area exams of Language Arts/Reading, Language Arts/Writing, Mathematics, Science, and Social Studies. In each test, you will need to apply some amount of subject-area knowledge. However, because all of the questions are multiple-choice items largely based on text or visuals (such as tables, charts, or graphs), the emphasis in *High School Equivalency Test Preparation* is on helping learners like you build and develop core reading and thinking skills. As part of the overall strategy, various test-taking tips are included below and throughout the book to help you improve your performance on the tests. For example:

◆ *Always thoroughly read the directions so that you know exactly what to do.* For example, on many tests direction lines explicitly state which questions are to be answered using information in a passage, visual, map, or chart. Pay attention to these directions in order to make sure you are correctly matching up these test elements.

◆ *Read each question carefully so that you fully understand what it is asking.* Some questions, for example, may present more information than you need to correctly answer them.

◆ *Manage your time with each question.* Because the tests are timed exams, you'll want to spend enough time with each question, but not *too* much time. You can save time by first reading each question and its answer options before reading the passage or examining the graphic. Once you understand what the question is asking, review the passage or visual for the appropriate information.

◆ *Note any unfamiliar words in questions.* First, attempt to reread the question by omitting the unfamiliar word(s). Next, try to substitute another word in its place.

◆ *Answer all questions, regardless of whether you know the answer or are guessing at it.* There is no benefit in leaving questions unanswered. Keep in mind the time that you have for each test and manage it accordingly. For time purposes, you may decide to initially skip one or more questions. However, note each with a light mark beside the question and try to return to it before the end of the test.

◆ *Narrow answer options by rereading each question and the text or graphic that goes with it.* Although all answer choices are *possible*, keep in mind that only one of them is *correct*. You may be able to eliminate one or two answers immediately; others may take more time and involve the use of either logic or assumptions. In some cases, you may need to make your best guess between two options. If so, keep in mind that test makers often avoid answer patterns; that is, if you know the previous answer is **B** and are unsure of the answer to the next question but have narrowed it to options **B** and **D**, you may want to choose **D**.

◆ *Read all answer choices.* Even though the first or second answer choice may appear to be correct, be sure to thoroughly read all answer choices. Then go with your instinct when answering questions. For example, if your first instinct is to mark **A** in response to a question, it's best to stick with that answer unless you later determine that answer to be incorrect. Usually, the first answer you choose is the correct one.

◆ *Correctly complete your answer sheet by marking one lettered space on the answer sheet beside the number that corresponds to it.* Mark only one answer for each item; multiple answers will be scored as incorrect. If time permits, double-check your answer sheet after completing the test to ensure that you have made as many marks—no more, no less—as there are questions.

Y ou've already made two very smart decisions in trying to earn your high school equivalency certificate and in purchasing *High School Equivalency Test Preparation* to help you to do so. The following are additional strategies to help you optimize your success on the tests.

3 weeks out ...

- ◆ Set a study schedule. Choose times in which you are most alert, and places, such as a library, that provide the best study environment.
- ◆ Thoroughly review all material in *High School Equivalency Test Preparation.*
- ◆ Make sure that you have the necessary tools for the job: sharpened pencils, pens, paper, and, for mathematics, a calculator.
- ◆ Keep notebooks for each of the subject areas that you are studying. Folders with pockets are useful for storing loose papers.
- ◆ When taking notes, restate thoughts or ideas in your own words rather than copying them directly from a book. You can phrase these notes as complete sentences, as questions (with answers), or as fragments, provided you understand them.

1 week out ...

- ◆ Take the pretests, noting any troublesome subject areas. Focus your remaining study around those subject areas.
- ◆ Prepare the items you will need for the test day: admission ticket (if necessary), acceptable form of identification, some sharpened No. 2 pencils (with erasers), a watch, eyeglasses (if necessary), a sweater or jacket, and a high-protein snack to eat during breaks.
- ◆ Map out the course to the test center, and visit it a day or two before your scheduled exam. If you drive, find a place to park at the center.
- ◆ Get a good night's sleep the night before the tests. Studies have shown that learners with sufficient rest perform better in testing situations.

The day of ...

- ◆ Eat a hearty breakfast high in protein. As with the rest of your body, your brain needs ample energy to perform well.
- ◆ Arrive 30 minutes early to the testing center. This will allow sufficient time in the event of a change to a different testing classroom.
- ◆ Pack a sizeable lunch, especially if you plan to be at the testing center most of the day.
- ◆ Focus and relax. You've come this far, spending weeks preparing and studying for the tests. It's your time to shine.

Before You Begin: Using Logic and Making Assumptions

At several hours in length, the high school equivalency tests are to testing what marathons are to running. Just like marathons, though, you may train for success on the tests. As you know, the exams test your ability to interpret and answer questions about various passages and visual elements. Your ability to answer such questions involves the development and use of core reading and thinking skills. Chief among these are the skills of reasoning, logic, and assumptions. **Reasoning** involves the ability to explain and describe ideas. **Logic** is the science of correct reasoning. Together, reasoning and logic guide our ability to make and understand assumptions. An **assumption** is an idea that we know to be true and which we use to understand the world around us.

You use logic and make assumptions every day, sometimes without even knowing that you're doing so. For example, you might go to bed one night knowing that your car outside is dry; you might awaken the next morning to discover that your car is wet. In that example, it would be *reasonable* for you to *assume* that your car is wet because it rained overnight. Even though you did not see it rain, it is the most *logical* explanation for the change in the car's appearance.

When thinking logically about items on the tests, you identify the consequences, or answers, from text or visuals. Next, you determine whether the text or visuals logically and correctly support the consequences. If so, they are considered valid. If not, they are considered invalid. For example, read the following text and determine whether it is valid or invalid:

Passage A

High school equivalency tests assess a person's reading comprehension skills. Ellen enjoys reading. Therefore, Ellen will do well on the tests.

Passage B

High school equivalency tests cover material in five different subject areas. Aaron has geared his studies toward the tests, and he has done well on practice tests. Therefore, Aaron may do well on the actual tests.

Each of the above situations has a consequence: *Ellen will* or *Aaron may* do well on the tests. By using reasoning and logic, you can make an assumption about which consequence is valid. In the example above, it is *un*reasonable to assume that Ellen will do well on the tests simply because she likes to read. However, it *is* reasonable to assume that Aaron may do well on the tests because he has studied for the tests and has done well on the practice tests in each of the five subject areas.

Use the same basic principles of reasoning, logic, and assumptions to determine which answer option logically and correctly supports a question on the science test. You may find occasions in which you have narrowed the field of possible correct answers to two, from which you must make a best, educated guess. In such cases, weigh both options and determine the one that, reasonably, makes the most sense.

You can apply these same skills when analyzing the questions on social studies high school equivalency tests. Use the sample question, annotated responses, and callouts below to begin developing your logic and reasoning skills. On the pages that follow, use these same strategies to analyze the questions. Remember to think about the most *reasonable* and *logical* conclusions or consequences before making any *assumptions*.

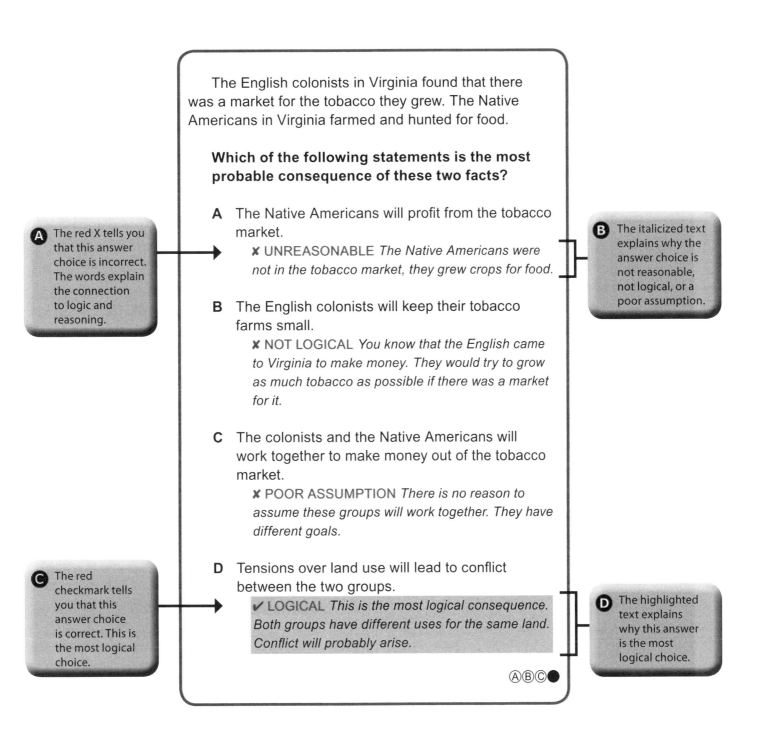

The English colonists in Virginia found that there was a market for the tobacco they grew. The Native Americans in Virginia farmed and hunted for food.

Which of the following statements is the most probable consequence of these two facts?

A The Native Americans will profit from the tobacco market.

A The red X tells you that this answer choice is incorrect. The words explain the connection to logic and reasoning.

✗ UNREASONABLE *The Native Americans were not in the tobacco market, they grew crops for food.*

B The italicized text explains why the answer choice is not reasonable, not logical, or a poor assumption.

B The English colonists will keep their tobacco farms small.

✗ NOT LOGICAL *You know that the English came to Virginia to make money. They would try to grow as much tobacco as possible if there was a market for it.*

C The colonists and the Native Americans will work together to make money out of the tobacco market.

✗ POOR ASSUMPTION *There is no reason to assume these groups will work together. They have different goals.*

C The red checkmark tells you that this answer choice is correct. This is the most logical choice.

D Tensions over land use will lead to conflict between the two groups.

✔ LOGICAL *This is the most logical consequence. Both groups have different uses for the same land. Conflict will probably arise.*

D The highlighted text explains why this answer is the most logical choice.

Ⓐ Ⓑ Ⓒ ●

These additional sample questions will assess your understanding of logic, reasoning, and assumptions. If you need help, annotated answers are located at the bottom of the page. You will have many more opportunities to answer questions using logic, reasoning, and assumptions throughout this book.

Directions: Question 1 refers to the following information.

In the 1790s, many Americans settled in the areas immediately west of the Appalachian Mountains.

[HINT: The date provides a clue. Locations are also helpful. Remember that the Appalachian Mountains run from western New York and Pennsylvania down into South Carolina.]

1 What event caused this growth in settlement?
   A the French and Indian War
   B the Proclamation of 1763
   C the American Revolution
   D the Louisiana Purchase

Ⓐ Ⓑ Ⓒ Ⓓ

Directions: Question 2 refers to the following map.

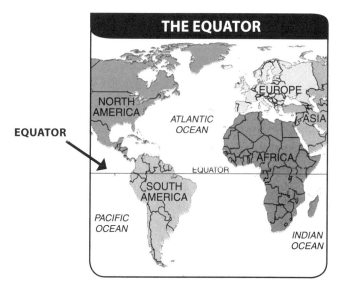

2 Which country is on the equator?
   [HINT: This question asks about a country, not a continent. The countries on the map are not labeled. You will have to use logic to find the answer]
   A the United States
   B China
   C Kenya
   D Cuba

Ⓐ Ⓑ Ⓒ Ⓓ

Answers

1 **A** ✗ POOR ASSUMPTION While the colonists may have thought they could settle in the area after the French and Indian War, the British forbade them. This was one of the reasons the colonists wanted independence.
B ✗ UNREASONABLE Do not be drawn in by an answer with a date. Remember that the proclamation forbid colonists from settling west of the Appalachian Mountains. Also, it was seventeen years before the settlement.
C ✔ LOGICAL The American Revolution ended in 1783. The Americans gained the territory west of the Appalachians from the British and opened the area to settlement. This event was the closest to the 1790s.
D ✗ NOT LOGICAL The Louisiana Purchase included land west of the Mississippi River, not the Appalachian Mountains. The purchase was not made until 1803.

2 **A** ✗ UNREASONABLE The United States is in North America. The equator does not cross North America.
B ✗ NOT LOGICAL China is in Asia. While the equator does cross parts of Asia, China is probably too far north. Also, China is not shown on this map.
C ✔ LOGICAL Kenya is in Africa. The equator crosses several African countries. Kenya is the only African country that is a choice. It is the most logical answer.
D ✗ UNREASONABLE Cuba is an island off the coast of Florida. Looking at the map, the islands near Florida are not on the equator.

Britain and France lost over 2.5 million men during World War I.

3   **How might this loss of life explain their relationship with Hitler's Germany in the 1930s?**

[HINT: Think about how Britain and France first reacted when Hitler used aggressive tactics to take over other European countries before World War II.]

The British and the French

A   declared war immediately when Hitler was elected chancellor of Germany.

B   did not want to have another costly war, so they appeased Hitler.

C   felt guilty that they were not more punitive towards Germany after World War I.

D   began a massive military build-up and eagerly waited for another war.

ⒶⒷⒸⒹ

U.S. Constitution Amendment I

Congress shall make no law respecting an establishment of religion, or prohibiting the free exercise thereof; or abridging the freedom of speech, or of the press; or the right of the people peaceably to assemble, and to petition the government for a redress of grievances.

4   **Which of the following would be a violation of the First Amendment?**

[HINT: This question is asking for a "violation" of the amendment, so look for an act that the amendment forbids.]

A   Congress declares Protestantism the official religion of the United States

B   college student protestors hold a peaceful rally

C   Catholics hold mass in St. Patrick Catholic Church in Washington, D.C.

D   a newspaper reporter writes a negative article about the president

ⒶⒷⒸⒹ

Answers

3   **A ✘ UNREASONABLE** Hitler was elected chancellor in 1932. World War II began in 1939.
B ✔ LOGICAL/BEST ASSUMPTION Both France and Britain were still recovering from the effects of World War I. They were anxious to do whatever it took to prevent another war, so they allowed Hitler to take over some countries.
C ✘ NOT LOGICAL Hitler's rise to power can be connected with the allies' punitive treatment of Germany after World War I. It was a cause of World War II.
D ✘ UNREASONABLE The French and British were not eager for a war. They did not have the money for a massive military build-up.

4   **A ✔ LOGICAL** This would be passing a law respecting an establishment of religion, which is expressly forbidden in the amendment.
B ✘ NOT LOGICAL Peaceable assembly is protected by the amendment.
C ✘ POOR ASSUMPTION Just because the church is in Washington, D.C., does not mean that it is an agent of the government. Free exercise of religion is protected.
D ✘ NOT LOGICAL Freedom of the press (newspapers, television, other media) is protected by the amendment.

MAP OF THE UNITED STATES

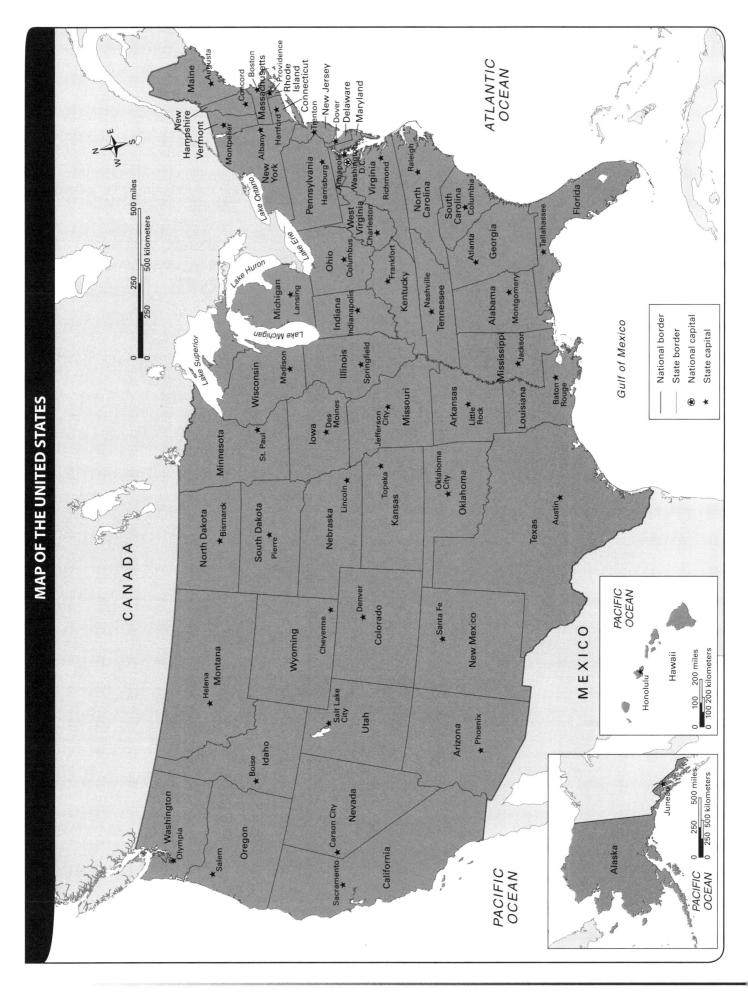

Map of the United States | Social Studies Student Book

MAP OF THE WESTERN HEMISPHERE

GREENLAND (DENMARK)

CANADA

Hudson Bay

Labrador Sea

Great Lakes

UNITED STATES

ATLANTIC OCEAN

Gulf of Mexico

MEXICO

CUBA

HAITI

DOMINICAN REPUBLIC

U.S. VIRGIN ISLANDS

BELIZE

JAMAICA

HONDURAS

ST. KITTS AND NEVIS

ST. LUCIA

GUATEMALA

BARBADOS

EL SALVADOR

NICARAGUA

GRENADA

COSTA RICA

VENEZUELA

GUYANA

SURINAME

PANAMA

COLOMBIA

FRENCH GUIANA (FRANCE)

ECUADOR

PACIFIC OCEAN

PERU

BRAZIL

BOLIVIA

PARAGUAY

N
W E
S

CHILE

URUGUAY

ARGENTINA

FALKLAND ISLANDS (U.K.)

| 0 | 500 | 1,000 miles |

| 0 | 500 | 1,000 kilometers |

—— National border

ANTARCTICA

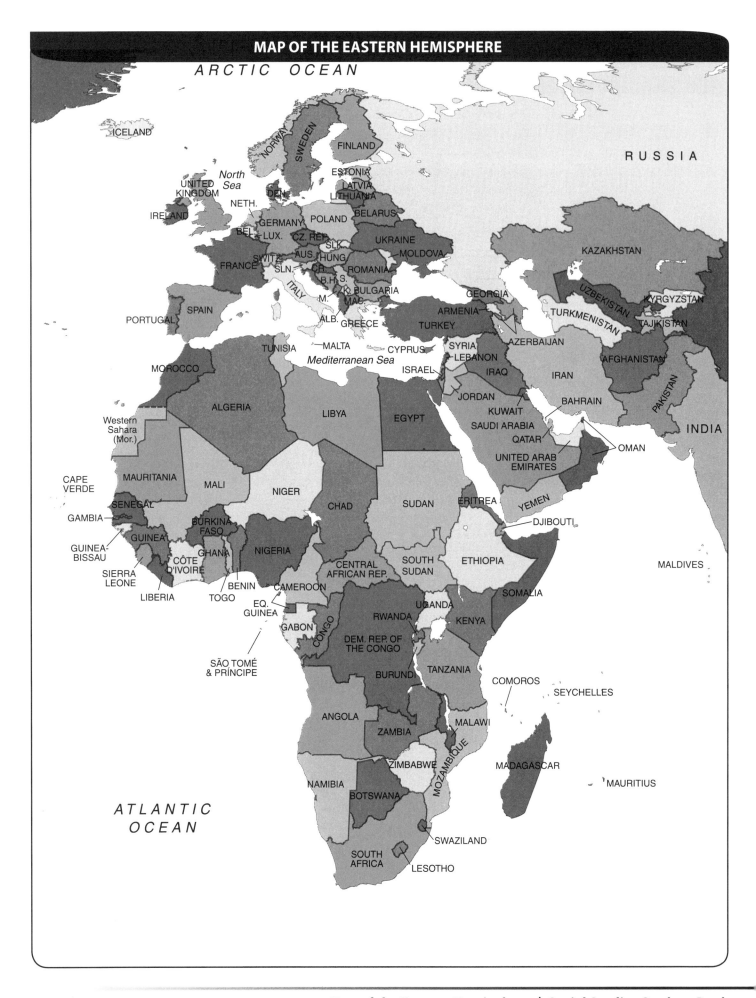

ARCTIC OCEAN

Abbreviations

ALB.	ALBANIA
AUS.	AUSTRIA
BEL.	BELGIUM
B.H.	BOSNIA AND HERZEGOVINA
CR.	CROATIA
CZ. REP.	CZECH REPUBLIC
DEN.	DENMARK
MAC.	MACEDONIA
HUNG.	HUNGARY
K.	KOSOVO
LUX.	LUXEMBOURG
M.	MONTENEGRO
NETH.	NETHERLANDS
S.	SERBIA
SLK.	SLOVAKIA
SLN.	SLOVENIA
SWITZ.	SWITZERLAND

MONGOLIA

N. KOREA

S. KOREA

JAPAN

CHINA

BHUTAN

NEPAL

INDIA

BANGLADESH

MYANMAR (BURMA)

LAOS

VIETNAM

THAILAND

CAMBODIA

TAIWAN

PACIFIC OCEAN

PHILIPPINES

SRI LANKA

BRUNEI

MALAYSIA

SINGAPORE

INDONESIA

MARSHALL IS.

PALAU

FEDERATED STATES OF MICRONESIA

NAURU

PAPUA NEW GUINEA

SOLOMON IS.

INDIAN OCEAN

EAST TIMOR

VANUATU

FIJI

N
W E
S

— National border

AUSTRALIA

| 0 | 500 | 1,000 miles |
| 0 | 500 | 1,000 kilometers |

NEW ZEALAND

Unit 1

Unit Overview

Geography shapes the world in which we live. Throughout history, geographic features have influenced important aspects of people's lives. Regions throughout the world have natural geographic barriers such as mountains, oceans, and rivers, and have thus been separated by cultural, economic, and language differences. The world today, however, is becoming a smaller place. Technologies such as various forms of satellite and wireless communications have enabled people to bridge geographic barriers and study and experience other cultures. Geography plays a major role in discovering your place in today's ever-changing world.

Similarly, geography plays a vital role in social studies high school equivalency tests, comprising approximately 15 percent of all questions. As with other areas of the social studies test, geography questions will test your ability to interpret various types of maps and to answer questions about them through the use of thinking skills such as comprehension, application, analysis, and evaluation. In Unit 1, the introduction of essential map-reading and analysis skills will help you prepare for these tests. For extra support, maps of the United States, the Western Hemisphere, and the Eastern Hemisphere are located on pages xiv–xvii in the frontmatter.

Table of Contents

Geography

absolute location: the position of a place on Earth according to coordinates of longitude and latitude

altitude: the height of a point in relation to sea level or ground level

capital city: the city that is the administrative center and seat of governance in a country or region

climate: the prevailing weather patterns in an area over a long period

compass rose: a symbol on a globe or a map used to indicate north, south, east, and west

continent: the world's main continuous expanses of land (Africa, Antarctica, Asia, Australia, Europe, North America, South America)

county: a territorial and local administrative division within a state; sometimes called a parish

cultural geography: the study of the patterns and interactions of people in relation to the place where they live

culture: the beliefs, customs, arts, and habits of the people in a particular group or society

elevation: the height above sea level of a point on land

equator: an imaginary line that runs around the middle of Earth, separating it into the Northern and Southern Hemispheres

geography: the study of the physical features of Earth

globe: a spherical model of Earth

hemisphere: half of Earth, as divided north-to-south by the equator or west-to-east by an imaginary plane passing through the poles

key: an area on a globe or a map that explains the meanings of colors and symbols

lines of latitude: imaginary, horizontal lines on Earth that run parallel to the equator and indicate north-south position between the poles

lines of longitude: imaginary lines on Earth running north-south in equal distances from one another and indicating east-west position

map: a visual representation of a place, usually shown on a flat surface

migrate: to move from one country or place in order to live or work in another place

natural border: a boundary between two locations that is formed by a natural feature such as a river, mountain range, or desert

peninsula: a piece of land that protrudes from a larger land area and is almost entirely surrounded by water

physical map: a map that shows land and water features of an area, such as mountains, plains, rivers, gulfs, and oceans, as well as climate and elevation

political border: an imaginary line separating places with different governing bodies

political map: a map that shows how people have divided Earth's area into identified regions, countries, states, counties, cities, and towns

population: the number of people living in a particular geographic place, such as a city or country

population density: a measurement of population per unit area, such as the number of people per square mile

precipitation: rain, snow, sleet, or hail that falls to the ground

relative location: the position of a point in relation to another point

scale: a map component that shows the ratio of distance on the map to the corresponding distance on Earth

special-purpose map: a map—such a tourist map, battle site map, product map, or congressional district map—used to convey information other than physical features or political borders

symbols: dots, stars, lines, arrows, or icons explained in a key and shown on a globe or map to indicate cities, capitals, movement, battles, or other data

trade route: a series of land or sea pathways used for the commercial transport of goods by merchants

Understand Geography

① Learn the Skill

Geography is more than just the study of maps. **Geography** is the study of Earth. In social studies, the focus is typically on cultural geography—the impact of human culture on Earth and how humans are impacted by their geographical surroundings.

To understand geography, it is important to know some key geographic terms. A **globe** is a model of Earth, while a **map** is a visual representation of a place that is usually shown on a flat surface. The three main types of maps are physical maps, political maps, and special-purpose maps. The **equator** is an imaginary line that runs around the middle of Earth.

② Practice the Skill

By mastering the skill of understanding geography, you will improve your study and test-taking skills, especially as they relate to social studies high school equivalency tests. Study the map and strategies below. Use this information to answer question 1.

A When reading a selection about geography, pay close attention to key geographic terms that may appear. In this case, *equator* and *climates* are helpful words to use in answering question 1.

The equator runs through fourteen countries spread over three continents. While it may seem that those countries should be the hottest on Earth, factors such as altitude and rainy climates keep temperatures down.

B Even though the countries on the map are not labeled, continents are. Use logic, prior knowledge, and your understanding of location to reason through the answer to question 1.

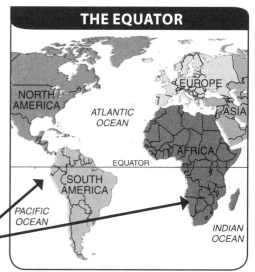

USING LOGIC

Find the equator on the map, and then locate the continents that it crosses. Use logic and your knowledge of geography to eliminate countries that are not within those continents.

1 Based on the text and map, which country lies on the equator?

   A Brazil

   B Mexico

   C Saudi Arabia

   D South Africa

Directions: Questions 2 through 5 are based on the map and information below.

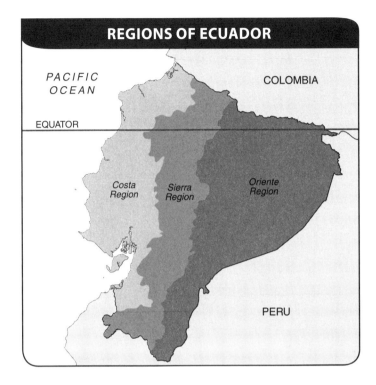

REGIONS OF ECUADOR

Ecuador is located along the equator on the western coast of South America. Ecuador has four geographic regions: the Costa, the Sierra, the Oriente, and the Galápagos Islands. The Costa runs between the coast and the Andes Mountains. The Sierra includes the Andes Mountains, and the Oriente to the east includes part of the Amazon rainforest. The Galápagos Islands, which are not shown on the map, lie west of the mainland along the equator.

Most of the population of Ecuador lives in the Costa and Sierra regions. Many people migrated to the Costa region in the 1950s when banana production increased in that area. The Sierra experienced a similar population boom when oil was discovered in that region in the 1970s.

2 Based on the map and the information, why does Ecuador have different climates?
  A Ecuador is on the equator.
  B Most people live near the cities.
  C Ecuador has several types of geographic features.
  D The geography is the same throughout the country.

3 Ecuadorians might have migrated to the Costa region in the 1950s because
  A they wanted to live in the Amazon.
  B they could find jobs in the oil industry.
  C the increase in banana production provided jobs.
  D tourism jobs were available in the rainforest.

4 Which statement best describes the Sierra region?
  A It is located along the eastern border of Ecuador.
  B It is located along the west coast of Ecuador.
  C Banana production caused a population boom.
  D It features the Andes Mountains.

5 Which two of Ecuador's geographic regions have an ocean border?
  A the Costa and Sierra regions
  B the Costa region and the Galápagos Islands
  C the Galápagos Islands and the Oriente region
  D the Sierra and Oriente regions

Directions: Questions 6 and 7 refer to the map and information below.

Directions: Questions 8 and 9 refer to the map and information below.

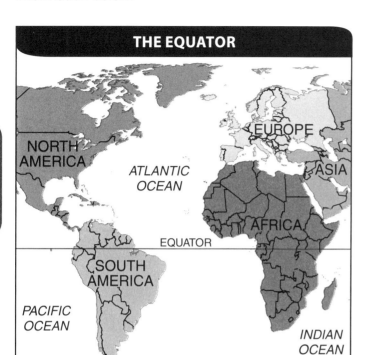

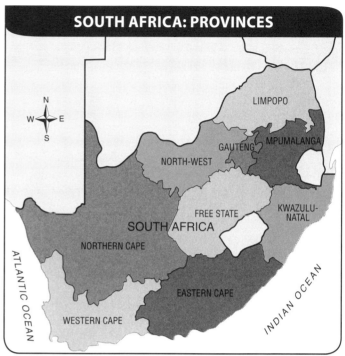

The equator runs through fourteen different countries. It is located, geographically, in the center of world maps. The equator divides Earth into the Northern and Southern hemispheres.

6   Which of the following countries is located north of the equator?
  A   South Africa
  B   Australia
  C   Egypt
  D   Chile

7   Which of the following countries is in the Southern Hemisphere?
  A   Argentina
  B   the United States
  C   Switzerland
  D   Libya

South Africa has a population of approximately 51 million people. There are several national parks in South Africa, including Kruger National Park in the Limpopo and Mpumalanga regions.

Mining in the interior plateau, which yields gold, diamonds, and coal, has sustained the economy of South Africa for decades. In the 1800s, South Africa was a target for British, Dutch, and German imperialist expansion.

8   Where is the Kruger National Park located?
  A   in the northeast
  B   in the southeast
  C   in the northwest
  D   in the southwest

9   What most likely attracted European imperialists to South Africa?
  A   national parks
  B   coastlines
  C   plateaus
  D   gold

Directions: Questions 10 through 13 refer to the map and information below.

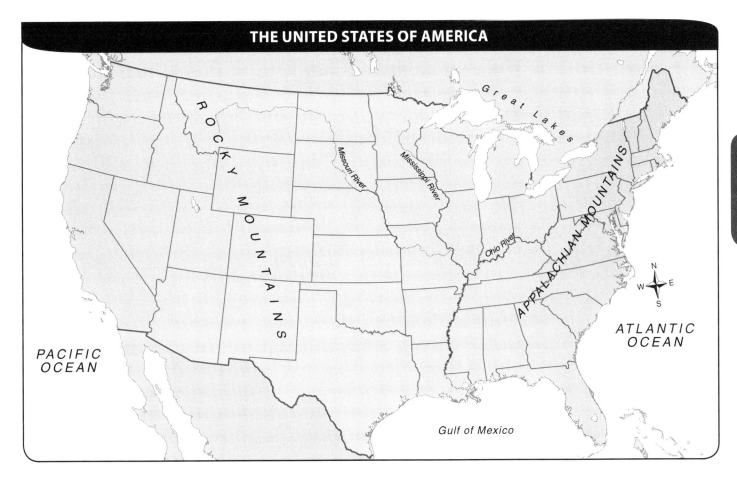

THE UNITED STATES OF AMERICA

Oceans, lakes, rivers, and mountain ranges are natural geographic features. Such features might have aided or hindered the settlement of or transportation through what is now the United States by newcomers wishing to make their homes in this country. The country was settled from the outside in, meaning the coastal areas were settled before the interior.

10 **Which natural features are located in the western region?**
  A   the Great Lakes and the Pacific Ocean
  B   the Atlantic Ocean and the Mississippi River
  C   the Rocky Mountains and the Great Lakes
  D   the Pacific Ocean and the Rocky Mountains

11 **Based on the map and the paragraph, which state was probably settled by Europeans first?**
  A   Kentucky
  B   Wyoming
  C   North Carolina
  D   Illinois

12 **What might have aided settlement of the Midwest region?**
  A   the Rocky Mountains
  B   the Appalachian Mountains
  C   the Ohio River
  D   the Pacific Ocean

13 **Which natural geographic feature probably hindered settlers moving from the Midwest to the West Coast?**
  A   The Mississippi River
  B   The Rocky Mountains
  C   The Gulf of Mexico
  D   The Appalachian Mountains

Directions: Questions 14 through 16 are based on the following map and information.

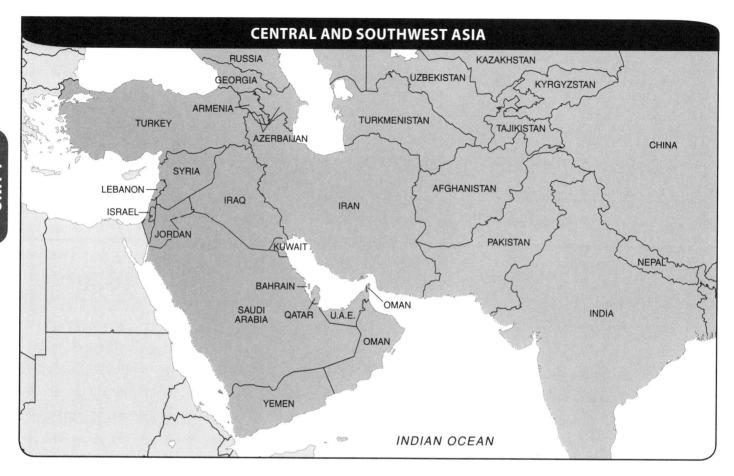

CENTRAL AND SOUTHWEST ASIA

Asia is the largest continent on Earth. It stretches from Russia in the north, to India in the south, to the islands of Japan and Indonesia in the east. The Middle East region is located in central and southwest Asia. The term "Middle East" originated with early European exploration, which divided Asia into the Near East, the Middle East, and the Far East.

14 Based on the map and paragraph, which of the following countries is in the Middle East?
A   China
B   Saudi Arabia
C   Russia
D   Japan

15 Which country was probably considered to be in the Far East?
A   China
B   Turkey
C   Pakistan
D   Egypt

16 Based on the map and information, which of the following statements about Asia is accurate?
A   Asia has a shared culture.
B   Asia borders the Indian and Atlantic Oceans.
C   Asia includes part of Africa.
D   Asia has a diverse climate.

Understand Map Components

① Learn the Skill

When you begin to analyze maps, you must first **understand map components.** Maps often include the following components: 1. **Scales** have small marks that stand for miles and kilometers. Scales help measure real distances on Earth. 2. **Lines of longitude** and **lines of latitude** are used to find exact, or absolute, locations of places. Lines of longitude run north-south, while lines of latitude run east-west. Relative location describes the position of a place in relation to other places. 3. **Symbols** such as dots for cities, stars for capital cities, or icons for special events, such as battles, can help you understand details on a map. Symbols are explained in the **map key.** Different types of maps use different symbols. Map titles, compass roses, and labels are also useful tools on a map.

② Practice the Skill

By mastering the skill of understanding map components, you will improve your study and test-taking skills, especially as they relate to social studies high school equivalency tests. Analyze the map below. Use this information to answer question 1.

A When you start to analyze a map, examine all of the components, such as the title and key. This will help you determine the purpose of the map.

B Use the scale to measure distances between cities.

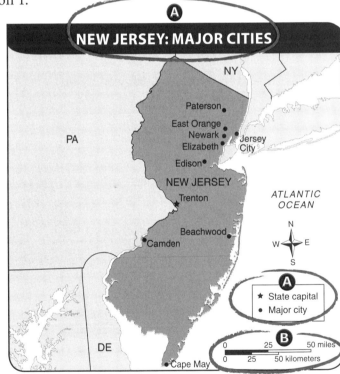

A NEW JERSEY: MAJOR CITIES

A
★ State capital
• Major city

B
0   25   50 miles
0   25   50 kilometers

USING LOGIC

A compass rose is a multipurpose map symbol. It can help you find in what direction a city is located. It can also help you make generalizations about the relative locations of places.

1   **Which area of New Jersey has the most major cities?**
A   northwest
B   west
C   south
D   northeast

Directions: Questions 2 and 3 refer to the following map.

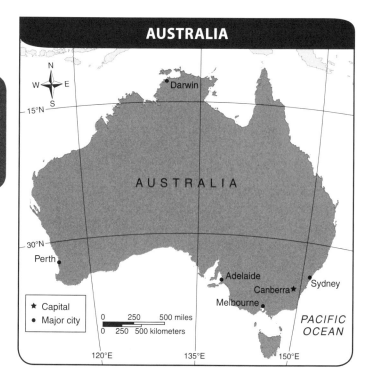

Directions: Questions 4 through 6 refer to the following map.

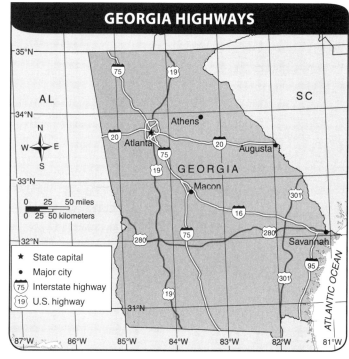

2   **Based on the map, which statement about Sydney is accurate?**
   A   Sydney is the capital of Australia.
   B   Sydney is located on the west coast of Australia.
   C   Sydney is east of 150°E longitude.
   D   Sydney is north of 30°N latitude.

3   **Based on the map, what can you assume about Australia?**
   A   Most of the cities are located west of 120°E.
   B   Most of the cities are located north of 15°N.
   C   Most of the cities are located south of 30°N.
   D   Most of the cities are located between 0 and 15°N.

4   **Which interstate highway goes through Georgia's capital?**
   A   19
   B   75
   C   95
   D   280

5   **Which city is near state highway 280 and interstate highway 16?**
   A   Athens
   B   Augusta
   C   Macon
   D   Savannah

6   **Which city's absolute location is closest to 81°W, 32°N?**
   A   Athens
   B   Augusta
   C   Macon
   D   Savannah

Directions: Questions 7 through 10 refer to the following map.

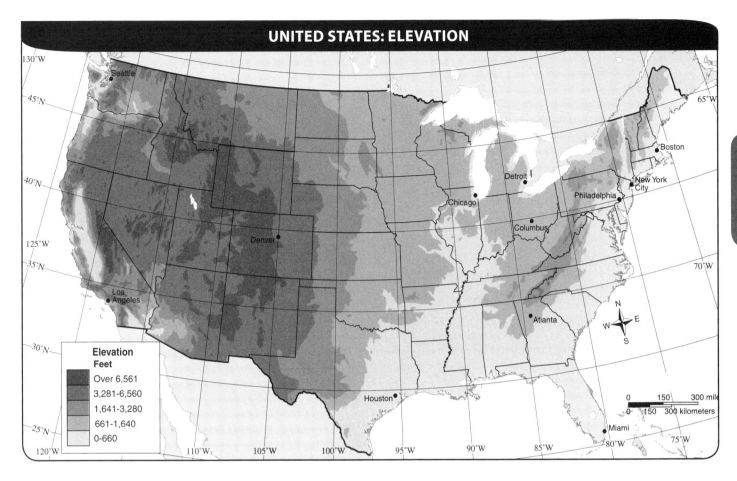

UNITED STATES: ELEVATION

7 **What is the distance between two cities in the southeast with an elevation that ranges from 0 to 1,600 feet?**

A 625 miles
B 900 miles
C 1,275 miles
D 1,500 miles

8 **Based on the map, which state would most likely have one of the highest points in the nation?**

A Oregon
B Colorado
C Texas
D Maine

9 **Which city is located between 35° to 30°N and 85° to 80° W?**

A Philadelphia
B Columbus
C Atlanta
D Miami

10 **Based on the map, what is the relative location of Detroit?**

A north of Columbus
B south of Atlanta
C 45°N, 80°W
D 40°N, 90°W

UNIT 1

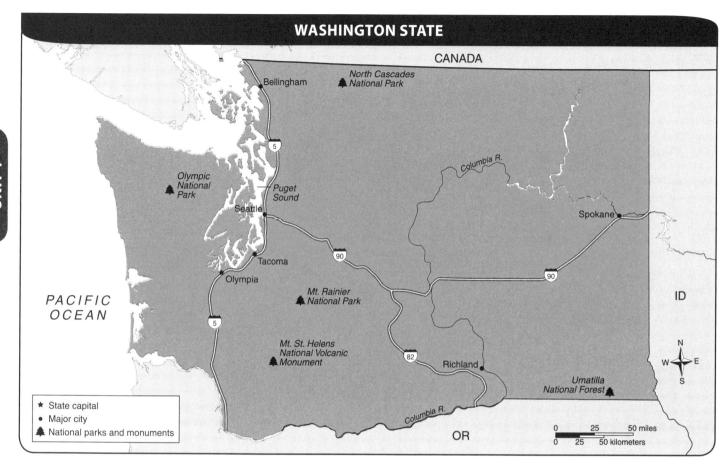

11 **Which national park is closest to the capital?**
 A Olympic National Park
 B Mt. Rainier National Park
 C Mt. St. Helens National Volcanic Monument
 D North Cascades National Park

12 **Based on the map, which of the following statements is accurate?**
 A I-90 connects Spokane and Richland
 B I-90 runs north to south
 C I-5 connects 4 major cities
 D I-82 merges with I-5

13 **Based on the information in the map, which of the following best describes Washington State?**
 A Washington State is most populated in the west.
 B Washington State is mostly urban and industrial.
 C Washington State borders Canada and California.
 D Washington State features few natural areas.

14 **Why might Puget Sound be an important waterway?**
 A Puget Sound is close to all of the National Parks.
 B Puget Sound is the source of the Columbia River.
 C Puget Sound extends into Oregon.
 D Puget Sound connects major cities to the Pacific Ocean.

Directions: Questions 15 through 17 refer to the following information.

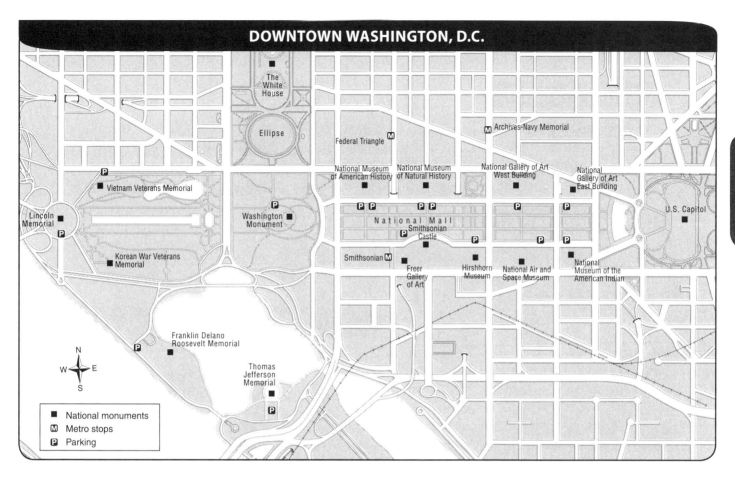

DOWNTOWN WASHINGTON, D.C.

- ■ National monuments
- Ⓜ Metro stops
- Ⓟ Parking

Each year close to 20 million people visit the United States' capital, Washington, D.C. Most of the main government buildings and national monuments are located in one area of the city. Visitors can walk, ride on a tour bus, or take the Metro, the city's subway system, to visit these sites. Although some attractions, such as the White House tour, require advance tickets, all government buildings, including the White House and the National Archives, as well as all monuments, memorials, and Smithsonian museums, are free. They are supported by and belong to the American taxpayers.

15 **Where is most of the parking located?**
   A near the White House
   B near the Vietnam Veterans Memorial
   C by the U.S. Capitol
   D near the Smithsonian museums

16 **Of those shown on the map, which Metro station is closest to the White House?**
   A Smithsonian
   B Federal Triangle
   C Ellipse
   D Lafayette Park

17 **Which is the most logical route for a walking tour?**
   A U.S. Capitol to National Gallery, to Washington Monument, to F.D.R. Memorial, to Jefferson Memorial
   B Lincoln Memorial to Jefferson Memorial, to Korean War Veterans Memorial, to White House, to Washington Monument
   C Vietnam Veterans Memorial to Lincoln Memorial, to White House, to U.S. Capitol, to Washington Monument
   D Washington Monument to Lincoln Memorial, to White House, to National Gallery, to Vietnam Veterans Memorial

Physical Maps

① Learn the Skill

A **physical map** shows the geographic land and water features of an area, such as mountains, plains, rivers, gulfs, and oceans. Physical maps can also show **climate** and **elevation**. Physical maps often use shading or different colors for elevation and climate, and symbols for features that can be identified using the map key. Scientists study physical maps for settlement and migration patterns.

② Practice the Skill

By mastering the skill of analyzing physical maps, you will improve your study and test-taking skills, especially as they relate to social studies high school equivalency tests. Study the map below. Use this information to answer question 1.

Ⓐ To identify a physical map, look for landforms and bodies of water such as rivers or oceans.

Ⓑ Use the map key to learn about the meaning of the shading on a map.

CALIFORNIA: PHYSICAL

CASCADE RANGE

Ⓐ

COAST RANGES

SIERRA NEVADA

PACIFIC OCEAN

SACRAMENTO VALLEY

Lake Tahoe

San Francisco Bay

Monterey Bay

San Joaquin River

SAN JOAQUIN VALLEY

CALIFORNIA

DEATH VALLEY

COAST RANGES

MOJAVE DESERT

SAN BERNADINO MTS.

Salton Sea

0   100   200 miles
0   100   200 kilometers

Ⓑ Elevation Feet
- Over 6,561
- 3,281-6,560
- 1,641-3,280
- 661-1,640
- 0-660
- Below sea level

🧩 MAKING ASSUMPTIONS

You might assume that physical maps do not show national or state boundaries, but they usually do. However, keep in mind that physical features cross over many borders.

1 **Based on the information in the map, which statement about the land in California is correct?**

   A The land is a mixture of low land, hills, and mountains.

   B The highest elevations are found along the coast.

   C The land on the coast is very low.

   D The land is mostly low with some hills.

Directions: Questions 2 and 3 refer to the map and information below.

MICHIGAN: NATURAL FEATURES

Michigan has over 11,000 lakes and ponds. Bordering the state are four of the five Great Lakes—Michigan, Huron, Erie, and Superior. Several of Michigan's more than 90 state parks are located near bodies of water, where visitors can swim, fish, and enjoy the natural beauty.

2 **Based on the passage and the map, which statement about Michigan is accurate?**
   A Michigan is south of Lake Erie.
   B Michigan is home to the Missouri River.
   C Michigan surrounds Lake Huron.
   D Michigan borders most of the Great Lakes.

3 **Based on the map, which of the following is accurate?**
   A Houghton is the name of a river.
   B Lake Michigan is east of the state of Michigan.
   C Silver Lake State Park is near Lake Michigan.
   D The Kalamazooo River flows into Lake Charlevoix.

Directions: Questions 4 and 5 refer to the map below.

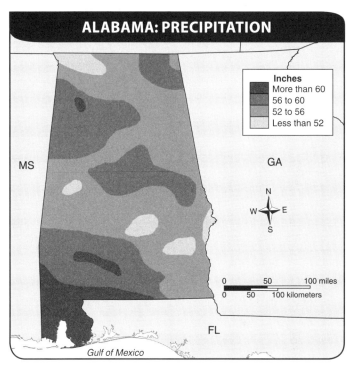

ALABAMA: PRECIPITATION

Inches
More than 60
56 to 60
52 to 56
Less than 52

4 **In general, where is the wettest area of Alabama?**
   A in the east
   B in the north
   C on the coast
   D in the southeast

5 **What is the least amount of precipitation that occurs along the Alabama/Florida border?**
   A less than 52 inches
   B 52 to 56 inches
   C 56 to 60 inches
   D more than 60 inches

UNIT 1

Directions: Questions 6 through 10 refer to the maps below.

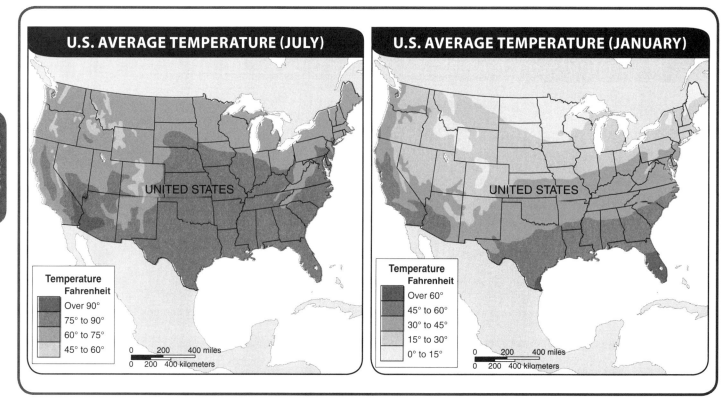

6   Based on the maps, which of the following
    are temperatures you might expect to occur
    in Virginia?
    A   20 degrees in January; 75 degrees in July
    B   30 degrees in January; 80 degrees in July
    C   50 degrees in January; 70 degrees in July
    D   60 degrees in January; 80 degrees in July

7   Which of the following states would you
    expect to be the coldest in January?
    A   Washington
    B   Ohio
    C   Pennsylvania
    D   Maine

8   Which of these states would have the
    highest probability of snow during January?
    A   Florida
    B   South Carolina
    C   Tennessee
    D   Louisiana

9   Which of the following statements best
    summarizes the content of the maps?
    A   The United States has a wide range of
        temperatures.
    B   The United States is a warm country.
    C   The United States is a cold country.
    D   The United States has a narrow range of
        temperatures.

10 Which of the following factors affects the
    climate of the southeastern part of the
    United States?
    A   its proximity to the equator
    B   its vegetation
    C   its longitude
    D   its numerous mountain ranges

Directions: Questions 11 and 12 refer to the map and information below.

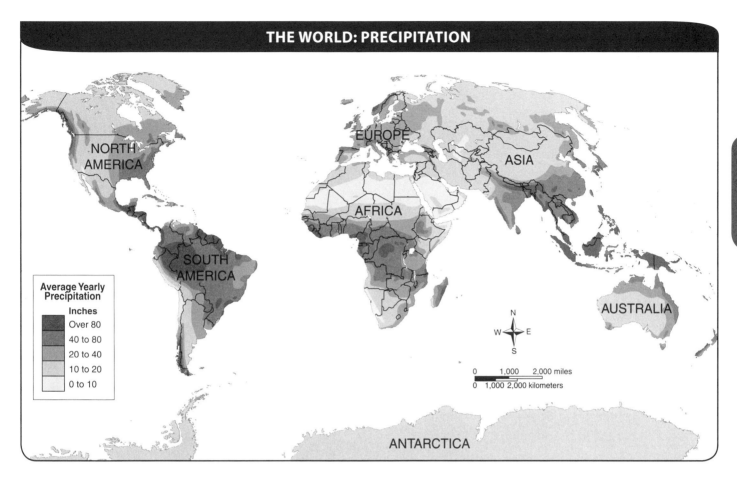

THE WORLD: PRECIPITATION

One of the wettest areas of the world is South Asia. Here, some parts of the region experience a monsoon, or rainy, season that lasts from June through October. During this season, these monsoon areas receive a large proportion of their rain for the year. The farmers depend on these rains to water their crops, knowing that there will be less rain the rest of the year.

Rainforests, such as those located in South America, are also very wet. However, the rainfall is steadier and spread throughout the year. There are two types of rainforests: tropical and temperate. Tropical rainforests are found closer to the equator, where it is warm. Tropical rainforests are known for their dense vegetation that prevents whatever sunlight there might be from reaching the ground. Temperate rainforests are found near the cooler coastal areas farther north or south of the equator. In the United States, for example, the state of Washington is home to an unspoiled temperate rainforest, which is located in the northern reaches of Olympic National Park.

11 Why is farming in parts of South Asia problematic?

  A There is never enough rain.

  B It is constantly raining in the region.

  C The region has three rainy seasons per year.

  D The region receives most of its yearly rain from June to October.

12 According to the map, which continent uniformly experiences yearly average precipitation of 10 to 20 inches?

  A Asia

  B North America

  C South America

  D Antarctica

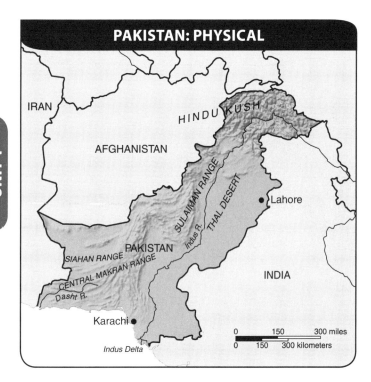

PAKISTAN: PHYSICAL

Pakistan is located in South Asia and extends from the Himalayas to the Arabian Sea. The four geographic regions of Pakistan include mountains and plateaus in western Pakistan, mountains in the north, plains in the valley of the Indus River, and hills in the northwest.

Pakistan's land is as diverse as its people. Because of the area's vast, rugged land, agriculture is not an economic mainstay of many of the country's regions. However, the use of irrigation has helped in the raising of crops such as wheat, rice, and cotton. About 40 percent of the population lives in urban areas; the remainder live in rural areas. Karachi, a port city along the coast in the south, and Lahore, in the east-central part of the country, are the most populated cities.

13 Based on the map and the passage, Pakistan's urban population is concentrated in areas with which physical features?
  A plains and coast
  B mountains and coast
  C hills and mountains
  D plains and hills

14 About what percentage of Pakistan is covered with mountains or hills?
  A 10%
  B 25%
  C 30%
  D 50%

15 Which of the following best describes why the Indus River is important to Pakistan?
  A It has a large delta.
  B It separates the mountains from the desert.
  C It runs the entire length of Pakistan.
  D It is a tributary of the Dasht River.

16 In what way did the Pakistanis modify their geography to improve their lives?
  A They flattened mountains to aid in transportation.
  B They built large cities, such as Karachi, in the Hindu Kush mountains.
  C They changed the flow of the Indus River into the Thal Desert.
  D They used irrigation to create arable land.

UNIT 1

Political Maps

① Learn the Skill

A **political map** shows how humans have divided the surface of Earth. It shows **borders** between counties, states, territories, and countries. It can also show **human-made features** such as roads, buildings, and cities. Some political maps use shading or dots to illustrate areas where people live. This is known as **population density**. Areas with fewer dots or lighter shading generally are less populated.

② Practice the Skill

By mastering the skill of understanding political maps, you will improve your study and test-taking skills, especially as they relate to social studies high school equivalency tests. Study the map below. Use this information to answer question 1.

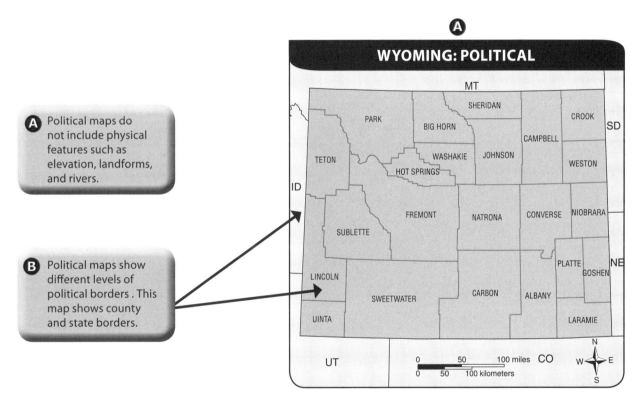

A Political maps do not include physical features such as elevation, landforms, and rivers.

B Political maps show different levels of political borders. This map shows county and state borders.

TEST-TAKING TIPS

The map key changes for different types of maps. Some maps do not have a key. Be sure to study each map carefully to determine that map's features.

1 **Which of the following is the best description of what this map shows?**
   A the states that border Wyoming
   B the counties of Wyoming
   C the counties of Wyoming and the states that border Wyoming
   D the counties and elevation of Wyoming

UNIT 1

Directions: Questions 2 and 3 refer to the map below.

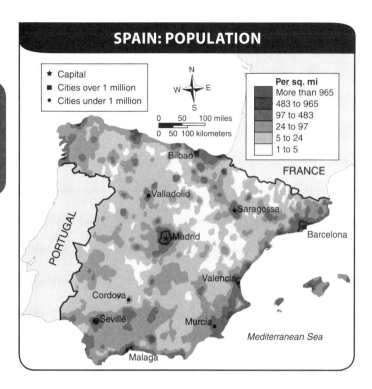

SPAIN: POPULATION

2   **In which area of Spain is the population density the greatest?**
    A   between Madrid and Saragossa
    B   along the Portuguese border
    C   along the French border
    D   near most major cities

3   **Based on the map, which statement about Spain is accurate?**
    A   Madrid has the highest population.
    B   All areas of Spain have more than 10 people per square mile.
    C   Few people live along the Mediterranean Coast.
    D   Murcia has areas with more than 965 people per square mile.

Directions: Questions 4 through 6 refer to the map below.

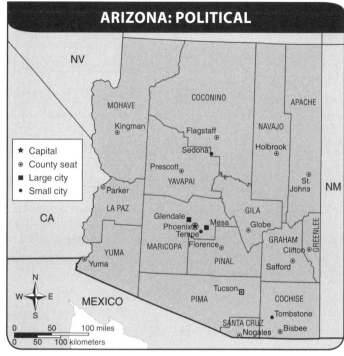

ARIZONA: POLITICAL

4   **What does the symbol next to Tucson probably represent?**
    A   county seat and small city
    B   county seat and large city
    C   state capital and county seat
    D   state capital and large city

5   **Based on the map, which area of the state is least populated?**
    A   Maricopa County
    B   Far northern Arizona
    C   Pima County
    D   southeastern Arizona

6   **Based on the map, what can be assumed about Arizona?**
    A   Maricopa County has the largest population.
    B   Coconino County has the largest population.
    C   The state's population is evenly distributed across all counties.
    D   Most of the population is near the California border.

Directions: Questions 7 through 11 are based on the map and information below.

BRAZIL: POPULATION DENSITY

Per sq. mi
- More than 965
- 483 to 965
- 97 to 483
- 24 to 97
- 5 to 24
- 1 to 5

Almost 200 million people live in Brazil. The country, the fifth largest in the world, is home to the Amazon River delta. In the north and west, Brazil has well over 1,000,00 square miles of rainforest in the Amazon basin.

Unlike the other countries of South America, in which the official language is Spanish, the official language of Brazil is Portuguese. Brazil's indigenous population traded with the colonizers from Portugal who arrived in the 1500s. Because the majority of the native population perished due to wars and disease, enslaved Africans were imported to work the fields. Of the 9.5 million people captured in Africa and brought to the Americas between the sixteenth and the nineteenth centuries, nearly 4 million landed in Brazil—ten times more than those sent to the United States.

Brazil won its independence from the Portuguese in 1822 after more than 300 years as a colony. Brazil became the last American nation to abolish slavery, on May 13, 1888. At that time Rio de Janeiro, Brazil's second-largest city, had the largest urban concentration of enslaved people—more than 40% of its population—since the end of the Roman Empire.

7   **Based on the map, where are Brazil's major cities probably located?**
   A   along the Bolivian border
   B   along the east coast
   C   in the Amazon basin
   D   in the center of the country

8   **Which geographic factors most likely affected the growth of Brazil's population centers?**
   A   the Amazon rainforest and the mountains
   B   the Amazon rainforest and the Atlantic Ocean
   C   the Amazon Delta and the Peruvian border
   D   the equator and the Pacific Ocean

9   **According to the passage, how is the population of modern Brazil similar to the population during the early period of colonization?**
   A   It is low in the Amazon area.
   B   It is low in the coastal area.
   C   It is high in the Amazon area.
   D   It is high near the Bolivian border.

10 **Based on the passage, how many years elapsed between Brazil's independence and its abolishment of slavery?**
   A   45 years
   B   46 years
   C   56 years
   D   66 years

11 **Based on the information, which of the following statements about Brazil is correct?**
   A   Brazil's population is a mixture of people of different ethnicities.
   B   Brazil's population is mostly Portuguese.
   C   Brazil's population is distributed evenly throughout the country.
   D   Brazil's only peaceful neighbor is Uruguay.

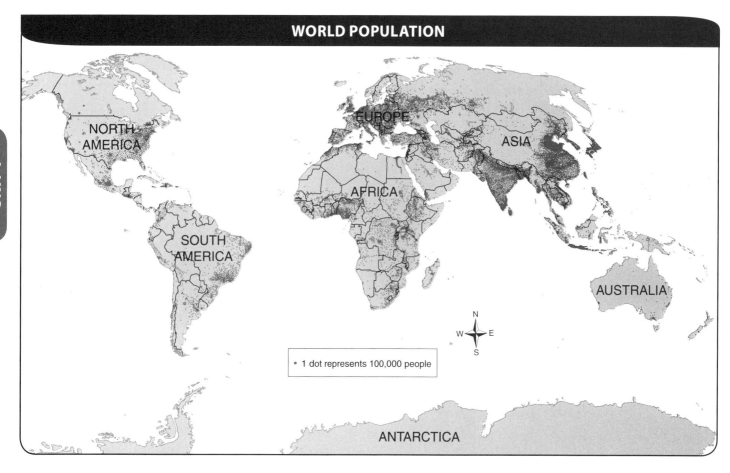

WORLD POPULATION

NORTH AMERICA

SOUTH AMERICA

EUROPE

ASIA

AFRICA

AUSTRALIA

ANTARCTICA

• 1 dot represents 100,000 people

12 **Based on the map, which continent has the largest population?**

   A Asia

   B North America

   C South America

   D Africa

13 **Which of the following best describes the population density of North America?**

   A It is densely populated in the central part of the continent.

   B It is densely populated across almost the entire continent.

   C It is less densely populated than Europe.

   D It is densely populated along the coastal areas.

14 **What is one way that scientists might use this map for environmental purposes?**

   A to find the absolute location of places

   B to find areas where pollution might be the greatest

   C to find areas with high land

   D to find areas with a hot, dry climate

15 **Based on the map, which continent is most densely populated?**

   A North America

   B South America

   C Asia

   D Europe

Directions: Questions 16 through 18 refer to the map below.

Directions: Questions 19 and 20 refer to the map and information below.

IRELAND: COUNTIES AND COUNTY SEATS

UNITED STATES: MIDWEST REGION

16 Which of the following counties in Ireland is not landlocked?

  A Tipperary

  B Roscommon

  C Dublin

  D Monaghan

17 Based on the map, which of the following statements about Ireland is accurate?

  A All of the counties are around the same size.

  B Several county capitals share the same name as the county.

  C The complete area north of Dublin belongs to the United Kingdom.

  D The Celtic Sea is east of County Wicklow.

18 Which of the following cities is the seat of County Tipperary?

  A Kilkenny

  B Tipperary

  C Clonmel

  D Limerick

The Midwest region of the United States includes the Great Lakes states, as well as Missouri, Iowa, Kansas, Nebraska, and North and South Dakota. In 2010, almost 70 million people called the Midwest region home. The state with the largest population is Illinois. North Dakota had the smallest population in the region.

19 Based on the map and the paragraph, which of the following statements is accurate?

  A The Midwest region features the largest state in the United States.

  B Illinois has the highest population among all fifty states.

  C There are only six states in the Midwest region.

  D Wisconsin is in the Midwest region.

20 Which of the following cities is a Midwest city?

  A Albany

  B Chicago

  C Baltimore

  D Pittsburgh

Movement on Maps

① Learn the Skill

To understand **movement on maps,** it is important to know the symbols and map elements that are commonly used to show movement. Symbols such as **arrows** or **lines** can show the movement, direction, or route of people, goods, or ideas. **Colors, shading,** and **patterns** can also be used to show when movements occurred or to illustrate the forces or factors that caused the movement. Some maps that show movement are special-purpose maps. There is more information about special-purpose maps in Unit 4. Movement, or migration, is an important factor in understanding geography.

② Practice the Skill

By mastering the skill of understanding movement on maps, you will improve your study and test-taking skills, especially as they relate to social studies high school equivalency tests. Study the map below. Use this information to answer question 1.

A Look at the arrows to understand the direction of the movements.

B When dealing with movement on maps, be sure to note the geographical areas involved. Which areas are the movements going to, or from, or between? What do you know about those areas during the time period specified on the map?

☑ TEST-TAKING TIPS

Use the map key to determine the meaning of the map's different colors and shadings. Map keys provide information about movement on maps, such as who or what group is moving to or from which direction.

ATLANTIC SLAVE TRADE ROUTES

Key:
- ‹--- Slave traders' routes early 1500s
- ←— Slave traders' routes 1600s
- ←— Slave traders' routes after 1619
- Gathering areas for enslaved people
- Major concentration of enslaved people

NORTH AMERICA
Great Lakes
Mississippi R.
Gulf of Mexico
CUBA   HISPANIOLA
SOUTH AMERICA
PACIFIC OCEAN
ATLANTIC OCEAN
EUROPE
AFRICA

Scale: 0   1,000   2,000 miles
0   1,000 2,000 kilometers

1 **Jamestown Colony was founded in Virginia in 1609. According to the map, what changes occurred after the founding of Jamestown?**
   A The slave-gathering areas of Africa increased.
   B Areas with major concentrations of enslaved people moved from South America to Africa.
   C More enslaved people were sent from South America.
   D The trade routes extended to North America.

Directions: Questions 2 through 5 refer to the information and map below.

The Silk Road was a series of ancient trade routes that stretched more than 4,000 miles from the Far East to the West. The main overland route extended from China to the Mediterranean Sea. Besides goods, travelers on the Silk Road exchanged ideas, philosophies, and cultures.

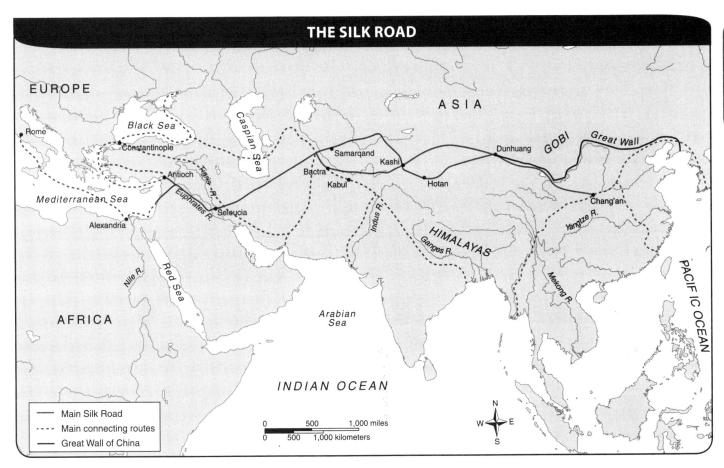

THE SILK ROAD

2 **Why was the Silk Road important?**
   A It boosted the economy of Africa.
   B It prevented cultural exchange between East and West.
   C It provided silk to wealthy Asians.
   D It allowed for goods and ideas to be exchanged between Asia and Europe.

3 **How might goods from Alexandria have reached Kabul?**
   A via Rome and Constantinople
   B via Seleucia and Bactra
   C across the Great Wall of China
   D via Antioch and Samarqand

4 **What connection can you make about the cities of Samarqand, Bactra, Kashi, and Kabul?**
   A These cities were not located on the main connecting routes of the Silk Road.
   B These cities were located north of the Great Wall of China.
   C These cities were centrally located on the Silk Road.
   D Kashi and Kabul were west of Bactra and Samarqand.

5 **How is it likely that traders from Rome reached the Silk Road?**
   A by wagon
   B by horse
   C by foot
   D by boat

Directions: Questions 6 through 9 refer to the map below.

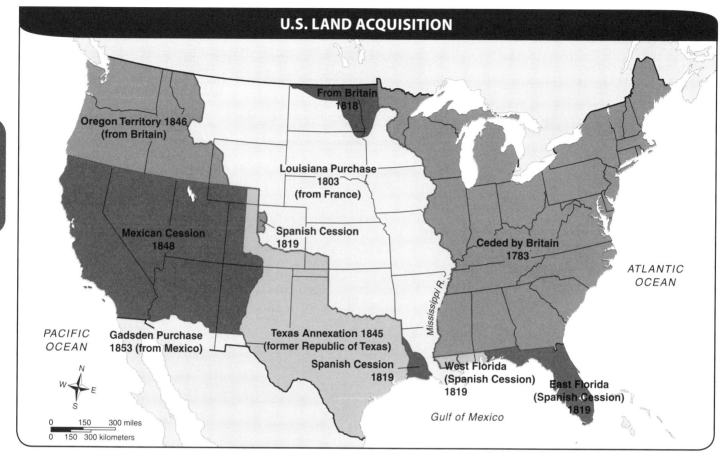

U.S. LAND ACQUISITION

Oregon Territory 1846 (from Britain)

From Britain 1818

Louisiana Purchase 1803 (from France)

Mexican Cession 1848

Spanish Cession 1819

Ceded by Britain 1783

Mississippi R.

ATLANTIC OCEAN

PACIFIC OCEAN

Gadsden Purchase 1853 (from Mexico)

Texas Annexation 1845 (former Republic of Texas)

Spanish Cession 1819

West Florida (Spanish Cession) 1819

East Florida (Spanish Cession) 1819

Gulf of Mexico

N W E S

0   150   300 miles
0   150   300 kilometers

6 Which statement best describes the map?

A The map shows how the United States expanded over time through land acquisitions.

B The map illustrates the acquisition of territories after 1819.

C The map shows the battles fought for western expansion.

D The map shows the sequence of events that led to eastern expansion.

7 Which of the following nations ceded the most land along the Gulf of Mexico?

A Britain

B Spain

C Mexico

D France

8 Based on the information on the map, when was much of the land west of the Mississippi River first opened for settlement?

A in 1783, with the British cession

B in 1803, with the Louisiana Purchase

C in 1819, with the Spanish cession

D in 1853, with the Gadsden Purchase

9 Which of the following states was included in the Mexican Cession of 1848?

A Florida

B Illinois

C Oklahoma

D California

UNIT 1

Directions: Questions 10 through 12 refer to the map and information below.

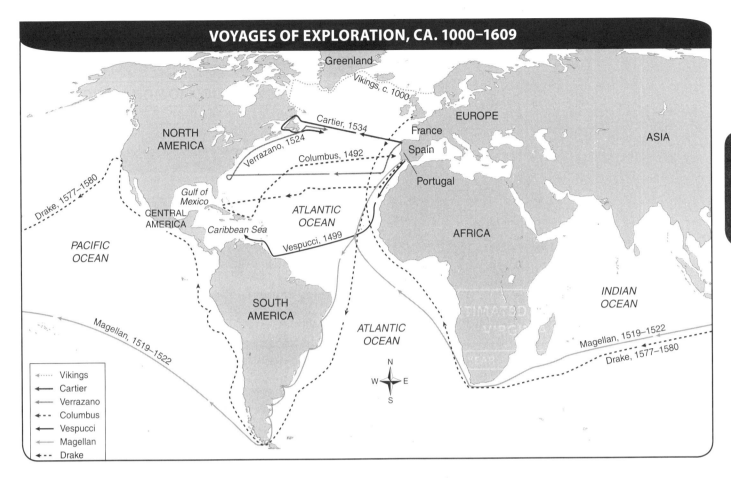

VOYAGES OF EXPLORATION, CA. 1000–1609

In the 1400s, Henry the Navigator of Portugal helped start the Age of Discovery in Europe by funding numerous expeditions abroad. One of his goals was to find a sea route to Asia. He also wanted to gain geographic knowledge. Before the 1400s, exploration did exist, but on a smaller scale. However, sea and ocean expeditions did not venture very far away from their home bases. It was not until the Viking explorations of the Atlantic that expeditions penetrated distant waters.

10 Which of the following best describes the direction the majority of the explorers initially traveled?

A   east-bound

B   west-bound

C   north-bound

D   south-bound

11 Based on the map, who was the first to reach North America?

A   Columbus

B   Cartier

C   Verrazano

D   the Vikings

12 Which of the following best describes the effects of European exploration on North America?

A   the discovery of riches and a water route to Asia

B   colonization, increased trade, and indigenous peoples' loss of land

C   the discovery of gold, silver, and natural resources; increased trade

D   the discovery of the Northwest Passage and increased trade

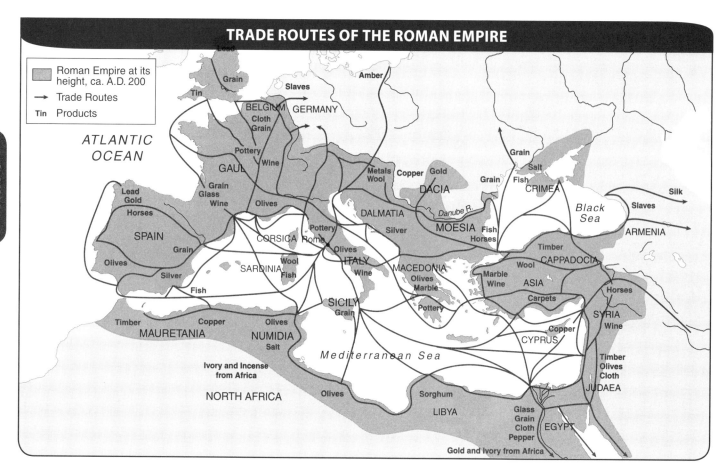

TRADE ROUTES OF THE ROMAN EMPIRE

13 **Based on the map, which of the following best describes the trade activity of the Roman Empire?**

A The Roman Empire was so large that only trade within the empire was required.

B The Romans preferred not to trade with people to the north and south of Rome.

C The Romans traded only within their empire.

D The Romans traded extensively, including outside their empire.

14 **What product might the Roman Empire hope to receive through trade with people in Spain?**

A wine

B grain

C timber

D copper

15 **Based on the map, which of the following statements is accurate?**

A The Roman traders used only water routes.

B The Roman Empire traded over three continents.

C The greatest variety of goods was found in Libya.

D The Roman Empire included all of present-day Europe.

16 **Which of the following was most likely a consequence of the Roman trade routes?**

A The trade routes caused the Romans to become increasingly isolated.

B The trade routes allowed Rome to enforce its laws throughout the world.

C Trade allowed for an exchange of cultural knowledge.

D The trade routes were the main cause of the Roman economic collapse.

Relate Geography and History

① Learn the Skill

To understand how to **relate geography and history,** it is important to analyze the context of the physical, political, or special-purpose map and how it connects with a historical period or event. All of the map skills you have learned so far will help you make these connections.

② Practice the Skill

By mastering the skill of relating geography and history, you will improve your study and test-taking skills, especially as they relate to social studies high school equivalency tests. Study the map and information below. Use this information to answer question 1.

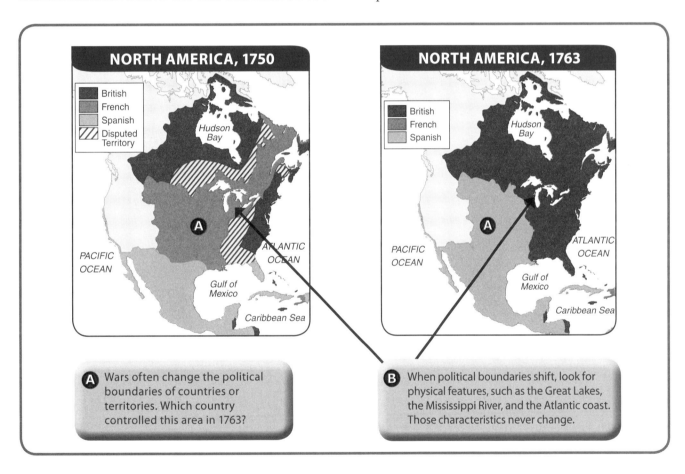

NORTH AMERICA, 1750

British
French
Spanish
Disputed Territory

Hudson Bay

PACIFIC OCEAN

ATLANTIC OCEAN

Gulf of Mexico

Caribbean Sea

NORTH AMERICA, 1763

British
French
Spanish

Hudson Bay

PACIFIC OCEAN

ATLANTIC OCEAN

Gulf of Mexico

Caribbean Sea

A Wars often change the political boundaries of countries or territories. Which country controlled this area in 1763?

B When political boundaries shift, look for physical features, such as the Great Lakes, the Mississippi River, and the Atlantic coast. Those characteristics never change.

MAKING ASSUMPTIONS

Use dates and other facts presented on the maps to place the geography into a historical context. Remember that the French and Indian War ended in 1763.

1 Which of the following was a consequence of the French and Indian War?
   A The French gained territory in North America.
   B The British gained territory in North America.
   C The French controlled the Mississippi River.
   D The British gained control of Texas.

③ **Apply the Skill**

Directions: Question 2 refers to the map below.

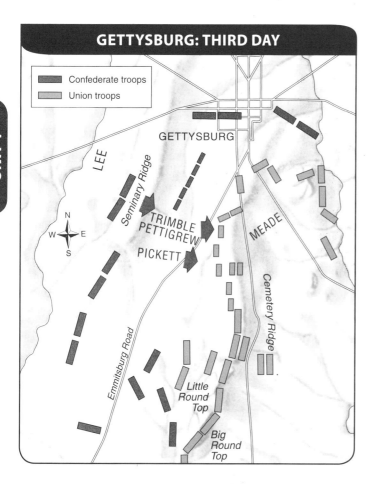

GETTYSBURG: THIRD DAY

- Confederate troops
- Union troops

Directions: Question 3 refers to the maps below.

EUROPE: 1914

EUROPE: 1919

2 **In 1863, the Confederacy lost the Battle of Gettysburg and retreated. Analyze the map. On the third day of the battle, the Confederacy**

- **A** attacked Little Round Top.
- **B** waited for the Union to cross the Emmitsburg Road and attack.
- **C** advanced over open ground and their troops were stretched thin.
- **D** focused on defending the town of Gettysburg.

3 **Which countries were most affected by World War I?**

- **A** Austria-Hungary and Serbia
- **B** Germany and the Netherlands
- **C** the United Kingdom and Russia
- **D** Spain and Montenegro

Lesson 6 | Relate Geography and History

Directions: Questions 4 through 6 refer to the map and information below.

WESTERN EUROPE: RELIGIOUS DIVISIONS, CA. 1555

Catholic

Lutheran

Catholic and Lutheran

Calvinist

Catholic and Calvinist

Anglican

Catholic and Bohemian and Moravian Brethren (Hussite)

In 1517, German Catholic monk Martin Luther released his Ninety-five Theses, or ways in which the Catholic Church should be reformed. Church leaders, including Pope Leo X, disagreed and believed that Luther's ideas were heretical. He was excommunicated, or officially separated from the church and all of its sacraments, in 1521. However, Luther had many supporters in some of the German states (then part of the Holy Roman Empire). His followers would establish the Lutheran form of Christian religion in protest to what they perceived as faults in the early modern Catholic Church.

4 According to information on the map, where might Anglicanism have originated?
A   England
B   Spain
C   Ireland
D   the Holy Roman Empire

5 In what area was Lutheranism the most prominent religion?
A   in England
B   in France
C   in Spain
D   in Denmark

6 Based on the map, where were religious conflicts most likely to occur?
A   in the Papal States
B   in the Holy Roman Empire
C   in Sweden
D   in France

UNIT 1

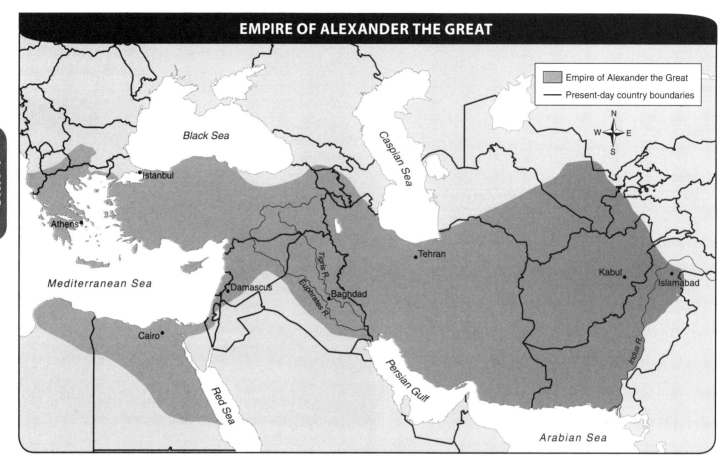

Alexander III was the King of Macedonia (modern Greece) from 336 to 323 B.C.E. During his reign, he established a vast empire stretching eastward from Macedonia, across the Mediterranean Sea, through the Middle East, to India. Alexander's campaigns led to a sharing of trade goods, ideas, and cultures. He became known as Alexander the Great.

7 **Which modern countries were a part of Alexander's empire?**
  A Russia and India
  B Saudi Arabia and Italy
  C Turkey and Iran
  D Iraq and China

8 **Based on the map, what difficulty might Alexander and his troops have experienced during their campaigns?**
  A communication
  B finding food
  C crossing the oceans
  D mostly cold weather

9 **Based on the map and the information, which of the following can be assumed to be true about Alexander?**
  A Alexander was a poor military leader whose army was usually in disarray.
  B Alexander was a disorganized leader whose expeditions were usually failures.
  C Alexander forced all people in his empire to learn Greek and embrace Macedonian culture.
  D Alexander was an accomplished military commander.

Directions: Questions 10 and 11 refer to map and information below.

THE SCHLIEFFEN PLAN, 1914

BRITAIN

HOLLAND

English Channel

Somme R.

BELGIUM

GERMANY

LUXEMBOURG

Paris

Seine R.

FRANCE

N W E S

⬡ French fortifications

← German advance

SWITZERLAND

Directions: Questions 12 and 13 refer to the map below.

THE BATTLE OF IWO JIMA

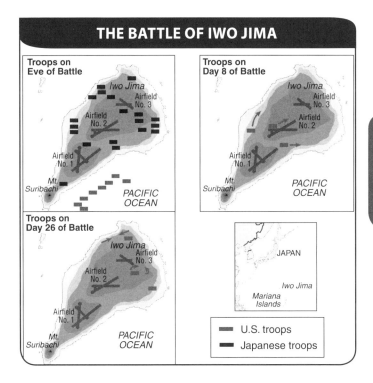

Ongoing conflict between Germany and France caused the Chief of the German Great General Staff, Alfred von Schlieffen, to plan for a possible invasion of France in 1905. When war was declared between the two countries in 1914, the Schlieffen Plan was put into action.

10 Why did Schlieffen not plan to attack on the Franco/German border?

A   He favored a water route.

B   He wanted to secure Paris.

C   He wanted to secure the Somme.

D   The French had fortified the border.

11 Britain was pledged to protect Belgian neutrality. How might the Schlieffen Plan involve Britain?

A   Schlieffen planned to attack Britain.

B   Belgium would declare war on Britain.

C   Belgium would declare war on France.

D   Britain would join the war to help Belgium.

12 Based on the map, why was Iwo Jima significant?

A   because of its airfields

B   because the United States wanted to control all islands in the South Pacific

C   because of the inspiration caused by raising the American flag on Mount Suribachi

D   because it showed that the Japanese had lost the will to fight

13 How did gaining control of Iwo Jima support the strategic plans of the United States for victory in the Pacific during World War II?

A   The U.S. Navy could use it as a base of supply.

B   The United States could use it to house the building of the atomic bomb.

C   It was a closer base than the Mariana Islands to launch an invasion of Japan.

D   Because of its size, Iwo Jima could support hundreds of thousands of American troops.

The Unit Review is structured to resemble high school equivalency tests. Be sure to read each question and all possible answers very carefully before choosing your answer.

To record your answers, fill in the circle that corresponds to the answer you select for each question in the Unit Review.

Do not rest your pencil on the answer area while considering your answer. Make no stray or unnecessary marks. If you change an answer, erase your first mark completely.

Mark only one answer space for each question; multiple answers will be scored as incorrect.

Sample Question

How can historians use geography?
  A to study how animals relate to their habitat
  B to understand cultures in different areas of the world
  C to determine county divisions within states
  D to determine which historical event happened as a result of another historical event

Directions: Questions 1 and 2 are based on the map below.

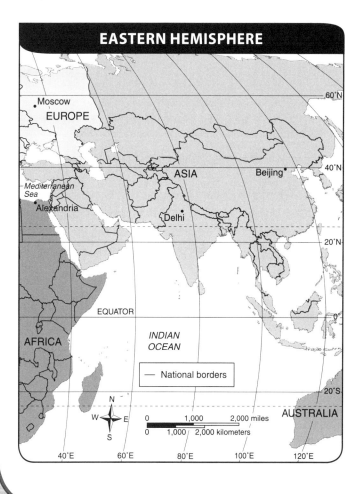

1 Based on the information on the map, what is the relative location of Beijing, China?
  A northeast of Delhi
  B 40N°, 80°E
  C 40S°, 80°W
  D west of Moscow

Ⓐ Ⓑ Ⓒ Ⓓ

2 What tool could you use to find the absolute location of a place?
  A a scale
  B a key
  C latitude and longitude
  D map symbols

Ⓐ Ⓑ Ⓒ Ⓓ

Directions: Questions 3 through 6 are based on the map below.

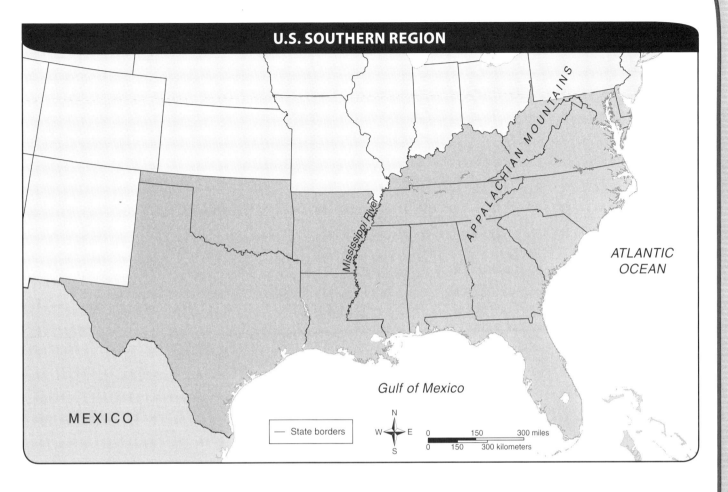

U.S. SOUTHERN REGION

APPALACHIAN MOUNTAINS

Mississippi River

ATLANTIC OCEAN

Gulf of Mexico

MEXICO

State borders

N
W E
S

0   150   300 miles
0   150   300 kilometers

3 **Based on the map, the southern region of the United States**

   A includes all states east of the Mississippi River.

   B includes Virginia, but not West Virginia.

   C includes all states that feature the Appalachian Mountains.

   D includes all states that border the Gulf of Mexico.

Ⓐ Ⓑ Ⓒ Ⓓ

4 **Which southern state shares a border with seven other states in the southern region?**

   A Arkansas

   B Georgia

   C Mississippi

   D Tennessee

Ⓐ Ⓑ Ⓒ Ⓓ

5 **Which of the following cities is located in the southern region of the United States?**

   A Los Angeles

   B Nashville

   C Chicago

   D Phoenix

Ⓐ Ⓑ Ⓒ Ⓓ

6 **About how far away are east Texas and west South Carolina?**

   A about 300 miles

   B about 500 miles

   C about 700 miles

   D about 900 miles

Ⓐ Ⓑ Ⓒ Ⓓ

Directions: Questions 7 through 10 are based on the map below.

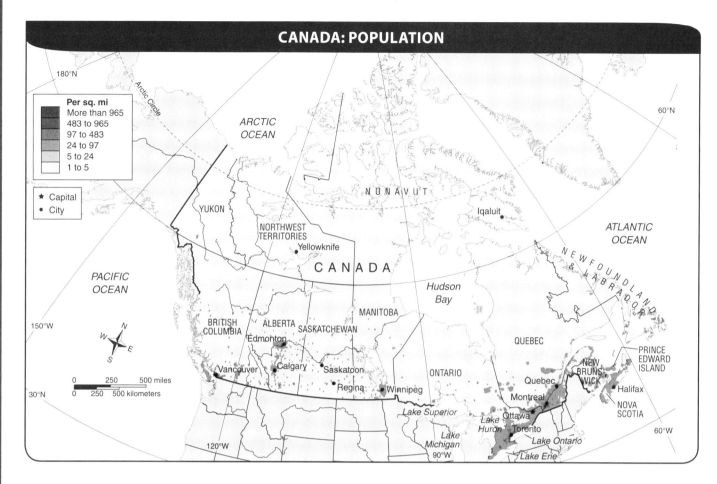

CANADA: POPULATION

Per sq. mi
More than 965
483 to 965
97 to 483
24 to 97
5 to 24
1 to 5

★ Capital
● City

7 **According to the map, where is most of the population of Canada located?**
  A between 60°N and 75°N
  B near Edmonton
  C near the capital
  D west of 120°W

ⒶⒷⒸⒹ

8 **Based on the map, which of the following provinces or territories probably has the highest total income?**
  A British Columbia
  B Manitoba
  C Saskatchewan
  D Alberta

ⒶⒷⒸⒹ

9 **Based on the map, which statement best describes Canada?**
  A There is plenty of quality farmland near the Arctic Circle.
  B Fishing and shipping have always been important to Canada.
  C Many Canadians have settled on the country's west coast.
  D Canadians do not value their relationship with the United States.

ⒶⒷⒸⒹ

10 **Which city is closest to 60°N, 120°W?**
  A Yellowknife
  B Edmonton
  C Calgary
  D Halifax

ⒶⒷⒸⒹ

Directions: Questions 11 through 14 are based on the map and information below.

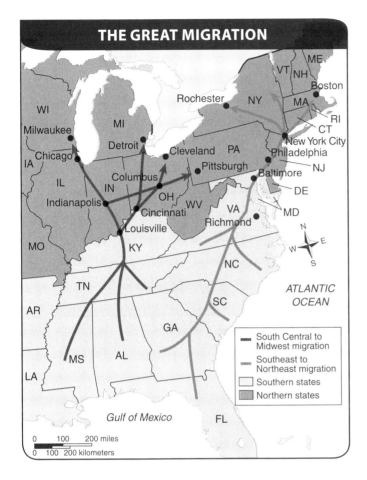

THE GREAT MIGRATION

South Central to Midwest migration

Southeast to Northeast migration

Southern states

Northern states

In the early 1900s, more than 1 million African Americans, pushed by discrimination and poor economic conditions in the rural South, migrated north and west in an event that became known as the Great Migration. The migration began around 1916, lessened during the Great Depression, and increased again during World War II and after. Northern cities such as New York, Chicago, Cleveland, and Detroit saw the greatest African American population increases. Manufacturing and other urban jobs led African Americans to these cities. Moving to cities also caused a growth in African American literacy and an African American cultural explosion. Many Southern African American artists, authors, and musicians converged on New York City because it was seen as a cultural center of the United States.

11 **Where were African Americans from Georgia most likely to have migrated?**
- **A** Ohio
- **B** West Virginia
- **C** Illinois
- **D** New York

Ⓐ Ⓑ Ⓒ Ⓓ

12 **Which of the following factors contributed to the Great Migration?**
- **A** the Great Depression and an increase in rural jobs
- **B** World War II and an increase in Southern factory jobs
- **C** World War I and Jim Crow laws
- **D** crop failure and lack of jobs in Detroit

Ⓐ Ⓑ Ⓒ Ⓓ

13 **Which of the following was a result of the Great Migration?**
- **A** World War I
- **B** World War II
- **C** Jim Crow laws
- **D** the Harlem Renaissance

Ⓐ Ⓑ Ⓒ Ⓓ

14 **How was the United States affected by the Great Migration?**
- **A** increased urban workforce
- **B** increased rural workforce
- **C** decreased literacy
- **D** decreased crop failures

Ⓐ Ⓑ Ⓒ Ⓓ

Directions: Questions 15 and 16 are based on the map and information below.

Directions: Questions 17 and 18 are based on the map below.

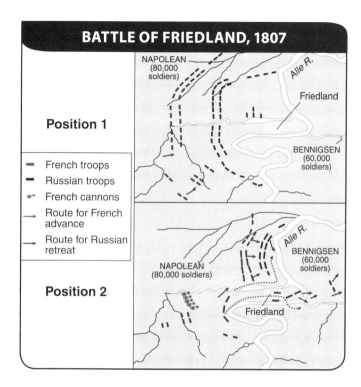

BATTLE OF FRIEDLAND, 1807

NAPOLEAN (80,000 soldiers)

Alle R.

Friedland

Position 1

BENNIGSEN (60,000 soldiers)

— French troops
— Russian troops
— French cannons
→ Route for French advance
→ Route for Russian retreat

Alle R.

BENNIGSEN (60,000 soldiers)

NAPOLEAN (80,000 soldiers)

Position 2

Friedland

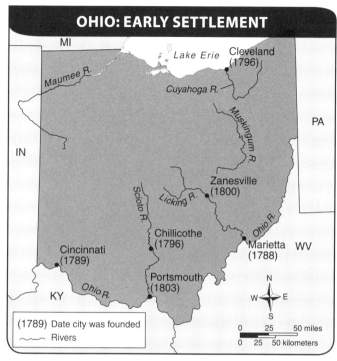

OHIO: EARLY SETTLEMENT

MI

Lake Erie   Cleveland (1796)

Maumee R.   Cuyahoga R.

IN   PA

Muskingum R.

Zanesville (1800)

Scioto R.   Licking R.

Chillicothe (1796)   Ohio R.   Marietta (1788)   WV

Cincinnati (1789)

Portsmouth (1803)

N
W   E
S

KY   Ohio R.

(1789) Date city was founded
~~~ Rivers

0   25   50 miles
0   25   50 kilometers

Napoleon's victory over Russia at the Battle of Friedland ended the Third Coalition of European countries' attempt to stop the Emperor from controlling the entire continent.

15 What advantages did the French have?

   A The French had cannons and more troops.

   B The French controlled Friedland and were led by Napoleon.

   C The French controlled the Alle River and had cannons.

   D The French had more troops and were led by Bennigsen.

Ⓐ Ⓑ Ⓒ Ⓓ

16 How did geography help the French win?

   A The Russians could transport troops using the Alle River.

   B The Russians were trapped against the Alle River and could not retreat quickly.

   C The French were unable to place their cannons because of the terrain.

   D The French controlled the high ground.

Ⓐ Ⓑ Ⓒ Ⓓ

17 Based on the map, the early settlements in Ohio

   A were near Pennsylvania so they could be protected.

   B were mostly along Lake Erie.

   C were all built along waterways.

   D were mostly in the interior of the territory.

Ⓐ Ⓑ Ⓒ Ⓓ

18 Soon after which historical event were most of the settlements in Ohio founded?

   A the American Revolution

   B the French and Indian War

   C the War of 1812

   D the Iroquois Wars

Ⓐ Ⓑ Ⓒ Ⓓ

Notes

Unit 2

Unit Overview

American history is dynamic, ever changing with the times. Throughout its short but momentous history, the United States has defended its citizens and millions worldwide through its progressive military strength and intelligence forces. As history changes, so too does the role of the military.

Women have served in the our armed forces since 1775. They nursed the wounded, laundered clothes, and cooked for the troops. In 1944, as Allied Forces fought in World War II, Women's Army Corps (WAC) units supported combat troops. But it was not until 2013 that the Defense Department authorized women to serve on an equal basis alongside their male counterparts, removing the remaining barrier to equality in the services. Recent wars such as Iraq and Afghanistan lacked real front lines and thousands of women soldiers found themselves in combat situations. Whether as members of the armed forces or in a host of other areas, it is important that, as United States citizens, we safeguard our country's future. To do that, we first must understand its—and our—past.

The importance of understanding our history extends to social studies high school equivalency tests, where U.S. history comprises approximately 25 percent of all questions. As with other areas of the social studies test, U.S. history questions will test your ability to interpret text and visuals, such as tables, charts, graphs, and political cartoons, through the use of thinking skills such as comprehension, application, analysis, and evaluation. In Unit 2, the introduction of core reading and thinking skills will help you prepare for social studies high school equivalency tests.

Table of Contents

Key U. S. History Terms

amendment: an official change to the words and meaning of a law or other document

Articles of Confederation: the agreement among the 13 founding states that established the United States of America as a confederation and served as its first constitution

candidate: a person who is seeking to be elected to office or chosen for a position

colonial: relating to the original 13 colonies forming the United States of America

colony: an area that is apart from but controlled by a distant country

Confederacy: the group of Southern states that separated themselves from the United States during the Civil War

constitution: the documented beliefs and laws by which a country, state, or organization is governed

Constitutional Convention: the 1787 meeting of delegates in Philadelphia to revise the Articles of Confederation and frame the federal Constitution

electoral vote: a vote cast by an elector in the electoral college system that is determined by the popular vote of the people in the elector's congressional district

Emancipation Proclamation: the 1863 presidential proclamation issued by Abraham Lincoln declaring freedom for people enslaved in the states in rebellion during the Civil War

Federalists: supporters of the newly written constitution who became identified as a political party that favored a strong central government

Great Society: an agenda of social programs launched by President Lyndon B. Johnson in 1964 and characterized as a "war on poverty"

immigrant: a person who moves to live permanently in a foreign country

impeach: to charge a holder of public office with misconduct

inaugural: marking the beginning of a period in office

Industrial Revolution: the period ending the 18th and into the 19th centuries during which agriculture, manufacturing, transportation, and mining were all advanced dramatically by technology, changing almost every aspect of daily life for people in a modernizing society

League of Nations: an international organization formed after World War II for the purpose of promoting cooperation and peace among nations

levy: to impose an involuntary tax or fee on citizens

popular vote: the total of the votes made by the electorate, the collection of individual qualified voters

prohibition: the act of forbidding something, such as a law prohibiting the sale and manufacture of alcohol

proportional representation: a system in which the power a political party has in a legislature is related to the number of votes its candidates receive in an election

Radical Republicans: a faction of the Republican Party during and after the Civil War committed to the emancipation of enslaved people and their equal treatment during Reconstruction.

ratification: to make a document official by a vote and/or authorizing signature

Reconstruction: the period in United States history immediately following the Civil War, during which the federal government imposed conditions of transformation on Southern states before they were permitted to rejoin the union

Representative: a congressman or congresswoman elected to represent the people of a specific congressional district

secession: the formal withdrawal from a union or organization

sharecropping: a system in which a landowner permits a tenant to use land for agriculture in return for a predetermined share of the crops

suffrage: the right to vote in an election

treaty: an official agreement between countries or groups

Interpret Tables

① Learn the Skill

One way to present facts, statistics, and other details in a clear, well-organized manner is to use a **table**. Tables allow authors to visually present information that might be too lengthy or complex to describe in a narrative passage.

Tables organize information into **rows** and **columns**. Rows run across the table from left to right. Columns run up and down the table from top to bottom. A monthly calendar is a good example of a table. Reading the title of a table, as well as the headings for its rows and columns, can help you interpret and use the information presented in the table.

② Practice the Skill

By mastering the skill of interpreting tables, you will improve your study and test-taking skills, especially as they relate to social studies high school equivalency tests. Examine the table and strategies below. Use this information to answer question 1.

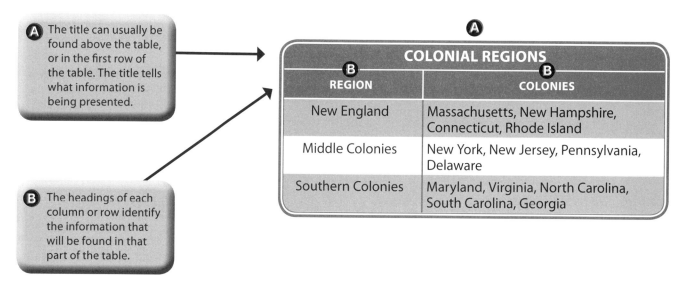

Ⓐ The title can usually be found above the table, or in the first row of the table. The title tells what information is being presented.

Ⓑ The headings of each column or row identify the information that will be found in that part of the table.

COLONIAL REGIONS	
REGION	**COLONIES**
New England	Massachusetts, New Hampshire, Connecticut, Rhode Island
Middle Colonies	New York, New Jersey, Pennsylvania, Delaware
Southern Colonies	Maryland, Virginia, North Carolina, South Carolina, Georgia

✓ TEST-TAKING TIPS

Use the headings of the rows and columns of a table in order to determine how the information in these parts of the table relates to each other. In this table, you can see that the region named in each row is related to the colonies listed to the right.

1 Based on the table, which statement best describes the New England colonies?

The New England colonies
- **A** included all colonies north of Virginia.
- **B** included Connecticut and New Hampshire.
- **C** had the highest number of colonies.
- **D** were the largest group geographically.

Directions: Questions 2 and 3 refer to the following table.

POPULATION OF COLONIES, 1750	
COLONY	**POPULATION**
Connecticut	111,300
Delaware	28,700
Georgia	5,200
Maryland	141,100
Massachusetts	188,000
New Hampshire	27,500
New Jersey	71,400
New York	76,700
North Carolina	73,000
Pennsylvania	119,700
Rhode Island	33,200
South Carolina	64,000
Virginia	231,000

2 The information presented in the table supports which of the following statements?

A Most of the colonies had populations of more than 100,000 people.

B New York had a larger population than Delaware.

C Rhode Island had the smallest population of any colony.

D The population of Massachusetts was more than twice that of Maryland.

3 Based on the table and your knowledge of history, which statement best describes the colonial American population?

A The colonies that covered the smallest geographic areas also had the smallest populations.

B The Southern Colonies had the largest populations of any colonies.

C Each region featured one populous colony and several other much more sparse colonies.

D The earliest colonies most likely had larger populations than those colonies established closer to 1750.

Directions: Question 4 refers to the following table.

ESTIMATED POPULATION OF VIRGINIA COLONY	
YEAR	**POPULATION**
1650	18,700
1700	58,600
1750	231,000

4 The details in the table support which of the following assumptions?

A Many people left Virginia to settle in other colonies between 1700 and 1750.

B Virginia's colonial population peaked before 1750.

C Virginia had one of the smallest colonial populations in 1750.

D Between 1700 and 1750, Virginia's agricultural economy diversified and its population grew significantly.

Directions: Questions 5 through 7 refer to the following table.

COLONIAL POPULATIONS OF ENSLAVED PEOPLE			
COLONY	1720	1750	1770
Connecticut	1,093	3,010	5,689
New York	5,740	11,014	19,062
Maryland	12,499	43,450	63,818
Virginia	26,550	107,100	187,600
South Carolina	11,828	39,000	75,178

5 Which colony's population of enslaved people increased the least from 1720 to 1750?
   A South Carolina
   B New York
   C Maryland
   D Connecticut

6 Which colony's population of enslaved people increased by the greatest number from 1720 to 1750?
   A New York
   B Virginia
   C Maryland
   D South Carolina

7 Based on the table, which statement is accurate?
   A South Carolina's population of enslaved people doubled between 1720 and 1750.
   B New England colonies typically had larger populations of enslaved people than Middle Colonies.
   C Virginia's population of enslaved people increased by more than 150,000 between 1720 and 1770.
   D Connecticut's population of enslaved people began to decrease after 1750.

Directions: Questions 8 and 9 refer to the following table and information.

ESTIMATED REGIONAL POPULATION OF COLONIES, 1770	
REGION	POPULATION
New England	539,800
Middle Colonies	555,900
Southern Colonies	994,400

As the late 1700s approached, the English colonies began to grow at an extremely fast rate. In fact, by 1775, the colonial population would reach nearly ten times the size it had been in 1700. Some of this growth resulted from continued immigration to the colonies. However, the bulk of this population growth was caused by very high birth rates, coupled with low death rates.

8 Based on the information in the table, which statement accurately describes the Middle Colonies?
   A The Middle Colonies had the smallest population of any colonial region.
   B Massachusetts represented more than half of the Middle Colonies' population.
   C About 400,000 fewer people lived in the Middle Colonies than in the Southern Colonies.
   D The Middle Colonies had a smaller average population per colony than New England.

9 Which of the following best accounts for the population growth in the colonies?
   A The colonies experienced natural increases due to birth and death rates.
   B German and Scots-Irish settlers began moving to the colonies.
   C The health of the colonists declined over time.
   D Many people moved to the colonies to find manufacturing jobs.

Directions: Questions 10 through 13 refer to the following table.

NATIVE AMERICAN CONFLICTS IN COLONIAL AMERICA		
CONFLICT (DATE)	**REGION**	**EVENTS/OUTCOME**
Pequot Revolt (1636–1637)	New England	Conflict grows as colonists move west into Massachusetts and Connecticut; colonists accuse a Pequot Indian of killing a settler, and they burn a village in retaliation; Pequot attack Connecticut town; settlers and Narrangansatt Indians then burn and destroy Pequot's primary village; many Pequot lose their lives
King Philip's War (1675–1676)	New England	Wampanoag and other groups respond to encroachment on lands in southeastern Massachusetts with armed conflict; many losses for colonists and Native Americans; Native American forces eventually weaken; many Native Americans forced to leave their homes
Yamassee War (1715)	Southern Colonies	Conflict grows between colonists seeking new lands and Creek Indians; colonists enlist help from Cherokee and Yamassee to defeat Creek
Raid on Kittanning (1756)	Middle Colonies	Pennsylvania colonists raid Delaware village of Kittanning; part of a series of violent conflicts between Native Americans and colonists over rights to land

UNIT 2

10 In which region did the earliest conflict occur?

The earliest conflict was in
A New England.
B the Middle Colonies.
C the Southern Colonies.
D the Pequot region.

11 Based on the information in the table, which statement is the most accurate?
A Few people lost their lives during these conflicts.
B Conflicts between colonists and Native Americans occurred throughout all regions of the colonies.
C Most Native American groups lived in large villages.
D Native American groups rarely battled against one another.

12 What can be assumed about Native American conflicts in colonial America?
A Colonists usually rejected the help of other Native American groups.
B Most colonial conflicts began in the Southern Colonies.
C Colonists and Native Americans usually found peaceful solutions to their conflicts.
D Most conflicts between colonists and Native Americans began over land disputes.

13 Based on the information in the table, how is colonial population growth connected to conflict?

The colonial population
A decreased in some areas because of conflict with Native Americans.
B decreased because people in Europe were afraid to move to America.
C increased, and more land was needed.
D increased because all of the Native Americans were forced out of North America.

Directions: Questions 14 through 18 refer to the following information and table.

While the original Thirteen Colonies were united under British rule, each region developed different ways of life. In New England, most colonists lived in towns. Many colonists in the region farmed, but others worked in industries such as fishing, shipping, lumber, and trade. In the Middle Colonies, most people lived and worked on small farms. However, some large cities, such as Philadelphia and New York, grew in the region. Trade and some small industries were also important. The Southern Colonies featured many large plantations. Agriculture was the dominant economic activity in this region.

REGIONAL DIFFERENCES

REGION	ECONOMY	SETTLEMENT PATTERNS
New England	Agriculture, fishing, shipping, lumbering, trade	Towns
Middle Colonies	Agriculture, trade, small industries	Small farms, some large cities
Southern Colonies	Agriculture	Large plantations and small farms

14 Based on the table and the passage, which economic activity occurred in each region?
- A agriculture
- B commerce
- C fishing
- D small industries

15 What does the middle column of the table contain?

The middle column of the table contains information about
- A the Middle Colonies.
- B the regions of the Thirteen Colonies.
- C the economic activities of each region.
- D the settlement patterns of each region.

16 What information could you learn from the passage that you could not find in the table?

The information in the text provides
- A the number of people living in each colonial region.
- B specific examples of large cities in the Middle Colonies.
- C the types of plantations found in the Southern Colonies.
- D the industries in which New England colonists worked.

17 In which colony might people be more quickly informed about news and events?
- A New Hampshire
- B South Carolina
- C Massachusetts
- D Georgia

18 Which of the following assumptions can you logically make about the reason for the differences among the colonies?
- A Geography and climate played a large part in the differences among the colonies.
- B The temperate New England climate fostered the growth of large plantations.
- C Because the Southern Colonies were farthest south, their climate and geography encouraged industries.
- D The large forests and rocky lands of the Middle Colonies encouraged fur trapping and the lumber industry.

Main Idea and Details

① Learn the Skill

The **main idea** is the most important point of a passage or a story. The main idea may come at the beginning, middle, or end of a passage. A main idea may be clearly stated or it may be implied. If it is implied, you must use reasoning and supporting details to determine the main idea. You usually find the main idea within the **topic sentence**, or the first or last sentence of a given paragraph.

Supporting details provide additional information about the main idea. Such details include facts, statistics, explanations, and descriptions.

② Practice the Skill

By mastering the skill of identifying the main idea and supporting details, you will improve your study and test-taking skills, especially as they relate to social studies high school equivalency tests. Read the excerpt and strategies below. Use this information to answer question 1.

A The main idea expresses the key point of a passage or story. It usually can be found in the topic sentence.

B Supporting details usually follow and provide additional information about the main idea.

From Thomas Paine's *Common Sense* (1776):

. . . The infant state of the Colonies, as it is called, so far from being against, is an argument in favour of independence. We are sufficiently numerous, and were we more so we might be less united. 'Tis a matter worthy of observation that the more a country is peopled, the smaller their armies are. In military numbers, the ancients far exceeded the moderns; and the reason is evident, for trade being the consequence of population, men became too much absorbed thereby to attend to anything else. Commerce diminishes the spirit both of patriotism and military defense. And history sufficiently informs us that the bravest achievements were always accomplished in the non-age of a nation. . . .

✓ TEST-TAKING TIPS

Identify supporting details by first finding the main idea and then locating the parts of the text that include information related to the main idea. These likely are the supporting details.

1 **Which detail supports the main idea that Paine believes the colonies should seek independence from Britain?**
   A Growing commerce leads to increased feelings of independence.
   B The bravest achievements, such as independence, come in a nation's early years.
   C The colonies lack a sizeable military presence with which to pursue independence.
   D Independence and trade are consequences of growing populations.

UNIT 2

Directions: Questions 2 and 3 refer to the following information and excerpt.

War between Britain and its colonies began on April 19, 1775, but few Americans wanted to break from Britain. Instead, most colonists wanted to gain rights under the British Government. As the war continued, however, many Americans began to want economic freedom in addition to personal liberty.

On April 12, 1776, North Carolina's delegates voted for independence. A month later, Virginia's delegates did the same. In June 1776, a committee including John Adams, Benjamin Franklin, and Thomas Jefferson met to prepare a document explaining the need for independence. That document was the Declaration of Independence.

From the Declaration of Independence:

. . . We hold these truths to be self-evident, that all men are created equal, that they are endowed by their Creator with certain unalienable rights, that among these are life, liberty and the pursuit of happiness. That to secure these rights, governments are instituted among men, deriving their just powers from the consent of the governed. That whenever any form of government becomes destructive to these ends, it is the right of the people to alter or abolish it, and to institute new government, laying its foundation of such principles and organizing its powers in such form, as to them shall seem most likely to effect their safety and happiness.

2   What is the main idea in this excerpt from the Declaration of Independence?
   A   All men are endowed with unalienable rights.
   B   Governments are responsible for the happiness of the people.
   C   People have the right to end destructive governments and form new ones.
   D   Life, liberty, and the pursuit of happiness are important freedoms.

3   The details in the paragraph and the excerpt support which of the following main ideas?
   A   After war broke out in 1775, the colonists wanted to be independent of Britain.
   B   North Carolina's and Virginia's delegates were at odds over independence.
   C   The colonists cautiously approached independence only after the British continued to violently oppress them.
   D   John Adams, Thomas Jefferson, and Benjamin Franklin believed that all men were created equal and with certain rights.

Directions: Question 4 refers to the following paragraph and table.

A total of 56 men from thirteen colonies representing New England, the Middle Colonies, and the Southern Colonies signed the Declaration of Independence. The signers ranged in age from 26 to 70 and included two future presidents, John Adams and Thomas Jefferson.

COLONIES	NUMBER OF SIGNERS
Connecticut	4
Delaware	3
Georgia	3
Maryland	4
Massachusetts	5
New Hampshire	3
New Jersey	5
New York	4
North Carolina	3
Pennsylvania	9
Rhode Island	2
South Carolina	4
Virginia	7

4   The details in the table support which of the following assumptions?
   A   Pennsylvania and Virginia were large and important colonies.
   B   Both signers who became president were from Massachusetts.
   C   North Carolina was smaller in size than Connecticut in 1776.
   D   New England supported independence more than the Southern Colonies.

Directions: Questions 5 and 6 refer to the following information and map.

The original territory of the United States, as defined by the treaties of November 30, 1782, and September 3, 1783, with Great Britain, was bounded on the north by Canada, on the south by the Spanish Colonies of East and West Florida, on the east by the Atlantic Ocean, and on the west by the Mississippi River. It included the Thirteen Original Colonies and the areas claimed by them. One of the difficult problems of the new nation was the existence of extensive unoccupied territory between the Thirteen Original Colonies and the Mississippi River. Seven of the Colonies claimed large parts of this territory and some of the claims were conflicting.

From nationalatlas.gov, accessed 2014

5 What is the main idea of the passage?
A The colonies were in conflict with Great Britain over parts of Canada.
B There were disputed land claims among the colonies.
C The colonies were arguing with Spain over ownership of West and East Florida.
D There were conflicting claims among the colonies over land west of the Mississippi River.

6 How does the map provide a supporting detail for the main idea in the passage?
A It shows the Thirteen Colonies.
B It shows West and East Florida.
C It shows the large size of the unoccupied territory.
D It shows that the Great Lakes border Canada.

Directions: Questions 7 and 8 refer to the following excerpt from the Declaration of Independence.

We, therefore, the representatives of the United States of America, in General Congress, assembled . . . do, in the name, and by the authority of the good people of these colonies, solemnly publish and declare, that these united colonies are, and of right ought to be free and independent states; that they are absolved from all allegiance to the British Crown, and that all political connection between them and the state of Great Britain, is and ought to be totally dissolved; and that as free and independent states, they have full power to levy war, conclude peace, contract alliances, establish commerce, and to do all other acts and things which independent states may of right do.

7 The main idea can establish purpose. What is the main idea and purpose of the Declaration of Independence?

The purpose of the Declaration of Independence was to
A overthrow Britain's government.
B end political loyalty to Britain.
C declare war on Britain.
D end oppressive governments everywhere.

8 Which detail supports the main idea that the colonists will govern themselves?
A "We, . . . in the name, and by the authority of the good people of these colonies"
B "these united colonies are . . . free and independent"
C "all political connection between them and the state of Great Britain, is . . . dissolved"
D "as free and independent states, they have full power to levy war"

Directions: Questions 9 through 11 refer to the following paragraph and table about the Articles of Confederation.

After declaring independence from Britain, the American colonies set forth to govern themselves. First, however, they needed a plan of government. In 1776 and 1777, colonial leaders wrote the Articles of Confederation. American leaders purposefully designed the Articles to limit the national government's power to make and enforce laws. The Articles were adopted by Congress on November 15, 1777, and fully ratified by all states on March 1, 1781. Some important achievements occurred under the Articles, including a plan for new states in the Northwest Ordinance of 1787. However, the weak central government made it difficult for the states to function as one nation. In particular, under the Articles of Confederation, the national government was unable to tax or regulate trade between states. In 1787, American leaders proposed the United States Constitution, which established a strong national government.

COMPARING GOVERNMENT PLANS		
	ARTICLES OF CONFEDERATION	**U.S. CONSTITUTION**
Government	Weak central government, with no executive	Strong central government, with president
Legislature	One house; one vote per state	Two houses; one vote per senator or representative
Taxes	Collected by states	Collected by national government
New states	Admitted through agreement of nine states	Admitted through agreement by Congress
Amendments	Agreed upon by all states	Agreed upon by three-fourths of states

9 Which of the following titles best expresses the main idea of the paragraph?

A Birth of the Northwest Ordinance

B End of the American Revolution

C The First Plan of Government

D The United States Constitution

10 Based on the details in the table, which act would have been possible under the Articles of Confederation?

A Members of the House of Representatives and senators vote to declare war.

B The state of Virginia collects taxes.

C All states must agree to admit a new state.

D Pennsylvania receives more representatives than New Jersey.

11 Why did American leaders choose to limit the national government's powers under the Articles of Confederation?

A They wanted to reflect Britain's national government.

B They wanted most of the power to rest with individual states.

C They believed that representatives and senators should make and enforce laws.

D They wanted the states to function as one nation.

Directions: Question 12 refers to the table on this page and the following paragraph.

After the American Revolution ended in 1783, the United States had a large amount of debt. The situation was so bad that the government could not pay many soldiers for their service during the war. Also, they did not have money to pay government officials. The United States had a national debt of around $40 million and owed $12 million to foreign countries. The individual states carried a combined debt of $25 million.

12 Why would the structure of the Articles of Confederation make solving this debt problem difficult?

A There was no president to submit a national budget.

B The states had no economic plan.

C Congress had to negotiate for loans with foreign governments.

D Only the states had the power to levy taxes.

Directions: Questions 13 through 16 refer to the following paragraph and table about the U.S. Constitution.

In the summer of 1787, a total of 55 delegates attended the Constitutional Convention in Philadelphia. The U.S. Constitution they submitted for ratification in September was vastly different from the Articles of Confederation. The Constitution established a strong national government, with a president, a bicameral (two houses) legislature, and a supreme court. The legislature was a mixture of equal and proportional representation. All three branches of national government were powerful, but checked one another. At the time it was submitted for ratification, the Constitution had no provisions for protecting personal freedoms. Many states remembered how the oppression of those freedoms caused the colonies to break from Britain and were concerned about having a strong national government that did not secure freedoms in the United States. Nevertheless, the Constitution would become law once ratified by nine states. The Bill of Rights, which guaranteed a number of personal freedoms, was added in 1791.

RATIFICATION OF U.S. CONSTITUTION		
DATE	STATE	VOTE
Dec. 7, 1787	Delaware	30-0
Dec. 12, 1787	Pennsylvania	46-23
Dec. 18, 1787	New Jersey	38-0
Jan. 9, 1788	Connecticut	128-40
Feb. 2, 1788	Georgia	26-0
Feb. 6, 1788	Massachusetts	187-168
April 28, 1788	Maryland	63-11
May 23, 1788	South Carolina	149-73
June 21, 1788	New Hampshire	57-47
June 25, 1788	Virginia	89-79
July 26, 1788	New York	30-27
Nov. 21, 1789	North Carolina	194-77
May 29, 1790	Rhode Island	34-32

13 Based on the details in the passage and table, which small state might have been most concerned about proportional representation in Congress?
A Rhode Island
B Pennsylvania
C New York
D South Carolina

14 Based on the details in the passage and table, why might have the vote in Massachusetts been close?

Massachusetts might have had a close vote for ratification because
A John Adams was not elected as the first president.
B Boston was the birthplace of the American Revolution.
C leaders were concerned that personal liberties were not protected.
D it wanted to wait and see how New York would vote it had few delegates.

15 Which of the following titles best expresses the main idea of the information provided by the passage and table?
A Checks and Balances
B The Constitutional Convention
C Protecting Personal Freedoms
D From Convention to Ratification

16 Which of the following best expresses the main idea of the passage and the table?
A New York and Virginia preferred the Articles of Confederation over the Constitution.
B States had various concerns about the Constitution and different timetables for ratification.
C New Hampshire's ratification of the Constitution led New York and Virginia to do the same.
D Most states ratified the Constitution unanimously.

Categorize

① *Learn the Skill*

A good way to organize information about people, places, dates, and events is to **categorize** it. To categorize means to place information in a group of similar or related items. For instance, when learning about a particular time period in history, you might categorize events into groups such as political events, military events, or economic events.

By sorting information into categories in this way, you can better examine how things are alike and different. Categorizing information can also help you understand patterns or trends throughout social studies. When you organize specific information into larger categories, it helps you see the big picture.

② *Practice the Skill*

By mastering the skill of categorizing, you will improve your study and test-taking skills, especially as they relate to social studies high school equivalency tests. Examine the table and strategies below. Use this information to answer question 1.

Ⓐ The two main categories shown in this table are Federalists and Anti-Federalists. You can use the content of the table to determine whether other people or ideas should be categorized as Federalist or Anti-Federalist.

Ⓑ Tables are useful tools for organizing the information that you categorize. Here, additional information about these groups has been categorized according to their views on government, views on the United States Constitution, and leaders.

FEDERALISTS AND ANTI-FEDERALISTS

GROUP	Ⓑ VIEW ON GOVERNMENT	Ⓑ VIEW ON CONSTITUTION	Ⓑ LEADER
Federalist	Supported strong national government; wanted large military force; supported commerce and industry over agriculture	Supported adoption of Constitution	Alexander Hamilton
Anti-Federalists	Wanted to limit power of national government; believed states should keep as much power as possible; favored agriculture over commerce and industry	Opposed adoption of Constitution	Thomas Jefferson

USING LOGIC

When categorizing information, determine the most general categories into which your information can be grouped. From there, you can further group each set of information into more specific categories.

1 **Which of the following statements could be categorized as expressing an Anti-Federalist viewpoint?**

A The Constitution should be ratified as quickly as possible.

B The national government must be capable of enforcing its own laws.

C The future of the nation depends upon the work of farmers throughout the nation.

D Taxes should be raised in order to support industrial growth.

Directions: Questions 2 and 3 refer to the following excerpts.

From *The Federalist Papers: No. 2* by John Jay:

It has until lately been a received and uncontradicted opinion that the prosperity of the people of America depended on their continuing firmly united, and the wishes, prayers, and efforts of our best and wisest citizens have been constantly directed to that object. But politicians now appear, who insist that this opinion is erroneous, and that instead of looking for safety and happiness in union, we ought to seek it in a division of the States into distinct confederacies or sovereignties.

From *Anti-Federalist Letters from the Federal Farmer to the Republican:*

There are certain unalienable and fundamental rights, which in forming the social compact, ought to be explicitly ascertained and fixed—a free and enlightened people, in forming this compact, will not resign all their rights to those who govern, and they will fix limits to their legislators and rulers. . . .

2   **Which two categories of individuals does John Jay identify in the first excerpt?**
   A   his supporters and supporters of Alexander Hamilton
   B   people who believe in a strong central government and people who believe in a number of strong state governments
   C   people who favor industry and people who favor agriculture
   D   delegates who supported the Constitution and delegates who opposed the Constitution

3   **How might the author of the second excerpt have categorized the citizens of the United States?**

   The author might have categorized citizens as
   A   people who do not possess unalienable and fundamental rights.
   B   individuals who support a strong national government.
   C   a group that has resigned all of their rights to the government.
   D   people who want limited government.

Directions: Questions 4 and 5 refer to the following information.

Georgia was the southernmost colony and bordered Spanish Florida. In 1739, when England and Spain were at war, colonists were successful in beating back a Spanish retaliation attack on the colony. To help defend against the possibility of invasion, the city of Savannah, Georgia was fortified. By the time of the American Revolution, Georgia remained the least-populated colony, with its land still mostly wilderness.

After the American Revolution, the states tried to expand their territory. In 1785, Georgia established a claim to land in what is now present-day Alabama and Mississippi. Spain, who had first claimed the territory, ordered the Georgian settlers to leave. In 1789, land companies purchased more land from the Georgia legislature, further complicating the issue of ownership. At that time, Spain still claimed a portion of this territory.

4   **Into which category is this information best placed?**
   A   economic history
   B   international political history
   C   military history
   D   social history

5   **Which of the following could be reason why Georgia categorized the Spanish as a threat?**
   A   Georgia was the least-populated colony at the time of the American Revolution.
   B   The land in Georgia was mostly a wilderness.
   C   British and Spanish forces were at war over Georgia.
   D   Georgia bordered Florida and had been previously attacked by the Spanish.

Directions: Questions 6 and 7 refer to the following information and excerpt.

George Washington believed that political parties would prove harmful to the new United States. In his 1796 farewell address as president, he discussed his views of these parties and his concerns for their impact on the country:

"... the common and continual mischiefs of the spirit of party are sufficient to make it the interest and duty of a wise people to discourage and restrain it.

It serves always to distract the public councils and enfeeble public administration. It agitates the community with ill-founded jealousies and false alarms, kindles the animosity of one against another, foments occasionally riot and insurrection. It opens the door to foreign influence and corruption, which finds a facilitated access to the government itself through the channels of party passions."

6   How could Washington's speech be categorized?
  A   motivational
  B   cautionary
  C   thankful
  D   frightened

7   In this excerpt, Washington describes several types of potential harmful effects of political parties.

  Under which of these would you categorize the bribery of an elected official by another government?
  A   feeble public administration
  B   animosity between groups
  C   riot and insurrection
  D   foreign influence and corruption

Directions: Questions 8 through 10 refer to the following map.

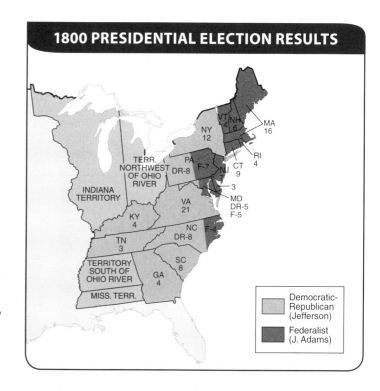

8   Which category below would list the greatest number of places?
  A   territories
  B   Democratic-Republican states
  C   Federalist states
  D   states that divided electoral votes between the Federalists and Democratic-Republicans

9   Which of the following would belong to a category titled "States with Ten or More Electoral Votes"?
  A   Kentucky
  B   South Carolina
  C   Connecticut
  D   Pennsylvania

10 Based on the map, in which category would you place the state of Vermont?
  A   Democratic-Republican state
  B   territory
  C   Federalist state
  D   Middle Colony

Directions: Questions 11 through 13 refer to the following information.

In 1803, French Emperor Napoleon Bonaparte, faced with an imminent war with Britain, finally agreed to sell the Louisiana Territory to the United States. Napoleon feared that Britain might try to occupy the territory. The Louisiana Purchase, as it became known, included more than 800,000 square miles of land west of the Mississippi River. The United States paid $15 million for the land. President Thomas Jefferson had wanted to acquire the land to continue westward expansion of the United States and to gain full control of the Mississippi River.

11 How is Napoleon's agreement to sell the Louisiana Territory best categorized?

- A economic
- B religious
- C political
- D social

12 Jefferson's decision to make the Louisiana Purchase falls into which two categories?

Jefferson's decision is best categorized as
- A a military and geographic decision.
- B an international political and military decision.
- C a national political and military decision.
- D a geographic and economic decision.

13 Into which category does the desire to control the Mississippi River fall?

- A economics
- B international politics
- C national politics
- D social

Directions: Questions 14 and 15 refer to the following table.

THE LEWIS AND CLARK EXPEDITION
Commissioned by President Thomas Jefferson; officially called The Corps of Discovery; main goal was to find northern water route between Atlantic and Pacific oceans
Led by army officers Meriwether Lewis and William Clark; lasted from May 1804 through September 1806
Journey began and ended in St. Louis; the Corps reached the Pacific Ocean bordering present-day Oregon
Clark served as naturalist and kept a detailed journal of the new plants and animal species discovered
Failed in main mission to find Northwest Passage; information gathered about the land, plants, and animals and successful interaction with Native American groups proved valuable

14 How can Jefferson's original goal for the mission be categorized?

- A Native American interaction
- B western expansion
- C national security
- D commercial and trade

15 Overall, how is the journey of The Corps of Discovery best categorized?

The journey is best categorized as
- A a failure for not achieving anything.
- B worthwhile for increasing knowledge about the American west.
- C political for being ordered by President Jefferson.
- D controversial for causing conflict with Native Americans.

Directions: Questions 16 and 17 refer to the following table and passage.

NORTHWEST TERRITORY STATES		
STATE	YEAR OF STATEHOOD	STATE NUMBER
Ohio	1803	17th
Indiana	1816	19th
Illinois	1818	21st
Michigan	1837	26th
Wisconsin	1848	30th

When Congress passed the Northwest Ordinance in July of 1787, the Northwest Territory was created. The new territory was a sizeable area of federal land east of the Mississippi River between the Great Lakes and the Ohio River. At the same time, Congress established a form of government for the territory and declared how various areas of land might eventually become states. The Ordinance required the creation of at least three but not more than five states from the Northwest Territory, and the boundaries of each new state were defined. The Ordinance prohibited slavery and required each new state to number at least 60,000 inhabitants to qualify for statehood.

16 **The information presented in the table and the passage categorizes states created from the Northwest Territory. How else could this group of states be categorized?**

These states could also be categorized as
A western states.
B free states.
C states west of the Mississippi River.
D original colonies.

17 **Which state could be placed in a category of states formed after 1840?**
A Ohio
B Indiana
C Michigan
D Wisconsin

Directions: Questions 18 and 19 refer to the following information.

In October of 1803, President Thomas Jefferson addressed Congress and encouraged the lawmakers to approve the Louisiana Purchase.

From Thomas Jefferson's Annual Message to Congress, 1803:

While the prosperity and sovereignty of the Mississippi and its waters secure an independent outlet for the produce of the western States, and an uncontrolled navigation through their whole course, free from collision with other powers and the dangers to our peace from that source, the fertility of the country, its climate and extent, promise in due season important aids to our treasury, an ample provision for our posterity, and a wide-spread field for the blessings of freedom and equal laws.

18 **Jefferson describes two categories of benefits the United States will receive from the Louisiana Purchase. What are they?**
A alliances with Spain and control of the Gulf of Mexico
B opportunities for building factories and the use of military facilities in the region
C safe passage through the area and financial gain from the area's resources
D peaceful relations with Native Americans and control of the Ohio River

19 **How could the tone of Jefferson's address be categorized?**

Jefferson's address can be categorized as
A stern.
B hopeful.
C defeated.
D judgmental.

Sequence

① Learn the Skill

When you **sequence** events, you place them in an order, most often chronologically (from earliest to latest). By understanding the order in which events occurred, you can examine how one event led to another to produce a certain outcome. The ability to sequence further enables you to recognize how a past event might affect a current event, which could lead to a future result. In this way, sequencing events can help you make predictions about future outcomes.

② Practice the Skill

By mastering the skill of sequencing, you will improve your study and test-taking skills, especially as they relate to social studies high school equivalency tests. Read the information and strategies below. Use this information to answer question 1.

A The final event or outcome of a sequence of events is sometimes described at the beginning or end of a passage.

B Look for words such as *first, next, later, finally,* and so on, that provide clues about the order in which events occurred. Times and dates also provide hints that you can use when sequencing events.

🧩 MAKING ASSUMPTIONS

When reading information about history, you can usually assume that it is written in chronological order. However, sometimes historians organize material by themes. For example, a World War II historian may describe European battles and then Pacific battles, even though they may have taken place at the same time.

A <u>By the 1840s, only a very small number of Native Americans remained in the southern United States between the Atlantic Ocean and the Mississippi River</u>. Much of the Native Americans' removal from this area occurred through a series of treaties and legislation encouraged by President Andrew Jackson. After taking office in 1829, Jackson spurred Congress to pass the Indian Removal Act of 1830. This allowed Jackson to offer Native Americans territory in the west in exchange for leaving their native lands in the east. He also signed many removal treaties that forced Native Americans off their homelands.

One such group, the Cherokee Nation, disputed government policies in Georgia that limited their freedoms. The Supreme Court decided in 1832 that Native American groups were not subject to state laws. **B** <u>Later</u>, Jackson negotiated his own removal treaty with a Cherokee chief. Congress approved the treaty in 1835. When many Cherokee resisted leaving their lands, Jackson ordered a military response. **B** <u>Finally</u>, in 1838, troops led the Cherokee to the Indian Territory along the Trail of Tears.

1 **Which of the following events occurred immediately after Jackson became president?**

A Jackson negotiated a removal treaty with the Cherokee.
B Congress approved the Indian Removal Act of 1830.
C The Cherokee disputed government policies that limited their freedoms.
D U.S. troops led the Cherokee along the Trail of Tears.

Directions: Questions 2 and 3 review to the following information.

The War of 1812 began after a long period of escalating tensions between Britain and the United States. Tensions grew when British forces disrupted American ships carrying goods to Europe. However, another important cause of the conflict proved to be Americans' desire for additional lands along the frontier. Many settlers suspected that the British supported Native Americans in their conflicts with settlers. After the Battle of Tippecanoe in 1811, settlers became especially eager to remove the British from the area.

WAR OF 1812

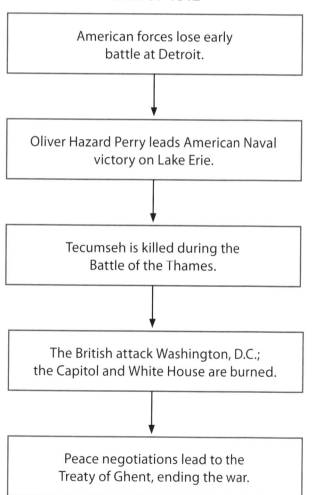

American forces lose early battle at Detroit.

Oliver Hazard Perry leads American Naval victory on Lake Erie.

Tecumseh is killed during the Battle of the Thames.

The British attack Washington, D.C.; the Capitol and White House are burned.

Peace negotiations lead to the Treaty of Ghent, ending the war.

2 **Which event preceded the War of 1812?**
  A the Battle of the Thames
  B the British attack on Washington, D.C.
  C the signing of the Treaty of Ghent
  D the Battle of Tippecanoe

3 **Which of the following events might logically be placed last on the sequence graphic organizer showing the sequence of events of the War of 1812?**
  A Britain ceded Canada to the United States.
  B The British defeated Andrew Jackson's forces at the Battle of New Orleans.
  C The United States became the most powerful nation in the world.
  D Nationalism began to grow in the United States.

Directions: Question 4 refers to the following information.

In the early 1800s, Texas was a part of northeastern Mexico. However, many American settlers started migrating to the area during this time. Texas gained its independence in 1821. However, the Mexican government insisted that Texans become Mexican citizens and convert to Catholicism. Texans also received orders to accept the Mexican government's ban on slavery in their territory. Texans largely disregarded these orders, and settlers continued to arrive. In 1835, about 30,000 Americans lived in Texas. When the Mexican government attempted to assert its power there, many American settlers revolted. This event became known as the Texas Revolution. The Texans gained a victory in 1836, and asked to join the United States.

4 **When did Texas gain its independence?**
  A during the same year that the population of Texas reached 30,000
  B more than 10 years before the Texas Revolution
  C after the settlers' victory in 1836
  D after joining the United States

Directions: Questions 5 through 7 refer to the following excerpt from James Monroe's first inaugural address.

Such, then, being the highly favored condition of our country, it is in the interest of every citizen to maintain it. What are the dangers which menace us? If any exist they ought to be ascertained and guarded against.

In explaining my sentiments on this subject it may be asked, What raised us to the present happy state? How did we accomplish the Revolution? How remedy the defects of the first instrument of our Union . . . ? How sustain and pass with glory through the late war? The Government has been in the hands of the people.

5 **Which of the following events occurred first?**
   A   Monroe's inauguration
   B   the election of 1816
   C   the American Revolution
   D   the writing of the Articles of·Confederation

6 **What was the last challenge to which Monroe referred?**

   When Monroe spoke about "glory through the late war," he meant
   A   the Civil War.
   B   the French and Indian War.
   C   the War of 1812.
   D   the American Revolution.

7 **To which most recent document is President Monroe likely referring when he states, "The Government has been in the hands of the people"?**
   A   the Articles of Confederation
   B   the Treaty of Ghent
   C   the Declaration of Independence
   D   a Massachusetts news article

Directions: Questions 8 and 9 refer to the following sequence chart.

BATTLE OF NEW ORLEANS

British hope to gain access to Mississippi Valley by capturing New Orleans.

↓

British and American forces arrive near New Orleans in late 1814.

↓

On December 24, 1814, British and American diplomats in Belgium make peace and agree to Treaty of Ghent.

↓

Many small conflicts occur near New Orleans in late 1814 and early 1815. News of the signing of the treaty has not yet reached the United States.

↓

The main battle of New Orleans occurs on January 8, 1815.

↓

The Americans win a decisive victory.

↓

The British give up plans and leave for Britain.

8 **What happened after the British and American forces arrived at New Orleans?**
   A   Americans won a decisive victory.
   B   A number of small conflicts broke out.
   C   Britain gave up plans for additional conflicts.
   D   The British planned to gain access to the Mississippi Valley.

9 **Why did the Battle of New Orleans occur after the Treaty of Ghent was signed?**
   A   The British wanted to control New Orleans despite the treaty.
   B   Andrew Jackson was determined to beat the British.
   C   The troops in New Orleans did not know that the treaty had been signed.
   D   Americans did not agree with the terms of the treaty.

Directions: Questions 10 and 11 refer to the following excerpt from Andrew Jackson's "Message to Congress on Indian Removal," 1830.

It gives me pleasure to announce to Congress that the benevolent policy of the Government, steadily pursued for nearly thirty years, in relation to the removal of the Indians beyond the white settlements is approaching to a happy consummation. Two important tribes have accepted the provision made for their removal at the last session of Congress, and it is believed that their example will induce the remaining tribes also to seek the same obvious advantages. ...

The present policy of the Government is but a continuation of the same progressive change by a milder process. The tribes which occupied the countries now constituting the Eastern States were annihilated or have melted away to make room for the whites. The waves of population and civilization are rolling to the westward, and we now propose to acquire the countries occupied by the red men of the South and West by a fair exchange, and, at the expense of the United States, to send them to land where their existence may be prolonged and perhaps made perpetual.

10 According to Jackson's speech, which of the following events has already taken place?
   A   Most Native American groups are gone from the eastern United States.
   B   The final two Native American groups in the eastern United States refused to leave their lands.
   C   The policy the government has used for the past thirty years to relocate Native Americans has failed.
   D   Migration of white settlers to the western portions of the United States has slowed.

11 What does Jackson suggest about the evolution of the policies of the United States toward Native Americans?

   The policies have
   A   been only moderately successful over time.
   B   become less harsh and confrontational toward Native Americans.
   C   led to a consensus agreement with all Native American groups facing relocation.
   D   been inconsistent between presidencies.

Directions: Questions 12 and 13 refer to the following information.

After serving as Secretary of State, James Monroe received the Democratic-Republican nomination for President in 1816, and handily won the general election. Monroe faced many foreign policy challenges. In 1817, an agreement led to the reduction of both British and American forces on the Great Lakes. Another agreement determined the boundary between the United States and Canada. In 1819, a treaty with Spain made official the United States' control of Florida.

Monroe won reelection in 1820. The most notable event of his second term proved to be his endorsement of Manifest Destiny and the proposal of the Monroe Doctrine in 1823. The Monroe Doctrine became one of the foundations of foreign policy for the young nation. The United States government has upheld this doctrine ever since. The Monroe Doctrine states that European Nations must not interfere with any nations in the Western Hemisphere or try to acquire new territory there.

12 How many years passed between when Monroe was first elected president and his proposal of the Monroe Doctrine?
   A   two years
   B   four years
   C   five years
   D   seven years

13 Why might voters have reelected Monroe in 1820?
   A   He proposed the Monroe Doctrine.
   B   He saved the Federalist Party.
   C   He had been Secretary of State.
   D   He settled many disputes with foreign countries.

Directions: Questions 14 and 15 refer to the following information.

After the War of 1812, many political leaders in the United States believed that the nation should look to expand its boundaries. One such leader was James Monroe's secretary of state, John Quincy Adams. He helped to develop the policy that became known as the Monroe Doctrine. This policy stated that European colonization in the Americas would be viewed as an act of aggression toward the United States. However, the Monroe Doctrine also allowed for the possibility of future U.S. expansion within the Americas.

From James Monroe's "Seventh Annual Message to Congress," December 2, 1823:

With the existing colonies or dependencies of any European power we have not interfered and shall not interfere. But with the Governments who have declared their independence and maintain it, and whose independence we have . . . acknowledged, we could not view any interposition for the purpose of oppressing them, or controlling in any other manner their destiny, by any European power in any other light than as the manifestation of an unfriendly disposition toward the United States.

14 **The Monroe Doctrine was likely issued after which event?**
   A   the United States' annexation of Texas
   B   John Quincy Adams became president
   C   Britain agreed to stop continued expansion into western North America
   D   Spain asked other European nations to help stop revolts in Spanish-American colonies

15 **Which later event reflected the Monroe Doctrine's importance to U.S. foreign policy?**
   A   the Vietnam War
   B   the Mexican War
   C   the Civil War
   D   the Great Depression

Directions: Questions 16 and 17 refer to the following sequence chart.

U.S. EXPANSION IN THE EARLY 1800s

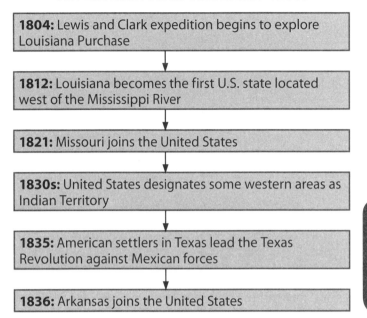

1804: Lewis and Clark expedition begins to explore Louisiana Purchase

1812: Louisiana becomes the first U.S. state located west of the Mississippi River

1821: Missouri joins the United States

1830s: United States designates some western areas as Indian Territory

1835: American settlers in Texas lead the Texas Revolution against Mexican forces

1836: Arkansas joins the United States

16 **Which of the following states gained statehood before Missouri?**
   A   Texas
   B   Arkansas
   C   Louisiana
   D   California

17 **Based on the chart, which of the following statements is accurate?**
   A   Arkansas and Missouri gained statehood less than ten years apart.
   B   The Texas Revolution took place during the same decade in which Missouri became a state.
   C   Texas became a state sometime after 1835.
   D   Every present-day U.S. state located east of the Mississippi River became a state before 1812.

Cause and Effect

① Learn the Skill

A **cause** is an action that makes another event happen. Sometimes causes will be directly stated in text. However, at times, authors may only imply the causes of certain events. An **effect** is something that happens as a result of a cause.

A single cause often produces more than one effect. On the other hand, multiple causes can work together to produce a single effect. By identifying causes and effects in social studies texts, you can better understand the connections between events and more fully comprehend what you have read.

② Practice the Skill

By mastering the skill of analyzing cause and effect, you will improve your study and test-taking skills, especially as they relate to social studies high school equivalency tests. Read the information and strategies below. Use this information to answer question 1.

Ⓐ Here, the author of the passage directly states that one event has caused another.

Ⓑ Other causes and effects are implied rather than explicitly described.

During the Revolutionary era, Northern and Southern states had united behind the common goal of gaining independence from Britain. However, over time, differences between the two regions grew more pronounced. As the 1800s began, the South remained primarily agricultural. The Southern economy centered on plantations and the use of enslaved African laborers. The Northern economy, on the other hand, featured growing commercial and industrial sectors in addition to agriculture. **Ⓐ** These differences caused economic and ideological friction between the two regions. **Ⓑ** Disputes over states' rights emerged as questions arose about the legality of slavery in U.S. territories.

USING LOGIC

Look for key words and phrases such as *caused, affected, led to,* and *resulted from* that signal a cause-and-effect relationship. To confirm that you have correctly identified a cause-and-effect relationship, you should be able to logically restate the events as *A caused B*.

1 **What is one effect of the sectional differences that emerged between the North and the South in the early-to mid-1800s?**
   A The Northern states strongly supported states' rights.
   B The South began using the labor of enslaved people.
   C The Northern economy became increasingly diverse.
   D Northern farmers began establishing plantations.

Directions: Questions 2 and 3 refer to the following table.

SOUTH CAROLINA POPULATION		
YEAR	WHITES	ENSLAVED AFRICAN AMERICANS
1790	140,178	107,094
1820	237,440	258,475
1840	259,084	327,038
1860	291,300	402,406

Source: U.S. Census Bureau

2 **Which of the following would have most likely caused an increase in the enslaved African American population?**
   A New fugitive slave laws were passed in 1850.
   B Many slaves escaped to the North along the routes of the Underground Railroad.
   C Agriculture remained the most common way of making a living in the South.
   D Most Southern farmers worked on small farms.

3 **Which of the following is the most likely effect of population data found in the table?**
   A Northern abolition groups increased their membership.
   B Whites became increasingly nervous about possible violence from the enslaved African American population.
   C The slave trade ended because there was no longer a need for enslaved workers.
   D Enslaved African Americans had to find jobs in towns and cities because plantations had too many workers.

Directions: Questions 4 and 5 refer to the following information.

Nat Turner was an enslaved person on a Virginia plantation. In 1831, Turner organized a group of fellow enslaved people and planned a revolt against their owners. With a group of about 60 people, he attacked slave owners in the surrounding area. Slave owners quickly retaliated. By the time the revolt ended, two days later, more than 50 people had lost their lives. Turner and his followers received harsh punishments and many of them were executed.

4 **What was one probable effect of Nat Turner's revolt?**

Nat Turner's revolt most likely caused
   A slave owners to offer additional rights to enslaved people.
   B additional slave revolts to break out across the South.
   C slave owners to seek a diplomatic solution to the conflict.
   D Southern officials to develop more restrictive policies towards enslaved people.

5 **What might have caused Turner and his followers to plan their revolt?**
   A anger over the harsh conditions under which they lived
   B a desire to share in the profits made by the plantations at which they worked
   C support for the leaders of the Underground Railroad
   D resentment at the passage of new fugitive slave laws

UNIT 2

Directions: Questions 6 and 7 refer to the following information.

As Abraham Lincoln campaigned for president in 1860, many Southern leaders feared that, if elected, he would attempt to bring an end to slavery in the South. When Lincoln won the presidency that November, several Southern states moved toward seceding from the Union. South Carolina became the first to secede on December 20, 1860. Soon, six other Southern states followed suit. Together, these seven states—South Carolina, Mississippi, Florida, Alabama, Georgia, Louisiana, and Texas—formed a new nation called the Confederate States of America. In response to the formation of the Confederacy, Lincoln and other Union leaders sought to claim federal forts and other property located in the South.

6   **How did Lincoln's election in 1860 affect the United States?**
   A   It led to the secession of seven Southern states.
   B   It caused the nation to seize forts and other property from other nations.
   C   It brought an immediate end to slavery in the South.
   D   It encouraged Southern leaders to compromise with the federal government.

7   **Based on the information, which action is the best example of both a cause and an effect?**
   A   the secession of Florida
   B   the formation of the Confederacy
   C   the government's attempts to claim federal property in the South
   D   Southern leaders' fears about Lincoln's anti-slavery policies

Directions: Questions 8 and 9 refer to the following map.

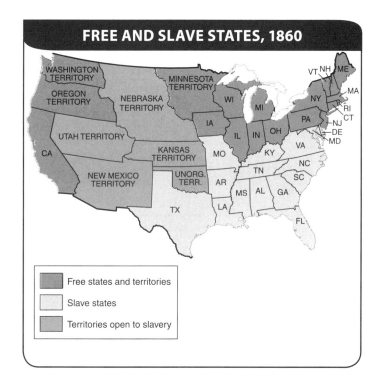

FREE AND SLAVE STATES, 1860

Free states and territories

Slave states

Territories open to slavery

8   **How would the secession of the Southern states have affected this map?**
   A   West Virginia would become a slave state.
   B   California would no longer be labeled as part of the United States.
   C   The Southern states would be labeled as a separate nation.
   D   Atlanta, Georgia, would be identified as the Confederate capital.

9   **What may have caused conflict over slavery in the territories?**

   The map suggests that conflict arose over slavery in the territories because
   A   these territories had become some of the most populous areas in the nation.
   B   more territories were open to slavery than not.
   C   most territories were located in the northern United States.
   D   many of the territories offered valuable access to transportation routes.

Directions: Questions 10 and 11 refer to the following information.

The Civil War officially began on April 12, 1861. On that day, Confederate troops fired on Fort Sumter in South Carolina. At the time, the Union still controlled the fort. However, prior to the attack, the Union commander Major Robert Anderson and his troops were running low on supplies. President Lincoln informed South Carolina's governor that much-needed supplies would be sent to Fort Sumter. However, while Union troops waited for these supplies to arrive, Confederate General P.G.T. Beauregard demanded that Anderson surrender the fort. When Anderson refused, the Confederates launched their attack. Although no lives were lost in the attack, Anderson eventually had to surrender and leave the fort. In response to the attack, Lincoln called for volunteers to join the army to battle against the Confederacy.

10 What prompted Confederate troops to fire upon Fort Sumter?

The Confederates fired on the fort because
   A   of orders from Confederate political leaders.
   B   of Lincoln's call for volunteers to battle the Confederacy.
   C   President Lincoln ordered supplies to be sent to the fort.
   D   Major Robert Anderson refused to surrender the fort.

11 What was the most significant effect of the attack on Fort Sumter?
   A   Lincoln's decision to call for volunteers to battle the Confederacy
   B   the surrender of the fort to Confederate forces
   C   the emergence of P.G.T. Beauregard as a military leader
   D   the loss of morale experienced by the Union

Directions: Questions 12 and 13 refer to the following excerpt from Lincoln's Gettysburg Address.

Fourscore and seven years ago our fathers brought forth on this continent a new nation, conceived in liberty and dedicated to the proposition that all men are created equal. Now we are engaged in a great civil war, testing whether that nation or any nation so conceived and so dedicated can long endure. We are met on a great battlefield of that war. We have come to dedicate a portion of that field as a final resting-place for those who here gave their lives that that nation might live.

12 What does Lincoln's address suggest to be one cause of the Civil War?

The Confederacy
   A   limited the rights of enslaved African Americans.
   B   believed that representatives and senators should make and enforce laws.
   C   wanted the states to function as one nation.
   D   supported rewriting the Declaration of Independence.

13 What effect did Lincoln hope that the Battle of Gettysburg would have?

Lincoln hoped that the soldiers' sacrifice would
   A   end slavery throughout the nation.
   B   preserve the ideals of the founding fathers.
   C   make future battles less costly for the Union Army.
   D   win citizens' support for the war effort.

Directions: Questions 14 through 17 refer to the following excerpt from the Emancipation Proclamation.

That on the first day of January, in the year of our Lord one thousand eight hundred and sixty-three, all persons held as slaves within any State or designated part of a State, the people whereof shall then be in rebellion against the United States, shall be then, thenceforward, and forever free; and the Executive Government of the United States, including the military and naval authority thereof, will recognize and maintain the freedom of such persons, and will do no act or acts to repress such persons, or any of them, in any efforts they may make for their actual freedom.

That the Executive will, on the first day of January aforesaid . . . designate the States and parts of States . . . in which the people hereof, respectively, shall then be in rebellion against the United States; and the fact that any State, or the people thereof, shall on that day be, in good faith, represented in the Congress of the United States by members chosen thereto at elections wherein a majority of the qualified voters of such State shall have participated, shall . . . be deemed conclusive evidence that such State, and the people thereof, are not then in rebellion against the United States.

14 **How did the Emancipation Proclamation affect enslaved persons in the United States and the Confederacy?**
   A   It offered them the opportunity to earn their freedom by serving in the U.S. military.
   B   It freed enslaved persons living in Southern states fighting against the Union.
   C   It freed all enslaved people in the United States and Confederacy.
   D   It promised enslaved people their freedom at the conclusion of the Civil War.

15 **According to this excerpt, how might a state that was not in rebellion against the United States be identified?**

That state would
   A   sign the Emancipation Proclamation.
   B   accept the Fourteenth and Fifteenth amendments.
   C   have elected members in the U.S. Congress.
   D   be willing to abolish slavery in certain counties.

16 **What effect did Lincoln hope to accomplish by offering these terms?**

Lincoln
   A   hoped to punish Southern states for allowing slavery.
   B   wished to add troops to the Union military.
   C   hoped to rally the support of Southern representatives in Congress.
   D   wanted to preserve the United States at all costs.

17 **How did the Emancipation Proclamation affect the course of the Civil War?**
   A   It caused the surrender of numerous Southern states.
   B   It cemented Lincoln's popularity and guaranteed his reelection in 1864.
   C   It generated support for the Union from other nations, such as Britain and France, who had already outlawed slavery.
   D   It severely reduced the labor force in the South.

Compare and Contrast

① Learn the Skill

When you **compare** two or more items, you consider both the similarities and differences between them. The study of history, geography, civics, and other social studies subjects often requires you to compare details about people, places, and events.

To **contrast** means to focus only on the differences between items. By focusing on the ways in which things are alike and different, you gain a deeper understanding of the material you read.

② Practice the Skill

By mastering the skill of comparing and contrasting, you will improve your study and test-taking skills, especially as they relate to social studies high school equivalency tests. Read the information and strategies below. Use this information to answer question 1.

A You may find information to compare and contrast in both text and visuals, such as tables, charts, or graphs.

B Words and phrases such as *similarly, likewise, on the other hand,* and *however* often signal that an author is comparing or contrasting information.

As the Civil War came to a close, President Abraham Lincoln began to consider how the United States should be rebuilt. His plan for reconstructing the South called for generous terms that would allow the nation to heal with as little animosity between the North and the South as possible. <u>On the other hand</u>, Radical Republicans in Congress strongly opposed this plan. They believed that the Confederacy should receive harsh penalties for the difficulties of the Civil War.

MAKING ASSUMPTIONS

You may assume that most parallel items described in a text or visual can be compared and contrasted. For instance, the text on this page compares and contrasts the Reconstruction plans of Abraham Lincoln and the plans of Radical Republicans. Make sure, however, that the items you compare and contrast relate to each other in a similar way, such as two different plans or two different fruits.

1 **When comparing or contrasting the plans of Lincoln and the Radical Republicans, which of the following statements is accurate?**

   The Reconstruction plans of Lincoln and the Radical Republicans
   A both aimed to rebuild the nation as quickly as possible.
   B featured different objectives for the process of Reconstruction.
   C imposed similarly harsh penalties on the Confederacy.
   D featured different timetables for bringing the nation together.

UNIT 2

③ *Apply the Skill*

Directions: Questions 2 and 3 are based on the following table.

RECONSTRUCTION PLANS

LINCOLN	RADICAL REPUBLICANS
Aimed at reconciliation	Hoped to institute harsh punishments for Confederates
Offered pardons to former Confederates who agreed to support the Constitution and the United States	Refused to seat any former Confederates in Congress
Allowed Southern states to elect former Confederates to Congress	Placed Southern states under military rule
Allowed Confederate states to rejoin the Union if they established anti-slavery governments	Established Freedmen's Bureau to assist former slaves

2 **How could you compare the plans of Lincoln and the Radical Republicans?**

The plans of Lincoln and the Radical Republicans were similar in that they both

- **A** made rejoining the nation simple for former Confederate states.
- **B** hoped to successfully rebuild the United States.
- **C** allowed former Confederates to participate in the rebuilding process.
- **D** called for Northern officials to oversee the establishment of new governments.

3 **In contrast to the radical plan for Reconstruction, how is Lincoln's plan best described?**

- **A** peacemaking
- **B** punitive
- **C** bold
- **D** ambitious

Directions: Questions 4 and 5 are based on the following information.

In early June 1863, General Robert E. Lee led his Army of Northern Virginia into Pennsylvania. Lee's aim was to capture the railroad hub at Harrisburg, Pennsylvania, and force Union troops in Virginia to move north to engage him. While marching through the fields of Pennsylvania, Lee forbade his troops from looting the farms or destroying any homes. The Confederate troops "paid" for the food they took to support their army with useless Confederate money.

Nearly a year later in May 1864, Union General William T. Sherman began his march through Georgia to the sea. Sherman encouraged his men to take all of the food and livestock from the farms they passed. Sherman needed food because he was cut off from Union supplies. He also burned homes and barns. Sherman's aim was to demoralize the South and destroy any supplies that could be used to aid the Confederate Army.

4 **How do Lee's actions contrast with those of Sherman?**

Lee

- **A** wanted to destroy the farms of the Pennsylvanians.
- **B** wanted to fight a battle at Gettysburg.
- **C** wanted to demoralize the South.
- **D** believed that by being kind to Northerners the Confederacy might win their support.

5 **In what way were Lee's and Sherman's ultimate goals similar?**

- **A** Both wanted to take food and livestock from farmers.
- **B** Both wanted to control new territories.
- **C** Both wanted to destroy the fighting spirit of the opposition.
- **D** Both wanted to find a way to win the war.

Directions: Questions 6 and 7 refer to the following information.

A system known as sharecropping emerged in the South at the end of the Civil War. Planters hired many former slaves to once again work at cultivating crops such as cotton. These workers came to Southern farms with their families and provided the labor that planters required to continue producing their crops. The planters supplied nearly all of the equipment and supplies needed for growing these crops. They often extended credit to the workers in order to cover their expenses. At the end of the growing season, workers typically received half of the proceeds the crops garnered. However, planters usually deducted expenses and interest from the workers' portion of the profits. These factors, as well as other dishonest actions practiced by many planters, prevented many workers from making a living at sharecropping.

6 How did the system of sharecropping differ from slavery in the South before the Civil War?
   A Workers on plantations were often mistreated.
   B Planters relied on the labor of others to produce their crops.
   C Workers could receive payment for their work on a plantation.
   D Planters provided the materials used to produce crops.

7 How was sharecropping similar to slavery?

   As during the era of slavery, many sharecroppers
   A received credit to cover the cost of their living expenses.
   B traveled together with their families.
   C had some control over the cultivation process.
   D worked at agricultural tasks under difficult conditions.

Directions: Questions 8 and 9 refer to the following amendments to the U.S. Constitution.

Thirteenth Amendment to the U.S. Constitution

Section 1. Neither slavery nor involuntary servitude, except as a punishment for crime whereof the party shall have been duly convicted, shall exist within the United States, or any place subject to their jurisdiction.

Section 2. Congress shall have the power to enforce this article by appropriate legislation

Fifteenth Amendment to the U.S. Constitution

Section 1. The right of citizens of the United States to vote shall not be denied or abridged by the United States or by any State on account of race, color, or previous condition of servitude.

Section 2. The Congress shall have power to enforce this article by appropriate legislation.

8 How are these amendments similar?

   Both the Thirteenth and Fifteenth Amendments
   A deal with the voting rights of American citizens.
   B were ratified before the conclusion of the Civil War.
   C grant Congress the authority to enforce their provisions.
   D prohibit slavery.

9 Which of the following would be illegal under the Fifteenth Amendment but is not addressed in the Thirteenth Amendment?
   A poll taxes for certain ethnic groups
   B voter registration drives
   C involuntary servitude in United States territories
   D the formation of controversial political parties

Directions: Questions 10 through 13 refer to the following information and table.

After Reconstruction, 22 African Americans from the South represented their states in Congress. By the end of the 19th century, however, Jim Crow laws began to influence the results of elections in the South. No African Americans from any state served in the Senate between 1881 and 1967. Similarly, the House of Representatives had no African American members between 1901 and 1929. Since then, however, Congress has continually had African American members.

EARLY AFRICAN AMERICAN LEGISLATORS FROM FORMER CONFEDERATE STATES

NAME	STATE	ACCOMPLISHMENT
Hiram Revels	Mississippi	First African American member of U.S. Senate; elected by Mississippi state legislature on February 23, 1870
Blanche K. Bruce	Mississippi	First African American to serve a full term in U.S. Senate, from 1875–1881; elected by Mississippi state legislature; last African American senator until 1967
Joseph Hayne Rainey	South Carolina	First African American popularly elected to Congress; a former slave, he joined Congress in 1870 and served four more terms in the House
George Henry White	North Carolina	The last former slave to serve in Congress and last African American in the House until 1929; served from 1897–1901

10 Which of the following describes a way in which the Senate and House of Representatives were similar?

A Both experienced lengthy periods in the 1900s with no African American members.

B Hiram Revels served in both houses of Congress.

C Both have had at least one African American member since 1929.

D African Americans were popularly elected to both houses in 1870.

11 In what way were Hiram Revels and Joseph Hayne Rainey different?

A key difference between Revels and Rainey was that

A Revels was elected years later than Rainey.

B Rainey served in the Senate, while Revels joined the House of Representatives.

C Revels was formerly enslaved, while Rainey was not.

D Rainey was popularly elected to serve in Congress, but Revels was not.

12 Which of the following statements accurately compares or contrasts Jim Crow laws and the Fugitive Slave Acts?

A Jim Crow laws, unlike the Fugitive Slave Acts, were not actual legislation.

B Both were established to prevent African Americans from serving in government.

C The Fugitive Slave Acts were federal laws, but Jim Crow laws were state or local acts.

D Both were enacted to preserve slavery in the South.

13 In which of the following ways were the careers of Blanche K. Bruce and George Henry White the same?

A Both served only one term.

B They were the last African Americans to serve in their respective branch of Congress for many years.

C Both were popularly elected to office.

D Both represented the same state in Congress.

- **1863:** Lincoln proposes plan for Reconstruction
- **1864:** Congress passes Wade-Davis Bill requiring 50 percent of states' male voters to take a loyalty oath; Lincoln vetoes the bill
- **1865:** Lincoln is assassinated
- **1865:** President Andrew Johnson issues amnesty proclamation designed to take control of Reconstruction from Southern aristocracy
- **1865:** Most states ratify the Thirteenth Amendment and set up civil governments
- **1865:** Congress denies seats to former Confederates; President Johnson criticizes Republicans and vetoes their Reconstruction legislation
- **1866:** Congress passes Civil Rights Act
- **1866:** The Fourteenth Amendment, which guarantees citizenship to all people born in the United States, including formerly enslaved people, is rejected by most Southern states
- **1867:** Reconstruction Acts pass Congress and establish military districts to govern the South
- **1868:** Congress impeaches President Johnson but falls short of removing him from office
- **1868:** Six Confederate states rejoin the Union
- **1870:** The remaining Confederate states rejoin the Union
- **1870:** The Fifteenth Amendment is ratified, guaranteeing all citizens the right to vote, regardless of race, color, or previous condition of servitude
- **1876:** Reconstruction ends with the election of Rutherford B. Hayes as president

14 **Andrew Johnson's Reconstruction policies were most similar to whose?**

Johnson's policies were most similar to those of
A   the Radical Republicans.
B   Rutherford B. Hayes.
C   Abraham Lincoln.
D   the former Confederates.

15 **In which of the following ways did the Thirteenth and Fourteenth Amendment differ?**
A   One dealt with Reconstruction, while the other dealt with foreign policy.
B   One was adopted quickly, while the other was initially rejected by most Southern states.
C   Abraham Lincoln authored one amendment, while Congressional leaders wrote the other.
D   Radical Republicans supported one amendment, but not the other.

16 **With which action did Andrew Johnson demonstrate a Reconstruction strategy similar to that of the Radical Republicans?**
A   vetoing the Reconstruction Acts
B   criticizing the decision to not seat former Confederates in Congress
C   arguing against the establishment of military districts in the South
D   taking control of Reconstruction away from the Southern aristocracy

17 **In which of the following ways were the Fourteenth and Fifteenth Amendments similar?**
A   Both guaranteed rights that African Americans had not previously had.
B   Both were rejected by the Southern states.
C   Both established civil governments in the South.
D   Both were supported by President Rutherford B. Hayes.

Interpret Charts and Graphs

① Learn the Skill

Charts and **graphs** are another way to present information visually. Like tables, charts and graphs can present a great deal of information in a relatively small amount of space. In social studies, authors often use these elements to show information that would be too lengthy to describe in a narrative passage. Charts and graphs also have the additional benefit of clearly showing change over time.

② Practice the Skill

By mastering the skill of interpreting charts and graphs, you will improve your study and test-taking skills, especially as they relate to social studies high school equivalency tests. Examine the line graph and strategies below. Use this information to answer question 1.

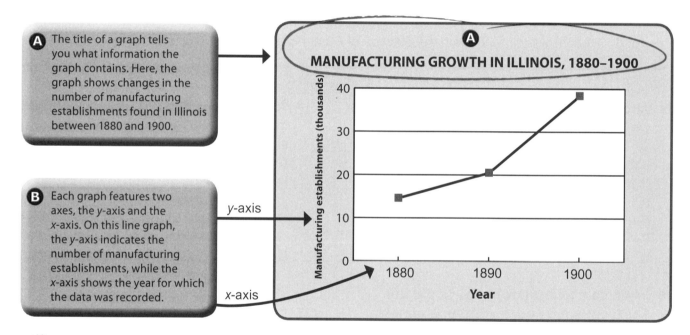

A The title of a graph tells you what information the graph contains. Here, the graph shows changes in the number of manufacturing establishments found in Illinois between 1880 and 1900.

B Each graph features two axes, the *y*-axis and the *x*-axis. On this line graph, the *y*-axis indicates the number of manufacturing establishments, while the *x*-axis shows the year for which the data was recorded.

y-axis

x-axis

A

MANUFACTURING GROWTH IN ILLINOIS, 1880–1900

Manufacturing establishments (thousands)

40

30

20

10

0

1880   1890   1900

Year

USING LOGIC

To interpret a graph, refer to both axes and determine how they relate to one another at certain points on the graph. For instance, to determine the number of manufacturing establishments found in Illinois in 1890, you would scan up from the point on the *x*-axis for 1890 and find the number on the *y*-axis.

1 During the 1890s, what happened to the number of manufacturing establishments in Illinois?

A They increased slightly.

B They decreased slightly.

C They remained nearly the same.

D They increased dramatically.

UNIT 2

Directions: Questions 2 and 3 refer to the following bar graph.

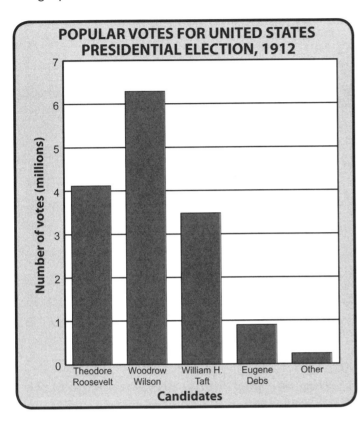

POPULAR VOTES FOR UNITED STATES PRESIDENTIAL ELECTION, 1912

Directions: Questions 4 and 5 refer to the following circle graphs.

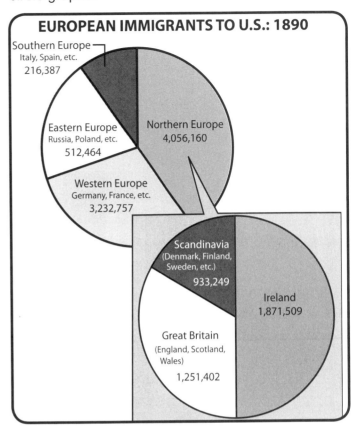

EUROPEAN IMMIGRANTS TO U.S.: 1890

Southern Europe — Italy, Spain, etc. 216,387

Eastern Europe Russia, Poland, etc. 512,464

Northern Europe 4,056,160

Western Europe Germany, France, etc. 3,232,757

Scandinavia (Denmark, Finland, Sweden, etc.) 933,249

Ireland 1,871,509

Great Britain (England, Scotland, Wales) 1,251,402

UNIT 2

2   Which statement best describes the results for William H. Taft?

   William H. Taft received
   A   more popular votes than Theodore Roosevelt and Eugene Debs.
   B   the fourth highest number of popular votes.
   C   approximately 3.5 million popular votes.
   D   around 5 million fewer votes than Woodrow Wilson.

3   Based on the information in the graph, which of the following statements is accurate?
   A   The election of 1912 was a multi-party race.
   B   Theodore Roosevelt became vice president.
   C   Woodrow Wilson won the presidency in a overwhelming victory.
   D   Eugene Debs received nearly 1 million Electoral College votes.

4   Based on the information in the graphs, which of the following statements is accurate?

   In 1890,
   A   it is likely that more immigrants to the United States came from Germany than from Russia.
   B   southern European countries, such as Italy and Spain, provided the majority of the immigrants.
   C   twice as many immigrants were from Northern Europe than were from Western Europe.
   D   more immigrants came from Asia and Africa than from Europe.

5   Which historical event most likely caused the immigration rates in the second circle graph?
   A   war between Sweden and Norway
   B   continued eviction of poor Irish farmers
   C   increase in British factory jobs
   D   World War I

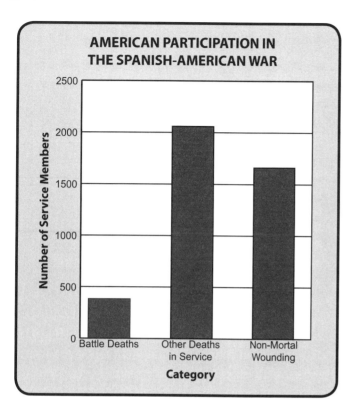

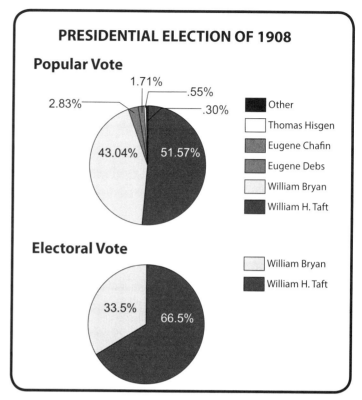

6   Based on the graph, which of the following statements is accurate?

During the Spanish-American War, U.S. troops
A   numbered only 2,000.
B   suffered fewer than 500 deaths in battle.
C   incurred more than 2,000 non-mortal injuries.
D   suffered more than 5,000 total casualties.

7   Based on the information in the graph, what can be assumed about war?
A   Almost everyone who fights in a war becomes injured.
B   The Spanish-American War was one of America's largest wars.
C   Wars are fought by small armies.
D   Death by disease or accident was more likely than death in battle.

8   Who won the third largest percentage of the popular vote in the 1908 election?
A   William H. Taft
B   Eugene Chafin
C   William Bryan
D   Eugene Debs

9   Based on the graphs, which of the following statements is accurate?

These graphs indicate that
A   three of the candidates received no electoral votes.
B   Taft won a larger percentage of the popular vote than he did of the electoral vote.
C   three of the candidates each received more than 10 percent of the popular vote.
D   the two top candidates combined to receive less than 75 percent of the popular and electoral vote.

Directions: Questions 10 and 11 refer to the following graph.

Directions: Questions 12 and 13 refer to the following graph.

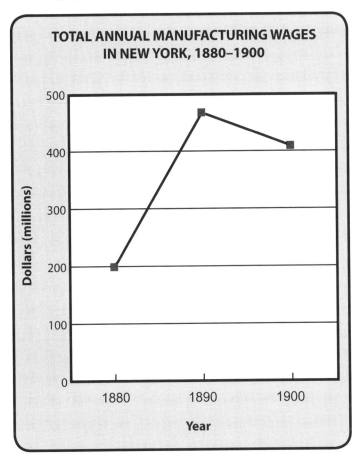

TOTAL ANNUAL MANUFACTURING WAGES IN NEW YORK, 1880–1900

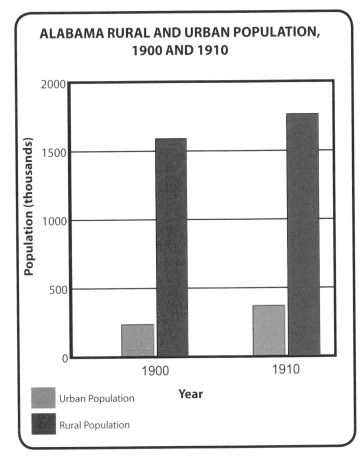

ALABAMA RURAL AND URBAN POPULATION, 1900 AND 1910

10 Which of the following would help explain the changes in total manufacturing wages shown on the graph?

A Manufacturing companies began to pay higher wages during the 1890s.

B New York added many new manufacturing jobs during the 1880s.

C The growth of manufacturing continued to accelerate in New York during the 1890s.

D Manufacturing became a consistently expanding part of New York's economy.

11 How were manufacturing wages affected between 1890 and 1900?

Between 1890 and 1900, manufacturing wages

A increased slightly.

B returned to their 1880 levels.

C decreased by about 70 million dollars.

D decreased by about 120 million dollars.

12 How could Alabama's population in both 1900 and 1910 best be described?

Alabama's population in 1900 and 1910 was

A divided almost evenly between urban and rural areas.

B heavily urbanized.

C mostly rural.

D more than 2,000,000 people.

13 By 1910, how had Alabama's population changed?

A The population had become slightly more urbanized.

B The population was more than 90 percent urban.

C The population had experienced decreases in both rural and urban areas.

D The population was showing dramatic growth in its urban areas.

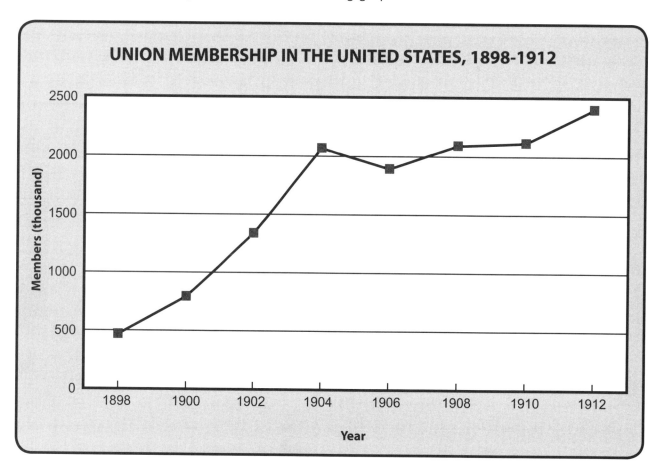

UNION MEMBERSHIP IN THE UNITED STATES, 1898-1912

14 During which two-year period did union membership in the United States decrease?
   A 1902–1904
   B 1904–1906
   C 1908–1910
   D 1910–1912

15 When did union membership in the United States increase most dramatically?

Union membership increased most dramatically between
   A 1898 and 1900.
   B 1902 and 1904.
   C 1906 and 1908.
   D 1910 and 1912.

16 The changes shown on this graph would be most closely associated with which historical theme?
   A the Progressive Era
   B Yellow Journalism
   C the Spanish-American War
   D imperialism

17 How is labor union membership in the United States over the course of the time period shown on the graph best described?

Labor union membership
   A both increased and decreased sharply.
   B reached its highest level in 1908.
   C began to decline gradually after 1910.
   D first grew rapidly, then increased more gradually.

Make Inferences

① Learn the Skill

An **inference** is an educated guess based on facts or evidence. When you make an inference, you put two or more pieces of information together to determine what they might mean. In this way, making an inference is similar to putting together the pieces of a puzzle. Even before you have assembled the complete puzzle, you can begin to determine what it will look like. As you study historical information, making inferences will help you to better understand the connections between people, places, and events that might not initially seem to be related.

② Practice the Skill

By mastering the skill of making inferences, you will improve your study and test-taking skills, especially as they relate to social studies high school equivalency tests. Read the information and strategies below. Use this information to answer question 1.

A This sentence states Wilson's intentions about U.S. involvement in World War I. This fact can be combined with another to make an inference.

B This information can be combined with the information above to make an educated guess about the way the American public felt about the war.

> After becoming president in 1913, Woodrow Wilson's first term was dominated by the outbreak of World War I in Europe. **A** Throughout his first term, Wilson sought for the United States to remain neutral. Tensions grew when German submarines attacked American ships. Britain also interfered with American ships in an attempt to blockade Germany. Despite these incidents, Wilson worked to keep the United States out of the war. **B** For his re-election campaign in 1916, Wilson ran under the slogan, "He kept us out of war." Wilson won the election and began his second term in 1917.

USING LOGIC

When making inferences, be sure that your educated guesses can be logically supported by the facts available. Even though an inference is a guess, it should still be a guess that has a strong chance of turning out to be true.

1   **What can you infer about the American public's feelings toward involvement in World War I during Wilson's first term?**
   A   Most Americans felt that the United States should support Britain's blockade.
   B   Many Americans supported Wilson's policy of neutrality.
   C   Americans were angered by Wilson's diplomatic approach to foreign policy.
   D   Many Americans wanted Wilson to devote more time to domestic affairs.

Directions: Question 2 refers to the following information.

Beginning in the second half of the 1800s, many women in the United States worked to gain the right to vote. Organizations such as the National Woman Suffrage Association and the American Woman Suffrage Association worked to gain this right through a national constitutional amendment and individual state constitutional amendments. After a number of states granted suffrage, women began to use their new voting rights to once again push for a national amendment. The Nineteenth Amendment granted women throughout the United States the right to vote in 1920.

2   Susan B. Anthony (1820–1906) served as a leader in the National Woman Suffrage Association.

Which of the following inferences can you make about Anthony?

Susan B. Anthony
   A   lived in one of the first states to grant women the right to vote.
   B   remained bitterly opposed to the leaders of the American Woman Suffrage Association.
   C   traveled and lectured on the importance of woman suffrage.
   D   opposed anti-slavery and temperance amendments.

Directions: Question 3 refers to the following information and table.

In 1917, the National Woman Suffrage Association published *The Blue Book* in an effort to dispute some objections to women having the right to vote.

THE SUFFRAGE DEBATE	
OBJECTION	**ANSWER TO THE OBJECTION**
It would double the ignorant vote.	Statistics show that more girls than boys are graduating from high school. Equal suffrage would increase the number of voters with more education.
Most women are against suffrage.	The organizations of women that support suffrage are much larger than those organizations that oppose suffrage.
Women are overburdened. Voting would stop them from caring for their families.	The act of voting takes very little time. Almost all women can find some time in their day to read newspapers or otherwise educate themselves on issues before voting.
Women are too emotional and sentimental and cannot be trusted with the ballot.	The authors of *The Blue Book* point out several instances of how men in government have made emotional and sentimental decisions about war and economic policy instead of relying on logic.

3   What can you infer about the authors of *The Blue Book*?
   A   They were extremely angry at the objections raised to women's suffrage.
   B   Even though some of the objections were true, they still felt that women should vote.
   C   They believed that violent protests were their only chance to secure the vote.
   D   They believed in using a logical, methodical approach to win an argument.

Directions: Questions 4 and 5 refer to the following information.

By August 1918, more than one million United States soldiers had been deployed to France. Their French and British allies, who had been fighting Germany and its allies for four years, were not impressed with the military skills of the conscripted 'doughboys' of the American Expeditionary Force (AEF). They believed that the Americans should be used only as replacements in French or British divisions. However, American commander General John J. Pershing refused to allow this. He insisted that the U.S. Army fight together as one unit.

4   **Based on Pershing's response to France and Britain, what can be inferred?**

     Pershing
     A   felt intimidated by the French and British commanders.
     B   wanted to make a private peace with Germany.
     C   wanted the U.S. forces to get credit for their victories.
     D   believed that soldiers who were drafted could fight better than regular army troops.

5   **Based on the information, which of the following can be inferred?**
     A   The French and British commanders believed that the U.S. soldiers were not skilled enough to fight as a separate unit.
     B   The American troops were weak and doughy.
     C   America's allies had won many victories and had nearly ended the war.
     D   The United States joined the fighting early in the war.

Directions: Questions 6 and 7 refer to the following information and excerpt.

In 1872, Susan B. Anthony voted in the presidential election and was arrested and fined. She refused to pay her fine and used her arrest to highlight her beliefs about women's rights, especially the right to vote.

From an 1873 speech by Susan B. Anthony:

"Friends and fellow citizens: I stand before you tonight under indictment for the alleged crime of having voted at the last presidential election, without having a lawful right to vote. It shall be my work this evening to prove to you that in thus voting, I not only committed no crime, but, instead, simply exercised my citizen's rights, guaranteed to me and all United States citizens by the National Constitution, beyond the power of any state to deny.

It was we, the people; not we, the white male citizens; nor yet we, the male citizens; but we, the whole people, who formed the Union ... . And it is a downright mockery to talk to women of their enjoyment of the blessings of liberty while they are denied the use of the only means of securing them provided by this democratic-republican government–the ballot."

6   **To what text is Anthony referring in the second paragraph of her speech?**
     A   the Preamble to the U.S. Constitution
     B   the Declaration of Independence
     C   the Twentieth Amendment
     D   a speech by President Grant

7   **What can you infer based on the information?**
     A   Anthony is mocking the Constitution.
     B   Anthony believes that women enjoy liberty.
     C   Anthony believes that the Constitution already guarantees women the right to vote.
     D   Anthony is speaking to a group of her closest friends.

Directions: Questions 8 and 9 refer to the following information.

Prohibition was a condition in which the making, transporting, and selling of alcoholic beverages was made illegal. In the United States, a large prohibition movement began in the mid-1800s and quickly rose to national attention. During World War I, the conservation of resources reduced alcohol consumption in the nation. Afterwards, the Eighteenth Amendment to the U.S. Constitution instituted Prohibition as a national law. However, this law proved very difficult to enforce. Many Americans participated in illegal production of alcohol, known as bootlegging. Underground drinking establishments and organized criminal activity flourished. By 1933, the Twenty-First Amendment had repealed Prohibition. However, the amendment did not prevent states from banning alcohol, and some states continued to enforce their own prohibition laws. As of 1966, no state prohibition laws remained in effect.

8 **What can be inferred based on the repeal of Prohibition by the Twenty-First Amendment?**
- **A** The Great Depression led people to reduce alcohol consumption.
- **B** For many people, the problems caused by Prohibition outweighed the benefits.
- **C** Bootlegging proved to be unprofitable.
- **D** Prohibition was more difficult to enforce at the local level.

9 **What can you infer about state prohibition laws from the passage above?**
- **A** These laws were superseded by the Twenty-First Amendment.
- **B** State laws focused on stopping the practice of bootlegging.
- **C** These laws proved easier to enforce than national prohibition measures.
- **D** Some state legislatures believed that consumption of alcohol was dangerous and immoral.

Directions: Questions 10 and 11 refer to the following information.

Spain ceded Puerto Rico to the United States following the Spanish-American War. It was placed under military rule until 1900, when the United States established an administrative government. The 1917 Jones Act officially made Puerto Rico a territory of the United States.

From the Eighteenth Amendment:

Section 1. After one year from the ratification of this article the manufacture, sale, or transportation of intoxicating liquors within, the importation thereof into, or the exportation thereof from the United States and all territory subject to the jurisdiction thereof for beverage purposes is herby prohibited.

Section 2. The Congress and the several States shall have concurrent powers to enforce this article by appropriate legislation.

10 **What can be inferred about Puerto Rico?**

Puerto Rico
- **A** objected to Spanish rule.
- **B** was subject to the same prohibition policies as the states.
- **C** was allowed to continue some production of alcoholic beverages.
- **D** had to ratify the Eighteenth Amendment before it could become law.

11 **The Eighteenth Amendment was ratified in 1919.**

In what year can you infer that the amendment's measures took effect?
- **A** 1919
- **B** 1920
- **C** 1921
- **D** 1922

Directions: Questions 12 and 13 refer to the following information.

The League of Nations was an international organization established after World War I. Created as part of the peace treaty that ended the war, the purpose of the League was to preserve international peace and prevent the outbreak of future conflicts. The League of Nations strove to achieve its goals through the protection of member countries and their boundaries against aggressor nations, the establishment of a world court, and disarmament. United States President Woodrow Wilson was a strong supporter of the League of Nations. However, many members of Congress opposed the United States' joining the organization.

PERMANENT MEMBERS OF THE LEAGUE OF NATIONS COUNCIL

Great Britain
France
Italy
Japan
Germany
USSR

Directions: Questions 14 and 15 refer to the following table.

MILESTONES OF THE 1920s	
World's Firsts	1927: Charles Lindbergh makes first transatlantic airplane flight
	1927: First 'talking' movie, *The Jazz Singer*, released
Arts/ Culture	1921: Louis Armstrong joins "King" Oliver's Creole Jazz Band
	1921: Edith Wharton wins Pulitzer Prize for novel *The Age of Innocence*
Society	1925: Women cut their hair and shed their corsets to embrace "flapper" fashion
	1929: Chicago organized crime members killed in "St. Valentine's Day Massacre"
Labor	1923: U.S. Steel institutes 8-hour work day
	1929: Ford Motor Company increases minimum wage from $6 to $7 a day

12 **What can you infer based on the information provided?**
   A   The United States never joined the League of Nations.
   B   The League of Nations only allowed Allied nations and neutral countries to join.
   C   Woodrow Wilson served as a member of the League of Nations world court.
   D   Germany was not allowed to join the League of Nations following World War I.

13 **What can be inferred about the long-term success of the League of Nations?**
   A   It stopped invasions by aggressor nations for more than 50 years.
   B   It did not achieve its goal of preserving world peace.
   C   The member nations of the council enjoyed peaceful relations for many decades.
   D   Its council required a two-thirds majority in order to take action.

14 **Based on the milestones, what can be inferred about the 1920s?**
   A   The 1920s were very similar to the 1910s.
   B   Life for working people was more difficult in the 1920s than in the decades before.
   C   Women suffered oppression in the 1920s.
   D   The 1920s was a time of exciting innovation.

15 **Which of the following can you infer empowered women in the 1920s?**
   A   working in factories during World War II
   B   being wives and mothers
   C   gaining the right to vote
   D   being allowed to drive cars

Interpret Political Cartoons

① Learn the Skill

Political cartoons are drawings that are intended to make political or social statements. These cartoons usually reflect the opinions of the artists who draw them. These individuals, known as **political cartoonists**, often use humor or satire to make their points. They may also use a **caricature**, or an exaggerated representation of a thing or a person's physical features, to present their point of view. By interpreting political cartoons, you can gain valuable first-hand knowledge of the different ways that people viewed historical events during the time in which they were happening.

② Practice the Skill

By mastering the skill of interpreting political cartoons, you will improve your study and test-taking skills, especially as they relate to social studies high school equivalency tests. Examine the cartoon and strategies below. Use this information to answer question 1.

Ⓐ Symbols often help convey meaning in political cartoons through the use of words and images, such as the axe blade (vote) chopping into the tree (saloon).

Ⓑ Political cartoons often include labels or captions that identify items shown in the cartoon. These labels or captions may appear within a cartoon or in the space below it.

Ⓒ The man to the right of the tree is a caricature of a politician. He is the one saying the words at the bottom of the cartoon.

The Prohibition Party formed in the late 1800s and worked for many years to outlaw the production, sale, and transportation of alcoholic beverages.

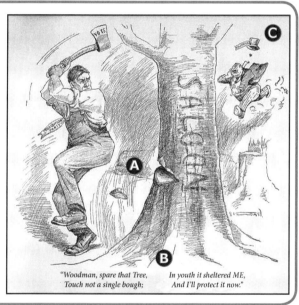

"*Woodman, spare that Tree,   In youth it sheltered ME,*
Touch not a single bough;   And I'll protect it now."

👉 MAKING ASSUMPTIONS

You can assume that most political cartoons express some type of commentary or opinion from the cartoonist. As you examine the words, pictures, or symbols that make up a cartoon, think about how these items work together to express the cartoonist's views.

1 **What do the depictions of the two figures in this cartoon suggest about the cartoonist's view on Prohibition?**

   A   The cartoonist believes that politicians are rightfully concerned about Prohibition.

   B   The cartoonist believes that the Prohibition Party is right in trying to outlaw alcohol.

   C   The cartoonist fears that the Prohibition Party is pursuing its goals recklessly.

   D   The cartoonist suggests that many politicians support the work of the Prohibition Party.

Directions: Questions 2 and 3 refer to the following political cartoon.

2   What do the figures standing along the outside of this cartoon represent?

A   nations about to begin fighting in World War I

B   groups competing for their own best interests in the League of Nations

C   groups opposed to the formation of the League of Nations

D   nations opposed to United States foreign policy in the early 1900s

3   The cartoonist believes that the actions of the nations shown in the cartoon have negatively affected the world. Which of the following is accurate according to the cartoon?

According to the cartoon, the actions of these parties have

A   prompted the United States to take sides in disputes between other nations.

B   led to the outbreak of new wars.

C   prevented the United States from taking any action of its own regarding the League of Nations.

D   forced the United States to quit the League of Nations and join the United Nations.

Directions: Question 4 and 5 refer to the following political cartoon.

Following the stock market crash in 1929, President Herbert Hoover sought to minimize the effects of the crash on the U.S. economy. Part of his plan involved working with business and labor leaders to maintain wages and employment in the nation.

4   Which statement best describes the depiction of President Hoover?

The cartoonist suggests that Hoover is

A   a weak and ineffective leader.

B   guiding the country's economy back to stability.

C   unsure of the correct course of action to improve the economy.

D   wary of supporting big business during this crisis.

5   Which of the following does the cartoon identify as the cause of the economic crash?

A   The cartoonist blames President Hoover.

B   The cartoonist thinks labor is the source of the problem.

C   The cartoonist points to speculation as the cause.

D   The cartoonist states that detours from regular business practices are to blame.

Directions: Questions 6 and 7 refer to the following political cartoon.

It IS a New Deal

6   In this cartoon, who is the figure holding the cards supposed to represent?

The figure represents
A   Herbert Hoover.
B   Woodrow Wilson.
C   the United Nations.
D   the United States.

7   **The cartoonist uses the images and text together to convey what kind of feeling?**
A   optimism
B   skepticism
C   confusion
D   calmness

Directions: Questions 8 and 9 refer to the following political cartoon.

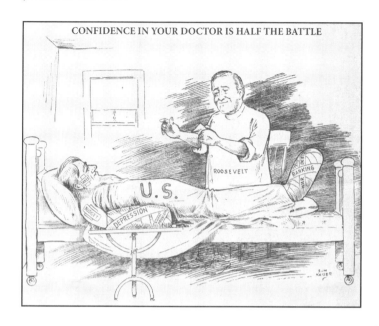

CONFIDENCE IN YOUR DOCTOR IS HALF THE BATTLE

8   **In this cartoon, what do the patient's injuries represent?**
A   the problems facing the United States
B   Roosevelt's New Deal programs
C   the outbreak of conflict in Europe
D   the presidency of Herbert Hoover

9   **Which of the following ideas is the cartoonist trying to express through this illustration?**
A   Citizens of the United States had lost faith in Roosevelt's ability to lead.
B   The Depression had brought the nation to the brink of collapse.
C   Americans should trust Roosevelt to fix many of the nation's problems.
D   The United States needed to grow stronger to protect itself from other nations.

Directions: Questions 10 and 11 refer to the following information and poster.

Similar to political cartoons, political posters are created by artists to editorialize or express messages or beliefs. These posters are sometimes used as propaganda, which is something designed to promote a particular idea or doctrine. This poster promotes one of the New Deal's most popular programs, the Civilian Conservation Corps. Known as the "CCC," it provided labor-intensive work for unskilled men who lived away from home in campsites where the work was located.

10 Which of the following best describes the way the artist depicts the young Civilian Conservation Corps worker on this poster?

   A angry

   B proud

   C courteous

   D exhausted

11 What was the program featured in this poster most likely designed to confront?

The program was probably designed to confront

   A bank failures.

   B political corruption.

   C outbreaks of disease.

   D unemployment.

Directions: Questions 12 and 13 refer to the following poster.

12 To what does "REMEMBER DEC. 7th!" refer?

"REMEMBER DEC. 7th!" refers to

   A the Japanese attack on Pearl Harbor.

   B the beginning of World War II.

   C the dropping of the atomic bomb.

   D the D-Day invasion.

13 Which of the following best describes the artist's purpose for creating this poster?

   A to inspire loyalty and resolve

   B to provoke outrage

   C to defend a course of action

   D to report a piece of news

Directions: Questions 14 and 15 refer to the following poster.

14 **Based on the information presented in the poster, what is a "Victory Home"?**
   A a home at which several residents own war bonds
   B a home that displays a victory sticker in its window
   C a home that flies the American flag
   D a home that finds ways to support the war effort

15 **Which of the measures listed on the poster is aimed directly at preventing shortages of gasoline?**
   A finding time to work for the war
   B raising and sharing food
   C walking and carrying packages
   D conserving everything you have

Directions: Questions 16 and 17 refer to the following political cartoon about the Great Depression.

"THE PHILANTHROPIST," A 1930 Herblock Cartoon,
© The Herb Block Foundation

16 **Which element in this cartoon could be considered a caricature?**
   A the sign
   B the man standing beside the light pole
   C the man eating the apples
   D the city pictured in the background

17 **What statement is the cartoonist making about the Great Depression?**
   A It caused unemployment to increase.
   B It caused the price of food in the nation to increase.
   C It affected people in urban areas more than in rural areas.
   D It affected the wealthy as well as the poor.

Summarize

① Learn the Skill

To **summarize** means to briefly restate in your own words the main points of a passage or a visual element. When reading about historical events, you will often be presented with a great deal of detailed information. Through summarizing, you can determine which details are important and which are unimportant to understanding events and their relationship to one another.

② Practice the Skill

By mastering the skill of summarizing, you will improve your study and test-taking skills, especially as they relate to social studies high school equivalency tests. Read the information and strategies below. Use this information to answer question 1.

A When summarizing, leave out details that lack significance, or importance. Instead, concentrate on details that are important for understanding the main point of a passage.

B Look for the main points in a passage and think of ways to restate them in your own words.

A Many scholars consider the launch of the first Soviet satellite, called *Sputnik,* in 1957 to be the beginning of the space race between the Soviet Union and the United States. **B** Striving for both scientific and political gain during the Cold War era, the two nations competed to achieve important milestones in space exploration. In 1961, President John F. Kennedy told the U.S. Congress of his goal of landing a man on the moon before the end of the decade. That declaration led to the creation of the Apollo program in the United States. The Soviet Union and the United States each wanted to become the first nation to place an astronaut on the moon. The United States won that part of the space race, landing astronauts on the moon with the Apollo 11 mission in 1969. Following this achievement, both nations began to scale back their space programs. As Cold War tensions gradually eased, a period of increased cooperation in space exploration between the two rival nations began.

USING LOGIC

Use logic to classify pieces of information as either main ideas or details. Think logically about whether each piece of information is the dominant theme of the passage or if it is a specific fact that supports a larger point.

1 Which of the following statements provides the best summary of the passage above?

A President Kennedy was a leader of the U.S. space initiative.

B The United States and the Soviet Union competed in a space race for scientific and political gains.

C Apollo 11 was the first mission to place astronauts on the moon.

D The space race slowed as Cold War tensions gradually eased.

Directions: Questions 2 and 3 refer to the following information.

Joseph McCarthy was elected to the United States Senate from Wisconsin in 1946. His early Senate career attracted little attention. However, McCarthy gained notoriety following a 1950 speech in which he claimed to have evidence of more than 200 Communist Party members working in the U.S. State Department. Soon, McCarthy became a powerful figure in the Republican Party. He was named the chair of the Permanent Subcommittee on Investigations. From this post, McCarthy held many hearings in which he accused numerous government officials of Communist ties. Over time, McCarthy's accusations became increasingly reckless and unpopular, even with members of his own party. His attacks on members of the U.S. Army proved especially divisive. McCarthy's investigations ended when the Senate censured him in December 1954.

2 **A summary of this passage would likely include which type of information?**

A direct quotations from the passage

B the names of some of the accused State Department officials

C the circumstances surrounding McCarthy's election to the U.S. Senate

D an overview of McCarthy's accusations and his eventual downfall

3 **Which of the following statements best summarizes this passage?**

A McCarthy's accusations divided Republicans in the Senate.

B McCarthy correctly identified many Communist members in the State Department.

C McCarthy gained power through his hearings on Communism, but then lost it with a series of unfounded accusations.

D McCarthy became an important chair of the Permanent Subcommittee on Investigations.

Directions: Question 4 refers to the following information and map.

On June 25, 1950, North Korean forces crossed the 38th parallel into South Korea, marking the beginning of the Korean War. Within three days, the South Korean capital of Seoul had fallen. The United Nations advocated that its members send forces to help restore peace in the nation. By July 30, 1950, President Truman stated that he had authorized U.S. air, sea, and ground forces to assist South Korean forces in the conflict against North Korea.

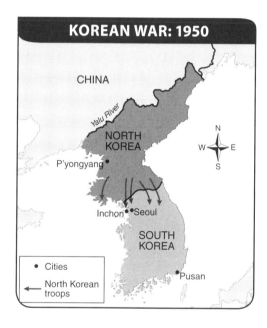

4 **What can you summarize about North Korea's invasion of South Korea?**

A North Korean forces quickly captured Seoul and Pusan.

B United States forces quickly arrived at Seoul and recaptured the capital.

C President Truman authorized various types of U.S. troops to aid South Korean forces.

D Within five days of battle, the North Koreans reached the southern tip of the peninsula.

Directions: Questions 5 and 6 refer to the following excerpt from John F. Kennedy's Inaugural Address.

We dare not forget today that we are the heirs of that first revolution. Let the word go forth from this time and place, to friend and foe alike, that the torch has been passed to a new generation of Americans—born in this century, tempered by war, disciplined by a hard and bitter peace, proud of our ancient heritage—and unwilling to witness or permit the slow undoing of those human rights to which this Nation has always been committed, and to which we are committed today at home and around the world.

Let every nation know, whether it wishes us well or ill, that we shall pay any price, bear any burden, meet any hardship, support any friend, oppose any foe, in order to assure the survival and the success of liberty.

5 **What is the main point of Kennedy's speech?**
   A   A new generation of Americans have been born.
   B   Americans have been made bitter by war.
   C   Many other nations wish to restrict the human rights of their citizens.
   D   The United States will defend the principles of freedom upon which it was founded.

6 **How is this passage from Kennedy's speech best described?**
   A   as a tribute
   B   as an announcement
   C   as an expression of gratitude
   D   as a description of strategy

Directions: Questions 7 and 8 refer to the following information.

President Lyndon Johnson signed the Civil Rights Act of 1964 into law on July 2, 1964. This marked the realization of a 1963 proposal made by President Kennedy for Congress to enact legislation that would guarantee civil rights in many different areas, including voting, education, and public facilities. With the Civil Rights Act of 1964, all forms of discrimination based on race, religion, or nationality became prohibited. The new act made segregation illegal both in private businesses, such as restaurants and theaters, and public places, such as libraries and schools. It also provided protection against employment discrimination. The enforcement of these new freedoms became the duty of the federal government.

7 **Which of the following pieces of information, if added to the paragraph, could be included in a summary?**
   A   the time of day at which the Act was signed
   B   the immediate impact of the Act on the nation
   C   other similar measures proposed by President Kennedy
   D   later measures aimed at instituting fair employment practices

8 **What is the main point of this paragraph?**

The main point is that
   A   President Johnson received credit for signing the Act.
   B   the new freedoms granted by the Act proved difficult to enforce.
   C   the Act granted new rights and protections to people of all races, religions, and nationalities.
   D   state governments did not support the passage of this legislation.

JOHNSON'S GREAT SOCIETY PROGRAMS

AREA OF FOCUS	SUMMARY
Poverty	The "War on Poverty" legislation established many programs aimed at relieving poverty; programs sought to empower impoverished citizens to help formulate solutions to problems.
Health Care	Medicare and Medicaid programs were established to provide health care to the elderly and the poor, respectively.
Employment	The Job Corps provided vocational training for young people.
Arts	The National Endowment for the Arts and Humanities was established; it provided financial support to writers, performers, and artists.
Education	Numerous measures helped to fund classroom improvements, provide low-interest loans for students, and establish scholarships for minority students; the Head Start program provided early education for young children from disadvantaged families.

9 **Which of the following best summarizes the content of the table?**

A Johnson's Great Society programs focused primarily on fighting poverty.

B The Great Society helped children and young adults prepare for life in the working world.

C Medicare and Medicaid are among the Great Society programs that continue today.

D The Great Society programs targeted many domestic issues facing the nation.

10 **Read the statement below.**

These measures represented an early example of affirmative action programs.

This statement could be added to the "Summary" column for which area of focus?

A arts

B poverty

C health care

D education

Mired in the midst of the Watergate scandal, in which staff members of his reelection campaign had been caught breaking into the Democratic Party's national headquarters, President Richard M. Nixon resigned in a speech on August 8, 1974. The following is an excerpt from his resignation speech.

"From the discussions I have had with Congressional and other leaders, I have concluded that because of the Watergate matter I might not have had the support of the Congress that I would consider necessary to back the very difficult decisions and carry out the duties of this office in the way the interests of the nation would require.

I have never been a quitter. To leave office before my term is completed is abhorrent to every instinct in my body. But as president, I must put the interest of America first. America needs a full-time president and a full-time Congress, particularly at this time with problems we face at home and abroad.

To continue to fight through the months ahead for my personal vindication would almost totally absorb the time and attention of both the president and the Congress in a period when our entire focus should be on the great issues of peace abroad and prosperity without inflation at home."

11 **Which of the following statements best summarizes the first paragraph of this excerpt?**

A Nixon has discussed the Watergate incident with Congressional leaders.

B Nixon lacks the Congressional support to carry out the duties of the president.

C The president and Congress must work together to make important decisions.

D Nixon feels he does not need the support of Congress to continue as president.

12 **In summarizing Nixon's address, how could his tone be described?**

Nixon's tone could be described as

A defiant.

B joyful.

C regretful.

D confused.

UNIT 2

Directions: Questions 13 and 14 refer to the following information.

President Ronald Reagan delivered the following speech at Germany's Berlin Wall in June 1987. The wall divided free West Berlin from Communist-controlled East Berlin and the rest of East Germany. In this speech, Reagan addresses Soviet leader Mikhail Gorbachev.

"And now the Soviets may, in a limited way, be coming to understand the importance of freedom. We hear much from Moscow about a new policy of reform and openness ... .

Are these the beginnings of profound changes in the Soviet state? Or are they token gestures, intended to raise false hopes in the West, or to strengthen the Soviet system without changing it?... There is one sign the Soviets can make that would be unmistakable, that would advance dramatically the cause of freedom and peace.

General Secretary Gorbachev, if you seek peace, if you seek prosperity for the Soviet Union and Eastern Europe, if you seek liberalization: Come here to this gate! Mr. Gorbachev, open this gate! Mr. Gorbachev, tear down this wall!"

13 **Which of the following best summarizes Reagan's purpose for delivering this speech?**
   A   to proclaim American support for West Germany
   B   to propose a treaty between the United States and Soviet Union
   C   to encourage Soviet leadership to acknowledge the importance of freedom
   D   to predict changes in the Soviet government

14 **What is the main concept that Reagan wishes the Soviets to adopt?**

   The main concept is
   A   freedom.
   B   peace.
   C   prosperity.
   D   liberalization.

Directions: Questions 15 and 16 refer to the following information.

The presidency of William J. (Bill) Clinton, from 1993 to 2001, was a period of significant economic growth and prosperity in the United States. This period featured low unemployment, as well as a booming stock market. New technologies and innovations became an important part of the economic expansion experienced during Clinton's presidency. In 1997, the president and Congress reached an agreement that balanced the federal budget for the first time in 30 years. By 2000, the nation recorded its largest surplus ever.

15 **Which of the following statements best summarizes this passage?**
   A   President Clinton presided over a time of significant change in the United States.
   B   The economy experienced booms and busts during Clinton's presidency.
   C   Congress and President Clinton worked well together during his terms in office.
   D   President Clinton oversaw a period of significant economic expansion.

16 **What can be determined from reading this passage?**

   It can be determined that
   A   before Clinton, other recent presidents had not balanced the federal budget.
   B   changing technologies caused many people to lose their jobs.
   C   the stock market experienced many cyclical drops during Clinton's presidency.
   D   the budget for the year 2000 was vastly different than the budgets of the previous three years.

The Unit Review is structured to resemble social studies high school equivalency tests. Be sure to read each question and all possible answers very carefully before choosing your answer.

To record your answers, fill in the circle that corresponds to the answer you select for each question in the Unit Review.

Do not rest your pencil on the answer area while considering your answer. Make no stray or unnecessary marks. If you change an answer, erase your first mark completely.

Mark only one answer space for each question; multiple answers will be scored as incorrect.

Sample Question

What was the period of economic growth in the late 1800s known as?
 A   the Industrial Revolution
 B   the Golden Age
 C   the Civil War
 D   the Great Migration

Directions: Question 1 refers to the following information.

Though woman suffrage workers had previously been divided in their course of action, by 1916, most suffragists had joined together to work towards a national constitutional amendment. Several events built momentum for the passage of this amendment. In 1917, the state of New York approved suffrage for women. The following year, President Woodrow Wilson offered his support for a constitutional amendment. The Nineteenth Amendment passed the House of Representatives on May 21, 1919. The Senate passed the amendment two weeks later. The amendment received the necessary support of three-quarters of all states on August 18, 1920, when Tennessee became the 36th state to ratify it. The amendment was officially enacted on August 26, 1920.

1 Which detail supports the idea that the suffrage movement had been divided before 1916?
 A   Many Americans considered suffrage for women to be a radical change to the nation's Constitution.
 B   Supporters of women's suffrage often met with harsh resistance during their campaigns.
 C   The first suffrage amendment was introduced in Congress more than 40 years before the Nineteenth Amendment gained approval.
 D   Some suffragists worked for suffrage acts in individual states, while others worked for a national constitutional amendment granting women the right to vote.

ⒶⒷⒸⒹ

Directions: Questions 2 and 3 refer to the following table.

U.S. PRESIDENTS SINCE 1960			
NAME	**TERM**	**PARTY**	**STATE REPRESENTED**
John F. Kennedy	1961–1963	Democrat	Massachusetts
Lyndon B. Johnson	1963–1969	Democrat	Texas
Richard M. Nixon	1969–1974	Republican	New York / California
Gerald R. Ford	1974–1977	Republican	Michigan
Jimmy Carter	1977–1981	Democrat	Georgia
Ronald Reagan	1981–1989	Republican	California
George H.W. Bush	1989–1993	Republican	Texas
Bill Clinton	1993–2001	Democrat	Arkansas
George W. Bush	2001–2009	Republican	Texas
Barack Obama	2009–	Democrat	Illinois

2 Who served as president between 1963 and 1969?

The president between 1963 and 1969 was
A Ronald Reagan.
B Lyndon B. Johnson.
C Richard M. Nixon.
D Jimmy Carter.

ⒶⒷⒸⒹ

3 Based on the information in the table, which of the following statements is accurate?
A Candidates of the Republican Party dominated national politics during the 1960s.
B Most presidents since 1960 have only served a single term in office.
C Only the Democratic Party had two of its candidates serve consecutive terms in office.
D Most presidents since 1960 have represented states with large populations.

ⒶⒷⒸⒹ

Directions: Questions 4 and 5 refer to the following map.

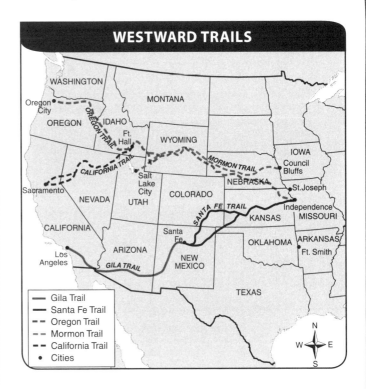

4 What is the main idea of this map?
A Settlers followed several different trails to reach the western United States.
B Independence marked the halfway point of the Oregon Trail.
C All trails to the west began in Independence, Missouri.
D Lewis and Clark took a more circuitous route to reach what is now Oregon.

ⒶⒷⒸⒹ

5 Which of the following details supports the main idea that settlers' journeys along the Oregon Trail were very dangerous?
A Very few settlers died from conflicts with Native Americans.
B Many settlers traveled west to escape economic difficulties in the east.
C Many Oregon Trail settlers traveled using prairie schooner wagons.
D Many settlers along the trail died from diseases such as cholera.

ⒶⒷⒸⒹ

Directions: Questions 6 through 8 refer to the line graph.

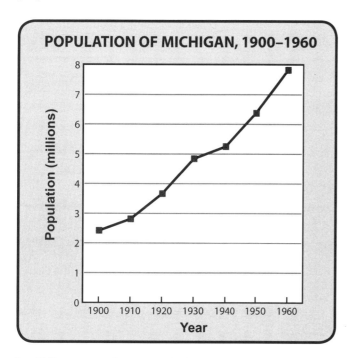

POPULATION OF MICHIGAN, 1900–1960

(Graph: x-axis labeled "Year" from 1900 to 1960 in ten-year intervals; y-axis labeled "Population (millions)" from 0 to 8.)

6 What was the population of Michigan in 1940?
- A slightly less than 5 million
- B less than 3 million
- C more than 6 million
- D approximately 5.25 million

Ⓐ Ⓑ Ⓒ Ⓓ

7 During which decade did Michigan experience its greatest population growth?
- A 1910–1920
- B 1920–1930
- C 1930–1940
- D 1950–1960

Ⓐ Ⓑ Ⓒ Ⓓ

8 Based on the graph, which of the following trends is correct?

Michigan's population
- A grew dramatically between 1900 and 1910.
- B growth slowed after 1940.
- C was affected by the automotive industry.
- D grew at the same rate every decade.

Ⓐ Ⓑ Ⓒ Ⓓ

Directions: Questions 9 and 10 refer to the following information.

Following the Constitutional Convention, the leaders who supported the adoption of the Constitution became known as Federalists. Figures such as Alexander Hamilton, James Madison, and John Jay wrote in support of the Constitution. Federalists supported a strong national government. They also favored industries and big business. The Federalists became popular among wealthy merchants and Northern property owners. They also frequently supported the British in matters of foreign policy.

Thomas Jefferson led a group opposed to Federalist policies, called the Anti-Federalists. The Anti-Federalists, including James Monroe, opposed the adoption of the Constitution, favoring states' rights over a strong central government. The Anti-Federalists were also concerned about the Constitution's lack of protection for personal liberties. They gained support among Southern landholders and many less privileged citizens.

9 Why could James Monroe be categorized as an Anti-Federalist?

James Monroe
- A was from Virginia.
- B supported the Monroe Doctrine.
- C served as president of the United States.
- D supported the Virginia Declaration of Rights.

. Ⓐ Ⓑ Ⓒ Ⓓ

10 Which of the following statements could be categorized as describing a Federalist point of view?
- A Support for industry and trade should come before support for small farmers.
- B The United States should support the French in matters of foreign policy.
- C The states should refuse to ratify the United States Constitution.
- D The federal government should not restrict the rights of the individual states.

Ⓐ Ⓑ Ⓒ Ⓓ

Directions: Questions 11 and 12 refer to the 1858 debate between Abraham Lincoln and Stephen Douglas.

Douglas: . . . Now, I hold that Illinois had a right to abolish and prohibit slavery as she did, and I hold that Kentucky has the same right to continue and protect slavery that Illinois had to abolish it. . . . that each and every State of this Union is a sovereign power, with the right to do as it pleases upon this question of slavery, and upon all its domestic institutions.

Lincoln: . . . I will say here, while upon this subject, that I have no purpose, directly or indirectly, to interfere with the institution of slavery in the States where it exists. . . . but . . . there is no reason in the world why the negro is not entitled to all the natural rights enumerated in the Declaration of Independence, the right to life, liberty, and the pursuit of happiness. I hold that he is as much entitled to those as the white man.

11   How are Douglas's and Lincoln's views on slavery similar?
   A   They both propose to make slavery illegal.
   B   Neither intends to interfere with slavery where it already exists.
   C   They both believe that states should have the right to decide whether slavery is illegal.
   D   They both believe that slavery does not restrict the natural rights of enslaved people.

Ⓐ Ⓑ Ⓒ Ⓓ

12   With what assertion of Douglas's would Lincoln disagree?

Lincoln would disagree with Douglas's assertion that
   A   slavery should still exist in the South.
   B   the Declaration of Independence applies to all citizens.
   C   the federal government has authority over state's rights.
   D   each state has sovereign power.

Ⓐ Ⓑ Ⓒ Ⓓ

Directions: Questions 13 and 14 refer to the following political cartoon.

"BACKLASH,"
A 1966 Herblock Cartoon, © by The Herb Block Foundation

13   Who is the figure depicted on the left in this cartoon?
   A   Franklin D. Roosevelt
   B   Abraham Lincoln
   C   Lyndon B. Johnson
   D   George W. Bush

Ⓐ Ⓑ Ⓒ Ⓓ

14   What idea is the cartoonist trying to convey through this cartoon?
   A   Unlike the New Deal, the Great Society has not proven beneficial to the United States.
   B   Stopping the spread of Communism in the Vietnam War is more important than funding the programs of the Great Society.
   C   The president accidentally neglected the Great Society while tending to the Vietnam War.
   D   The costs of taking part in the Vietnam War would take away vital money from the Great Society programs.

Ⓐ Ⓑ Ⓒ Ⓓ

Directions: Questions 15 and 16 refer to the following information.

In 1819, the United States included 22 states. These states were equally divided between those that allowed slavery and those that did not. However, when Missouri was poised to become the 23rd state, disagreements arose in Congress regarding whether the new state would be permitted to allow slavery. To solve this dispute, Congress reached what came to be known as the Missouri Compromise. This agreement allowed the northern part of Massachusetts to join the nation as the free state of Maine. In turn, Missouri would enter the nation as a slave state. This preserved the balance of free and slave states in the nation. Ultimately, the Missouri Compromise ensured that nine of the states created from the Louisiana Territory remained free.

15 What was the main cause of the Missouri Compromise?

The Missouri Compromise was ultimately caused by
A the disagreement over the borders of what would become the state of Missouri.
B conflict between members of Congress regarding the balance of Northern and Southern states.
C fears over the spread of slavery.
D disputes over the control of valuable resources found in Missouri.

Ⓐ Ⓑ Ⓒ Ⓓ

16 Which of the following effects of the Missouri Compromise is implied in the paragraph?
A Representation in the Senate would remain equal for free states and slave states.
B The plantation system would diminish in the South.
C Only free states would be admitted to the United States in the future.
D Hostilities broke out between Missouri and Maine.

Ⓐ Ⓑ Ⓒ Ⓓ

Directions: Question 17 refers to the following information.

The early portion of George W. Bush's first term in office was notable for his efforts to institute a program of tax cuts. He also strove to change or stop various policies that Bill Clinton had set forth in the final days of his term. Additionally, Bush proposed a number of measures designed to assist big business in the United States. His No Child Left Behind program instituted mandatory standardized testing for public schools throughout the nation. Bush's early foreign policy was dominated by the September 11, 2001 terrorist attacks and the United States' response to those attacks.

From the *Department of Homeland Security* June 2002:

"The President proposes to create a new Department of Homeland Security, the most significant transformation of the U.S. government in over half-century by largely transforming and realigning the current confusing patchwork of government activities into a single department whose primary mission is to protect our homeland. The creation of a Department of Homeland Security is one more key step in the President's national strategy for homeland security."

17 Based on the information above, what can be inferred about the Department of Homeland Security?

The Department of Homeland Security
A is not funded by federal tax revenue.
B was created in response to the September 11, 2001 terrorist attacks.
C was established to help big business in the United States.
D was originally proposed by Bill Clinton during his final days in office.

Ⓐ Ⓑ Ⓒ Ⓓ

Directions: Questions 18 through 20 refer to the following information.

THE TRANSCONTINENTAL RAILROAD

October 1861: Theodore Judah lobbies for federal funding of the Central Pacific Railroad Company.

↓

July 1862: The Pacific Railroad Bill authorizes the Central Pacific Railroad to build a railroad line from California. The bill also establishes the Union Pacific Railroad Company to construct a railroad westward from the Missouri River. The meeting of these will form the transcontinental railroad.

↓

January 1863: The Central Pacific breaks ground in Sacramento, California.

↓

December 1863: The Union Pacific breaks ground in Omaha, Nebraska.

↓

Late summer 1865: Central Pacific workers begin drilling 12 tunnels through the Sierra Nevadas by hand. Many Chinese immigrants contribute to this effort.

↓

October 1866: Union Pacific crews reach the 100th Meridian line. According to the Pacific Railroad Bill, this milestone allows the crews to continue building westward.

↓

August 1867: Central Pacific workers complete one of their greatest challenges by finishing the Summit Tunnel.

↓

April 1868: Union Pacific workers reach Sherman Summit in the Rocky Mountains, the highest point on either line.

↓

May 1871: The Central Pacific and Union Pacific meet. A golden spike is hammered into the ground to complete the transcontinental railroad.

18 Which of the following events occurred before 1867?

A   Railroad leaders agree on the meeting point of the Central Pacific and Union Pacific.

B   Union Pacific workers reach Sherman Summit.

C   The Central Pacific and Union Pacific lines meet in Promontory Summit, Utah.

D   Union Pacific crews reach the 100th Meridian line.

ⒶⒷⒸⒹ

19 Which of the following events happened first?

A   The Central Pacific breaks ground.

B   Central Pacific workers begin drilling tunnels through the Sierra Nevadas.

C   Union Pacific workers reach Sherman Summit.

D   The Pacific Railroad Bill is passed.

ⒶⒷⒸⒹ

20 Which of the following events likely happened after the completion of the transcontinental railroad?

A   Significant economic growth occurred along the railroad lines.

B   Construction on competing transcontinental lines ceased.

C   Population growth in the western United States slowed.

D   Renewed tensions broke out between Northern and Southern states.

ⒶⒷⒸⒹ

Unit 3

Unit Overview

Increasingly, we live in a globalized world in which the boundaries between countries, economies, ideas, and cultures separate us less than in the past. Technologies such as the Internet, satellite communication, and wireless devices have brought us closer together than ever before. As we look toward the future, countries must collaborate more than ever to ensure success. Before moving forward with our future, however, we must first understand the past. As citizens of a more globalized world, we must understand not only the history of our own country, but also the history of the world outside our borders.

The importance of world history also extends to social studies high school equivalency tests, where world history comprises approximately 15 percent of all questions. As with other areas of these tests, world history questions will test your ability to interpret information by using reading skills and thinking skills such as comprehension, application, analysis, and evaluation. In Unit 3, the introduction of more complex reading skills, along with visuals, such as diagrams and timelines, will help you prepare for social studies high school equivalency tests.

Table of Contents

Key World History Terms

Black Death: an outbreak of bubonic plague in the 1300s that killed about one third of the population of Europe

civilization: the organized and developed condition of human society

colonization: the act of setting up a colony away from a people's country of origin

Crusades: a series of military campaigns by the Roman Catholic Church during the Middle Ages for the purposes of spreading Christianity into the region that is generally now referred to as the Middle East

D-Day: June 6, 1944, the day on which Allied forces invaded Normandy during World War II

democracy: a form of government in which citizens choose leaders by voting and in which the importance of each individual's vote is the same

feudalism: a social system in which vassals, subservient residents, work for landowners who give them use of the land for subsistence

glasnost: a Soviet policy begun in the mid-1980s that permitted more open discussion of political and social issues

Gothic: relating to a style of architecture popular in Europe from roughly the 1100s to the 1500s and characterized by the frequent use of pointed arches

hieroglyphics: a system of writing using mainly pictorial characters

magistrate: a local official with administrative and sometimes judicial functions

Magna Carta: Latin for "Great Charter"; a 1215 document guaranteeing English political liberties signed by King John under pressure from English barons

medieval: relating to the period of European history from about AD 500 to about 1500

multicultural: including aspects from different cultures

NATO: the North Atlantic Treaty Organization, a military alliance of 28 nations situated primarily in the northern part of the Western Hemisphere

Nazi: a member of the National Socialist German Workers' Party; under Adolf Hitler, the Nazi Party was characterized by fascist, racist, and atheist beliefs

oligarchy: a country, organization, or business that is controlled by a small number of people

Peloponnesian War: a lengthy war between Athens and Sparta in Ancient Greece, from 431 to 404 BC

Renaissance: the period of European cultural history following the Middle Ages and characterized by a surge in learning and discovery

Roman Empire: the period of ancient Roman civilization, following the Roman Republic, during which a singular Emperor headed a vast territory that spanned most of Europe and into Asia and Africa

Shang Dynasty: the first period in China to produce recorded history and in which bronze work became common in that civilization

tomb: a vault, typically underground, for burying the dead

vassal: a person who receives protection and use of land from a feudal lord in exchange for the pledge of service

Categorize Concepts

① Learn the Skill

When learning about a social studies topic, you will find that information relates to the topic in many different ways. For instance, when learning about a country, you may read about its people, geography, government, economy, and history. By **categorizing concepts** under headings such as these, you can better organize and understand what you have learned.

② Practice the Skill

By mastering the skill of categorizing concepts, you will improve your study and test-taking skills, especially as they relate to social studies high school equivalency tests. Read the information and strategies below. Use this information to answer question 1.

A As you read, look for related topics or ideas in the text. Consider how you might group these ideas together or how you might draw distinctions between them.

B Consider how the information relates to subjects with which you are familiar. Do the ideas in this passage fit into a familiar category, such as history or government?

Some city-states in ancient Greece featured a system of government known as an oligarchy. In an oligarchy, only a select few citizens share ruling power. Sparta became the best-known oligarchic city-state. While its government **A** featured kings and an assembly of free men over 30, Sparta's government was actually controlled by a Council of Elders. This group included 28 members and five elected officials. They proposed laws to the assembly, but the assembly lacked the power to debate these proposals.

In the city-state of Athens, citizens established a **A** different type of government known as democracy. In Athens, every freeborn man older than 18 received an equal vote in government elections. Many government officials took office through a lottery system and served under term limits. In fact, elections only took place in order to select some of the most important government officials.

✓ TEST-TAKING TIPS

When preparing to categorize concepts, try to identify the main ideas and key details of a passage. Recognizing these items will often point you toward potential categories, such as government or geography, into which information can be placed.

1　**In what way could a community in which all adults received an equal vote in choosing local government officials be categorized?**

　A　as an oligarchy
　B　as a democracy
　C　as both an oligarchy and a democracy
　D　as a city-state

UNIT 3

Directions: Questions 2 and 3 refer to the following information.

Even though Ancient Egypt was in the desert, the Nile River and its tributaries allowed the Egyptians to have an agrarian society. Wheat and barley were grown in such abundance that the Egyptians could keep vast stores and trade part of their harvest. Domesticated animals, such as cattle, sheep, goats, and pigs, were raised for food, and dogs and cats were kept as pets.

Egyptian families typically consisted of parents and children in one household. Egyptian couples were monogamous, but there were no formal or legal requirements for marriage. Divorce was also possible. Women had almost the same legal rights as men. They could own property and do with it as they saw fit. Women could also begin divorce proceedings. Although they rarely held government office, many women had power as priestesses in Egypt's many religious sects.

2 **Which concepts are most important in the text above?**
   A marriage, domestic pets
   B military, agrarian
   C government, religious
   D agriculture, daily life

3 **How were women in Ancient Egypt best categorized?**

   Women in Ancient Egypt
   A were artistic.
   B had many rights.
   C had nuclear families.
   D kept cats as pets.

Directions: Questions 4 and 5 refer to the following information and map.

The Greek city-states of Athens and Sparta once cooperated to defend the Greek states from Persian invaders. The Greeks engaged in three major conflicts against these invaders, the last of which took place in 479 BC.

Disagreements developed between the two city-states regarding both land and sea trade routes and monies contributed to the rivals by smaller political states. In 431 BC, the Peloponnesian War began. It lasted for 28 years, with alternating periods of conflict and peace. While both sides had important victories, Sparta ultimately emerged victorious in 404 BC.

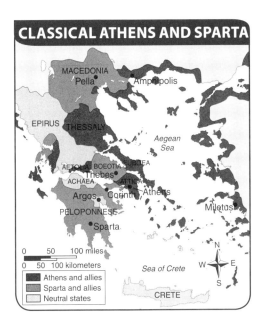

CLASSICAL ATHENS AND SPARTA

4 **Examine the map closely. How was Athens best categorized logically?**
   A as an imperial state
   B as a naval power
   C as controlled by a pacifist government
   D as a nation with many overland trade routes

5 **Into which of the following categories would you place the Peloponnesian War?**
   A skirmish
   B cold war
   C world war
   D civil war

UNIT 3

Directions: Questions 6 and 7 refer to the following information.

Ancestor worship became an important part of religion in ancient China. The people of this civilization believed that life did not end with death. They often called upon the spirits of their deceased ancestors in order to gain favor. They felt that the spirits of dead ancestors had the capability to influence and affect the lives of living family members.

The beliefs of the ancient Egyptians centered on various myths, as well as the worship of nature and many gods. For example, Egyptians believed that the life-force of humans consisted of various elements. The most important of these was the *ka*. This element was believed to leave the body at death and travel to the kingdom of the dead. Because they believed that the *ka* could not exist without the body, Egyptians developed elaborate funeral, mummification, and burial practices designed to preserve the body.

6 How could the Egyptian term *ka* could be categorized?

  A as a spiritual force
  B as a religious rite
  C as a funeral practice
  D as an ancient Egyptian god

7 Which of the following correctly pairs an item within a category?

Category—Item in Category

  A Egyptian religion—ancestor worship
  B ancestor worship—belief in life-force made of various elements
  C *Ka*—ability of the deceased to influence the lives of living family members
  D Egyptian burial practices—preservation of body

Directions: Questions 8 and 9 refer to the following table.

ANCIENT PYRAMIDS			
REGION	**DATE**	**MATERIALS**	**PURPOSE**
Egypt	2630 BC–1530 BC	Largest pyramids built from stone blocks; later smaller pyramids made from mud brick	Tombs for kings and queens; also served as centers of larger religious complexes
Americas	3000 BC–1500 AD	Stone	Various purposes, including burial sites, military defense sites, and bases for palaces and temples
Mesopotamia	4000 BC–600 BC	Mud brick with glazed brick on face	Religious temples or sanctuaries

8 Which of the following categories best differentiates the pyramids in the table?

  A the date of construction
  B durability
  C historical significance
  D geographic location

9 Which of the following categories could include pyramids built in the Americas?

  A pyramids built before 3500 BC
  B pyramids built in the Eastern Hemisphere
  C pyramids built after 1000 AD
  D pyramids with single uses

UNIT 3

Directions: Questions 10 through 12 refer to the following information.

The government of the Roman Republic included three main groups—the Senate, the magistrates, and the citizen assemblies. While the Senate officially acted only in an advisory role, its recommendations commanded great respect. The citizen assemblies had the power to declare war, elect magistrates, and pass laws. However, the assemblies did not represent all citizens equally. In the *comitia centuriata,* citizens voted in 193 blocks. Each block received a single vote. However, the blocks for wealthy citizens had few members, while blocks for non-landowners could contain thousands of people. The magistrates had several individuals serving in the same position in order to prevent any one person from becoming too powerful.

10 How is this information best categorized?
   A   military history
   B   political history
   C   geographic history
   D   economic history

11 How is the government of the Roman Republic best categorized?
   A   monarchial
   B   socialistic
   C   representational democratic
   D   dictatorship

12 In the *comitia centuriata*, each block received one vote. That characteristic is similar to which of the following documents?
   A   EU Charter
   B   *Magna Carta*
   C   Declaration of Independence
   D   Articles of Confederation

Directions: Questions 13 and 14 refer to the following map.

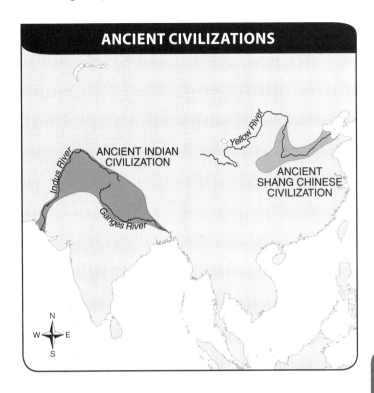

ANCIENT CIVILIZATIONS

ANCIENT INDIAN CIVILIZATION

ANCIENT SHANG CHINESE CIVILIZATION

Yellow River

Indus River

Ganges River

13 How could these civilizations be categoriezed?

Both of these civilizations could be categorized as
   A   early European civilizations.
   B   river civilizations.
   C   coastal civilizations.
   D   desert civilizations.

14 Which of the following civilizations could be placed in the same category as those in India and China?
   A   ancient Greece
   B   Mayan
   C   Incan
   D   ancient Egypt

Directions: Questions 15 and 16 refer to the following information.

The Inca were an advanced society. Inca medical men became adept at performing surgeries, such as amputations. They may have even performed bone transplants. The Inca also developed a lunar calendar to measure time, as well as units of measure for length and weight. Inca crafts included pottery, textiles, and metal ornaments and jewelry. A distinctive form of music also developed in the Inca culture.

The Maya boasted many similar advances. They developed a sophisticated calendar system that was employed to measure time and make astronomical observations. In doing so, the Maya also employed the mathematical concept of zero. In addition to these developments, the Maya also crafted a system of writing that used hieroglyphics to record information. In this way, they kept a record of scientific observations, historical data, and family histories.

15 **Which of the following developments could be categorized as a breakthrough in communication?**
  A the development of a lunar calendar
  B the practice of surgery
  C the production of metal items and pottery
  D the development of a system of writing

16 **How is the information in both paragraphs best categorized?**
  A military history
  B social history
  C political history
  D geographic history

Directions: Questions 17 and 18 refer to the following information.

Ancient Greece had many thinkers who made important contributions to culture and the arts. Greek sculptors carved statues that were often painted in vibrant colors. Statues of Greek gods could stand as high as 40 feet.

The designs that the Greeks painted on pottery became increasingly complex. These items often showed scenes from daily life, as well as events from Greek myths. The ancient Greeks also became known for their architecture. Greek architects designed palaces, as well as buildings such as government structures and temples.

Literature in ancient Greece began as the passing of stories orally from one person to another. Later, the Greeks developed a system of writing to record literary works. The Greeks also created notable dramas. These tragedies and comedies were often performed at outdoor festivals, which also served as competitions between the playwrights. Ancient Greek authors also began to write about history, recording the causes of important events and evaluating the roles of individuals in these events.

17 **Which of the following could be categorized as an ancient Greek contribution to literature?**
  A a statue of a Greek god
  B a comedic play
  C a large public building
  D a painting of a scene from a Greek myth

18 **The majority of the details in the information can be categorized under which concept?**
  A religious history
  B architectural history
  C sculptural history
  D cultural history

Lesson 1 | Categorize Concepts

Interpret Diagrams

① Learn the Skill

Diagrams are different from other types of graphics, such as charts or graphs, because they can show the relationships that exist between pieces of information. For instance, diagrams can show sequence, similarities, differences, and other comparisons. Authors often use diagrams to concisely present or summarize social studies information. By learning how to **interpret** diagrams, you can maximize your understanding of the information presented in these visuals.

② Practice the Skill

By mastering the skill of interpreting diagrams, you will improve your study and test-taking skills, especially as they relate to social studies high school equivalency tests. Examine the diagram and strategies below. Use this information to answer question 1.

Ⓐ The format of a diagram provides clues to its purpose and the type of information that it will include. A Venn diagram shows how two subjects are similar and different.

Ⓑ Pay close attention to the titles and headings of diagrams. What information can you learn from these items? Here, the headings above the two main circles identify the subjects that will be compared and contrasted.

12TH AND 13TH CENTURY MONARCHIES Ⓐ

England Ⓑ
- Instituted new justice system that established common law in England
- *Magna Carta* forced king to grant more authority to barons in 1215
- Parliament established in 1264

Both Ⓑ
- Centralized government
- Made rule over vassals more official
- Increased wealth from new tax systems

France Ⓑ
- In prior years, king only took authority of area near Paris
- Under Philip II, claimed lands from England
- Philip II established capable administration to facilitate tax collection

TEST-TAKING TIPS

When asked to use a diagram in a testing situation, first preview the questions related to the diagram. Determine what information you will need to locate in the diagram to correctly answer these questions.

1 **In which way did France strengthen its monarchy that England did not?**
- **A** France centralized its national government.
- **B** France established a new system of justice.
- **C** France increased wealth from a new tax system.
- **D** France claimed new territories for the nation.

Directions: Questions 2 and 3 refer to the following diagram.

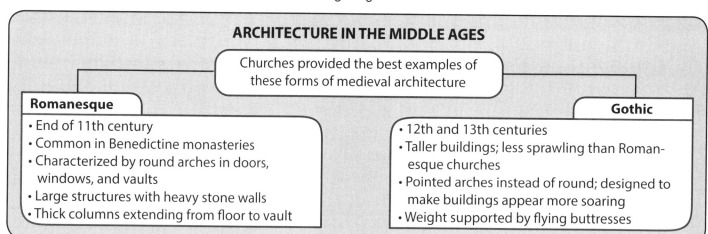

ARCHITECTURE IN THE MIDDLE AGES

Churches provided the best examples of these forms of medieval architecture

Romanesque
- End of 11th century
- Common in Benedictine monasteries
- Characterized by round arches in doors, windows, and vaults
- Large structures with heavy stone walls
- Thick columns extending from floor to vault

Gothic
- 12th and 13th centuries
- Taller buildings; less sprawling than Romanesque churches
- Pointed arches instead of round; designed to make buildings appear more soaring
- Weight supported by flying buttresses

2 Which of the following statements is true?
A Romanesque architecture became popular after Gothic architecture.
B Gothic structures were generally shorter than Romanesque buildings.
C Romanesque structures did not typically feature flying buttresses.
D Romanesque buildings covered a smaller area than Gothic structures.

3 Why might Gothic churches be more visually dramatic than Romanesque churches?

Gothic churches
A were built in the 12th and 13th centuries.
B had heavy stone walls.
C used flying buttresses to support round arches and vaults.
D were taller and appeared to be soaring.

Directions: Questions 4 and 5 refer to the following diagram.

LIFE IN MEDIEVAL COURTS

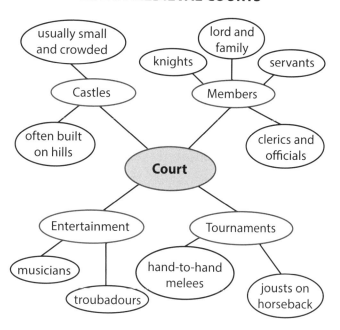

4 The tournaments held at medieval courts are most similar to which present-day event?

Tournaments were similar to present-day
A concerts.
B sporting events.
C town meetings.
D political rallies.

5 According to the diagram, how are knights best classified?
A as entertainment for the Court
B as living in castles
C as having hand-to-hand melees
D as members of the Court

Directions: Questions 6 and 7 refer to the following diagram.

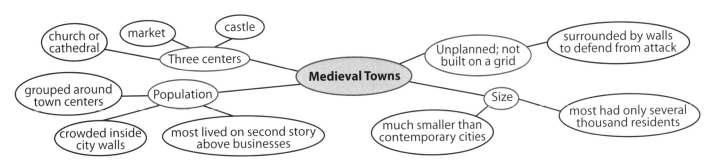

6   **Which of the following would you be unlikely to find in a medieval town?**

A   vendors
B   walls to keep out invaders
C   towers in which thousands of people lived
D   markets

7   **The population size in most medieval towns was most likely limited by which factor?**

The population was limited by
A   the outbreak and spread of diseases.
B   the available space within the city walls.
C   attacks from outside invaders.
D   quotas placed on city populations.

Directions: Questions 8 and 9 refer to the following diagram.

THE BLACK DEATH IN ENGLAND

Ship returning from Black Sea stops at Naples in November 1347; ship carries disease known as Black Death.

↓

Black Death reaches England in August 1348 and spreads to London in November 1348.

↓

Between 20 and 40 percent of England's population dies in only a year and a half. Victims are mostly adults.

↓

Black Death vanishes in 1350.

↓

Disease later returns in 1361, primarily affecting children.

↓

Further outbreaks occur over the course of the next 17 years.

↓

The outbreaks ultimately cause the English population to drop by 50 percent.

8   **What can be inferred about the Black Death?**

The Black Death
A   was introduced to Europe at several different locations.
B   had a greater effect in England than in other nations.
C   was spread through trade.
D   affected England for more than 30 consecutive years.

9   **Why did the 1361 outbreak mostly affect children?**
A   A new type of bacteria caused the outbreak.
B   Children had not developed immunity from the earlier outbreak.
C   The disease spread primarily in schools.
D   More than 50 percent of the adult population had already died.

Directions: Questions 10 through 13 refer to the following diagram.

THE FIRST THREE CRUSADES

First Crusade	Second Crusade	Third Crusade
• Pope Urban II calls Christians to unite in order to liberate Jerusalem from Muslims in 1095 • Thousands of people from many different backgrounds respond • First Crusade begins in 1096 and successfully conquers Jerusalem; many living in the city are massacred • Creates a military presence in Jerusalem that continues for nearly 200 years • After their victory, many crusaders return home; others hope to stay and create a lasting Christian establishment	• Muslims in the Near East recapture the city of Edessa in 1144 • Pope Eugenius III calls for the Second Crusade • Several important leaders, such as France's King Louis VII and Holy Roman Emperor Conrad III, join the crusade • Many troops are attacked on route and only part of the original force reaches Jerusalem in 1148; soon attack Muslims at Damascus • Many lives lost but no territorial gains made	• Following the Second Crusade, orders of knights that combined religious goals with military training grow in importance • Knights serve as Crusaders and help extend the influence of both the Church and national leaders • After Muslims reclaim Jerusalem in 1187, the Church calls for a new Crusade • The leaders of three western powers respond: France's Philip II, Holy Roman Emperor Frederick I, and England's Richard I • Only Richard I reaches the Holy Land; despite his heroic efforts, the Crusaders do not reclaim Jerusalem or other significant territory

All

- Wars waged by Christians from Western Europe in an effort to reclaim Holy Land from Muslims
- Early examples of European colonialism; combined religious, political, and military goals
- Made possible by growing influence and centralization of the church, as well as growing population and prosperity of Europe

10 **Which of the following figures was probably the most important in the history of the Crusades?**
- **A** Pope Urban II
- **B** Louis VII of France
- **C** Holy Roman Emperor Conrad III
- **D** Richard I of England

11 **What can be inferred about the Crusades?**

The Crusades
- **A** led to a period of peace and understanding between Christian and Muslim faiths.
- **B** served as a way for western men to be exposed to Middle Eastern culture.
- **C** were one of the main causes of the Protestant Reformation.
- **D** proved that Muslim military leaders were incapable of organizing a large military force.

12 **Based on the diagram, which of the following statements is true?**
- **A** The Second Crusade proved to be the most successful.
- **B** The Crusades were carried out for primarily military purposes.
- **C** Europe's rulers believed that the Crusades were great opportunities to gain territory and power.
- **D** Westerners gained additional territories with each Crusade.

13 **Which of the following continued a cultural trend that began with the Crusades?**
- **A** the Industrial Revolution
- **B** the rise of nationalism
- **C** the rise of isolationism
- **D** the Renaissance

Directions: Questions 14 through 17 refer to the following diagram.

FEUDALISM IN THE MIDDLE AGES

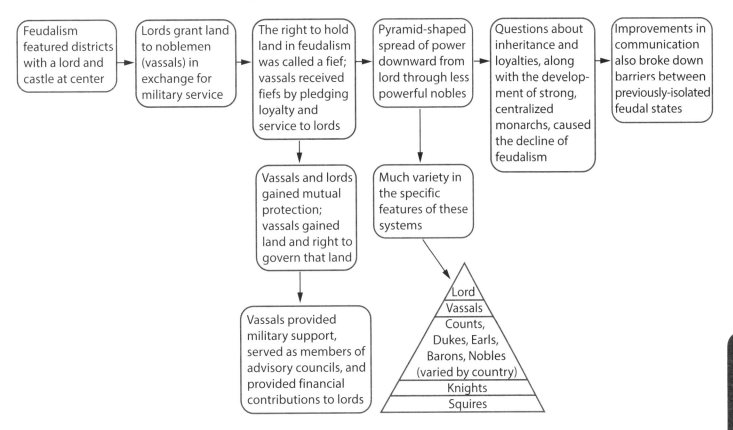

14 **What benefit did vassals gain from feudalism?**
   A payments from lords
   B authority over religious districts
   C direct communication with monarchs
   D the right to govern land

15 **What does the information in this diagram suggest?**

   Feudalism
   A lasted only a short time.
   B gave way to more regularized and firmly established systems of government.
   C facilitated communication across great distances.
   D relied on lawmaking bodies composed of members of each level of authority.

16 **Which group held the least power under feudalism?**
   A squires
   B vassals
   C earls
   D barons

17 **Why did lords likely require military commitments from their vassals?**

   This requirement was likely because
   A many knights had left to fight the Crusades.
   B they could expect loyalty in exchange for land.
   C centralized monarchs frequently tried to overthrow them.
   D vassals were responsible for spreading laws and other communications.

Determine Purpose and Point of View

① Learn the Skill

Authors write different types of material from a variety of **perspectives** and for a number of different **purposes**. For instance, a textbook author writes to inform or educate students. On the other hand, a newspaper editorial is written to persuade the reader. The perspective from which a work is written is called the **point of view**.

② Practice the Skill

By mastering the skill of understanding an author's purpose and point of view, you will improve your study and test-taking skills, especially as they relate to social studies high school equivalency tests. Read the excerpt and strategies below. Use this information to answer question 1.

A As you read a passage, think about the author's purpose for writing, and how that purpose relates to his or her point of view.

B To help determine an author's point of view, look for statements or passages that express opinions about the subjects being discussed. When considered collectively, these opinions will help you identify the author's point of view.

From the *Magna Carta* **(1297):**

… Know that we, at the prompting of God and for the health of our soul and the souls of our ancestors and successors, for the glory of holy Church and the improvement of our realm, freely and out of our good will have given and granted to the archbishops, bishops, abbots, priors, earls, barons and all of our realm these liberties written below to hold in our realm of England in perpetuity.

… No freeman is to be taken or imprisoned or disseised of his free tenement or of his liberties or free customs, or outlawed or exiled or in any way ruined, nor will we go against such a man or send against him save by lawful judgement of his peers or by the law of the land.

☑ TEST-TAKING TIPS

When answering test questions related to an author's point of view, first identify the subject or main idea of the writing. Then think about the different perspectives that someone could likely have regarding this topic. This step will allow you to narrow your focus and clarify the author's point of view more quickly.

1 Based on the authors' point of view, what is the purpose of the *Magna Carta*?

The *Magna Carta* was written to
A improve the Church.
B establish basic rights of Englishmen.
C overthrow the monarchy.
D establish church courts to ensure liberties.

Directions: Questions 2 through 4 refer to the following excerpt.

From John Locke's *Two Treatises of Government* (1690):

Sect. 4. To understand political power right, and derive it from its original, we must consider, what state all men are naturally in, and that is, a state of perfect freedom to order their actions, and dispose of their possessions and persons, as they think fit, within the bounds of the law of nature, without asking leave, or depending upon the will of any other man.

A state also of equality, wherein all the power and jurisdiction is reciprocal, no one having more than another; there being nothing more evident, than that creatures of the same species and rank, promiscuously born to all the same advantages of nature, and the use of the same faculties, should also be equal one amongst another without subordination or subjection, unless the lord and master of them all [God] should, by any manifest declaration of his will, set one above another, and confer on him, by an evident and clear appointment, an undoubted right to dominion and sovereignty.

2   In this passage, what is Locke's point of view about people?

Locke argues that people are naturally
A   selfish.
B   free.
C   trustworthy.
D   unequal.

3   What is Locke's point of view about government in this excerpt?
A   There should be no government because all men are free and natural.
B   Government should consist of people born into a certain rank.
C   Those in government should establish jurisdiction and subjection.
D   Government should promote equality and only be led by a divinely-appointed sovereign.

4   How does Locke's point of view compare with Thomas Jefferson's?
A   They both supported the monarchy.
B   They both believed that some men were born to rule others.
C   They both believed that man has natural rights.
D   They both supported a powerful national government.

Directions: Question 5 refers to the following quotation.

"The marble not yet carved can hold the form
Of every thought the greatest artist has."

From Michelangelo Buonarroti, *Sonnet 15*

5   Which of the following correctly states Michelangelo's point of view in the quotation above?

Michelangelo believed that
A   each new sculpture offers an opportunity for greatness.
B   sculpture is the most important form of fine art.
C   too many sculptors rely on the great ideas of other artists.
D   marble is the most challenging medium in which to perfect a sculpture.

Directions: Questions 6 and 7 refer to the following excerpt from Niccoló Machiavelli's *The Prince* (1532).

A prince must … appear to all who see and hear him to be completely pious, completely faithful, completely honest, completely humane, and completely religious. And nothing is more important than to appear to have that last quality …. Everyone can see how you appear, few can feel what you are, and these few will not dare to oppose the opinion of the multitude when it is defended by the majesty of the state. In actions of all men, especially princes, where there is no recourse to justice, the end is all that counts. A prince should only be concerned with conquering or maintaining a state, for the means will always be judged to be honorable and praiseworthy by each and every person, because the masses always follow appearances and the outcomes of affairs, and the world is nothing other than the masses.

6　**Which of the following statements best describes Machiavelli's point of view?**
　A　Religious piety is important for a leader.
　B　Appearance of belief is more important than actual belief.
　C　Support of the masses is not necessary for a good leader.
　D　The voices of a few dissenters will always counteract the voices of the masses.

7　**Which of the following best describes Machiavelli's purpose in writing this passage?**
　A　to advocate for a political candidate
　B　to complain about the role of monarchs
　C　to issue a warning to his fellow citizens
　D　to highlight the ways in which rulers maintain power

Directions: Questions 8 and 9 refer to the following information and excerpt.

King Henry VIII of England dissolved Catholic monasteries and other religious houses when he declared himself head of the Church of England in 1536. The poor, along with older people or people with disabilities, who had previously relied on those religious organizations for relief, had to instead rely on the government.

From an English "Poor Law" (1536) written by William Marshall:

"Therefore his highness, of his most blessed and godly disposition, like a virtuous prince and gracious head regarding as well the maintenance of the commonwealth of his realm, the body, as the relief of the poor, wretched and miserable people whereof be a great multitude in this his realm, and the redress and avoiding of all valiant beggars and idle persons within the same … has by the advice of the lords spiritual and temporary and the commons in this present Parliament assembled … provided certain remedies as well for the help and relief of such idle, valiant beggars as has been before remembered, as of such poor and miserable people as be before rehearsed, in manner and form following … "

8　**What can be determined about the King's point of view?**

　The King views poor people in England with as deserving of
　A　love
　B　scorn
　C　sympathy
　D　assistance

9　**Based on the tone of this law, which of the following was most likely a provision of the law?**
　A　Anyone expressing need for aid would receive it.
　B　Jobs were found for all poor people.
　C　Begging would be legal.
　D　Poor children would be provided apprenticeships.

Directions: Questions 10 and 11 refer to the following excerpt from René Descartes' *Discourse on Method* (1637).

I was nourished by study from my earliest childhood; and since I was convinced that this was the means to acquire a clear and certain knowledge of all that is useful in life, I had an extreme desire to learn. But as soon as I had finished a course of studies which usually culminates in one being accepted as one of the learned, I changed my opinion completely; for I found myself troubled by so many doubts and errors that the only profit I had gained in seeking to educate myself was to discover more and more clearly the extent of my ignorance. Nevertheless I had been at one of the most famous schools in Europe, where I thought there must be wise men if such existed anywhere on earth. There I had learned all that the others learned; and besides, not satisfied with the knowledge that we were taught, I had poured over all the unusual and strange books that I could lay my hands on … . Finally, our century seemed to me to abound in as many wise spirits as any preceding one, which led me to suppose that I could judge the experience of others by my own, and to think that there was no such knowledge in the world such as I had been led to hope for …

10 **Which statement best summarizes Descartes' point of view?**
   A Though he attended a well-known school, his instructors were not particularly wise.
   B He learned more from his own independent reading than he did from attending classes.
   C Over time, he realized that the certain knowledge he once sought did not exist.
   D He lamented that his century did not produce as many great thinkers as previous centuries.

11 **What can be inferred based on Descartes' point of view?**

   Descartes would most likely be interested in the study of
   A mathematics.
   B philosophy.
   C theology.
   D poetry.

Directions: Question 12 refers to the following description of the African kingdom of Timbuktu, from Leo Africanus's *The Description of Africa* (1526).

The royal court is magnificent and very well organized. When the king goes from one city to another with the people of his court, he rides a camel and the horses are led by hand by servants. If fighting becomes necessary, the servants mount the camels and all the soldiers mount on horseback. When someone wishes to speak to the king, he must kneel before him and bow down; but this is only required of those who have never before spoken to the king, or of ambassadors. The king has about 3,000 horsemen and infinity of foot-soldiers armed with bows made of wild fennel which they use to shoot poisoned arrows. This king makes war only upon neighboring enemies and upon those who do not want to pay him tribute. When he has gained victory, he has all of them—even the children—sold in the market at Timbuktu.

12 **What is the author's purpose in writing this excerpt?**
   A to offer an accurate description of court life in Timbuktu
   B to encourage people to come settle in Timbuktu
   C to advocate for reform in the kingdom of Timbuktu
   D to argue against the institution of slavery in Timbuktu

Directions: Questions 13 and 14 refer to the following excerpt from Chinese emperor K'ang Hsi's *The Sacred Edicts* (1670).

1. Highly esteem familial piety and the proper relations among brothers in order to give due importance to social relations.
2. Give due weight to kinship in order to promote harmony and peace.
3. Maintain good relations with the neighborhood in order to prevent quarrels and lawsuits.
4. Give due importance to farming and the cultivation of mulberry trees in order to ensure sufficient clothing and food.
5. Be moderate and economical in order to avoid wasting away your livelihood.
6. Make the most of schools and academies in order to honor the ways of scholars.
7. Denounce strange beliefs in order to elevate the true doctrine.
8. Explain laws and regulations in order to warn the ignorant and obstinate.
9. Show propriety and courtesy to improve customs and manners.
10. Work hard in your professions in order to quiet your ambitions.

13 **How can the second part of each edict listed above be characterized?**
A threatening
B commanding
C cryptic
D explanatory

14 **Think about the author's purpose for writing these edicts. To which of the following are these edicts most similar?**
A instructions for assembling an appliance
B a series of emails about a school project
C an advice manual
D a timeline showing important historical events

Directions: Questions 15 and 16 refer to the following excerpt from Nicolas Copernicus's *The Revolutions of the Heavenly Bodies* (1543).

FIRST WE must remark that the universe is spherical in form, partly because this form being a perfect whole requiring no joints, is the most complete of all, partly because it makes the most capacious form, which is best suited to contain and preserve everything; or again because all the constituent parts of the universe, that is the sun, moon and the planets appear in this form; or because everything strives to attain this form, as appears in the case of drops of water and other fluid bodies if they attempt to define themselves. So no one will doubt that this form belongs to the heavenly bodies.

15 **What is Copernicus's purpose for writing this passage?**

Copernicus's purpose is to
A entertain.
B persuade.
C tell a story.
D instruct.

16 **Which of the following accurately restates Copernicus's point of view?**

The universe is spherical
A because Earth, the moon, and the sun are spherical.
B because the sphere is the strongest shape.
C because all things are naturally spherical.
D because that is the ruling of the Catholic Church.

Draw Conclusions

① Learn the Skill

You have already learned that an inference is an educated guess based on facts or evidence. By combining several inferences to make a judgment, you can **draw conclusions**. The ability to draw conclusions enables you to develop new ideas about social studies material. In this way, you can gain a deeper understanding of the information you read.

② Practice the Skill

By mastering the skill of drawing conclusions, you will improve your study and test-taking skills, especially as they relate to social studies high school equivalency tests. Read the information and strategies below. Use this information to answer question 1.

A As you read, look for pieces of information about which you can ask questions, such as: *Why would Britain want a survey of India?* What pieces of information might you need to answer such a question?

B Remember that an inference is like a puzzle that must be put together using two or more pieces of information. These educated guesses can then be combined to form a larger conclusion. You can also call upon your own prior knowledge to help you draw conclusions.

One of the most important geographical projects of the 1800s was the Great Trigonometrical Survey of India. **A** Britain had expanded its commercial and colonial interests in India during the 1700s, and the government wished to learn more about the region. As a result, the government launched the Great Trigonometrical Survey of India in 1800. The goal of this project was to survey and map the Indian subcontinent, along with those areas extending north of the Himalayas. **B** Because Nepal and Tibet forbid the British surveyors from entering their borders, the British asked Indians to disguise themselves as Buddhist pilgrims and secretly survey these areas. These volunteers learned how to measure a mile by taking 2,000 steps. In all, the Great Trigonometrical Survey of India took 70 years to complete.

USING LOGIC

In order to answer this question, you will have to use logic and call upon your prior knowledge. Think about why a country would not want representatives of another country on its land.

1 **Why do you think the British surveyors were forbidden to travel in Nepal and Tibet?**
   A The nations were worried about British colonial ambitions.
   B The mountainous terrain was very dangerous.
   C The governments of these nations did not want maps made of their territories.
   D Leaders from these nations feared the spread of Buddhism to Britain.

UNIT 3

Directions: Questions 2 and 3 refer to the following information.

European exploration of Australia focused on the charting of the continent's coastal areas, as well as the exploration of its interior. Between 1798 and 1803, Matthew Flinders, a British navigator, sailed around the continent. Though Flinders had expected to locate numerous mouths of large rivers during this charting expedition, he identified far fewer of these places along the coast than he had anticipated. This stirred discussion that the rivers on the west side of the Great Dividing Range could empty into a sizable inland body of water. Explorers later determined that these rivers instead joined the Murray River and emptied into the Indian Ocean.

Early explorers who attempted to cross the continent often encountered great difficulty. Some individuals even lost their lives. Despite many conflicts with Aboriginal Australians along the way, Scottish explorer John McDouall Stuart successfully crossed the continent from south to north in 1862. Later, Aboriginal Australians served as guides for other European explorers. These explorers eventually helped to map the entire Australian continent.

2   **Why were the British so anxious to explore Australian rivers?**
   A   They wanted to find the Great Dividing Range.
   B   They wanted to create a map of the continent.
   C   They were searching for an easy way to explore the continent's interior.
   D   They were anxious to find gold or diamonds on the continent.

3   **Why did European explorers likely experience conflicts with Aboriginal Australians?**

   Conflict likely occurred because of
   A   political allegiances.
   B   the Aborigines' fear of British imperial ambitions.
   C   disagreements about routes across the continent.
   D   efforts to control the continent's large inland body of water.

Directions: Question 4 refers to the following table.

THE RACE TO THE SOUTH POLE		
EXPEDITION LEADER	DATE	OUTCOME
Robert Falcon Scott	1901–1904	Ventured closer to South Pole than any previous expeditions
Ernest Shackleton	1907–1909	Approached within 200 km of the South Pole
Roald Amundsen	1911	Led the first expedition to reach South Pole in December of 1911
Robert Falcon Scott	1911–1912	Arrived at South Pole five weeks after Amundsen expedition; Scott and crew died on return journey

4   **Which of the following most likely posed the greatest obstacle to reaching the South Pole?**
   A   dangerous animals
   B   native inhabitants
   C   poorly-built ships
   D   cold temperatures

Directions: Questions 5 and 6 refer to the following information and map.

Captain James Cook was a British explorer who led three voyages to the Pacific Ocean during the mid- and late-1700s. Cook died in a conflict with Hawaiian islanders on his third journey. His crew eventually returned safely to Britain.

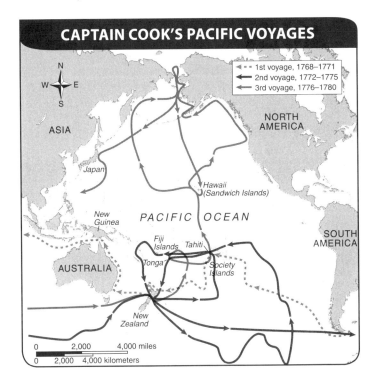

CAPTAIN COOK'S PACIFIC VOYAGES

- - - 1st voyage, 1768–1771
→ 2nd voyage, 1772–1775
→ 3rd voyage, 1776–1780

ASIA
NORTH AMERICA
Japan
Hawaii (Sandwich Islands)
New Guinea
PACIFIC OCEAN
SOUTH AMERICA
Fiji Islands Tahiti
Tonga Society Islands
AUSTRALIA
New Zealand

0   2,000   4,000 miles
0   2,000   4,000 kilometers

5 Why might Cook have taken different routes on each of his voyages?
  A The previous routes had proven too dangerous.
  B He hoped to keep exploring and acquiring new territories.
  C He was searching for the Northwest Passage.
  D He could not determine a route by which to circumnavigate the globe.

6 Which of the following conclusions can you accurately draw from the map?
  A Following his death, Cook's crew was eager to return directly to Britain.
  B Cook was interested in exploring many different areas of the world.
  C Cook did not believe it was safe to sail near the earth's polar regions.
  D Cook proved that North America was a large continent.

Directions: Questions 7 and 8 refer to the following information.

In order to foster the growth of trade in the East Indies, many European nations established organizations known as East India companies during the 1500s through the 1700s. The European national governments supported these companies to varying degrees, with some nations granting them charters. These charters allowed the companies to claim new lands, as well as perform certain governmental duties, such as lawmaking, declaring war, and negotiating treaties. The English East India Company received a charter from Queen Elizabeth I in 1600, and went on to play an important role in the government and economy of India for many years to follow.

7 What can be determined about the English East India Company?

The English East India Company
  A had no authority to claim new lands.
  B disbanded soon after it was established.
  C was the earliest East India company to be formed.
  D received support from the national government.

8 Which of the following best describes the primary goal of the East India companies?
  A to establish new monarchies
  B to learn about different cultures
  C to profit through trade
  D to establish new colonies

Directions: Questions 9 and 10 refer to the following information.

A Christian missionary and physician from Scotland, David Livingstone became a prominent explorer of southern and central Africa during the 1800s. Arriving at the southern tip of Africa in 1841, Livingstone soon began to travel throughout the region as part of his missionary work. He hoped to expose interior areas of Africa to the influence of western ideas. Between 1849 and 1852, he crossed the Kalahari Desert. Starting in 1855, Livingstone explored the Zambezi and other central African river systems and lakes. His work eventually drew the attention of the western world to Africa and helped spur additional missionary work on the continent. Livingstone's explorations eventually encouraged European nations to begin claiming African lands.

9 **Why might Livingstone have wanted to open interior areas of Africa to western ideas?**
  A to bring Christianity to the Africans
  B to establish trading companies
  C to locate a water route through the region
  D to make travel through the region safer

10 **Why might Livingstone's explorations have encouraged European nations to claim lands in Africa?**

  These nations
  A hoped to expand on Livingstone's missionary work.
  B learned the value of the continent's resources.
  C recognized the continent's strategic value for warfare.
  D hoped to improve the life of African people.

Directions: Questions 11 and 12 refer to the following table.

THE SILK ROAD	
ROUTE	• Connected traders from Europe, western Asia, Persia, central Asia, and China • Various principal routes • Emerged in order to avoid natural obstacles and dangerous political climates
TRADE	• Specialized in trade of expensive Chinese products, including silk • Few goods, but high prices • Greater economic impact on individual traders than on nations or empires
CULTURAL EXCHANGE	• Cultural impact proved greater than economic impact • Traders along the routes exchanged new ideas and ways of doing things

11 **What was the most enduring legacy of the Silk Road?**

  The most enduring legacy was the
  A development of permanent land routes.
  B economic growth of the nations involved.
  C altering of the landscape along its routes.
  D exchange of cultural elements among traders.

12 **Why would Silk Road traders have been more likely to sell fewer, more expensive items?**
  A These goods would have been easier to transport over land.
  B These goods would be more difficult for bandits to steal.
  C The sale of these goods produced wealth for the nations along the Silk Road routes.
  D These items were goods for daily use.

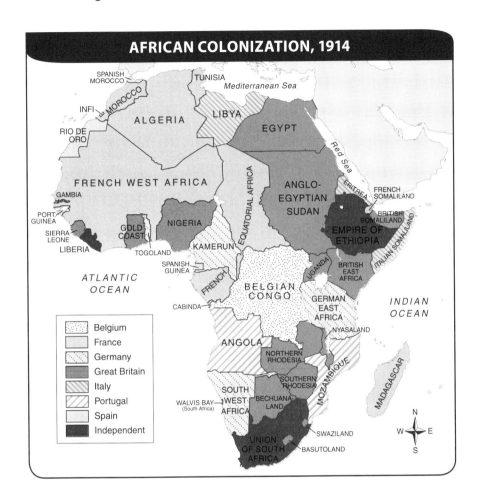

AFRICAN COLONIZATION, 1914

13 **Which nations controlled the most land in Africa in 1914?**
A   Belgium and Portugal
B   Italy and Spain
C   Great Britain and France
D   Germany and France

14 **Which of the following would have made Nigeria a valuable territory to possess?**

Nigeria was valuable because of its
A   large size.
B   access to the Nile River.
C   ocean harbors.
D   proximity to Indian Ocean commerce.

15 **In which of the following ways were these territories similar to the early North American colonies?**

They
A   covered an entire continent.
B   united together against a common opponent.
C   were located in the Southern Hemisphere.
D   were controlled by several different European nations.

16 **Of the following European languages, which was probably spoken the most in Africa?**
A   French
B   Italian
C   Spanish
D   Portuguese

Interpret Timelines

① Learn the Skill

The ability to **interpret timelines** proves especially valuable when studying history. Timelines present sequences of events in a visual manner. This enables the reader to determine not only the order in which the events occurred, but also the intervals between these events. Because timelines show key events in sequence, it is possible to identify historical trends that connect those events.

② Practice the Skill

By mastering the skill of interpreting timelines, you will improve your study and test-taking skills, especially as they relate to social studies high school equivalency tests. Read the timeline below. Use the timeline to answer question 1.

A The benchmark dates on a timeline show the equivalent intervals into which the full time span of the timeline is divided. In this case, the timeline shows the period from 1915 to 1935 divided into five-year intervals.

B This timeline illustrates the events that led to Hitler becoming chancellor of Germany. The trend here connects Germany's humiliation after World War I to Hitler building the Nazi Party into a national party, to economic depression and political dissatisfaction, and to the rise of Hitler and the Nazi Party.

POST-WORLD WAR I AND HITLER'S RISE TO POWER

1915–

1918: World War I ends

1919: **B** Treaty of Versailles imposes harsh penalties on Germany for its role in the war

1920–

1921: Hitler becomes leader of the Nazi Party in Germany

1923: Hitler leads a failed attempt to overthrow the Bavarian government

1925–

1925–1930: **B** Hitler works to build the Nazi Party throughout Germany

1929: **B** Depression reaches Germany, leading to dissatisfaction with other political parties

1930–

1932: **B** Nazi candidates receive most votes of any party in German elections

1933: Hitler becomes chancellor of Germany

1935–

USING LOGIC

Timelines typically show a trend in events. Events on the timeline are usually connected. By reviewing each event and what occurred before and after, you should be able to see a trend.

1 What directly led to the Nazi Party receiving the most votes in the 1932 German elections?

A the end of World War I in 1918

B victorious allies acting punitively towards the Germans at Versailles

C the people's unhappiness with other politicians because of the economic crisis

D the attempted overthrow of the Bavarian government

Directions: Questions 2 and 3 are based on the timeline below.

GERMAN INVASIONS

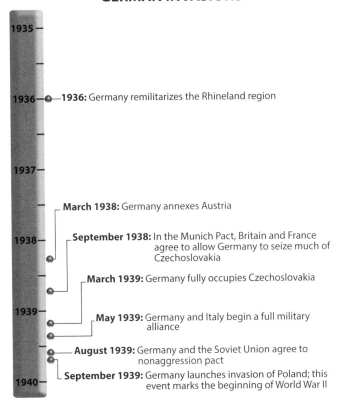

1936: Germany remilitarizes the Rhineland region

March 1938: Germany annexes Austria

September 1938: In the Munich Pact, Britain and France agree to allow Germany to seize much of Czechoslovakia

March 1939: Germany fully occupies Czechoslovakia

May 1939: Germany and Italy begin a full military alliance

August 1939: Germany and the Soviet Union agree to nonaggression pact

September 1939: Germany launches invasion of Poland; this event marks the beginning of World War II

Directions: Questions 4 and 5 are based on the timeline below.

ATTACKS ON BRITAIN AND FRANCE

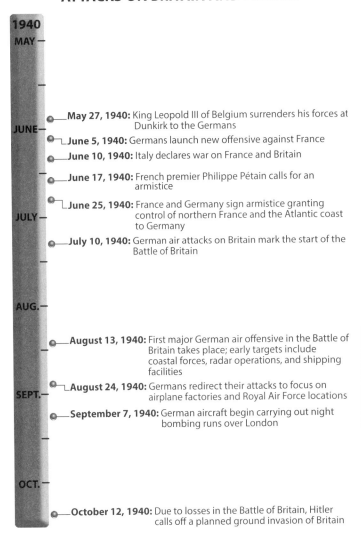

May 27, 1940: King Leopold III of Belgium surrenders his forces at Dunkirk to the Germans

June 5, 1940: Germans launch new offensive against France

June 10, 1940: Italy declares war on France and Britain

June 17, 1940: French premier Philippe Pétain calls for an armistice

June 25, 1940: France and Germany sign armistice granting control of northern France and the Atlantic coast to Germany

July 10, 1940: German air attacks on Britain mark the start of the Battle of Britain

August 13, 1940: First major German air offensive in the Battle of Britain takes place; early targets include coastal forces, radar operations, and shipping facilities

August 24, 1940: Germans redirect their attacks to focus on airplane factories and Royal Air Force locations

September 7, 1940: German aircraft begin carrying out night bombing runs over London

October 12, 1940: Due to losses in the Battle of Britain, Hitler calls off a planned ground invasion of Britain

2   **Which of the following trends is supported by the information in the timeline?**
   A   Germany's main desire was to conquer Britain.
   B   Germany showed its strength, and many European countries gave in.
   C   Germany was opposed at every turn by a united Europe.
   D   Germany and the Soviet Union would be allies in the upcoming war.

3   **Which prior event MOST affected the actions shown on the timeline?**
   A   the unification of German states
   B   the Great Depression
   C   the Franco-Prussian War
   D   World War I

4   **The information on the timeline supports which of the following conclusions?**
   A   Hitler focused his attacks on London.
   B   Germany won the Battle of Britain.
   C   The British refused to surrender to Germany.
   D   It took a year for Germany to secure France.

5   **The timeline supports which of the following statements?**
   A   Hitler was confident of victory in the summer of 1940.
   B   The German air force was invincible.
   C   Gaining France was not strategically beneficial to Germany.
   D   French premier Pétain gave Hitler his first victory.

UNIT 3

D-DAY INVASION

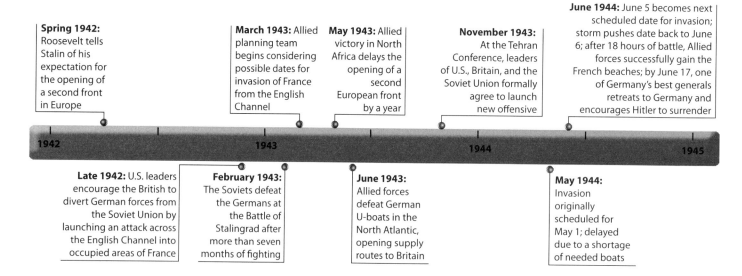

June 1944: June 5 becomes next scheduled date for invasion; storm pushes date back to June 6; after 18 hours of battle, Allied forces successfully gain the French beaches; by June 17, one of Germany's best generals retreats to Germany and encourages Hitler to surrender

Spring 1942: Roosevelt tells Stalin of his expectation for the opening of a second front in Europe

March 1943: Allied planning team begins considering possible dates for invasion of France from the English Channel

May 1943: Allied victory in North Africa delays the opening of a second European front by a year

November 1943: At the Tehran Conference, leaders of U.S., Britain, and the Soviet Union formally agree to launch new offensive

1942   1943   1944   1945

Late 1942: U.S. leaders encourage the British to divert German forces from the Soviet Union by launching an attack across the English Channel into occupied areas of France

February 1943: The Soviets defeat the Germans at the Battle of Stalingrad after more than seven months of fighting

June 1943: Allied forces defeat German U-boats in the North Atlantic, opening supply routes to Britain

May 1944: Invasion originally scheduled for May 1; delayed due to a shortage of needed boats

6 **Approximately how much time passed between the Allies' initial consideration of dates for the D-Day invasion and the date on which it was carried out?**
   A six months
   B one year
   C 15 months
   D 18 months

7 **Why did it take so long for the D-Day invasion to be realized?**
   A because the allies were focused elsewhere
   B because the allies could not agree on a plan
   C because Stalin made a separate peace with Germany
   D because of the outcome of the Tehran Conference

8 **Based on the information in the timeline, which of the following statements is true?**
   A The war effort was always focused on Europe.
   B The allies scored no victories between spring 1942 and June 1944.
   C Setbacks for the U.S. Navy in the Pacific delayed the D-Day invasion.
   D The allies worked together in a coordinated manner.

9 **The timeline supports which of the following trends?**
   A The Germans would remain strong until the very end of the war.
   B The allies garnered victories in the Soviet Union and in Africa before turning to France.
   C The United States and the Soviet Union would continue to work together to rebuild Europe after the war.
   D Britain's dominance over the other allied countries would amplify their post-war superpower status.

Directions: Questions 10 through 13 are based on the timeline below.

WORLD WAR II IN EUROPE AND THE PACIFIC

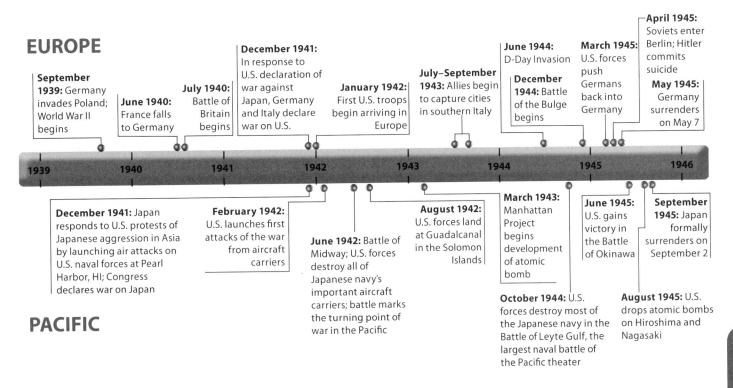

EUROPE

September 1939: Germany invades Poland; World War II begins

June 1940: France falls to Germany

July 1940: Battle of Britain begins

December 1941: In response to U.S. declaration of war against Japan, Germany and Italy declare war on U.S.

January 1942: First U.S. troops begin arriving in Europe

July–September 1943: Allies begin to capture cities in southern Italy

June 1944: D-Day Invasion

December 1944: Battle of the Bulge begins

March 1945: U.S. forces push Germans back into Germany

April 1945: Soviets enter Berlin; Hitler commits suicide

May 1945: Germany surrenders on May 7

1939 | 1940 | 1941 | 1942 | 1943 | 1944 | 1945 | 1946

December 1941: Japan responds to U.S. protests of Japanese aggression in Asia by launching air attacks on U.S. naval forces at Pearl Harbor, HI; Congress declares war on Japan

February 1942: U.S. launches first attacks of the war from aircraft carriers

June 1942: Battle of Midway; U.S. forces destroy all of Japanese navy's important aircraft carriers; battle marks the turning point of war in the Pacific

August 1942: U.S. forces land at Guadalcanal in the Solomon Islands

March 1943: Manhattan Project begins development of atomic bomb

October 1944: U.S. forces destroy most of the Japanese navy in the Battle of Leyte Gulf, the largest naval battle of the Pacific theater

June 1945: U.S. gains victory in the Battle of Okinawa

August 1945: U.S. drops atomic bombs on Hiroshima and Nagasaki

September 1945: Japan formally surrenders on September 2

PACIFIC

10 **Which of the following gives the dates of parallel events in Europe and the Pacific respectively?**
   A May 1945 and September 1945
   B September 1939 and February 1942
   C June 1941 and May 1942
   D April 1945 and December 1941

11 **Which event on the timeline eventually led to the dropping of atomic bombs on Hiroshima and Nagasaki?**
   A the German campaign at Stalingrad
   B the Battle of Midway
   C the launch of the Manhattan Project
   D the success of the D-Day invasion

12 **Based on the information in the timeline, which of the following statements is true?**
   A Hitler committed suicide during the Battle of the Bulge.
   B The Battle of Midway forced Japan to surrender.
   C The U.S. Navy was vital in the war against Japan.
   D Japan joined the war in defense of Germany.

13 **The timeline supports which of the following trends?**
   A D-Day was the first major turning point in the war.
   B The allied strategies for reaching Germany and Japan were similar.
   C The United States focused all its attention in 1944 in the Pacific.
   D The United States planned to use an atomic bomb all along.

INDIA: CONFLICT AND INDEPENDENCE

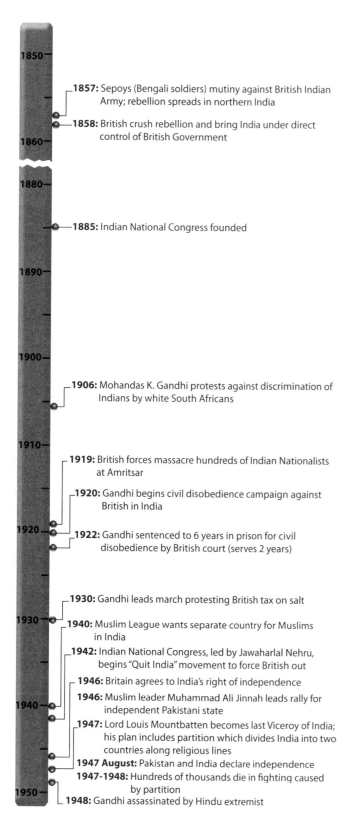

1850

1857: Sepoys (Bengali soldiers) mutiny against British Indian Army; rebellion spreads in northern India

1858: British crush rebellion and bring India under direct control of British Government

1860

1880

1885: Indian National Congress founded

1890

1900

1906: Mohandas K. Gandhi protests against discrimination of Indians by white South Africans

1910

1919: British forces massacre hundreds of Indian Nationalists at Amritsar

1920: Gandhi begins civil disobedience campaign against British in India

1920 **1922:** Gandhi sentenced to 6 years in prison for civil disobedience by British court (serves 2 years)

1930: Gandhi leads march protesting British tax on salt

1930 **1940:** Muslim League wants separate country for Muslims in India

1942: Indian National Congress, led by Jawaharlal Nehru, begins "Quit India" movement to force British out

1946: Britain agrees to India's right of independence

1946: Muslim leader Muhammad Ali Jinnah leads rally for independent Pakistani state

1940 **1947:** Lord Louis Mountbatten becomes last Viceroy of India; his plan includes partition which divides India into two countries along religious lines

1947 August: Pakistan and India declare independence

1947-1948: Hundreds of thousands die in fighting caused by partition

1950 **1948:** Gandhi assassinated by Hindu extremist

UNIT 3

14 Who was probably the most important leader for Indian independence?
A Nehru
B Jinnah
C Amritsar
D Gandhi

15 What caused the British to take control of India?
A Gandhi's protests
B the Sepoy Mutiny
C Amritsar
D the Muslim League

16 Why might the British have supported partition?
A because they wanted out of India quickly
B because of pressure from Jinnah
C because of pressure from Gandhi
D because all Muslims lived in the northwest and all Hindu lived in the southeast

17 Which of the following statements is supported by the events on the timeline?
A The British were anxious to leave India.
B Gandhi and Nehru had different goals.
C India was a valuable part of the British Empire.
D Britain reacted calmly to the Indian nationalist movement.

18 Gandhi's actions on the timeline mirror the actions of which other activist?
A Mother Teresa
B John Adams
C Princess Diana
D Martin Luther King, Jr.

Generalize

① Learn the Skill

When you **generalize,** you make a broad statement that applies to entire groups of people, places, events, and so on. These statements typically contain words such as *usually, all, everyone, many, few, often,* or *overall.* Generalizing is useful to draw a basic conclusion about something, for example, *The United States is a multicultural country.* However, beware of false conclusions and inaccurate generalizations. Be sure to examine all the information before making a generalization.

② Practice the Skill

By mastering the skill of generalizing, you will improve your study and test-taking skills, especially as they relate to social studies high school equivalency tests. Read the information and strategies below. Use this information to answer question 1.

A Look for words, such as *generally, most,* or *many,* as well as those listed above, that typically signal a generalization is being made. Then, look closely at the statement that follows to determine whether the writer applies it to a large group of items.

B When you identify a generalization in a passage of text, look closely to see what facts or evidence the author includes to support his or her statement.

USING LOGIC

As you encounter generalizations, you can classify them as either valid or invalid. A valid generalization is supported by facts and examples. On the other hand, an invalid generalization cannot be supported using facts and examples.

> The communist government of East Germany constructed the Berlin Wall in 1961 to prevent East Germans from fleeing the communist nation for the democratic nation of West Germany. East German troops heavily guarded the wall to prevent crossings. While a few citizens managed to cross this boundary, <u>most</u> people attempting to cross into West Berlin lost their lives. Those on the East German side of the wall <u>generally</u> had a lower standard of living compared to their Western counterparts, <u>similar to the way people in the Soviet Union lived versus people in France</u>. However, by the summer of 1989, the Hungarian government began to allow East Germans to travel through Hungary in order to reach Austria and West Germany. This development rendered the wall obsolete. By the fall of 1989, the East German government had nearly collapsed. On November 9, the government granted citizens the freedom to move across the boundary into West Germany. East Germany and West Germany reunited as a single nation the following year.

1 **Which generalization does the author make in this passage?**

  A East Germans generally did not cross successfully from East Germany to West Berlin.

  B East Germans generally directed their attempts to escape toward Hungary.

  C East Germans generally enjoyed the freedom to travel as they wished.

  D East Germans generally viewed West Germany as a hostile nation.

Directions: Questions 2 and 3 are based on the excerpt below.

Summary of the Dayton Peace Agreement on Bosnia-Herzegovina, released by the U.S. Department of State, November 30, 1995:

General Framework Agreement

- Bosnia and Herzegovina, Croatia and the Federal Republic of Yugoslavia [FRY] agree to fully respect the sovereign equality of one another and to settle disputes by peaceful means.

- The FRY and Bosnia and Herzegovina recognize each other, and agree to discuss further aspects of their mutual recognition.

- The parties agree to fully respect and promote fulfillment of the commitments made in the various Annexes, and they obligate themselves to respect human rights and the rights of refugees and displaced persons.

- The parties agree to cooperate fully with all entities, including those authorized by the United Nations Security Council, in implementing the peace settlement and investigating and prosecuting war crimes and other violations of international humanitarian law.

---

2   **Which of the following generalizations is supported by the excerpt?**
   A   The nations that signed this agreement are committed to preserving peace in the future.
   B   Bosnia and Yugoslavia will join together as one nation.
   C   The agreement was released by the U.S. Department of State on November 30, 1995.
   D   The parties will probably establish courts to prosecute war crimes and blame one another for all atrocities.

3   **Which generalization best describes the agreement?**

   It is primarily concerned with
   A   border disputes and war reparations.
   B   establishing peace, recognition of nations, and human rights.
   C   prosecution of war crimes.
   D   cooperation with the United Nations and commitments to Annexes.

Directions: Questions 4 and 5 are based on the information below.

The official currency of the European Union (EU), the euro, went into circulation for 11 of the 27 member states in 1999. These nations were Belgium, Germany, Ireland, Spain, France, Italy, Luxembourg, the Netherlands, Austria, Portugal, and Finland. Since then, Greece, Estonia, Latvia, Slovakia, Slovenia, Cyprus, and Malta have also adopted the euro. The euro was designed as part of a plan to unify the members of the EU around a single form of currency. Members of the EU had to meet a strict set of qualifications before adopting the euro in order to give the euro an acceptable level of stability.

4   **All members of the European Union adopted the euro as their unit of currency.**

   Which of the following nations could be cited to show that this generalization is invalid?
   A   Portugal
   B   Spain
   C   Ireland
   D   the United Kingdom

5   **The information supports which of the following generalizations?**
   A   Countries generally joined the European Union for economic reasons.
   B   Most of the countries in the European Union are in Eastern Europe.
   C   Overall, the currencies of European countries are unstable.
   D   New denominations of the euro are usually designed by different member countries.

Directions: Questions 6 and 7 are based on the excerpt below.

> ... RECALLING the historic importance of the ending of the division of the European continent and the need to create firm bases for the construction of the future Europe,
>
> "CONFIRMING their attachment to the principles of liberty, democracy and respect for human rights and fundamental freedoms and of the rule of law,
>
> "DESIRING to deepen the solidarity between their peoples while respecting their history, their culture and their traditions,
>
> "DESIRING to enhance further the democratic and efficient functioning of the institutions so as to enable them better to carry out, within a single institutional framework, the tasks entrusted to them, ...
>
> From the *Treaty on European Union*, 1992

6 **What generalization can you make about the goals of each item listed in the excerpt above?**

All of these items are aimed at
A unifying the nations of Europe.
B building Europe's tourism industry and other service industries.
C ending a long and costly conflict in Europe.
D building solidarity between Europe and the United States.

7 **Which of the following would the European leaders who signed this treaty likely oppose?**
A coalitions among European nations
B education about diverse European cultures
C diverse, separate European economies
D a single unit of currency for all of Europe

Directions: Questions 8 and 9 are based on the information below.

Glasnost was a key component of Soviet leader Mikhail Gorbachev's plan to reform the Soviet way of life. It referred to his attempts to encourage more free and open discussions of politics and culture. The Russian term *glasnost* can be translated to mean "openness." Under *glasnost*, Soviet citizens were allowed to voice their concerns and take part in activities that had long been prohibited. Cultural works that had been banned were published. Soviet scholars could freely discuss their ideas and collaborate more openly with their peers from around the world. Experts could also finally freely discuss the many economic problems facing the Soviet Union. *Glasnost* further allowed more freedom in the national government-run media, as well as the establishment of many independent groups.

8 **Which group of Soviets would have generally opposed *glasnost*?**
A artists
B scientists
C scholars
D communist leaders

9 **With which of the following does *glasnost* share many similarities?**
A the Star Spangled Banner
B the Preamble to the U.S. Constitution
C the First Amendment to the U.S. Constitution
D the Declaration of Independence

Directions: Questions 10 through 12 are based on the information below.

   In 1989, as nations across Eastern Europe began to transition from communist forms of government to democratic forms of government, Mikhail Gorbachev and the Soviet Union chose not to intervene. This allowed democratic reforms to take place in nations such as Hungary, Poland, and Bulgaria. Gorbachev's many reforms had also allowed opposition to communism to develop within the Soviet Union. Beginning in 1990, individual republics started to assert their own sovereignty over Soviet rule. In August of 1991, a failed coup by conservative communist leaders led to increased support for democratic reformers. By November of 1991, the Communist Party had been dissolved. Boris Yeltsin, a pro-democracy leader, negotiated the formation of the Commonwealth of Independent States the next month. Gorbachev resigned as president on December 25, and one day later the Soviet Union officially dissolved.

10 **Which of the following could be used to refute the generalization that all Eastern Europeans supported democratic reforms during this time?**
- **A** The Soviet Union chose not to intervene in outside conflicts.
- **B** Democratic governments rose to power in nations such as Hungary and Poland.
- **C** Individual Soviet republics began to assert their sovereignty.
- **D** Conservative leaders staged a coup against the Soviet government.

11 **Prior to this time, how did the Soviet Union most likely handle political unrest in Eastern Europe?**

Before this time, the Soviet Union had
- **A** used military force to stop uprisings.
- **B** mediated peaceful resolutions.
- **C** provided financial backing to communists.
- **D** avoided involvement in these movements.

12 **Based on this passage, which generalization can you make about the dissolution of the Soviet Union?**

The dissolution of the Soviet Union
- **A** was resisted by many of the republics.
- **B** happened very quickly.
- **C** was primarily due to intervention by the United States.
- **D** happened gradually over many years.

Directions: Question 13 is based on the map below.

COMMONWEALTH OF INDEPENDENT STATES

13 **Which factor probably led to the formation of the countries in the Commonwealth of Independent States?**
- **A** support of communism
- **B** historic rivalries
- **C** ethnic nationalism
- **D** geography

Directions: Questions 14 and 15 are based on the information below.

Hungary's contact with Western, non-Communist nations had grown steadily throughout the 1970s. By the mid-1980s, economic difficulties and high inflation caused many Hungarians to call for increased freedom of speech and reforms of the nation's Communist government. The government soon reduced censorship, permitted the establishment of independent political organizations, and allowed citizens to participate in demonstrations and strikes. By 1989, the Hungarian government reduced the constraints placed on immigration. It also reworked the national constitution in order to establish a democratic system of government. The nation's first democratic legislative election in 45 years took place in early 1990. In 2011, Hungary adopted a new constitution that provided for an elected president, who is head of state, a prime minister, who is nominated by the president and elected by the legislature, and a 386-member National Assembly.

14 **The changes taking place in Hungary during the late 1980s and early 1990s were similar to changes taking place in which nation?**
   A   Great Britain
   B   the United States
   C   Poland
   D   Japan

15 **What evidence from this passage supports the argument that nations such as Hungary generally allowed increased freedom of expression during the late 1980s and early 1990s?**
   A   Hungary relaxed restrictions on immigration.
   B   Hungary reduced censorship.
   C   Hungary revised its national constitution.
   D   Hungary held democratic elections.

Directions: Questions 16 and 17 are based on the information below.

During the civil war fought between former Yugoslavian republics, Serbian President Slobodan Milosevic launched attacks in Croatia and Bosnia. His policy of expelling or murdering non-Serbs received much criticism and drew many warnings from NATO countries.

"LINES IN THE SAND,"
A 1999 Herblock Cartoon, © by The Herb Block Foundation

16 **According to the cartoonist, how did Milosevic generally respond to NATO warnings?**
   A   He willingly accepted NATO's warnings.
   B   He accepted the warnings, but secretly disobeyed them.
   C   He accepted some warnings, but disobeyed others.
   D   He blatantly disregarded NATO's warnings.

17 **What does the symbol the cartoonist uses for Milosevic generally represent?**
   A   weakness
   B   aggression
   C   boundaries
   D   independence

Unit 3 Review

The Unit Review is structured to resemble social studies high school equivalency tests. Be sure to read each question and all possible answers very carefully before choosing your answer.

To record your answers, fill in the circle that corresponds to the answer you select for each question in the Unit Review.

Do not rest your pencil on the answer area while considering your answer. Make no stray or unnecessary marks. If you change an answer, erase your first mark completely.

Mark only one answer space for each question; multiple answers will be scored as incorrect.

Sample Question

What was the main cause for the Third Crusade?

A Pope Urban II wanted to control the Holy Land.

B Muslim leader Saladin had recaptured Jerusalem.

C English King Richard the Lionheart wanted to capture Constantinople.

D The Muslims had reclaimed Edessa.

Directions: Questions 1 and 2 refer to the following timeline.

THE UNITED NATIONS

1938—

late 1939: First concrete plan for a new international organization was started within the U.S. State Department

1940—

1942— **January 1942:** First official use of the name United Nations

October 1943: Moscow Declaration expresses need for a new organization to replace the League of Nations

August–October 1944: China, Britain, the Soviet Union, and the United States write proposals for new organization's charter

1944—

February 1945: Nations reach additional agreements on these measures

April–June 1945: Founding conference for United Nations is held in San Francisco

1946— **October 1945:** United Nations charter is ratified

January 1946: First meeting of General Assembly in London

December 1946: General Assembly receives $8.5 million from John D. Rockefeller, Jr., to buy land in New York City for its headquarters

1948—

1 **What was taking place when China, Britain, the Soviet Union, and the United States were writing proposals for the U.N. charter?**

A World War I

B World War II

C the Korean War

D the Cold War

Ⓐ Ⓑ Ⓒ Ⓓ

2 **Based on the timeline, why was this group of nations so eager to establish the United Nations by the end of 1945?**

The nations wanted

A to form a new group to take over when the League of Nations' charter ran out.

B to organize humanitarian aid for East Germany.

C to establish their organization before President Harry Truman left office.

D to help rebuild Europe and forestall another war.

Ⓐ Ⓑ Ⓒ Ⓓ

Directions: Questions 3 and 4 refer to the following information.

Although European explorers reached Australia during the 1600s, very few Europeans took an interest in the continent until British explorer James Cook studied the fertile land of its east coast in 1770. Cook claimed this area for Britain and paved the way for Australia's first European settlement. Built in 1788, this settlement served as a British penal colony. For many years, Britain continued to send individuals to Australia that had declared bankruptcy or been convicted of crimes. The entire Australian continent became a dependency of Britain in 1829. Exploration of Australia continued throughout much of the 1800s. Sheep and wheat became important agricultural products in the early part of the century. Beginning in 1851, a series of gold strikes made mining another important component of the Australian economy. The continent's growing economy also brought permanent settlements, which replaced the penal colonies by the middle of the 1800s.

3 What conclusion can you draw about Europeans' interest in Australia following James Cook's exploration of the continent's east coast?
A   They hoped to find gold.
B   They hoped to build permanent settlements.
C   They hoped to establish a port for shipping.
D   They hoped to farm the fertile soil.

Ⓐ Ⓑ Ⓒ Ⓓ

4 Why might the British have wanted to send debtors and people convicted of crimes to Australia?
A   They were experienced farmers.
B   It relieved the strain on the penal system in Britain.
C   It would prevent non-criminal British from moving to Australia.
D   They could explore the continent and send reports back to Britain.

Ⓐ Ⓑ Ⓒ Ⓓ

Directions: Questions 5 and 6 refer to the following information.

The arts were one of the many areas of life that changed significantly during the Renaissance. A spirit of innovation in society led artists working in media such as architecture, sculpture, and painting to introduce new techniques that differed from medieval methods. Renaissance communities provided supportive environments for artists as well. As towns gained wealth during this period, money was often set aside to support local artists. Whereas paintings and sculptures had previously been created primarily for use in churches, affluent citizens and royal court members gradually became important patrons of the arts. The arts also reflected the Renaissance's combining of the arts and science, as artists began to use principles of mathematics and geometry in order to create a sense of perspective and proportion in their work.

5 What generalization can you make about the arts during the Renaissance?

During the Renaissance, the arts generally
A   found little support in local communities.
B   received patronage only from churches.
C   became more respected and supported.
D   generated less enthusiasm than developments in mathematics and geometry.

Ⓐ Ⓑ Ⓒ Ⓓ

6 How does the author of this passage view the Renaissance?

The author views the Renaissance as a period of
A   innovation.
B   conflict.
C   despair.
D   reflection.

Ⓐ Ⓑ Ⓒ Ⓓ

Directions: Questions 7 and 8 refer to the following information.

In the early 1700s, India's once-powerful Mughal Empire had begun to decline, while British power expanded. The trading company known as the English East India Company arrived during the 1600s and constructed a fort at Calcutta. From this location, the company eventually conquered the Indian subcontinent. British officers commanded an army of Indians that helped to take over the region. This army remained a powerful force in Asia until India gained its independence in 1947.

7 What conclusion can you draw based on the information in this paragraph?

A The English East India Company struggled to make a profit in India.
B Calcutta was a small city.
C India gained its independence from Britain.
D The Mughal Empire declined due to a lack of trade.

ⒶⒷⒸⒹ

8 Under which of the following subjects would you categorize the main ideas of this paragraph?

The main ideas are best categorized as

A geography.
B ancient Indus Valley culture.
C colonialism.
D citizenship and government.

ⒶⒷⒸⒹ

Directions: Questions 9 and 10 refer to the following diagram.

THE INCA

The Inca gradually extended their authority over other groups living in the Andes region between 1200 and 1440.
↓
After 1493, the empire began a period of civil war. This conflict ended as Spanish explorers began to arrive.
↓
Spanish explorer Francisco Pizarro reached South America in 1532. He executed Inca emperor Atahualpa and began conquest of the Inca Empire.
↓
Pizarro's forces entered the central Inca city of Cuzco in 1533. The Inca eventually fell under Spanish rule and received subordinate status.

9 Based on the information in the diagram above, which of the following statements is correct?

A The Inca had significant interaction with European explorers prior to Pizarro's arrival in 1532.
B The period in which the Inca extended their influence lasted more than 200 years.
C A civil war within the Inca civilization broke out after 1533.
D The Inca remained dominant even after Spanish conquest.

ⒶⒷⒸⒹ

10 Inca leader Huayna Capac conquered the kingdom of Quito, or present-day Ecuador. This marked the height of Incan expansion and authority.

Where should the above information be added to the diagram?

A before the first box
B between the first and second boxes
C inside the second box
D after the fourth box

ⒶⒷⒸⒹ

Directions: Questions 11 and 12 refer to the following information.

The culture of ancient Greece valued diversity, and Greek mythology came to reflect this. The ancient Greeks worshipped many different deities and did not adhere to a strict set of beliefs. Instead, they told a wide variety of stories about Greek gods. These tales often differed according to whether they were told in the form of epic poetry, comedies, or tragedies.

In ancient Rome, the people originally viewed gods as a series of powers, rather than as individuals. The interaction of ancient Greek and Roman cultures during the 6th century BC influenced the Romans to describe gods in human form. During the final three centuries BC, Roman authors began to apply the names of Roman gods to Greek traditions. This practice created what is known as Greco-Roman mythology.

11 How might you best describe Greek mythology?

Greek mythology could best be described as
  A strict.
  B unchanging.
  C unified.
  D varied.

  Ⓐ Ⓑ Ⓒ Ⓓ

12 Under which of the following headings could you categorize Roman mythology?
  A common modern-day religions
  B highly-organized religions
  C intolerant systems of belief
  D influenced by Greek mythology

  Ⓐ Ⓑ Ⓒ Ⓓ

Directions: Questions 13 and 14 refer to the following table.

EUROPEAN ECONOMIC COMMUNITY/ EUROPEAN UNION MEMBERSHIP	
YEAR JOINED	**NATION**
1958	Belgium, West Germany, France, Italy, Luxembourg, the Netherlands
1973	Denmark, Ireland, the United Kingdom
1981	Greece
1986	Spain, Portugal
1990	territory from former East Germany
1995	Austria, Finland, Sweden
2004	Czech Republic, Estonia, Cyprus, Latvia, Lithuania, Hungary, Malta, Poland, Slovenia, Slovakia
2007	Bulgaria, Romania
2013	Croatia

13 Why did the majority of Eastern European countries not join the European Economic Community/European Union until 2004?

They did not join until 2004 because
  A they were barred by France and Germany.
  B they did not accept the euro as their currency until that time.
  C they had been part of the Soviet Union.
  D up until that time, the EU only allowed two countries to join per year.

  Ⓐ Ⓑ Ⓒ Ⓓ

14 Based on the information in the table, which of the following statements is correct?
  A Ireland joined the organization more than 20 years before Hungary.
  B Austria joined the organization in the same year as Hungary.
  C The United Kingdom was one of the original members of the organization.
  D Spain joined the organization earlier than France.

  Ⓐ Ⓑ Ⓒ Ⓓ

And because the condition of man … is a condition of war of every one against everyone, in which case every one is governed by his own reason, and there is nothing he can make use of that may not be a help unto him in preserving his life against his enemies; it followeth that in such a condition every man has a right to every thing, even to one another's body. And therefore, as long as this natural right of every man to every thing endureth, there can be no security to any man, how strong or wise soever he be, of living out the time which nature ordinarily alloweth men to live. And consequently it is a precept, or general rule of reason: that every man ought to endeavour peace, as far as he has hope of obtaining it; and when he cannot obtain it, that he may seek and use all helps and advantages of war. The first branch of which rule containeth the first and fundamental law of nature, which is: to seek peace and follow it. The second, the sum of the right of nature, which is: by all means we can defend ourselves.

15 What is Hobbes's point of view?

   A People should use whatever means necessary to defend themselves.

   B People should not seek to live together in peace.

   C No person has the right to take another's property.

   D Governments should not use the power of war, even when necessary.

        Ⓐ Ⓑ Ⓒ Ⓓ

16 Of the following, who might use Hobbes's writings to support his or her own point of view?

   A a person seeking to unite warring groups

   B a monarch offering protection in exchange for reduced individual rights

   C a political leader who does not support the use of force to defend a territory

   D a religious leader arguing that religious bodies should hold more power than political bodies

        Ⓐ Ⓑ Ⓒ Ⓓ

The Shang Dynasty ruled ancient China from approximately 1570 BC to 1045 BC. Archaeological evidence suggests that the Shang Dynasty featured a complex society. This society included agricultural workers, as well as urban artisans and priests. Because the earliest written records of ancient China date to this period, scholars consider the Shang to be China's first historical dynasty. Most of these Shang Dynasty writings are carvings or inscriptions on animal bones or shells. Shang Dynasty kings used these items to make predictions about the future, and the writings on these bones and shells record the kings' predictions. A king might issue predictions on topics as varied as military strategy, weather, harvests, family, and the construction of settlements. In this way, these inscriptions provide a valuable account of the daily lives of Shang Dynasty kings.

17 Why was the Shang Dynasty considered to be China's first historical dynasty?

   A because it featured a complex society

   B because both agricultural workers and urban artisans worked in the society

   C because the earliest written records of ancient China date to this period

   D because Shang kings used animal bones and shells to make predictions

        Ⓐ Ⓑ Ⓒ Ⓓ

18 How are the Shang Dynasty writings and carvings best categorized?

   A religious

   B wide-ranging

   C agricultural

   D geographical

        Ⓐ Ⓑ Ⓒ Ⓓ

Directions: Questions 19 through 22 refer to the following diagram.

WORLD WAR I

Causes

- Nationalism in Austria-Hungary
- Rivalry between France and Germany
- European nations' imperialism leads to territorial disputes in Asia and Africa
- Conflicts cause the formation of extensive alliances and an arms race
- Serbian nationalist assassinates Archduke Ferdinand of Austria-Hungary
- Following Ferdinand's assassination, alliances draw many nations into the conflict, making it a world war
- Britain is determined to keep its colonial territories and fears that unless it enters the war, Germany will control Western Europe

Outcomes

- Treaty of Versailles forces Germany to accept responsibility for war; ordered to pay costly reparations
- War brings end to Austro-Hungarian, Russian, and German empires
- League of Nations forms in an effort to promote cooperation to prevent future wars
- More than 10 million soldiers lose their lives
- Women enter many historically male occupations
- Many nations experience economic hardships due to the expense of war

19 Which of the following was most responsible for turning the conflicts that started World War I into a world war?

A nationalism in Austria-Hungary
B territorial disputes in Asia
C European imperialism in Africa
D extensive alliances formed among nations

Ⓐ Ⓑ Ⓒ Ⓓ

20 In which historically male occupation did women likely work during the war?

During World War I, women most likely worked as

A coal miners.
B physicians.
C industrial workers.
D soldiers.

Ⓐ Ⓑ Ⓒ Ⓓ

21 The rivalry between which two nations became an important cause of World War I?

A Austria and Hungary
B Serbia and Germany
C Britain and Germany
D the United States and France

Ⓐ Ⓑ Ⓒ Ⓓ

22 The information in the table supports which of the following generalizations?

A Compared to other wars, there were fewer casualties in World War I.
B Women's roles in society were largely unaffected by the war.
C The economies of most European nations were stronger in the years after the war.
D World War I had a major political and social impact on Europe and countries throughout the world.

Ⓐ Ⓑ Ⓒ Ⓓ

Unit 4

Unit Overview

The United States has a democratic form of government. In a democracy, leaders represent the interests of the citizens who elect them. As citizens of the United States, we have various rights and responsibilities. Every time you vote for leaders and issues, you are exercising one of those rights. Similarly, as citizens we also have certain responsibilities. One such responsibility involves staying informed about current events.

The importance of government and civics extends to social studies high school equivalency tests, where topics relating to U.S. government/civics make up approximately 30 percent of all questions. As with other areas of the social studies test, government and civics questions will test your ability to interpret information by using reading skills and thinking skills such as comprehension, application, analysis, and evaluation. In Unit 4, the introduction of various critical-thinking skills, along with specialized instruction about text and maps, will help you prepare for social studies high school equivalency tests.

Table of Contents

Key U.S. Government / Civics Terms

administration: the officials in the executive branch of a government or organization

appellate: the aspect of the court system that deals with applications (appeals) for decisions to be reversed

article: a separate part of a legal document

Bill of Rights: the first ten amendments of the U.S. Constitution

caucus: a group of people convened within a political party to choose a candidate or set a policy

checks and balances: the system within government in which different parts have powers that affect and control other parts so that no part becomes too powerful

civil rights movement: the social movement in the U.S. from the mid-1950s to late-1960s aimed at ending racial discrimination against African Americans

congressional district: one of 435 areas in the U.S. in which the population selects one member of congress

domestic policy: laws and programs that apply within a nation's borders

Electoral College: the process in which electors are selected and convened to officially cast votes to seat the president and vice president

executive branch: the part of government responsible for daily administration and carrying out laws

fascism: a centralized form of government that values nationalism and in which a dictator controls the lives of citizens who are not permitted to disagree with the government or the leader

federal: referring to a government structure in which power is shared between the central, national government and states or provinces

foreign policy: laws and programs that apply to how a nation conducts itself outside of its borders

judicial: referring to the system of courts that interprets and applies laws

jurisdiction: the power to govern an area or apply laws

legislature: the branch of government that enacts and revises laws

platform: the statement of the principles of a political party

political party: a group of people with shared values about governance who seek to have their members elected to positions of power

preamble: an introductory statement at the beginning of a document that usually explains the reason for the information that follows

primary election: a preliminary election that narrows the number of candidates running for political office

primary source: an original document or other material that consists only of that information provided by its creator and has not been altered in any way

secondary source: a document or record that discusses information originally presented elsewhere

suffrage: the right to vote in an election

Supreme Court: the court of highest authority in the U.S., consisting of the Chief Justice and eight associate justices

term: the period for which an official is elected to serve in office

UN Security Council: a group within the United Nations organization that is responsible for maintaining international peace and security

United States Constitution: the legal document that framed the U.S. government at its formation and continues to serve as the supreme body of laws for the nation

Use Context Clues

① Learn the Skill

The **context** of a word or term includes the words, details, and ideas surrounding it. **Context clues** are the pieces of information surrounding an unfamiliar term that help to clarify its meaning. By using context clues, you can determine the meaning of an unfamiliar word or clarify the main points of a confusing passage of text.

② Practice the Skill

By mastering the skill of using context clues, you will improve your study and test-taking skills, especially as they relate to social studies high school equivalency tests. Read the excerpt and strategies below. Use this information to answer question 1.

Ⓐ The context of this information tells you that it describes the content of a proposition, or a proposed law that voters will either approve or reject. The likely audience for this excerpt includes prospective voters.

Ⓑ Context clues can help you determine the meanings of unfamiliar terms such as *jurisdiction, fast-tracks,* and *rights-of-way.* Nearby terms and phrases, such as "regulatory matters," "approval," and "transmission of renewable energy," can help point you to the correct meaning of each term.

> ### Prop 7
> **Renewable Energy Generation. Initiative Statute.**
> - Requires utilities, including government-owned utilities, to generate 20% of their power from renewable energy by 2010, a standard currently applicable only to private electrical corporations.
> - Raises requirement for utilities to 40% by 2020 and 50% by 2025.
> - Imposes penalties, subject to waiver, for noncompliance.
> - Transfers some <u>jurisdiction</u> of regulatory matters from Public Utilities Commission to Energy Commission.
> - <u>Fast-tracks</u> approval for new renewable energy plants.
> - Requires utilities to sign longer contracts (20 year minimum) to procure renewable energy.
> - Creates account to purchase <u>rights-of-way</u> and facilities for the transmission of renewable energy.
>
> From Official Voter Information Guide, California General Election, 2008

✓ TEST-TAKING TIPS

When answering a difficult question, you can look for context clues that might suggest one possible answer over another. Further, when reading text passages for a test, use context clues to clarify any information that seems unclear or confusing.

1 What does "jurisdiction" probably mean?
A a list of rules
B the right to make judgments
C the obligation to lead meetings
D a regulatory agency

Directions: Question 2 refers to the following information.

From the city charter of Alexandria, Virginia
Section 3.01 Composition of the Council. The council shall consist of the mayor and six members at large, elected as provided in chapter 10 of this charter, and they shall serve for terms of three years or until their successors shall have been elected and take office ...

2 **Which of the following sentences means the same as the details in the charter?**
  A The council has six members who serve three terms until another member is elected.
  B The council consists of the mayor and six members from specific districts within the city who each serve three-year terms.
  C The council consists of the mayor and six members from any part of the city who serve three-year terms each or until a new member is elected.
  D The council consists of the mayor and six members who serve three terms each or until a new council member is elected to take his or her place.

Directions: Question 3 refers to the following table.

FEDERAL AND STATE POWERS	
FEDERAL	**STATE**
Has supremacy over conflicting state law	Maintain militia to be called on during local emergencies
Make treaties and declare war	Make marriage and divorce laws
Impose taxes on imports	Organize elections

3 **Based on the context of the table, which of the following is most likely a federal power?**
  A protect public safety
  B keep a peacetime army
  C organize education
  D run school boards

Directions: Questions 4 and 5 refer to the following information.

CREDIT CARD APPLICATION

Please complete all information below in ink. Missing information may affect our credit decision.

1. PERSONAL INFORMATION

FIRST NAME	MI	LAST NAME	SOCIAL SECURITY NUMBER	DATE OF BIRTH
				MO DAY YR

HOME ADDRESS: NUMBER, STREET NAME (APT. #)		HOME PHONE NUMBER ( )	PERMANENT ☐YES US RESIDENT ☐ NO
CITY	STATE ZIP	EMAIL ADDRESS	

PLACE OF RESIDENCE ☐OWN ☐RENT ☐PARENTS ☐OTHER	MO RENT/MORTGAGE PAYMENT $	HOW LONG AT CURRENT ADDRESS YRS. MOS.

PREVIOUS STREET ADDRESS IF LESS THAN 6 MONTHS AT CURRENT ADDRESS

PREVIOUS CITY	STATE ZIP

EMPLOYER/NAME	BUSINESS PHONE ( )

BUSINESS ADDRESS	YOUR POSITION
CITY	STATE ZIP	

HOW LONG EMPLOYED YRS MOS.	GROSS MONTHLY SALARY $	OTHER MONTHLY INCOME* $	OTHER INCOME SOURCE*

***OTHER INCOME: Alimony, child support or separate maintenance income need not be revealed if you do not wish to have it considered as a basis for repaying this obligation.**

4 **To what is the application referring with the phrase "this obligation?"**
  A alimony
  B child support
  C credit card debt
  D mortgage

5 **Based on the credit card application, what is probably the most important factor for creditors?**
  A employment history
  B citizenship status
  C place of residence
  D ability to pay debt

Directions: Questions 6 and 7 refer to the following voter registration application.

Voter Registration Application
Before completing this form, review the General, Application, and State specific instructions.

Are you a citizen of the United States of America? Will you be 18 years old on or before election day? **If you checked "No" in response to either of these questions, do not complete form.** (Please see state-specific instructions for rules regarding eligibility to register prior to age 18.)		This space for office use only.

1	(Circle one) Last Name First Name Middle Name(s) Mr. Mrs. Miss. Ms.	(Circle one) Jr Sr II III IV
2	Home Address Apt. or Lot# City/Town State	Zip Code
3	Address Where You Get Your Mail If Different From Above City/Town State	Zip Code
4	Date of Birth __/__/__ Month Day Year **5** Telephone Number (optional) **6**	ID Number - (see item 6 in the instructions for your state)
7	Choice of Party (see item 7 in the instructions for your state) **8** Race or Ethnic Group (see item 8 in the instructions for your state)	
9	I have reviewed my state's instructions and I swear/affirm that: • I am a United States citizen. • I meet the eligibility requirements of my state and subscribe to any oath required. • The information I have provided is true to the best of my knowledge under penalty of perjury. If I have provided false information, I may be fined, imprisoned, or (if not a U. S. citizen) deported from or refused entry to the United States.	Please sign full name (or put mark) Date: __/__/__ Month Day Year

---

6 Based on the context clues in this application, what is one requirement for voting in the United States?

In order to vote in the United States, a person must

- **A** declare his or her support for one political party.
- **B** be at least 18 years old.
- **C** have lived in the United States for six months.
- **D** provide a valid telephone number at which he or she can be reached.

7 Which of the following statements can you determine to be true based on the information in this application?

- **A** The United States has a two-party system of government.
- **B** Both federal and state governments have voting regulations.
- **C** Many states allow voters to cast ballots by mail.
- **D** No people younger than 18 can register to vote in the United States.

Directions: Questions 8 and 9 refer to the following table.

THE HARRISON GROUP		
NAME	**DEPARTMENT**	**LOCATION**
Chen, Karen	Accounting	Chicago
Garza, Tony	Corporate	Detroit
Greer, Angela	Marketing	New York
Patel, Vinay	Engineering	Chicago

8 Which of the company's facilities is located in Detroit?
- **A** manufacturing facilities
- **B** marketing department
- **C** engineering department
- **D** corporate headquarters

9 The context of the directory suggests that this company is what?
- **A** a large corporation
- **B** focused primarily on manufacturing goods
- **C** publicly traded
- **D** a leader in its field

Directions: Questions 10 through 13 refer to the following employment application.

```
COMPANY NAME: _____        POSITION APPLIED FOR: _____

┌─────────────────────────────────┐    APPLICANT TELEPHONE: _____
│  EMPLOYMENT APPLICATION         │    SOCIAL SECURITY NUMBER: _____
└─────────────────────────────────┘

YOUR NAME: _____
           Last                        First                          Middle
ADDRESS: _____
         _____
         _____

EDUCATION            Years Completed        Field of Study           (Graduate or Degree)

High School_____

College/University_____

Business/Technical_____

Other (May include grammar school) _____

REFERENCES:  List two personal references who are not relatives or former supervisors.
_____
Name          Address          Telephone          Occupation          Years known
_____
Name          Address          Telephone          Occupation          Years known

EMPLOYMENT:  List last employment first. Include summer or temporary jobs. Be sure all your experience or employers related
to this job are listed here, in the summary (following this section), or use an extra sheet of paper if necessary.
```

10 Based on the context clues in this excerpt, which of the following best describes a *personal reference?*

- **A** a person who can advocate for your character
- **B** an older family member who has known you for many years
- **C** a person you can turn to for advice and guidance
- **D** an individual who supervised you in your previous employment

11 What is the meaning of the term *position* in this context?

Context clues suggest that, in this usage, *position* means

- **A** a pose.
- **B** to move into place.
- **C** a job.
- **D** a point of view.

12 Which of the following could be correctly written in the *Graduate or Degree* column of the section titled Education?

- **A** one year
- **B** History
- **C** Associate of Applied Science
- **D** senior year

13 Which of the following represents a temporary job, as discussed in the Employment section of the application?

A temporary job would include

- **A** a one-year appointment to the board of a community group.
- **B** a volunteer project in the community.
- **C** a job from which one was fired after several months.
- **D** a short-term contract job.

Directions: Questions 14 through 18 refer to the following excerpt from then Secretary of State Colin Powell's testimony before the UN Security Council in February 2003.

This is all part of a system of hiding things and moving things out of the way and making sure <u>they</u> have left nothing behind. … [Powell plays intercepted message]

<u>This message</u> would have verified to the inspectors that they have been trying to turn over things. They were looking for things. But they don't want that message seen, because they were trying to clean up the area to leave no evidence behind of the presence of weapons of mass destruction. And they claim that nothing was there. And the inspectors can look all they want, and they will find nothing.

This effort to hide things from the inspectors is not one or two isolated incidents, quite the contrary. This is part and parcel of a policy of evasion and deception that <u>goes back 12 years</u>, a policy set at the highest levels of the Iraqi regime.

We know that Saddam Hussein has what is called quote, 'a higher committee for monitoring the inspections teams,' unquote. Think about that. Iraq has a high-level committee to monitor the inspectors who were sent in to monitor Iraq's disarmament.

Not to cooperate with them, not to assist them, but to spy on them and keep them from doing their jobs.

14 **Based on the context of this excerpt, what does Powell believe about the UN weapons inspections in Iraq?**

Secretary Powell believes
A that the Iraqi government is cooperating with the inspectors.
B that the United States should send in their own weapons inspectors.
C that the inspectors are being deliberately misled.
D that the UN inspectors are conspiring with the Iraqis to hide weapons from the United States.

15 **Based on the context clues in the excerpt, who is Powell referring to when he says "they" in the first paragraph?**
A the UN inspectors
B Iraqis who are hiding weapons
C Saddam's secret 'higher committee'
D the Iraqi Army

16 **What can be inferred about the message Powell played for the Security Council?**

The message
A tipped off UN inspectors where to find weapons.
B spread anti-American sentiment.
C came from high-ranking Iraqi officials.
D was sent by the UN inspectors.

17 **How does Powell's reference "goes back 12 years" put the situation in context?**

Powell was referring to
A when George W. Bush was elected president.
B when Powell became Secretary of State.
C the Iran-Iraq war.
D the Persian Gulf War.

18 **Based on the context of this excerpt, what was Powell's purpose in testifying before the UN Security Council?**

Powell wanted the Security Council
A to stop weapons inspections in Iraq.
B to support the use of force in Iraq.
C to send in more weapons inspectors.
D to revoke Iraq's UN membership.

Interpret the Constitution

① Learn the Skill

The **United States Constitution**, which outlines the basic principles on which the federal government operates, includes a preamble and seven articles. Twenty-seven amendments have also been added to this document. Because the Constitution describes these principles in a general manner, it becomes important to **interpret** the Constitution in order to understand how its principles apply to the everyday workings of our national government.

② Practice the Skill

By mastering the skill of interpreting the Constitution, you will improve your study and test-taking skills, especially as they relate to social studies high school equivalency tests. Read the excerpt and strategies below. Use this information to answer questions 1 and 2.

A The initial words of the Preamble identify the perspective from which the Constitution is written. With this phrase, the authors of the Constitution indicate that they have written this document on behalf of all Americans.

B These phrases represent examples of the types of general principles discussed in the U.S. Constitution.

From the Preamble to the United States Constitution:

A We the people of the United States, in order to form a more perfect union, establish justice, insure domestic tranquility, provide for the common defense, promote the general welfare, and secure the blessings of liberty to ourselves and our posterity, do ordain and establish this Constitution for the United States of America.

✓ TEST-TAKING TIPS

Because the original articles of the U.S. Constitution were written in the late 1700s, the language includes words that may seem confusing or unfamiliar. When interpreting information from the Constitution, look for familiar words and phrases that can provide clues to the meanings of these unfamiliar concepts.

1 Which of the following best describes the meaning of the phrase "insure domestic tranquility"?
- **A** protect the nation from outside threats
- **B** establish a fair and balanced court system
- **C** protect the rights of all people
- **D** maintain peace within the nation

2 Which of the following best describes the Preamble?
- **A** an outline
- **B** a declaration
- **C** an apology
- **D** a generalization

UNIT 4

Directions: Questions 3 and 4 refer to the following excerpt.

From Article I of the U.S. Constitution:

Section 7. All bills for raising revenue shall originate in the House of Representatives; but the Senate may propose or concur with amendments as on other bills.

Every bill which shall have passed the House of Representatives and the Senate, shall, before it become a law, be presented to the President of the United States; if he approve he shall sign it, but if not he shall return it, with his objections to that House in which it shall have originated, who shall enter the objections at large on their journal, and proceed to reconsider it. If after such reconsideration two thirds of that House shall agree to pass the bill, it shall be sent, together with the objections, to the other House, by which it shall likewise be reconsidered, and if approved by two thirds of that House, it shall become a law.

3 **How can the members of Congress override the president's veto?**
   A through unanimous approval from the house in which the bill originated
   B through approval from two-thirds of the house in which the bill originated
   C through gaining approval from the Speaker of the House of Representatives and the vice president
   D through approval from two-thirds of both houses

4 **Which of the following bills could not originate in the Senate?**

   The Senate could not originate a bill that
   A establishes new federal education standards.
   B institutes a higher tax on gasoline.
   C changes the nation's health care system.
   D places stricter emissions standards on automobiles.

Directions: Question 5 refers to the following excerpt.

From the Bill of Rights of the U.S. Constitution:

Amendment IX
   The enumeration in the Constitution, of certain rights, shall not be construed to deny or disparage others retained by the people.

5 **Which of the following offers the best interpretation of Amendment IX?**
   A The Constitution cannot be used to deny citizens their rights.
   B Each state has the authority to delegate rights to its citizens.
   C The fact that the Constitution describes certain rights does not mean that citizens do not have additional rights.
   D Citizens do not have the right to speak out against the provisions in the Bill of Rights.

Directions: Question 6 refers to the following excerpt.

From the Bill of Rights of the U.S. Constitution:

Amendment VI
   In all criminal prosecutions, the accused shall enjoy the right to a speedy and public trial, by an impartial jury of the state and district wherein the crime shall have been committed, which district shall have been previously ascertained by law, and to be informed of the nature and cause of the accusation; to be confronted with the witnesses against him; to have compulsory process for obtaining witnesses in his favor, and to have the assistance of counsel for his defense.

6 **Which of the following provides the best title for the content of Amendment VI?**
   A freedom of expression
   B rights of the accused
   C procedures for jury trials
   D witnesses in criminal proceedings

Directions: Questions 7 and 8 refer to the following excerpt from Article II of the U.S. Constitution.

Section 2. The President shall be commander in chief of the Army and Navy of the United States, and of the militia of the several states, when called into the actual service of the United States; he may require the opinion, in writing, of the principal officer in each of the executive departments, upon any subject relating to the duties of their respective offices, and he shall have power to grant reprieves and pardons for offenses against the United States, except in cases of impeachment.

He shall have power, by and with the advice and consent of the Senate, to make treaties, provided two thirds of the Senators present **concur**. …

7 **What powers does the U.S. Constitution grant the president of the United States?**

The Constitution grants the president the power to
  A pardon individuals convicted of state crimes.
  B reject treaties approved by the Senate.
  C request the advice of executive officers.
  D grant pardons in impeachment cases.

8 **Which of the following can be substituted for *concur* in order to provide the most accurate interpretation of the text?**
  A agree
  B admit
  C consider
  D refuse

Directions: Questions 9 and 10 refer to the following excerpt from Article V of the U.S. Constitution.

The Congress, whenever two thirds of both houses shall deem it necessary, shall propose amendments to this Constitution, or, on the application of the legislatures of two thirds of the several states, shall call a convention for proposing amendments, which, in either case, shall be valid to all intents and purposes, as part of this Constitution, when ratified by the legislatures of three fourths of the several states, or by conventions in three fourths thereof, as the one or the other mode of ratification may be proposed by the Congress; provided that no amendment which may be made prior to the year one thousand eight hundred and eight shall in any manner affect the first and fourth clauses in the ninth section of the first article; and that no state, without its consent, shall be deprived of its equal suffrage in the Senate.

9 **How do proposed amendments become part of the U.S. Constitution?**

Proposed amendments become part of the U.S. Constitution when
  A three fourths of state legislatures or conventions ratify them.
  B the president endorses them.
  C three fourths of the Senate ratifies them.
  D three fourths of Congress ratifies them.

10 **Which of the following has the authority to propose amendments to the U.S. Constitution?**
  A the Supreme Court
  B the officers of the executive branch
  C the president
  D state legislatures

Directions: Questions 11 and 12 refer to the following excerpt from the Bill of Rights of the U.S. Constitution.

Amendment I

Congress shall make no law respecting an establishment of religion, or prohibiting the free exercise thereof; or abridging the freedom of speech, or of the press; or the right of the people peaceably to assemble, and to petition the government for a redress of grievances.

Amendment II

A well regulated militia, being necessary to the security of a free state, the right of the people to keep and bear arms, shall not be infringed.

Amendment III

No soldier shall, in time of peace be quartered in any house, without the consent of the owner, nor in time of war, but in a manner to be prescribed by law.

11 The right to do which of the following is protected by the First Amendment?
  A organize violent demonstrations
  B refuse to house federal troops
  C publish criticisms of government policies
  D possess weapons

12 Which of the following is protected by the Second Amendment?
  A the refusal to house federal troops
  B the right of a militia to possess weapons
  C protection against unreasonable searches
  D the freedom to join the nation's armed forces

Directions: Questions 13 and 14 refer to the following excerpt from Article III of the U.S. Constitution.

Section 1. The judicial power of the United States, shall be vested in one Supreme Court, and in such inferior courts as the Congress may from time to time ordain and establish. The judges, both of the supreme and inferior courts, shall hold their offices during good behaviour, and shall, at stated times, receive for their services, a compensation, which shall not be diminished during their continuance in office.

Section 2. … In all cases affecting ambassadors, other public ministers and consuls, and those in which a state shall be party, the Supreme Court shall have original jurisdiction. In all the other cases before mentioned, the Supreme Court shall have appellate jurisdiction, both as to law and fact, with such exceptions, and under such regulations as the Congress shall make.

13 How does the Supreme Court handle appeals?

For cases in which the Supreme Court has appellate jurisdiction, it will
  A hear the original trial in the case.
  B review the decision of a lower court.
  C select a jury to decide the case.
  D receive no compensation for its work.

14 Which of the following has the authority to establish new federal courts?
  A the Supreme Court
  B the Chief Justice of the Supreme Court
  C the president and vice president
  D Congress

Directions: Questions 15 through 18 refer to the following information and diagram.

The United States Constitution sets up a system of checks and balances between the three branches of the federal government. Through this system, each branch of government has some type of authority over the other two branches. This system was devised in order to guarantee that no single branch of the government became too powerful.

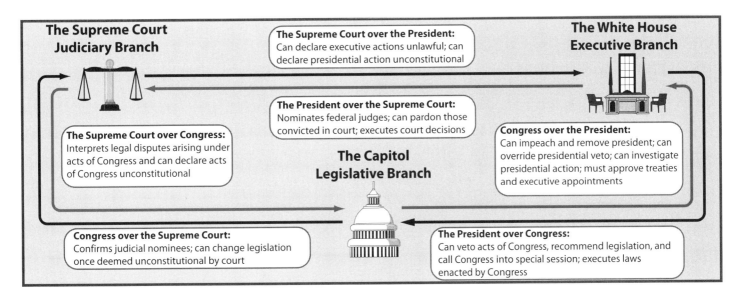

15 Which part of the federal government has the power to declare the actions of other government bodies unconstitutional?

- A the House of Representatives
- B the Senate
- C the Supreme Court
- D the president

16 How can Congress limit the power of the federal government's judicial branch?

Congress has the authority to

- A choose the individual court cases that go before the Supreme Court.
- B confirm judicial nominees.
- C override a Supreme Court ruling striking down a law passed in Congress.
- D determine the ways in which court decisions are implemented.

17 Which of the following checks on the power of Congress does the president possess?

- A the power to veto laws created by Congress
- B the authority to serve as president of the Senate
- C the authority to nominate replacements for members of Congress that do not serve their full terms
- D the right to rewrite legislation passed by Congress

18 Which of the following accurately describes the system of checks and balances established by the United States?

- A This system has been amended many times.
- B This system gives most authority to the executive branch.
- C This system was designed to keep one branch of government from becoming too powerful.
- D This system invests most of the legislative branch's ability to check the power of the other branches in the Senate.

Analyze Information Sources

① Learn the Skill

When learning about social studies, you will often be required to **analyze** many different types of **information sources**. **Primary sources** are original accounts of events written by people who actually experienced them at the time, like an eyewitness. These sources include speeches, documents, journal entries, and letters. **Secondary sources** interpret primary sources. Encyclopedias, newspaper articles, and history books are secondary sources. It is important to distinguish between primary and secondary sources to understand the author's purpose and point of view. Remember that all sources have a degree of **bias**, or partiality. Be sure to evaluate sources critically.

② Practice the Skill

By mastering the skill of analyzing information sources, you will improve your study and test-taking skills, especially as they relate to social studies high school equivalency tests. Read the excerpt and strategies below. Use this information to answer question 1.

A The language of this question and the repetition of the phrase "I think" suggest that this passage expresses the author's beliefs and opinions. If people are trying to promote something, it could be said that they have a bias towards it. If against something, then they are biased against it.

B Titles, labels, captions, and so on can provide valuable information for evaluating a source.

> <u>How many of you who are going to be doctors are willing to spend your days in Ghana</u>? Technicians or engineers: how many of you are willing to work in the Foreign Service and spend your lives traveling around the world? On your willingness to do that, not merely to serve one year or two years in the service, but on your willingness to contribute part of your life to this country, <u>I think</u> will depend the answer whether a free society can compete. <u>I think</u> it can. And <u>I think</u> Americans are willing to contribute. But the effort must be far greater than we've ever made in the past.
>
> **B**
>
> From John F. Kennedy, Campaign Speech in Ann Arbor, Michigan, 1960

TEST-TAKING TIPS

All sources have a degree of bias. Most scholarly works (secondary sources) attempt to prove a historical thesis, such as the role of economics during the American Revolution, and have to acknowledge the bias in the primary sources they use.

1 How does this excerpt show bias?

Kennedy is biased towards
A service programs.
B doctors.
C Americans.
D engineers.

UNIT 4

Directions: Questions 2 and 3 refer to the following excerpts.

From **.gov** Web site:

The Department of Homeland Security was established in 2002, in response to the terrorist attacks on the United States on September 11, 2001. The goal of this organization was to provide a unified anti-terrorism agency focused on raising awareness of terrorist threats in the nation, as well as preventing future terrorist attacks from occurring.

From **.com** Web site:

The Department of Homeland Security was formed on September 11, 2001 after the terrorist attacks that shocked the country. The founding of the Department of Homeland Security was a major achievement of the presidency of George H.W. Bush. It is now involved in tracking down terrorists around the world. This agency has been very successful.

2 **Which fact is directly disputed between the two excerpts?**
  A the creator of the Department of Homeland Security
  B the date on which the Department of Homeland Security was established
  C the reason for the creation of the Department of Homeland Security
  D the responsibilities of the Department of Homeland Security

3 **How do the tones of these two excerpts differ?**

  In comparison to that of the second excerpt, the tone of the first excerpt could be described as
  A scholarly.
  B informal.
  C biased.
  D emotional.

Directions: Questions 4 and 5 refer to the following graph.

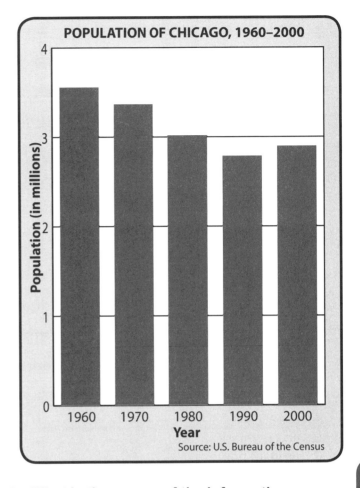

POPULATION OF CHICAGO, 1960–2000

Source: U.S. Bureau of the Census

4 **What is the source of the information presented in this graph?**
  A a corporation
  B the city of Chicago
  C a federal government agency
  D an encyclopedia

5 **Which of the following is an example of a biased interpretation of this graph?**
  A The population of Chicago has declined over time.
  B The decline in population was caused by an increase in violence by poor people.
  C Chicago's population was higher in 1960 than it was in 2000.
  D The population of Chicago has been declining over several decades for many reasons.

UNIT 4

Directions: Questions 6 and 7 refer to the following political cartoon published in 1963.

"WHAT DO YOU MEAN, 'NOT SO FAST',"

"WHAT DO YOU MEAN, 'NOT SO FAST'," by Bill Mauldin
Published in *Chicago Sun-Times,* May 10, 1963

6   **Which of the following best describes this cartoon as an information source?**
   A   impartial
   B   commentary
   C   propaganda
   D   critical of civil rights movement

7   **What does the date on which this cartoon was published suggest about its relevance to the study of the civil rights movement?**

   This cartoon
   A   was published many years after the end of the civil rights movement.
   B   preceded the civil rights movement by several years.
   C   has little relevance to the study of the civil rights movement.
   D   was published during the height of the civil rights movement.

Directions: Questions 8 and 9 refer to the following table.

SUPREME COURT JUSTICES		
NAME	**JOINED SUPREME COURT**	**APPOINTED BY**
Elena Kagan	2010	Barack Obama
Sonia Sotomayor	2009	Barack Obama
Chief Justice John Roberts	2005	George W. Bush
Samuel Alito	2006	George W. Bush
Stephen Breyer	1994	Bill Clinton
Ruth Bader Ginsburg	1993	Bill Clinton
Clarence Thomas	1991	George H.W. Bush
Anthony Kennedy	1988	Ronald Reagan
Antonin Scalia	1986	Ronald Reagan

8   **In which type of information source would you likely find this table?**
   A   newspaper editorial
   B   historical biography
   C   government Web site
   D   journal entry

9   **Which of the following can you determine using this information source?**
   A   the age of each justice
   B   the president who appointed each justice
   C   the year in which each justice was nominated for the Supreme Court
   D   the political party of each justice

UNIT 4

Directions: Questions 10 through 13 refer to the following excerpts.

From the 2000 presidential debate between Texas Governor George W. Bush and Vice President Al Gore:

GORE: This is a very important moment in the history of our country. Look, we've got the biggest surpluses in all of American history. The key question that has to be answered in this election is will we use that prosperity wisely in a way that benefits all of our people and doesn't just go to the few. Almost half of all the tax cut benefits, as I said under Governor Bush's plan, go to the wealthiest 1%. I think we have to make the right and responsible choices ... . For every new dollar that I propose for spending on health care, Governor Bush spends $3 for a tax cut for the wealthiest 1%. Now, for every dollar that I propose to spend on education, he spends $5 on a tax cut for the wealthiest 1%. Those are very clear differences.

BUSH: ... Under Vice President Gore's plan, he is going to grow the federal government in the largest increase since Lyndon Baines Johnson in 1965. We're talking about a massive government, folks. We're talking about adding to or increasing 200 programs, 20,000 new bureaucrats. Imagine how many IRS agents it is going to take to be able to figure out his targeted tax cut for the middle class that excludes 50 million Americans. There is a huge difference in this campaign. He says he's going to give you tax cuts. 50 million of you won't receive it ... . After my plan is in place, the wealthiest Americans will pay more tax, the poorest of Americans, six million families, won't pay any tax at all. It's a huge difference. A difference between big expanding federal government that wants to think on your behalf and a plan that meets priorities and liberates working people to be able to make decisions on your own.

10 How does each candidate seek to gain support for his arguments?
   A   offering statistics
   B   conceding a point to his opponent
   C   referencing a respected authority
   D   citing independent research studies

11 Why are both of these arguments biased?

   They are biased
   A   because only Bush uses facts.
   B   because Gore discusses tax policy.
   C   because both are trying to persuade voters.
   D   because both discuss American history.

12 For which purpose would these excerpts prove useful as information sources?

   These excerpts would prove useful as
   A   overviews of the U.S. tax system.
   B   historical summaries of presidential debates.
   C   impartial analyses of each candidate's plans for government.
   D   primary source documentation of the specific tax proposals of both candidates.

13 How would you characterize the tone of both candidates in these excerpts?
   A   indifferent
   B   anxious
   C   combative
   D   elusive

Directions: Questions 14 and 15 refer to the following excerpt.

Although there are special-purpose local government bodies (e.g., school boards in the United States), more important are those that carry out a broad range of public activities within a defined area and population. Almost all such local government bodies share certain characteristics: a continuing organization; the authority to undertake public activities; the ability to enter into contracts; the right to sue and be sued; and the ability to collect taxes and determine a budget. Areas of local government authority usually include public schools, local highways, municipal services, and some aspects of social welfare and public order.

From Columbia Encyclopedia article "Local Government," 6th edition, 2013

14 Which of the following would not likely appear in the remainder of this article?

The remainder of this article would be unlikely to contain
A   descriptions of different forms of local government.
B   details about local government structures.
C   opinions about the most successful types of local government.
D   descriptions of county governments.

15 Which of the following is a biased interpretation against local governments?
A   Local governments are often ineffective because they become saddled with petty arguments among residents.
B   Local governments are most effective in dealing with schools and local highways.
C   Local governments are responsible for local law enforcement.
D   Community organizers can be helpful to local governments.

Directions: Questions 16 and 17 refer to the following letter.

To the Editor:
It is essential that citizens approve the tax increase that has been proposed to fund a new downtown park for our community. This proposed park will provide a safe gathering place for many people in our community. Studies have indicated that it will also spur likely additional development in the neighborhood. In this way, our investment in this park will pay additional dividends for residents in the immediate vicinity and the rest of the community. While the tax increase proposed is not insubstantial, the benefits that each of our contributions will bring to the collective good of the community should more than offset this cost.

16 Which of the following best describes how this source is biased?

This letter is biased
A   against community development.
B   against taxes.
C   towards community parks.
D   towards substantial tax increases for the community.

17 How does the author of this excerpt support his or her argument?

The author
A   identifies examples of similar projects.
B   refers to studies conducted on the topic.
C   points out flaws in opposing arguments.
D   describes the reliability of his or her argument.

UNIT 4

Identify Problem and Solution

① Learn the Skill

Each day, people work to solve **problems** in their homes, schools, workplaces, and communities. The first step in solving a problem is to correctly identify and understand the problem in order to determine the best way to solve it. When determining a **solution**, it is important to identify a number of potential alternatives and evaluate the advantages and disadvantages of each.

② Practice the Skill

By mastering the skill of identifying problems and solutions, you will improve your study and test-taking skills, especially as they relate to social studies high school equivalency tests. Read the excerpt and strategies below. Use this information to answer question 1.

A In this passage, Henry Paulson, former secretary of the treasury, describes an economic problem. Examine the details and examples Paulson gives to clearly explain the problem.

B In this section, Paulson attempts to describe a solution to this problem. Do you think Paulson believes this solution will be simple?

USING LOGIC

When reading about social studies, the text may not specifically state both the problem and solution in a given situation. You must use the information provided about a problem to make inferences about possible solutions, and vice versa.

A The underlying weakness in our financial system today is the illiquid mortgage assets that have lost value as the housing correction has proceeded. These illiquid assets are choking off the flow of credit that is so vitally important to our economy. When the financial system works as it should, money and capital flow to and from households and businesses to pay for home loans, school loans and investments that create jobs. As illiquid mortgage assets block the system, the clogging of our financial markets has the potential to have significant effects on our financial system and our economy.

B … The federal government must implement a program to remove these illiquid assets that are weighing down our financial institutions and threatening our economy. … First, to provide critical additional funding to our mortgage markets … Second, to increase the availability of capital for new home loans … These two steps will provide some initial support to mortgage assets, but they are not enough.

From Statement by Treasury Secretary Henry M. Paulson, September 19, 2008

1 What is the main problem in this excerpt?
A home loans
B illiquid assets
C school loans
D the capitalist system

UNIT 4

Directions: Questions 2 and 3 refer to the following excerpt.

In order to assure that an increasing population, accompanied by expanding settlement and growing mechanization, does not occupy and modify all areas within the United States and its possessions, leaving no lands designated for preservation and protection in their natural condition, it is hereby declared to be the policy of the Congress to secure for the American people of present and future generations the benefit of an enduring resource of wilderness. For this purpose there is hereby established a National Wilderness Preservation System to be composed of federally owned areas designated by Congress as 'wilderness areas', and these shall be administered for the use and enjoyment of the American people in such manner as will leave them unimpaired for future use and enjoyment as wilderness …

From *The Wilderness Act of 1964*

2   What problem is outlined in this excerpt?

This excerpt describes the problem of
- A   deforestation for the lumber industry.
- B   habitat loss for endangered wildlife.
- C   financial complications from logging regulations.
- D   loss of wilderness due to increasing growth and development.

3   How does this legislation propose to solve the problem?
- A   by creating new national parks
- B   by establishing protected wilderness areas
- C   by limiting the number of trees that can be cut down in U.S. forests
- D   by protecting several species of wildlife

Directions: Questions 4 and 5 refer to the following excerpt from the United States Constitution.

Section 1. No person shall be elected to the office of the President more than twice, and no person who has held the office of President, or acted as President, for more than two years of a term to which some other person was elected President shall be elected to the office of the President more than once. But this article shall not apply to any person holding the office of President when this article was proposed by the Congress, and shall not prevent any person who may be holding the office of President, or acting as President, during the term within which this article becomes operative from holding the office of President or acting as President during the remainder of such term.

From the United States Constitution, Amendment XXII (1951)

4   This amendment proposes a solution. What problem is it designed to address?
- A   an unclear order of succession to the presidency
- B   the increasing power of the executive branch
- C   the contested election of the current president
- D   the lack of term limits for the presidency

5   Which historical event likely prompted the creation of this amendment?

The creation of this amendment was likely prompted by
- A   the assassination of President John F. Kennedy.
- B   President Richard Nixon's resignation.
- C   Franklin Delano Roosevelt's presidency.
- D   the election of Lyndon B. Johnson.

Directions: Questions 6 and 7 refer to the following speech by Barack Obama.

The truth is, an oil future is not a secure future for America. Indeed, the rest of the world is already moving away from oil, and the longer we wait, the more difficult and painful it will be for our companies and our workers to catch up. Countries like China and Japan are creating jobs and slowing oil consumption by churning out and buying millions of fuel-efficient cars. Brazil, a nation that once relied on foreign countries to import 80% of its crude oil, will now be entirely self-sufficient in a few years thanks to investment in biofuels. By getting more ethanol on the market and equipping their cars with the flexible-fuel engines that allow them to run on this fuel, Brazil has … secured its energy supply while still giving consumers a break at the pump.

So why can't we do this? Why can't this be one of the great American projects of the 21st century?

The answer is, it can. We can do this with technology we have on the shelves right now; we can do it by saving, not crippling, our ailing auto companies; and we can do it by using the kind of clean, renewable sources of energy that we can literally grow right here in America.

From speech by Illinois Senator Barack Obama, September 15, 2005

6   What is the main problem that Obama describes in this excerpt?
A   America's dependence on oil
B   the high cost of developing alternative fuel sources
C   the cost competition from other nations
D   the need to improve U.S. technology

7   How does Obama characterize the solutions that other nations have used to address this problem?

Obama characterizes these solutions as
A   well-intentioned.
B   worthy of evaluation.
C   inapplicable.
D   highly successful.

Directions: Question 8 refers to the following excerpt from the Supreme Court decision regarding the 2000 presidential election.

The closeness of this election, and the multitude of legal challenges which have followed in its wake, have brought into sharp focus a common, if heretofore unnoticed, phenomenon. Nationwide statistics reveal that an estimated 2% of ballots cast do not register a vote for President for whatever reason, including deliberately choosing no candidate at all or some voter error, such as voting for two candidates or insufficiently marking a ballot … . In certifying election results, the votes eligible for inclusion in the certification are the votes meeting the properly established legal requirements.

This case has shown that punch card balloting machines can produce an unfortunate number of ballots which are not punched in a clean, complete way by the voter. After the current counting, it is likely legislative bodies nationwide will examine ways to improve the mechanisms and machinery for voting.

8   Which group does the Supreme Court charge with solving this problem?
A   local boards of elections
B   state courts
C   lawmakers
D   the Federal Election Commission

Directions: Questions 9 and 10 refer to the following excerpt from the United States Constitution.

Section 1. The District constituting the seat of government of the United States shall appoint in such manner as the Congress may direct:

A number of electors of President and Vice President equal to the whole number of Senators and Representatives in Congress to which the District would be entitled if it were a state, but in no event more than the least populous state; they shall be in addition to those appointed by the states, but they shall be considered, for the purposes of the election of President and Vice President, to be electors appointed by a state; and they shall meet in the District and perform such duties as provided by the twelfth article of amendment.

From the United States Constitution Amendment XXIII, 1961

9 **What problem does this solution address?**
A confusion regarding the boundaries of Washington, D.C.
B disputes about the meeting place of the electoral college
C Washington, D.C.'s participation in presidential elections
D disagreement regarding congressional representation for Washington, D.C.

10 **Which of the following groups or individuals could have officially proposed this solution?**
A Washington, D.C. legislators
B Congress
C the citizens of Washington, D.C.
D the U.S. Supreme Court

Directions: Questions 11 and 12 refer to the following political cartoon.

11 **To what problem does the cartoonist seek to draw attention with this cartoon?**

The cartoonist tries to draw attention to the problem of
A violent riots in American cities.
B cutbacks in police department budgets.
C lack of punishment for police brutality.
D increases in violent crime.

12 **Which of the following best describes the cartoonist's assessment of the president's response to this problem?**
A timely
B insulting
C sympathetic
D decisive

Because of undermined confidence on the part of the public, there was a general rush by a large portion of our population to turn bank deposits into currency or gold—a rush so great that the soundest banks could not get enough currency to meet the demand. The reason for this was that on the spur of the moment it was, of course, impossible to sell perfectly sound assets of a bank and convert them into cash except at panic prices far below their real value … . It was then that I issued the proclamation providing for the nationwide bank holiday, and this was the first step in the Government's reconstruction of our financial and economic fabric. The second step was the legislation promptly and patriotically passed by the Congress confirming my proclamation and broadening my powers … to extend the holiday and lift the ban of that holiday gradually. This law also gave authority to develop a program of rehabilitation of our banking facilities.

13 **What caused Roosevelt to proclaim the bank holiday (closing banks)?**
  A Many people wanted their money out of banks.
  B He had a patriotic duty to do so.
  C Banks wanted to convert currency into gold.
  D The rush would have caused banks to sell assets for below real value.

14 **In what way could Roosevelt's solution be seen as dangerous?**

Roosevelt's solution
  A turned over all banks to the government.
  B closed banks when people wanted money.
  C called on the patriotism of Congress.
  D caused Congress to grant the president additional powers.

For many years, substances known as chlorofluorocarbons (CFCs) were used in a variety of products, such as solvents and refrigerants. However, beginning in the 1970s, scientists began to express concern over the impact of these substances on the earth's ozone layer. As new uses for CFCs emerged during the 1980s, fears about ozone layer damage became more urgent. With the signing of the Montreal Protocol, nations around the world agreed to cooperate in order to reduce CFCs. In the early 1990s, as new evidence came forth to show that ozone depletion was worse than previously expected, the same nations committed to ending production of all CFCs by 1996. As a result, emissions of ozone-depleting substances have already begun to fall. Some expect that the ozone layer will have naturally healed itself within approximately 50 years.

15 **Which of the following best describes the way in which the problem of CFCs was solved?**
  A citizen mobilization
  B international cooperation
  C stricter laws and regulations
  D collaboration of public interest groups

16 **How is this solution best characterized?**
  A immediate
  B divisive
  C controversial
  D long-term

UNIT 4

Special-Purpose Maps

① Learn the Skill

Special-purpose maps share many similarities with political maps. Both types of maps show political boundaries such as cities, states, regions, and countries. However, special-purpose maps show additional features that do not appear on simple political maps. These features may include things such as congressional districts, products and resources, and the use of symbols to represent key elements.

② Practice the Skill

By mastering the skill of interpreting special-purpose maps, you will improve your study and test-taking skills, especially as they relate to social studies high school equivalency tests. Examine the map and strategies below. Use this information to answer question 1.

Ⓐ This map shows political features typically associated with a political map. The political features on the map include the boundaries of the United States, as well as the locations of cities in which the branches of the Federal Reserve are located.

Ⓑ In addition to these political features, however, the map also indicates the boundaries of the twelve Federal Reserve districts in the United States. The addition of this extra layer of information makes this visual a special-purpose map.

U.S. FEDERAL RESERVE DISTRICTS

9 Minneapolis
Chicago 7
12 Kansas City Cleveland 2 Boston
San Francisco 10 3 New York
Ⓑ St. Louis 4 Philadelphia
8 5 Richmond
11 6 Atlanta Ⓐ
Dallas

Alaska and Hawaii
are part of the
San Francisco District

✓ TEST-TAKING TIPS

When interpreting a special-purpose map in a test-taking situation, study the map's title and contents to identify the purpose the map will serve. Try to summarize this purpose in a sentence or two.

1 In which Federal Reserve district is the state of Texas located?

Texas is located in the
A 8th District.
B 10th District.
C 11th District.
D 12th District.

UNIT 4

Directions: Questions 2 and 3 refer to the following map.

POPULATION OF GREAT LAKES STATES, 2010

👤 1 million people

Directions: Questions 4 and 5 refer to the following map and information.

ARKANSAS: CONGRESSIONAL DISTRICTS

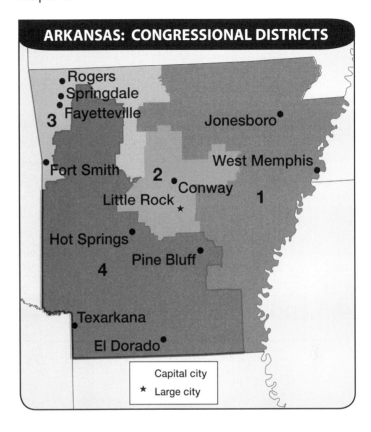

Capital city
★ Large city

The U.S. House of Representatives has 435 seats. The number of seats assigned to each state is based on its population, which is determined every 10 years by a national census. Based on the 2010 Census, each Congressional district now contains 710,767 people. In 2000, each Congressional district contained 647,000 people.

2 **Which state in this region had the largest population in 2010?**
A   Ohio
B   Illinois
C   Michigan
D   Wisconsin

3 **Which of the following statements is correct based on the information on the map?**

In 2010,
A   Minnesota had less than 5 million people.
B   Wisconsin had a larger population than Indiana.
C   Ohio and Michigan had a combined population of more than 20 million people.
D   the two most populous states share a border.

4 **What information could you learn from the passage that you could not find on the map?**
A   the number of large cities in the state
B   the basis for the census in districts
C   the number of districts in the state
D   the basis for the number of districts

5 **Why does Arkansas have 4 congressional districts?**
A   It has the fourth smallest population.
B   It is the population of Arkansas divided by total members of the U.S. Congress.
C   That is the number assigned when Arkansas was first made a state.
D   That is the number apportioned to Arkansas based on state population and the total number of U.S. representatives.

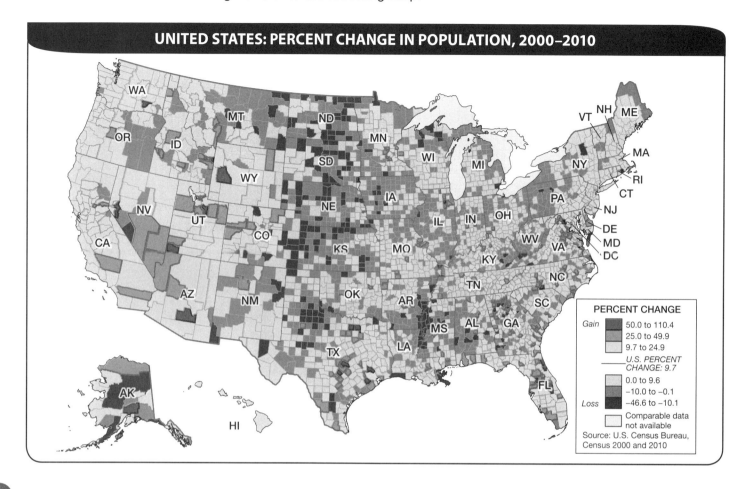

UNITED STATES: PERCENT CHANGE IN POPULATION, 2000–2010

PERCENT CHANGE

Gain
- 50.0 to 110.4
- 25.0 to 49.9
- 9.7 to 24.9

U.S. PERCENT CHANGE: 9.7

- 0.0 to 9.6
- −10.0 to −0.1

Loss
- −46.6 to −10.1

Comparable data not available

Source: U.S. Census Bureau, Census 2000 and 2010

6 Which of the following states experienced the greatest population loss between 2000 and 2010?

A North Dakota
B Florida
C Utah
D Hawai

7 In general, which part of the country experienced the greatest population losses?

A West Coast
B Mid-Atlantic
C Great Plains
D Florida

8 In general, which of the following parts of the country experienced the highest rate of population growth between 2000 and 2010?

A Northeast
B Southwest
C Hawaii and Alaska
D Great Plains

9 Based on the map, which of the following statements can you infer about the population of the United States between 2000 and 2010?

A The northern border area of the United States was more attractive to new residents than the southern border area.
B Neither Hawaii nor Alaska was attractive to new residents.
C Every state had areas that lost population each year.
D Of the three states on the West Coast, eastern Oregon was least attractive to new residents during this period.

Directions: Questions 10 and 11 refer to the following map.

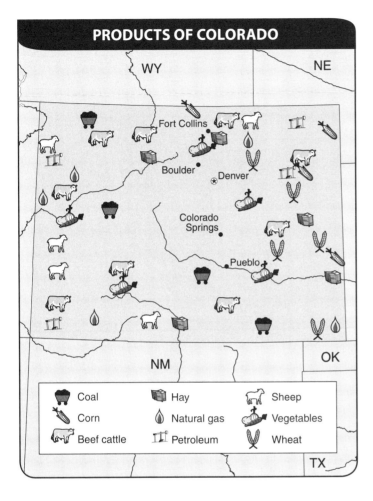

PRODUCTS OF COLORADO

Directions: Questions 12 and 13 refer to the following map showing the increase in percentage of primary voters from 2000 to 2008.

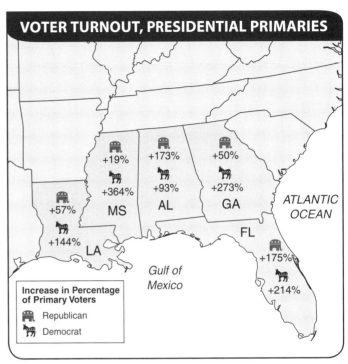

VOTER TURNOUT, PRESIDENTIAL PRIMARIES

10 Which of the following products is found around Pueblo?

   A coal

   B petroleum

   C corn

   D sheep

11 Based on the products listed on the map, where in Colorado are mountains most likely located?

   The mountains in Colorado are most likely located

   A along the Wyoming border.

   B in the east.

   C along the western border.

   D in the center-west of the state.

12 In which state did Republican primary turnout increase by a larger percentage than Democratic primary turnout?

   Republican primary turnout increased by a larger percentage in

   A Louisiana

   B Mississippi

   C Alabama

   D Georgia

13 In which state is it most likely that both Democrats and Republicans put the most money into voter registration programs?

   A Mississippi

   B Alabama

   C Georgia

   D Florida

UNIT 4

Directions: Questions 14 through 17 refer to the following map.

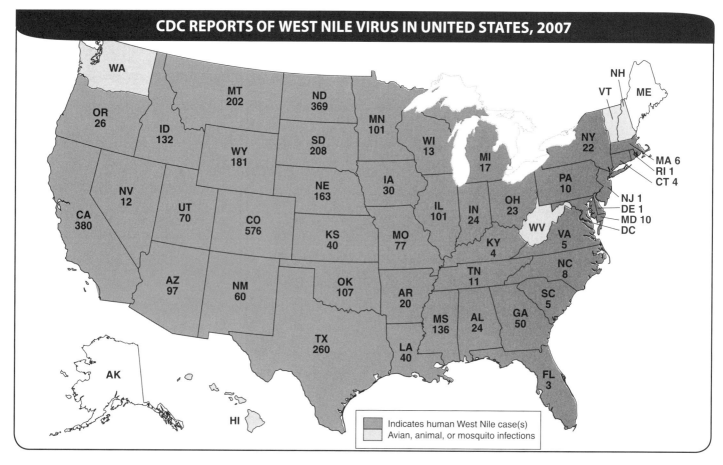

CDC REPORTS OF WEST NILE VIRUS IN UNITED STATES, 2007

WA

OR 26

MT 202

ND 369

MN 101

NH

VT ME

ID 132

WY 181

SD 208

WI 13

NY 22

MA 6
RI 1
CT 4

NV 12

UT 70

NE 163

IA 30

MI 17

PA 10

NJ 1
DE 1
MD 10
DC

CA 380

CO 576

KS 40

MO 77

IL 101

IN 24

OH 23

WV

VA 5

AZ 97

NM 60

OK 107

AR 20

KY 4

TN 11

NC 8

SC 5

TX 260

LA 40

MS 136

AL 24

GA 50

AK

HI

FL 3

Indicates human West Nile case(s)
Avian, animal, or mosquito infections

14 Which state reported the highest number of West Nile Virus cases in 2007?

The state reporting the highest number of cases was

A Colorado.
B Illinois.
C Texas.
D Wyoming.

15 The CDC would likely produce similar maps on which of the following subjects?

The CDC would likely produce a similar map about

A demographics in the United States.
B industries found in various locations across the United States.
C cases of Type 2 diabetes in the United States.
D the interstate highway system.

16 Which of the following states had no reports of human disease cases during 2007?

A Pennsylvania
B Washington
C Oklahoma
D Utah

17 Which of the following statements does this map support?

A Texas had one of the three highest numbers of cases reported.
B Ohio reported more than twice as many cases as Michigan.
C All of the states reporting more than 100 cases were located along a large body of water.
D Arizona, Minnesota, and Illinois each reported about 100 cases.

UNIT 4

Fact and Opinion

① Learn the Skill

A **fact** is a statement that can be proven true or untrue, while an **opinion** is a view or belief that cannot be proven true or untrue. Many times when reading about social studies, you will encounter statements of fact and opinion. The ability to distinguish between these two types of statements will enable you to better assess the accuracy of the information you read and determine how it relates to the subject you are studying.

② Practice the Skill

By mastering the skill of identifying fact and opinion, you will improve your study and test-taking skills, especially as they relate to social studies high school equivalency tests. Read the excerpt and strategies below. Use this information to answer question 1.

A Strongly worded or emotional sentiments such as these provide clues to the reader that the speaker or author is expressing an opinion.

B In these examples, the speaker uses statistical evidence that can be proven true or untrue. In social studies, facts are often used to support or discredit arguments.

A <u>We can't stand pat because it is essential with the conflict that we have around the world, that we not just hold our own</u>; that we not keep just freedom for ourselves. It is essential that we extend freedom—extend it to all the world. And this means more than what we've been doing. …

Now, looking at other parts of the world: South America, talking about our record and the previous one; we had a good neighbor policy, yes. It sounded fine. But let's look at it. <u>There were 11 dictators when we came into power in 1953 in Latin America. There are only three left</u>.

Let's look at Africa. <u>Twenty new countries in Africa during the course of this administration. Not one of them selected a Communist government</u>. All of them voted for freedom—a free type of government.

From Richard Nixon's remarks during the October 21, 1960 presidential debate

USING LOGIC

If you can name a piece of evidence that could logically prove a statement true, it is likely a fact. For opinions, you should not be able to think of pieces of evidence that could undeniably prove them true or false.

1 Which of the following ideas in Nixon's remarks expresses an opinion?

A Twenty new countries emerged in Africa during the Eisenhower administration.

B The United States should extend its freedom to the world.

C Numerous dictators left power during the Eisenhower administration.

D No new Communist governments were established in Africa.

UNIT 4

Directions: Questions 2 and 3 refer to the following information.

A debate has grown in the United States among defenders and critics of the Electoral College system. Some critics contend that this system has become outdated as the U.S. government has changed. Political leaders originally planned for the nation's government to take the form of a republic in which citizens elected officials to govern for them. Over time, though, the government has evolved into a democracy in which these officials are expected to govern according to the wishes of the people.

Additionally, critics argue that the Electoral College can allow a candidate to win the presidency while losing the popular vote. This has occurred during three presidential elections. Critics believe that this thwarts the will of the majority.

2 **Which of the following is a fact that a defender of the Electoral College might cite to support his or her position?**
  A The Electoral College has only failed to select the winner of the popular vote three times.
  B The Electoral College was established many years ago.
  C Abolishing the Electoral College would destabilize the U.S. political system.
  D The Electoral College is necessary to preserve a two-party system.

3 **What is one of the main opinions of Electoral College critics?**

  Critics of the Electoral College believe that the system is
  A biased.
  B controlled by a single party.
  C no longer needed.
  D too expensive.

Directions: Questions 4 and 5 refer to the following campaign poster from the 1944 presidential election.

4 **Why would campaign posters like this one be likely to feature opinions?**
  A to publicize the beliefs of experts
  B to appeal to the emotions of voters
  C to confuse Electoral College members
  D to promote candidates' platforms

5 **Which fact might an opponent use to refute the opinions on this poster?**
  A Roosevelt had taken the country into World War II.
  B Roosevelt was 62 years old when he ran for reelection in 1944.
  C Roosevelt had already served three terms as President.
  D Truman had replaced Roosevelt's previous vice president.

Directions: Questions 6 through 8 refer to the following information.

In the early stages of a presidential election cycle, political parties in the individual states select the delegates who will represent them at the parties' national nominating conventions. The two main methods by which these delegates are selected are by primary or caucus. In a primary election, voters elect delegates who will support their preferred candidate at the national convention. Ballots are cast in a manner similar to that of the general election. In a caucus, voters gather in groups at polling locations. At these locations, they listen to debates and speeches before a vote is taken.

6 **Which of the following statements about primaries and caucuses is a fact?**

   A Primary elections are easier to carry out than caucuses.

   B Primary elections are too similar to general elections.

   C Caucuses allow citizens to have too much influence on voting decisions.

   D Most states now hold primary elections, rather than caucuses.

7 **Which opinion below could cause a state to hold a primary rather than a caucus?**

   A Voters feel disconnected from candidates.

   B Voters are uninformed about candidates' platforms.

   C Many voters view the right to vote too casually.

   D Many voters wish to become more involved in the nomination process.

8 **Which Web site would be the best source of unbiased facts about primaries and caucuses?**

   A The League of Environmental Voters

   B The Library of Congress Voter Project

   C The White House Web site

   D The Texas Republican Party

Directions: Questions 9 and 10 refer to the following excerpt from Ronald Reagan's address accepting the Republican presidential nomination on July 17, 1980.

The first Republican president once said, 'While the people retain their virtue and their vigilance, no administration by any extreme of wickedness or folly can seriously injure the government in the short space of four years.'

If Mr. Lincoln could see what's happened in these last three-and-a half years, he might hedge a little on that statement. But, with the virtues that our legacy as a free people and with the vigilance that sustains liberty, we still have time to use our renewed compact to overcome the injuries that have been done to America these past three-and-a-half years.

First, we must overcome something the present administration has cooked up: a new and altogether indigestible economic stew, one part inflation, one part high unemployment, one part recession, one part runaway taxes, one part deficit spending and seasoned by an energy crisis. It's an economic stew that has turned the national stomach.

9 **In which of the following sources could you confirm the fact provided in the first paragraph?**

   A a historical atlas

   B a dictionary of quotations

   C an almanac

   D a political pamphlet

10 **Based on the information in this excerpt, how would you describe Reagan's opinion of the Carter administration?**

Reagan views the Carter administration as

   A cruel.

   B capable.

   C smart.

   D incompetent.

Directions: Questions 11 and 12 refer to the following information.

During presidential elections, the national Democratic and Republican parties have many responsibilities. The national parties must plan conventions, coordinate presidential debates, and assist their candidates in fundraising efforts. The national political parties also have the authority to refuse to acknowledge state delegates who they believe were chosen inappropriately. Although both parties usually adjust their methods for delegate selection after each election cycle, in the 2012 presidential election, the Democratic Party awarded state delegates to candidates based on the percentage of the popular vote they received in the primary or caucus, while the Republican Party allowed states to choose proportional representation or a winner-take-all plan. Under such a plan, the winning candidate of a state's primary or caucus receives all of that state's delegates.

11 Which of the following best describes this passage?

This passage features
A   many facts and no opinions.
B   mostly facts with a few opinions.
C   an even balance of fact and opinion.
D   many opinions with no facts.

12 Suppose a Republican presidential candidate lost a closely-contested primary election in a state.

Which of the following opinions might this candidate hold?
A   National political parties should insist on holding state caucuses.
B   Parties should tighten restrictions on campaign fundraising.
C   The state in which the primary was held should employ proportional representation.
D   All candidates should be given input into the planning of the nominating convention.

Directions: Questions 13 and 14 refer to the following excerpt from Al Gore's speech regarding the disputed 2000 presidential election.

This is a time to respect every voter and every vote. This is a time to honor the true will of the people. So our goal must be what is right for America.

There is a simple reason that Florida law and the law in many other states calls for a careful check by real people of the machine results in elections like this one.

The reason? Machines can sometimes misread or fail to detect the way ballots are cast, and when there are serious doubts, checking the machine count with a careful hand count is accepted far and wide as the best way to know the true intentions of the voters ... .

We need a resolution that is fair and final. We need to move expeditiously to the most complete and accurate count that is possible.

From Al Gore's speech regarding the disputed 2000 presidential election in Florida, November 15, 2000

13 Which of the following best describes Gore's opinion?

Gore holds the opinion that—first and foremost—the election should be decided
A   fairly.
B   using the latest available technology.
C   in a manner that is popular with all voters.
D   with no input from either political party.

14 Which statement below expresses a fact?
A   "... checking the machine count with a careful hand count is accepted ... as the best way to know the true intentions of voters ..."
B   "This is a time to respect every voter and every vote."
C   "This is a time to honor the true will of the people."
D   "So our goal must be what is right for America."

Directions: Questions 15 and 16 refer to the following information.

In the 1876 presidential election, Democratic candidate Samuel Tilden received nearly 51 percent of the popular vote, while Republican candidate Rutherford B. Hayes received just less than 48 percent of the vote. However, disputes about the eligibility of electors in certain states called into question the outcome in the Electoral College. Ultimately, a bipartisan group known as the Electoral Commission of 1877 formed in order to resolve the issue. The two parties compromised in order to settle the disputed election results. Hayes received the electoral votes needed to become President. In exchange, Hayes agreed to a series of Democratic proposals that effectively ended Southern Reconstruction.

15 **Which of the following parties would likely cite this election in order to support their opinions?**
   A   a third-party presidential candidate
   B   a political independent
   C   an opponent of government bureaucracy
   D   an opponent of the Electoral College

16 **What source could most likely be used to prove the accuracy of the popular vote results cited above?**

   These results could be best verified using
   A   a newspaper editorial from 1877 about the Electoral College.
   B   a biographical film on Rutherford B. Hayes.
   C   a university Web site with historic election results.
   D   a novel about Reconstruction.

Directions: Questions 17 and 18 refer to the following excerpt from Bill Clinton's closing remarks at the presidential debate on October 19, 1992.

I offer a new approach. It's not trickle-down economics; it's been tried for 12 years, and it's failed. More people are working harder for less, 100,000 people a month losing their health insurance, unemployment going up, our economy slowing down. We can do better. And it's not tax-and-spend economics. It's invest and grow, put our people first, control health care costs and provide basic health care to all Americans, have an education system second to none, and revitalize the private economy ... . I want a country where people who work hard and play by the rules are rewarded, not punished. I want a country where people are coming together across the lines of race and region and income. I know we can do better.

17 **Which of the following opinions does Clinton express in this excerpt?**
   A   The United States would benefit from additional taxation and spending.
   B   The nation has begun a period of economic recovery.
   C   The economic policies of Reagan and Bush have failed.
   D   The United States has one of the world's best health care systems.

18 **In which area does Clinton provide a fact?**
   A   unemployment
   B   health care
   C   education
   D   economy

Faulty Logic or Reasoning

① Learn the Skill

In Unit 3, you learned that generalizations are broad statements that apply to an entire group of people, things, or events. You also learned that these generalizations are considered invalid if they are not supported by facts. Such a generalization is also known as a **hasty generalization** and is an example of **faulty logic or reasoning**. You can find more information about logic and reasoning on pp. x–xiii.

② Practice the Skill

By mastering the skill of discerning faulty logic or reasoning, you will improve your study and test-taking skills, especially as they relate to social studies high school equivalency tests. Read the excerpt and strategies below. Use this information to answer question 1.

A Statements that make absolute or universal claims often exhibit faulty logic or reasoning. Because these statements can be disproven with a single piece of conflicting evidence, it makes it easier to highlight the faulty logic or reasoning used to make them.

B This statement provides another example of an absolute or universal claim ("no forces capable") that may be unlikely to hold up under close scrutiny.

> To the accusation that Cuba wants to export its revolution, we reply: <u>Revolutions are not exported, they are made by the people</u> … **A**
>
> What Cuba can give to the people, and has already given, is its example.
>
> And what does the Cuban Revolution teach? That revolution is possible, that the people can make it, that <u>in the contemporary world there are no forces capable of halting the liberation movement of the peoples</u>. **B**
>
> Our triumph would never have been feasible if the Revolution itself had not been inexorably destined to arise out of existing conditions in our socio-economic reality, a reality which exists to an even greater degree in a good number of Latin American countries.
>
> From Fidel Castro's "On the Export of Revolution"

🧩 MAKING ASSUMPTIONS

You can usually assume that an author or speaker uses reasoning and logic in order to explain some idea. When looking for faulty logic or reasoning, focus on statements that support the author or speaker's main ideas. Then, narrow your focus to those examples that appear to make unsupportable claims.

1 **Which of the following would reveal the underlined claim in the third paragraph as an example of faulty reasoning?**

  A a free election in Cuba
  B the removal of Castro from power
  C the military defeat of a liberation movement in Asia
  D United States support for liberation movements around the world

UNIT 4

Directions: Questions 2 and 3 refer to the following excerpt from Italian Prime Minister Benito Mussolini, who co-wrote this as part of an encyclopedia entry on fascism.

For Fascism, the growth of empire, that is to say the expansion of the nation, is an essential manifestation of vitality, and its opposite a sign of decadence. Peoples which are rising, or rising again after a period of decadence, are always imperialist; and renunciation is a sign of decay and of death. Fascism is the doctrine best adapted to represent the tendencies and the aspirations of a people, like the people of Italy, who are rising again after many centuries of abasement and foreign servitude ... for never before has the nation stood more in need of authority, of direction and order. If every age has its own characteristic doctrine, there are a thousand signs which point to Fascism as the characteristic doctrine of our time.

Benito Mussolini (with Giovanni Gentile), "What is Fascism?," 1932

2 **Mussolini makes an oversimplification by connecting which of the following?**

Mussolini's oversimplification connects
A   economic prosperity and decadence.
B   decadence and colonialism.
C   imperialism and decay.
D   imperialism and rising nations.

3 **Which of the following represents an error in logic or reasoning that Mussolini makes in this excerpt?**
A   He appeals to the beliefs of his audience.
B   He makes absolute and universal claims.
C   He defines the terminology that he uses to make his argument.
D   He uses vivid, descriptive language.

Directions: Question 4 refers to the following information and political cartoon.

Boris Pasternak was an acclaimed poet and author from the Soviet Union. His 1956 novel *Doctor Zhivago* criticized communism, and Soviet publishers refused to publish it. Pasternak received the 1958 Nobel Prize for literature for the novel. However, Soviet leaders would not permit him to travel in order to receive the award.

"I WON THE NOBEL PRIZE FOR LITERATURE. WHAT WAS YOUR CRIME?" by Bill Mauldin. Published in the *St. Louis Post-Dispatch*, October 30, 1958

4 **The cartoon criticizes the faulty reasoning of the Soviet government.**

Based on the information, which of the following oversimplifications does the cartoonist criticize?
A   All criminals should be treated the same way.
B   All travel outside the Soviet Union should be forbidden.
C   All authors should be regarded with suspicion.
D   All criticism of the government should be treated as a crime.

Directions: Questions 5 and 6 refer to the following excerpt.

Comrades, the 20th Congress of the Communist Party of the Soviet Union has manifested with a new strength the unshakable unity of our party, its cohesiveness around the central committee, its resolute will to accomplish the great task of building communism. And the fact that we present in all the ramifications the basic problems of overcoming the cult of the individual which is alien to Marxism-Leninism, as well as the problem of liquidating its burdensome consequences, is an evidence of the great moral and political strength of our party!

We are absolutely certain that our party, armed with the historical resolutions of the 20th Congress, will lead the Soviet people along the Leninist path to new successes, to new victories.

From Nikita Khrushchev's Secret Speech—"On the Cult of Personality," 1956

5 **Khrushchev asserts—but does not offer evidence to support—which of the following?**
   A the unity of his party
   B specific reforms taking place in the Soviet Union
   C economic prosperity in the Soviet Union
   D the spread of communism to other nations

6 **What does Khrushchev reason is the greatest threat to the Soviet Union's system of government?**

Khrushchev argues that the greatest threat is presented by
   A Marxism-Leninism.
   B the 20th Congress of the Communist Party.
   C the cult of personality.
   D the central committee of the Communist Party.

Directions: Question 7 refers to the following information and political cartoon.

In 1938, communism had begun to rise in Europe. In the United States, a Congressional committee led by Rep. Martin Dies of Texas had started investigating potential Communist activities within the nation. Cartoonist Herb Block references the committee in the title of this 1938 cartoon.

"WAIT TILL THE DIES COMMITTEE HEARS ABOUT THIS!"
A 1938 Herblock Cartoon, © by The Herb Block Foundation

7 **In this cartoon, Herb Block asserts that the Dies Committee makes which of the following errors in logic and reasoning?**

Herb Block suggests that the Dies Committee believes that
   A the celebration of Christmas is un-American.
   B all people who exhibit certain suspicious behaviors are Communists.
   C all Communist organizations are funded by state clubs.
   D the arrival of Communists will lead to the development of anti-U.S. plots.

Directions: Questions 8 and 9 refer to the following excerpt.

There are two sections of thought in South Africa in regard to the policy affecting the non-European community. On the one hand there is the policy of equality, which advocates equal rights within the same political structure for all civilized and educated persons ... .

On the other hand there is the policy of separation (apartheid) which has grown from the experience of established European population the country ... .

We can act in only one of two directions. Either we follow the course of equality, which must eventually mean national suicide for the White race, or we must take the course of separation (apartheid) through which the character and the future of every race will be protected and safeguarded with full opportunities for development and self-maintenance in their own ideas ... .

From a statement issued by the National Party of South Africa, 1948

8 **Which of the following is an example of faulty reasoning?**
   A South Africa is a divided nation.
   B The European population of South Africa oppose the policy of apartheid.
   C Equality will mean national suicide for the White race.
   D Apartheid will cause continued hardships for native South Africans.

9 **The faulty logic offered in support of apartheid most resembles that used to support which of the following?**
   A poll taxes
   B the doctrine of "separate but equal"
   C sharecropping
   D the Southern plantation system

Directions: Questions 10 and 11 refer to the following excerpt.

Never before in the history of this nation have so many human and property rights been destroyed by a single enactment of the Congress. It is an act of tyranny. It is the assassin's knife stuck in the back of liberty ... .

I am having nothing to do with enforcing a law that will destroy our free enterprise system.

I am having nothing to do with enforcing a law that will destroy neighborhood schools.

I am having nothing to do with enforcing a law that will destroy the rights of private property ... .

I am having nothing to do with this so-called civil rights bill.

From a speech by Alabama Governor George Wallace, July 4, 1964

10 **Which of Wallace's statements below is a hasty generalization?**
   A Never before in the history of this nation have so many human and property rights been destroyed by a single enactment of the Congress.
   B It is the assassin's knife stuck in the back of liberty.
   C I am having nothing to do with enforcing a law that will destroy our free enterprise system.
   D I am having nothing to do with this so-called civil rights bill.

11 **Based on the reasoning provided in this excerpt, you can determine that Wallace would likely support which of the following?**

   Wallace would likely support
   A the presence of federal troops in Alabama.
   B segregationist policies.
   C the creation of new integrated jobs in Alabama.
   D the right of the federal government to make similar policies for all states.

Directions: Questions 12 through 15 refer to the following information and political cartoon.

An African American man named James Meredith applied for admission to the University of Mississippi in 1962. Though the university attempted to deny him admission, a federal court ordered the university to desegregate and allow Meredith to enroll. When Mississippi's governor attempted to block Meredith's enrollment, the Kennedy administration ordered federal marshals to accompany Meredith to the university. Violence erupted when white students reacted hostilely to the arrival of the marshals. Two people died and hundreds were injured in the fighting.

"AND YOU INCITED THOSE INNOCENT RIOTERS
TO VIOLENCE ... " by Bill Mauldin

12 Whose use of faulty reasoning does the cartoonist call attention to in this cartoon?

The cartoonist calls attention to the faulty reasoning of

A James Meredith.
B the Kennedy administration.
C the federal marshals.
D Mississippi authorities.

13 This cartoon suggests that an invalid cause-and-effect relationship was drawn between which two items?

A the Mississippi governor's action and the decision of the Kennedy administration
B the work of the federal marshals and the outbreak of violence
C the earlier rulings of state courts and the final decision of the federal court
D the action of the Kennedy administration and Meredith's enrollment in the university

14 Which of the following best illustrates the dangers of faulty logic and reasoning?

A sending in federal marshals
B racial discrimination
C President Kennedy's policies
D civil rights

15 The faulty reasoning used by the Mississippi Grand Jury in the cartoon is most similar to which of the following situations?

A a pet owner blaming a new puppy for chewing up her shoes
B a teacher being blamed for students not passing a test
C a firefighter being blamed for the actions of an arsonist
D President Truman being blamed for the Japanese bombing of Pearl Harbor

Evaluate Information Critically

① Learn the Skill

Just as you have learned to analyze information sources, you will also need to evaluate the information that you find in these various sources. **Evaluating information** requires you to closely examine information for purpose, bias, faulty logic and reasoning, and facts or opinions in order to make judgments about its quality. This skill combines many of the skills you have learned previously.

② Practice the Skill

By mastering the skill of evaluating information, you will improve your study and test-taking skills, especially as they relate to social studies high school equivalency tests. Read the excerpt and strategies below. Use this information to answer questions 1 and 2.

Ⓐ The author provides support for a claim in the form of a list of duties the two men have fulfilled.

Ⓑ This phrase refers to the efficiency with which government programs have used the money devoted to funding them.

> Lyndon B. Johnson and Hubert Humphrey worked together long and closely to strengthen America at home and abroad—to build our moral, diplomatic, military and economic strength ... .
>
> But Lyndon B. Johnson and Hubert Humphrey both know, as their fellow Americans know, that military strength is not enough. **Ⓐ** They have worked tirelessly to strengthen our representation abroad, to create and guide the Peace Corps, to enact and to implement policies of expanded foreign trade, to assure peace, and, in the millions of miles both have traveled throughout the world, to bring to people everywhere a more vivid picture of America.
>
> And both men ... have made every possible effort to keep the nation fiscally strong by seeing to it that while needed programs were not ignored, **Ⓑ** the nation received a dollar's worth for every dollar spent.
>
> From Lyndon B. Johnson Campaign Brochure, 1964

UNIT 4

☑ TEST-TAKING TIPS

Evaluating information requires you to assess a text for numerous characteristics. You may find it useful to preview the questions you will have to answer. This will allow you to narrow your focus as you begin to read and evaluate the text.

1 Why does the author suggest that Johnson and Humphrey will be able to guide the nation's foreign policy?
A   their foreign policy experience
B   their career backgrounds
C   their educations
D   their personal strength

2 What characteristic of both Johnson and Humphrey does the author praise in the last paragraph?
A   courage
B   independence
C   character
D   fiscal responsibility

Directions: Questions 3 and 4 refer to the following excerpt.

In 1996, America will choose the President who will lead us from the millennium which saw the birth of our nation, and into a future that has all the potential to be even greater than our magnificent past. …

Opportunity. Responsibility. Community. These are the values that made America strong. These are the values of the Democratic Party. These are the values that must guide us into the future.

Today, America is moving forward with the strong Presidential leadership it deserves. The economy is stronger, the deficit is lower, and government is smaller. Education is better, our environment is cleaner, families are healthier, and our streets are safer. There is more opportunity in America, more responsibility in our homes, and more peace in the world.

From the Democratic Party Platform of 1996

3 **What was the purpose of the information in this excerpt?**

The information in the excerpt was designed
A to provide details about new policies supported by Democrats.
B to foster a sense of well-being and to encourage the reelection of Bill Clinton.
C to gain support for new health care policies.
D to defend the Democratic Party against charges leveled by the Republicans.

4 **Which of the following claims made in this excerpt could be most easily supported?**
A There is more responsibility in our homes.
B There is more peace in the world.
C There is more opportunity in America.
D The deficit is lower.

Directions: Questions 5 and 6 refer to the following excerpt.

On domestic issues, the choice is also clear. In critical areas such as public education and health care, Bush's emphasis is on greater competition. His No Child Left Behind Act has flaws, but its requirements have created a new climate of expectation and accountability. On both of these important fronts, but especially with his expensive health-care plan, Kerry primarily sees a need to raise and spend more money. …

John Kerry has been a discerning critic of where Bush has erred. But Kerry's message—a more restrained assault on global threats, earnest comfort with the international community's noble inaction—suggests what many voters sense: After 20 years in the Senate, the moral certitude Kerry once displayed has evaporated. There is no landmark Kennedy-Kerry Education Act, no Kerry-Frist Health Bill. Today's Kerry is more about plans and process than solutions. He is better suited to analysis than to action. He has not delivered a compelling blueprint for change.

From the *Chicago Tribune*: "George W. Bush for president" 2004

5 **Which of the following does the author cite in order to validate an endorsement of one candidate's domestic policies?**
A Bush's landmark health care plan
B the No Child Left Behind Act
C the Kennedy-Kerry Education Act
D the Kerry-Frist Health Bill

6 **What is the main purpose of this editorial?**

This editorial was designed
A to explain why the writer voted for George W. Bush.
B to convince voters that John Kerry's policies were failures.
C to convince voters that George W. Bush's policies were successful.
D to convince people to vote for George W. Bush.

Directions: Questions 7 and 8 refer to the following excerpt.

The choices this year are not just between two different personalities or between two political parties. They're between two different visions of the future, two fundamentally different ways of governing—their government of pessimism, fear, and limits, or ours of hope, confidence, and growth.

Their government sees people only as members of groups; ours serves all the people of America as individuals. Theirs lives in the past, seeking to apply the old and failed policies to an era that has passed them by. Ours learns from the past and strives to change by boldly charting a new course for the future. Theirs lives by promises, the bigger, the better. We offer proven, workable answers.

From Ronald Reagan's remarks accepting the Republican presidential nomination, August 23, 1984

7 How does President Reagan portray his opponent's approach to governing?

President Reagan portrays his opponent's approach as
A   sneaky.
B   uncompromising.
C   outdated.
D   optimistic.

8 How does President Reagan try to build credibility for his plan for governing?

President Reagan tries to build credibility by arguing that his plan
A   is proven.
B   is less expensive than his opponent's plan.
C   is unworkable.
D   cannot fail.

Directions: Questions 9 and 10 refer to the following excerpt.

We look back on the past four years with hearts nearly breaking, both for the lives unnecessarily lost and for the opportunities so casually wasted. Time and again, history invited George W. Bush to play a heroic role, and time and again he chose the wrong course. We believe that with John Kerry as president, the nation will do better.

Voting for president is a leap of faith. A candidate can explain his positions in minute detail and wind up governing with a hostile Congress that refuses to let him deliver. A disaster can upend the best-laid plans. All citizens can do is mix guesswork and hope, examining what the candidates have done in the past, their apparent priorities and their general character. It's on those three grounds that we enthusiastically endorse John Kerry for president.

From "John Kerry for President," *The New York Times*, October 17, 2004

9 In which section of the *New York Times* would you expect to find this article?
A   Politics
B   World News
C   National News
D   Opinion

10 How might this excerpt be valuable to students studying the 2004 election?

This excerpt would be most useful to students
A   writing a biography about Kerry.
B   tracking Kerry's supporters.
C   looking for a strong quote from Kerry.
D   studying 20th-century election trends.

Twice before, our Party gave the people of America leadership at a time of crisis—leadership which won us peace in place of war, unity in place of discord, compassion in place of bitterness ... .

... Today, we are in turmoil.
Tens of thousands of young men have died or been wounded in Vietnam.
Many young people are losing faith in our society.
Our inner cities have become centers of despair.
Millions of Americans are caught in the cycle of poverty ... .
Inflation has eroded confidence in the dollar at home and abroad ... .

Today's Americans are uncertain about the future, and frustrated about the recent past.

America urgently needs new leadership— leadership courageous and understanding— leadership ... restoring our confidence in ourselves and in our future.

From the Republican Party Platform of 1968

11 Which of the following sources could you use to assess the validity of the list of problems presented in this excerpt?
  A Democratic Party Platform of 1968
  B encyclopedia article about 1968
  C present-day newspapers
  D a biography of John F. Kennedy

12 How does the Party seek to highlight the effectiveness of its ideas?

The Party seeks to highlight the effectiveness of its ideas by
  A detailing the problems facing the Democratic administration.
  B discussing the concerns of average Americans.
  C explaining the causes of poverty in the United States.
  D referring to its track record of providing leadership in times of crisis.

'Our whole system depends on trust. The only way I know to be trusted is to be trustworthy. To be open, direct and honest. It's as simple as that.'

Jimmy Carter believes that secrecy has caused distrust of government at all levels. Americans are sick of half-truths and shallow promises. They want a President who will state the facts, be accessible to the people and responsive to their needs.

From "Jimmy Carter for President 1976" campaign brochure, 1976

13 What format does this brochure follow in an effort to effectively persuade readers?

This format uses
  A an opposing viewpoint, followed by Carter's rebuttal.
  B a question, followed by Carter's answer.
  C a quotation from Carter, followed by an explanation of the quotation.
  D a description of Carter's policies as governor, followed by an explanation of how those policies relate to the presidency.

14 This brochure is written to resonate with which of the following biases held by the public at the time?
  A The nation's tax system is unfair.
  B Government is inefficient.
  C U.S. educational standards have deteriorated.
  D Government is dishonest.

UNIT 4

Directions: Question 15 refers to the following excerpt.

A century ago, Teddy Roosevelt called together leaders from business and government to develop a plan for the next century's infrastructure. It falls to us to do the same. Right now, we are spending less than at any time in recent history and far less than our international competitors on this critical component of our nation's strength. We will start a National Infrastructure Reinvestment Bank that can leverage private investment in infrastructure improvement, and create nearly two million new good jobs. We will undertake projects that maximize our safety and security and ability to compete ...

In this time of economic transformation and crisis, we must be stewards of this economy more than ever before. We will maintain fiscal responsibility, so that we do not mortgage our children's future on a mountain of debt. We can do this at the same time that we invest in our future. We will restore fairness and responsibility to our tax code. We will bring balance back to the housing markets, so that people do not have to lose their homes. And we will encourage personal savings, so that our economy remains strong and Americans can live well in their retirements.

From the Democratic Party Platform of 2008

15 Which of the following tactics do the Democrats use to persuade the public?
- **A** They offer specific changes they will make.
- **B** They promise to consult the public on what is important.
- **C** They offer assurance that successful past practices will continue.
- **D** They list general changes that are likely to appeal to voters without offering specifics.

Directions: Questions 16 through 18 refer to the following excerpt from a campaign speech by Barack Obama in 2012.

On issue after issue, we are moving forward. After losing 9 million jobs in the great recession, our businesses have now added more than 5 million new jobs over the past 2 1/2 years. Manufacturing is coming back to our shores. The unemployment rate has fallen. Home values and home sales are rising. Our assembly lines are humming. ...

We cannot go back to the same policies ... We've got to keep moving forward ... And that's why I'm running for a second term as President of the United States.

I've got a plan that will actually create jobs, a plan that will actually create middle class security. ...

So I want you to compare my plan to Governor Romney's. See which plan you think is better for you. See which plan is better for America's future.

16 Which of the following claims by President Obama would be most difficult to verify?
- **A** More than 5 million jobs were created.
- **B** The unemployment rate has fallen.
- **C** Home sales are rising.
- **D** His plan will create jobs.

17 How does President Obama encourage the public to evaluate what he says?
- **A** Trust his leadership.
- **B** Compare his plan to his opponent's.
- **C** Believe the facts in his speech.
- **D** Realize that there has been real progress.

18 President Obama made this speech during his second presidential campaign. How might this speech differ from one he might have given during his first campaign?
- **A** It can include facts about his accomplishments as president.
- **B** He can blame the problems of the country on his predecessor.
- **C** More money can be spent on ads.
- **D** He does not have to use facts to explain his plans.

Analyze Effectiveness of Arguments

1 Learn the Skill

In reading texts, particularly those focusing on social studies material, you will often need to **identify strong and weak arguments**. A strong argument is persuasive and backed by accurate sources. On the other hand, a weak argument lacks the factual support needed to make it convincing. In order to **analyze the effectiveness of an argument**, look for the supporting evidence that the author or speaker provides and consider whether it is convincing.

2 Practice the Skill

By mastering the skill of analyzing the effectiveness of arguments, you will improve your study and test-taking skills, especially as they relate to social studies high school equivalency tests. Read the excerpt and strategies below. Use this information to answer question 1.

A The arguments made in this excerpt follow a repeating pattern. How does the repetition of this pattern make the argument more or less effective?

B The speaker continues to draw distinctions between his proposals and those of his opponent. What support could be offered for these arguments in order to make them more convincing?

> <u>I will</u> keep taxes low and cut them where I can. <u>My opponent</u> will raise them. <u>I will</u> open new markets to our goods and services. <u>My opponent</u> will close them. I will cut government spending. He will increase it.
>
> <u>My tax cuts will create jobs. His tax increases will eliminate them. My health care plan will make it easier for more Americans to find and keep good health care insurance.</u> His plan will force small businesses to cut jobs, reduce wages, and force families into a government run health care system where a bureaucrat stands between you and your doctor.
>
> From John McCain's address accepting the Republican Party presidential nomination, September 4, 2008

TEST-TAKING TIPS

When analyzing the effectiveness of an argument, you should first try to formulate a brief summary of the argument that the author is trying to make. With this summary in mind, you can then look more closely at the supporting details provided in order to assess the effectiveness of the argument.

1 McCain argues that his economic and health care proposals will be more effective than those of his opponent.

Which of the following would strengthen McCain's argument?

A additional details about his efforts to reform health care as a senator

B reflections on Democratic and Republican views about taxes

C details from both candidates' proposed federal budgets

D a list of Democratic presidents who have increased taxes

UNIT 4

Directions: Questions 2 and 3 refer to the following excerpt.

Senator William Fulbright: As I stated, section I is intended to deal primarily with aggression against our forces … . I do not know what the limits are. I do not think this resolution can be determinative of that fact. I think it would indicate that he [President Johnson] would take reasonable means first to prevent any further aggression, or repel further aggression against our own forces. … I do not know how to answer the Senator's question and give him an absolute assurance that large numbers of troops would not be put ashore. I would deplore it … .

Senator Ernest Gruening: Regrettably, I find myself in disagreement with the President's Southeast Asian policy … The serious events of the past few days, the attack by North Vietnamese vessels on American warships and our reprisal, strikes me as the inevitable and foreseeable concomitant and consequence of U.S. unilateral military aggressive policy in Southeast Asia. … We now are about to authorize the President if he sees fit to move our Armed Forces … not only into South Vietnam, but also into North Vietnam, Laos, Cambodia, Thailand, and of course the authorization includes all the rest of the SEATO nations. … This resolution is a further authorization for escalation unlimited. I am opposed to sacrificing a single American boy in this venture. We have lost far too many already. …

From Senate Debates on the Tonkin Gulf Resolution, August 6–7, 1964

2 **Which of the following does Fulbright use to support his argument?**
   A statistics regarding the conflict in Vietnam
   B details about the meaning of the resolution
   C his beliefs about the president's intent
   D recommendations from foreign policy experts

3 **What is the argument made by Senator Gruening in this excerpt?**

   Senator Gruening argues that
   A the resolution will lead to unchecked U.S. aggression in Southeast Asia.
   B the resolution will enable the United States to defend its forces overseas.
   C the North Vietnamese attack on U.S. forces was unprovoked.
   D the United States should devote more troops to preserving peace in Asia.

Directions: Question 4 refers to the following excerpt.

You see, we Democrats have a very different measure of what constitutes progress in this country.

We measure progress by how many people can find a job that pays the mortgage; whether you can put a little extra money away at the end of each month so you can someday watch your child receive her college diploma. We measure progress in the 23 million new jobs that were created when Bill Clinton was President—when the average American family saw its income go up $7,500 instead of down $2,000 like it has under George Bush.

From Barack Obama's address accepting the Democratic Party presidential nomination, August 28, 2008

4 **How does Obama best strengthen his argument that Democrats can improve the nation's economy?**
   A He refutes the economic gains of the sitting Republican administration.
   B He describes his definition of the word progress.
   C He details a plan for college savings.
   D He cites the economic improvements of the last Democratic administration.

Directions: Questions 5 through 8 refer to the following excerpts.

The first thing which strikes our attention is, that the executive authority, with few exceptions, is to be vested in a single magistrate. This will scarcely, however, be considered as a point upon which any comparison can be grounded; for if, in this particular, there be a resemblance to the king of Great Britain, there is not less a resemblance to the Grand Seignior, to the khan of Tartary, to the Man of the Seven Mountains, or to the governor of New York.

The magistrate is to be elected for FOUR years; and is to be re-eligible as often as the people of the United States shall think him worthy of their confidence. In these circumstances there is a total dissimilitude between HIM and a king of Great Britain … but there is a close analogy between HIM and a governor of NEW YORK, who is elected for THREE years, and is re-eligible without limitation or intermission … .

From *The Federalist Papers: No. 69*, by Alexander Hamilton, 1788

In my last number I endeavoured to prove that the language of the article relative to the establishment of the executive of this new government was vague and inexplicit, that the great powers of the President, connected with his duration in office would lead to oppression and ruin. That he would be governed by favorites and flatterers, or that a dangerous council would be collected from the great officers of state … . [T]hat if you adopt this government, you will incline to an arbitrary and odious aristocracy or monarchy that the president possessed of the power, given him by this frame of government differs but very immaterially from the establishment of monarchy in Great Britain, and I warned you to beware of the fallacious resemblance that is held out to you by the advocates of this new system between it and your own state governments.

From "Cato" Letter V, *The New-York Journal*, November 22, 1787

5　Hamilton argues that the U.S. president will be the most like which of the following?
  A　the khan of Tartary
  B　the Man of the Seven Mountains
  C　the authors of the Constitution
  D　the governor of New York

6　Which of the following pieces of evidence does Hamilton use to argue that the president will not have unlimited power?
  A　checks and balances
  B　the consolidation of authority in a single magistrate
  C　the length of the president's term in office
  D　examples of similar government systems from around the world

7　The author of the second excerpt argues that the adoption of the Constitution will lead to which form of government in the nation?
  A　dictatorship
  B　democratic republic
  C　oligarchy
  D　monarchy or aristocracy

8　Which of the following could strengthen the argument made in the second excerpt?
  A　examples of the difference between the proposed government and state governments
  B　suggestions for making the language of the Constitution less specific
  C　a plan for forming a council from state officers
  D　a comparison of aristocracies and monarchies

Directions: Questions 9 through 12 refer to the following excerpts from the 2004 Presidential Debate in Tempe, Arizona between President George W. Bush and Senator John Kerry.

KERRY: The measurement is not: Are we safer? The measurement is: Are we as safe as we ought to be? And there are a host of options that this President had available to him, like making sure that at all our ports in America, containers are inspected. … 95 percent come in today uninspected. That's not good enough. People who fly on airplanes today—the cargo hold is not X-rayed, but the baggage is. That's not good enough. …

BUSH: So we can do a better job of homeland security. I can do a better job of waging a smarter, more effective war on terror and guarantee that we go after the terrorists.

Yes, we can be safe and secure if we stay on the offense against the terrorists and if we spread freedom and liberty around the world. I have got a comprehensive strategy to not only chase down al-Qaeda, wherever it exists—and we're making progress; three-quarters of al-Qaeda leaders have been brought to justice—but to make sure that countries who harbor terrorists are held to account. As a result of securing ourselves and ridding the Taliban out of Afghanistan, the Afghan people had elections this weekend. And the first voter was a 19-year-old woman. … Freedom is on the march. We held to account a terrorist regime in Saddam Hussein. …

9 **Which of the following correctly describes the argument strategy of one of the candidates?**
A Bush describes his domestic homeland security policies.
B Kerry advocates a more aggressive pursuit of al-Qaeda leaders.
C Bush highlights accomplishments of the war on terror abroad.
D Kerry requests the passage of a new homeland security bill.

10 **How does Kerry use statistics to strengthen his argument?**

Kerry uses statistics to
A point out the cost of the war on terror.
B identify areas in which the United States can be made safer.
C detail the gains made against al-Qaeda.
D identify the percentage of luggage that goes uninspected.

11 **What does Bush argue the nation should do to remain safe and secure from terrorist threats?**
A better allocate resources for fighting terror
B hire new law enforcement officials
C work collaboratively with other nations
D help install free governments around the world

12 **How does Bush strengthen his argument?**

Bush strengthens his argument by
A listing nations supporting the U.S. policy.
B detailing achievements in the war on terror.
C discrediting Kerry's recommendations.
D referencing the execution of Saddam Hussein.

Directions: Questions 13 through 16 refer to the following information and excerpts.

During the 1984 Republican National Convention in Dallas, Gregory Lee Johnson burned an American flag as a political protest and was eventually convicted under Texas law. The case reached the U.S. Supreme Court in order to determine whether Johnson's conviction violated the First Amendment.

"If there is a bedrock principle underlying the First Amendment, it is that the government may not prohibit the expression of an idea simply because society finds the idea itself offensive or disagreeable. …

In short, nothing in our precedents suggests that a State may foster its own view of the flag by prohibiting expressive conduct relating to it … .

The First Amendment does not guarantee that other concepts virtually sacred to our Nation as a whole—such as the principle that discrimination on the basis of race is odious and destructive—will go unquestioned in the marketplace of ideas … . We decline, therefore, to create for the flag an exception to the joust of principles protected by the First Amendment."

Justice William Brennan, Opinion of the Court, *Texas v. Johnson*, June 21, 1989

"Uncritical extension of constitutional protection to the burning of the flag risks the frustration of the very purpose for which organized governments are instituted. The Court decides that the American flag is just another symbol, about which not only must opinions pro and con be tolerated, but for which the most minimal public respect may not be enjoined. The government may conscript men into the Armed Forces where they must fight and perhaps die for the flag, but the government may not prohibit the public burning of the banner under which they fight. I would uphold the Texas statute as applied in this case."

Chief Justice William Rehnquist, Dissenting Opinion, *Texas v. Johnson*, June 21, 1989

13 Which statement accurately describes the argument made by the majority of the Supreme Court?
A Johnson's conviction should stand according to Texas law.
B The First Amendment protects destruction of national symbols.
C The U.S. government cannot prevent free expression, even if the expression is offensive.
D Certain ideals or beliefs of the United States cannot be questioned or disputed.

14 On what basis does Brennan build his argument?

Brennan supports his argument with
A facts about the flag and its history.
B a majority vote of the court.
C public opinion.
D legal precedent.

15 This Supreme Court ruling confirms that the Constitution protects which of the following acts?
A threatening speech toward another citizen
B stealing of property from a public building
C voting in primary and general elections
D recording of a song that features curse words

16 On which of the following does Rehnquist base his argument?

Rehnquist bases his argument on
A the history of the American flag.
B the flag's symbolic value.
C the flag as a piece of public property.
D the military significance of the flag.

Lesson 9 | Analyze Effectiveness of Arguments

Unit 4 Review

The Unit Review is structured to resemble social studies high school equivalency tests. Be sure to read each question and all possible answers very carefully before choosing your answer.

To record your answers, fill in the circle that corresponds to the answer you select for each question in the Unit Review.

Do not rest your pencil on the answer area while considering your answer. Make no stray or unnecessary marks. If you change an answer, erase your first mark completely.

Mark only one answer space for each question; multiple answers will be scored as incorrect.

Sample Question

Which of the following accurately describes the contents of the U. S. Constitution?

A articles

B articles and amendments

C articles, amendments, and bills

D articles, amendments, bills, checks and balances, and three branches of government

Directions: Questions 1 and 2 refer to the following table.

1992 PRESIDENTIAL ELECTION RESULTS

CANDIDATE (PARTY)	ELECTORAL VOTES (%)	POPULAR VOTES (%)	STATES WON
Bill Clinton (Democratic)	370 (68.8%)	44,909,326 (43.0%)	32 (also won Washington, D.C.)
George H.W. Bush (Republican)	168 (31.2%)	39,103,882 (37.4%)	18
H. Ross Perot (Independent)	0 (0%)	19,741,657 (18.9%)	0

1 Which of the following statements about the table expresses an opinion?

A Clinton won both the electoral vote and the popular vote.

B If Perot had not entered the election, Bush would have been reelected as president.

C Despite receiving almost 20 million popular votes, Perot did not receive a vote in the Electoral College.

D Bush received approximately double the number of popular votes Perot received.

Ⓐ Ⓑ Ⓒ Ⓓ

2 Suppose you are assigned to write a research report on the presidential election of 1992. What primary sources might you consult in order to learn more about the results shown in the table?

You might consult a primary source such as

A an American history textbook.

B a biography of Perot.

C an encyclopedia entry on political parties.

D an interview of one of the candidates' campaign managers.

Directions: Questions 3 and 4 refer to the following information.

In the United States, affirmative action programs have been designed to create greater opportunities for underrepresented minority groups in areas such as the workplace, college admissions, and the issuing of government contracts. The policies have been instituted with the intent of offsetting the harmful effects of past discrimination.

Affirmative action has proven to be highly controversial in the United States. Opponents argue that these policies violate citizens' right to equal protection by the nation's laws. They further claim that discriminating against members of a present-day group to make amends for past discrimination against a different group is unfair.

Supporters of affirmative action counter that people experience discrimination specifically because they belong to a particular group. As a result, they believe it is necessary to institute systematic measures to guarantee that equal rights remain **inviolable** for all citizens.

3   **What problem have affirmative action programs been established to address?**
  A   the difficulty of interpreting cases involving equal protection disputes
  B   conflicts arising between different ethnic and religious groups in U.S. communities
  C   the harmful effects of past discrimination
  D   the lack of high-paying jobs for many Americans

ⒶⒷⒸⒹ

4   **By using context clues, what can you determine about the meaning of the word *inviolable*?**

  The meaning of the word *inviolable* is
  A   involuntary.
  B   optional.
  C   safe from violation.
  D   varied from person to person.

ⒶⒷⒸⒹ

Directions: Questions 5 and 6 refer to the following excerpt from Article IV of the United States Constitution.

Section 3. New states may be admitted by the Congress into this union; but no new states shall be formed or erected within the jurisdiction of any other state; nor any state be formed by the junction of two or more states, or parts of states, without the consent of the legislatures of the states concerned as well as of the Congress.

The Congress shall have power to dispose of and make all needful rules and regulations respecting the territory or other property belonging to the United States; and nothing in this Constitution shall be so construed as to prejudice any claims of the United States, or of any particular state.

Section 4. The United States shall guarantee to every state in this union a republican form of government, and shall protect each of them against invasion; and on application of the legislature, or of the executive (when the legislature cannot be **convened**) against domestic violence.

5   **What is the main focus of Section 3 of Article IV of the United States Constitution?**
  A   federal protection of the states
  B   the formation of new states
  C   the negotiation of treaties between the states
  D   the interactions of state and federal legislatures

ⒶⒷⒸⒹ

6   **Use context clues to determine the meaning of the word *convened* in the above excerpt.**

  In this excerpt, the meaning of *convened* is
  A   brought together.
  B   established.
  C   disbanded.
  D   elected.

ⒶⒷⒸⒹ

Directions: Questions 7 through 10 refer to the following excerpts.

BUSH: Well, I think one thing that distinguishes is experience. I think we've dramatically changed the world. I'll talk about that a little bit later, but the changes are mind-boggling for world peace. Kids go to bed at night without the same fear of nuclear war. And change for change's sake isn't enough. We saw that message in the late seventies when we heard a lot about change. And what happened? That 'misery index' went right through the roof.

But my economic program, I think, is the kind of change we want. And the way we're going to get it done is we're going to have a brand new Congress. A lot of them are thrown out because of all the scandals. I'll sit down with them, Democrats and Republicans alike, and work for my Agenda for American Renewal which represents real change. But I'd say, if you had to separate out, I think it's experience at this level.

CLINTON: I believe experience counts, but it's not everything. Values, judgment, and the record that I have amassed in my state also should count for something. I've worked hard to create good jobs and to educate people. My state now ranks first in the country in job growth this year, fourth in income growth, fourth in the reduction of poverty, third in overall economic performance, according to a major news magazine. That's because we believe in investing in education and in jobs. …

Experience is important, yes. I've gotten a lot of good experience in dealing with ordinary people over the last year and a month. … And I think the American people deserve better than they're getting. We have gone from first to 13th in the world in wages in the last 12 years since Mr. Bush and Mr. Reagan have been in. Personal income has dropped while people have worked harder in the last 4 years. There have been twice as many bankruptcies as new jobs created.

We need a new approach. The same old experience is not relevant. We're living in a new world after the Cold War. … And you can have the right kind of experience and the wrong kind of experience. Mine is rooted in the lives of real people. And it will bring real results if we have the courage to change.

From the Presidential Debate: St. Louis, October 11, 1992

7 Which of the following serves as the basis of Bush's argument in this excerpt?

A his presidential experience

B his economic program

C his expectations for changes in Congress

D his understanding of the "misery index"

Ⓐ Ⓑ Ⓒ Ⓓ

8 Which best describes the way in which Bush claims to have solved a foreign policy problem?

Bush suggests that his administration has

A restored alliances with former allies.

B brought an end to many violent uprisings around the world.

C remained a neutral peacemaker in many important world conflicts.

D reduced the fear of nuclear war.

Ⓐ Ⓑ Ⓒ Ⓓ

9 How does Clinton strengthen his argument about his experience to lead the nation?

Clinton strengthens his argument by including statistics about

A his proposed economic initiatives.

B his budgetary planning experience.

C economic improvements in Arkansas during his tenure as governor.

D the limited economic growth that occurred during the Bush administration.

Ⓐ Ⓑ Ⓒ Ⓓ

10 Which of Clinton's statements below presents a fact?

A We need a new approach.

B I think the American people deserve better than what they're getting.

C I believe experience counts, but it's not everything.

D There have been twice as many bankruptcies as new jobs created.

Ⓐ Ⓑ Ⓒ Ⓓ

UNIT 4

Directions: Questions 11 and 12 refer to the following political cartoon.

THE PRE-PRIMARY VOTE

"THE PRE-PRIMARY VOTE,"
A 1999 Herblock Cartoon, © by The Herb Block Foundation

11 Which of the following best describes the problem to which the cartoonist is trying to draw attention?
   A   the unreliability of presidential elections
   B   the increasing importance of campaign fundraising in the electoral process
   C   the unwillingness of Americans to financially support the candidates that share their ideas
   D   the secretive manner in which parties encourage candidates to run for office

Ⓐ Ⓑ Ⓒ Ⓓ

12 How would you evaluate this cartoon as an information source?

As an information source, this cartoon could best be described as
   A   impartial.
   B   unreliable.
   C   commentary.
   D   factually accurate.

Ⓐ Ⓑ Ⓒ Ⓓ

Directions: Questions 13 and 14 refer to the following map of the 2012 presidential election results.

ELECTORAL MAP, 2012

Democrat victory: Barack Obama
Republican victory: Mitt Romney

13 Which of the following states likely provided the greatest electoral benefit for the winning candidate?
   A   California
   B   New York
   C   Georgia
   D   Texas

Ⓐ Ⓑ Ⓒ Ⓓ

14 Based on the map, which of the following statements is accurate?
   A   The candidate who won the most states did not win the election.
   B   The victorious candidate won the three largest electoral states.
   C   The West Coast largely supported the Republican.
   D   Most states in New England supported the Democrat.

Ⓐ Ⓑ Ⓒ Ⓓ

Directions: Questions 15 and 16 refer to the following political cartoon.

"BY TH' WAY, WHAT'S THAT BIG WORD?"
by Bill Mauldin

15 How do the figures shown in this cartoon demonstrate faulty logic?

These figures demonstrate faulty logic because

A they cannot agree on the best method for testing voters.
B they cannot justify their choices of selected candidates.
C they have oversimplified the qualifications for voting.
D an honest literacy test would prevent them from voting.

Ⓐ Ⓑ Ⓒ Ⓓ

16 Under which of the following headings could this cartoon best be categorized?
A presidential elections
B government spending
C civil rights
D the U.S. Constitution

Ⓐ Ⓑ Ⓒ Ⓓ

Directions: Questions 17 and 18 refer to the following excerpt.

Twenty years ago, the economy was in shambles. Unemployment was at 7.1 percent, inflation at 13.5 percent, and interest rates at 15.3 percent. The Democratic Party accepted that malaise as the price the nation had to pay for Big Government, and in doing so lost the confidence of the American people. Inspired by Presidents Reagan and Bush, Republicans hammered into place the framework for today's prosperity and surpluses. We cut taxes, simplified the tax code, deregulated industries, and opened world markets to American enterprise. The result was the tremendous growth in the 1980s that created the venture capital to launch the technology revolution of the 1990s.

That's the origin of what is now called the New Economy: the longest economic boom in the Twentieth Century, 40 million new jobs, the lowest inflation and unemployment in memory.

From the Republican Party Platform of 2000

17 Which of the following claims is best supported by facts listed in the platform?
A Republicans were inspired by Reagan and Bush during the 1980s and early 1990s.
B Twenty years ago, the economy was in shambles.
C The Democratic Party viewed economic difficulties as a necessary consequence of Big Government.
D The U.S. economy experienced significant growth during the 1980s.

Ⓐ Ⓑ Ⓒ Ⓓ

18 How does this party platform show bias?
A It discusses the economic growth of the 1980s.
B President Clinton's accomplishments are not included.
C The technology revolution is attributed to the simplified tax code.
D Presidents Reagan and Bush are not discussed.

Ⓐ Ⓑ Ⓒ Ⓓ

Unit 5

Unit Overview

Many of the choices we make each day revolve around economics. For example, we collect paychecks, make deposits and withdrawals, shop, and pay bills and taxes. Economics is the study of the decisions involved in the production, distribution, and consumption of goods and services. By understanding economics, we become better at determining when and how we use our time and money.

Likewise, economics plays an important part in social studies high school equivalency tests, comprising approximately 15 percent of all questions. As with other parts of high school equivalency tests, economics will test your ability to interpret text and graphics using the thinking skills of comprehension, application, analysis, and evaluation. In Unit 5, the continuation of core skills and the introduction of others will help you prepare for the social studies test.

Table of Contents

Economics

Key Economics Terms

capitalism: a system in which individuals and corporations own the land, factories, and resources used to make and transport products and provide services

competition: the act of trying to win something, such as when businesses compete for consumers to choose and purchase their goods or services

consumer: a person who buys and uses goods and services

currency: the accepted money that is used in a country to buy goods and services

deficit: an amount of money that is less than what is needed to meet an obligation

demand: the condition of being desired or having a market for purchase, such as the *demand* for oil to meet energy needs

distribution: the process of delivering goods from the point where they are made to sellers and on to consumers

equilibrium point: the point at which the available supply of a product and the demand for it are equal

Federal Reserve System: the central bank of the U.S., which regulates the nation's financial system

free trade: a policy wherein governments do not restrict the import or export of goods to and from other countries

free-market economy: a capitalist system in which competition, supply, and demand determine prices without government control

goods: tangible property that people sell and buy

gross domestic product (GDP): the total value of all the goods and services produced by a country in a year

inflation: a general increase in the prices of goods and services, while the amount that can be purchased for a given sum of money decreases

interest: an amount of money paid, usually as a percentage, for money borrowed in a loan

laissez-faire: the policy of allowing businesses to operate generally without government involvement or interference

macroeconomics: the study of factors, such as employment and inflation, that affect the economy on its largest scale

microeconomics: the study of small-scale interactions within an economy, such as the supply, demand, and consumer decision making in an individual market for one type of product

monopoly: complete ownership or control, without competition, of an entire supply of something within a market

mortgage rate: the percentage of interest charged by a lender to a borrower taking a loan to buy property

output: something produced by a person, machine, or industry

profit: the amount of money earned for a sale of something that exceeds what it cost to produce that thing

recession: a period in which the buying and production within an economy are decreased or slowed down

revenue: money collected by a person or business

socialism: an economic system in which the government, as opposed to individuals and corporations, owns the property and resources used to produce and distribute goods and services

stock market: the collective system of buyers and sellers who exchange money for ownership shares of companies

supply: the available amount of something

surplus: the amount of something that is left over after the demand for it has been met

tariff: a tax on goods imported to or exported from a country

tax: an amount of money that is required to be paid to a government by an individual or corporation

unemployment rate: the measure, by percentage, of people who are seeking paid jobs but are not part of the labor force

wages: the amount of money that a worker is paid

Understand Economics

① Learn the Skill

Economics is the study of the ways in which goods and services are exchanged. It includes exchanges between people, groups, businesses, and governments. It borrows from human psychology, ethics, and history in its attempts to explain and predict behaviors related to buying and selling. **Understanding economics** is essential for making sense of societal behaviors and world events.

② Practice the Skill

By mastering the skill of understanding economics, you will improve your study and test-taking skills, especially as they relate to social studies high school equivalency tests. Examine the information below. Use this information to answer question 1.

A The table highlights some of the main economic indicators and how they apply to microeconomics versus macroeconomics.

<u>Microeconomics</u> involves economic decision making at an individual level or company level. This includes individuals, households, businesses, and industries. <u>Macroeconomics</u> studies the behavior of the entire economy. The table illustrates some of the differences between microeconomics and macroeconomics.

B To help you remember the difference between micro- and macroeconomics, remember that *micro* means "small" and *macro* means "large."

	A PRODUCTION	PRICES	INCOME	EMPLOYMENT
Microeconomics **B**	How many bottles of juice does Company A produce?	What is the price of a bottle of juice from Company A?	What are the wages of the employees at Company A?	How many people are employed at Company A?
Macroeconomics **B**	How many goods and services does the U.S. produce?	What is the U.S. Gross Domestic Product (GDP)?	What are the total wages and salaries of employees in the U.S.?	What is the unemployment rate in the U.S.?

UNIT 5

✓ TEST-TAKING TIPS

Try to think of an example that illustrates unfamiliar terms or concepts. For example, you might differentiate between micro- and macroeconomics by thinking about your personal spending habits versus the economic policies of the United States.

1   **Which of the following is an example of microeconomics?**
   A   The United States produced more oranges this year than last year.
   B   A can of frozen orange juice costs $2.09 at the supermarket.
   C   Oranges are one of the primary crops in Florida.
   D   Millions of gallons of orange juice are exported each year.

Directions: Questions 2 through 4 are based on the information below.

Adam Smith lived in Scotland during the time of America's Revolutionary War. In 1776, he published *The Wealth of Nations*. The book was the first to seriously examine the ways in which wealth is produced and distributed.

Smith believed that a country's economy works best when its government does not interfere with it. He asserted that when people were left to produce wealth without interference, they were led by an "invisible hand" to the benefit of all.

From Adam Smith's *The Wealth of Nations*:

The annual labour of every nation is the fund which originally supplies it with all the necessaries and conveniences of life which it annually consumes, and which consist always either in the immediate produce of that labour, or in what is purchased with that produce from other nations.

According therefore, as this produce, or what is purchased with it, bears a greater or smaller proportion to the number of those who are to consume it, the nation will be better or worse supplied with all the necessaries and conveniences for which it has occasion.

2 **Another way of expressing Smith's economic philosophy is to state that the best economies are**
A planned economies.
B centralized economies.
C free-market economies.
D government-controlled economies.

3 **According to Smith, which of the following can you infer should be a function of government?**
A to remove obstacles to business growth
B to give people money to start businesses
C to limit the profit a business can make
D to set the prices of goods and services

4 **According to Smith, what produces a nation's wealth?**
A produce from other nations
B the labor of its workforce
C its necessaries
D its luxuries

Directions: Questions 5 and 6 are based on the information below.

Capitalism, socialism, and communism are examples of economic systems. They vary by the amount of control the government or central authority has over businesses. The capitalist system has the least amount of government interference. The United States has a capitalist economic system.

Adam Smith and other economists favored a type of capitalism known as *laissez-faire*. This is a French term that means to let people do as they choose. In economics, it means that the government should not interfere. This theory was seen as inadequate by economist John Maynard Keynes. During the Great Depression, Keynes began to support the idea that government should make investments in society and businesses to spur the economy. Keynesian economists called for the same investment during the "Great Recession" of 2008–2009.

5 **What type of economic system is most often practiced in the United States?**
A Keynesian capitalism
B *laissez-faire* capitalism
C socialism
D *laissez-faire* socialism

6 **Keynes might have supported government investment during the Great Depression because Keynes believed that the United States government**
A should create jobs to lower unemployment.
B should run a deficit at all times.
C should follow the *laissez-faire* philosophy.
D would cure the recession by raising taxes.

UNIT 5

Directions: Questions 7 and 8 are based on the information below.

Communism is an economic theory that advocates the elimination of private property. In a Communist economy, goods are considered the property of everyone, to be used by individuals as needed.

Communism is distinguished by being a centrally-planned (or "command") economy. In a Communist system, the government owns all means of production—farms, factories, stores, and anything else that generates goods. The government decides what goods are produced and in what quantities, as well as the prices at which they are sold. In practice, Communist economies have tended to use resources for military development at the expense of consumer goods.

Belief in national self-reliance was originally another feature of communism. There was little international trade, and most of it was with other centrally-planned economies. In recent years, however, Communist countries have broken from this tendency.

7   **What feature is common to both communism and capitalism?**
   A   Both are heavily regulated by the government.
   B   Both engage in a minimum amount of international trade.
   C   Both rely heavily on the influence of free markets.
   D   Both concern themselves with the distribution of goods and services.

8   **Which is true about Communist economies?**
   A   they still do not participate in international trade
   B   the free market decides what goods are produced
   C   they promote private property
   D   production of consumer goods may suffer because of military advances

Directions: Questions 9 and 10 are based on the information below.

The United States engages in free trade with countries such as Canada and Mexico under the North American Free Trade Agreement, or NAFTA. But with many other countries, the United States imposes tariffs on imported goods. A tariff is essentially a tax. It is a cost added by the government to an imported good.

There are many reasons that a country may choose to impose a tariff. One reason is competition. A tariff helps protect domestic industries from competition from non-domestic industries. If an international country can produce a product or good more cheaply than the United States, people may be more likely to buy the less expensive good, and the industry in the United States will suffer.

9   **Which of the following best explains how tariffs protect domestic industry from competition?**
   A   The tariff makes it easier for stores in the United States to import the good.
   B   By adding a tariff to an imported good, the country exporting the good will stop sending it to the United States.
   C   When the tariff is added to the price of the imported good, it raises the price above that of the domestic good.
   D   People are less inclined to purchase goods that have tariffs attached.

10   **International countries may also assess tariffs on goods the United States exports to them. How would this type of tariff affect a U.S. company's profit, as compared to the prices of their goods?**
   A   Their goods will be more expensive, and their profit will increase.
   B   Their goods will be more expensive, but their profit will remain the same.
   C   Their goods will be less expensive, and their profit will increase.
   D   Their goods will be less expensive, and their profit will decrease.

Directions: Questions 11 through 14 are based on the information below:

Many people think the terms "communism" and "socialism" refer to the same economic system. While this was mostly true several decades ago, socialism has changed greatly over time.

Today, there are important differences between the two economic systems. Socialist systems place essential industries and services, such as health care, under government control. Because the government is answerable to the voters, they can influence the socialist systems indirectly. Tax revenue from a free market economy is used to finance these socialized services. While this has proven effective in some countries, it often results in very high rates of taxation.

A degree of socialism exists in nearly every established economy. There is a particularly strong tradition of socialism in Europe. For instance, childcare is widely subsidized. Due in large part to government assistance, the child-poverty rates in France and Sweden are much lower than those in the United States.

Almost every developed country guarantees its citizens access to health care or subsidizes a national health system. In the United States, socialism exists in the form of welfare programs and Social Security.

11 Which of the following best describes the socialist economic system?
A a stronger form of communism
B a free market economy
C an independent system of international trade
D a government-run distribution of essential goods and services

12 The difference between tax rates in the United States and those of European countries is due in part to
A free market supply and demand.
B the communist economies of European nations.
C the socialist nature of European economies.
D the socialist nature of the U.S. economy.

13 Why can Social Security and welfare be classified as socialism?
A They help the quality of life of many people.
B They are government-administered programs funded by a free market economy.
C They are an aspect of the national economy.
D They are part of a universal health care program.

14 Who ultimately decides what is to be funded in a socialist economy?
A the government
B the recipients of government assistance
C the tax officials
D the voters

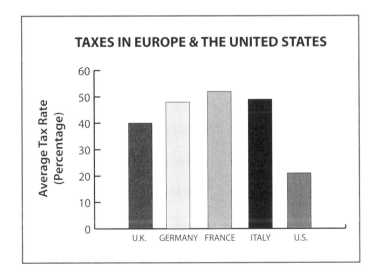

TAXES IN EUROPE & THE UNITED STATES

UNIT 5

Directions: Questions 15 and 16 are based on the information below.

A market is a place or infrastructure in which the exchange of goods and services takes place. In the most literal sense, a market is a physical place in which things are bought and sold, like a farmer's market, for example. To economists, a market is not necessarily a specific place, but a structure in which buyers and sellers are free to trade with one another. This freedom for buyers and sellers leads to similar prices for the same goods.

Sellers that sell cucumbers at a farmers market, for example, will tend to have their cucumbers priced similarly. Competition between sellers keeps the price of cucumbers from going too high. Sellers know that if they raise prices too high, their buyers will move to other sellers that have lower prices. Some sellers may add incentives to persuade buyers to purchase their produce or product. In this case, a seller with a higher-priced cucumber might incentivize customers by giving them a free tomato with each cucumber purchase.

Some markets are not competitive, but have monopolies. If there were only one seller of cucumbers at the farmers market and no other sellers of cucumbers could get a spot at the market, this seller could form a monopoly. Without any government regulation, this seller could set the price of cucumbers at whatever level he or she wanted.

15 **Which of the following holds prices for the same goods at about the same level in a market?**
   A   competition between sellers
   B   high demand for the goods
   C   incentives for consumers
   D   quantity of goods available

16 **Which of the following describes when a monopoly can occur?**
   A   A small number of companies control the market for a good or product.
   B   Each company produces goods that are different and appeal to different customers.
   C   One company sells a good or product that has no substitutes and other companies are blocked from entering the market.
   D   Many companies produce the same product, leading to low prices that cannot sustain companies.

Directions: Questions 17 and 18 are based on the information below.

Businesses rely on economic indicators to guide their decision making. An economic indicator is an economic statistic. The unemployment rate, or percentage of people unemployed, is an economic indicator. The purpose of an economic indicator is to indicate how well an economy is currently doing and will do in the future.

Some indicators are leading, meaning they change before the economy changes, so they are helpful in making predictions. The stock market, for example, often begins to decline or improve before the larger economy. Leading economic indicators are helpful to investors as they make decisions about where to invest their money.

Other indicators are lagging, meaning they change after the economy changes. The unemployment rate, for example, may continue to increase for several months after the economy has started to improve.

17 **Gross domestic product, or GDP, represents the total value of a country's production. Which of the following is an investor most likely to do if the GDP of the United States is consistently increasing?**
   A   invest in foreign-manufactured goods
   B   sell investments in foreign companies
   C   sell investments in U.S. businesses
   D   invest in U.S.-based companies

18 **Leading indicators are used to predict economic trends, while lagging indicators confirm long-term trends. Which of the following is a lagging indicator?**
   A   the stock market
   B   unemployment
   C   money supply
   D   building permits

UNIT 5

Analyze Consumer Behavior

① Learn the Skill

When learning about economics, you will often be required to **analyze** information about **consumer behavior**. The concept of consumer behavior draws on both economics and psychology to describe the actions of consumers in deciding what goods and services they should purchase, and when they should purchase them. When analyzing consumer behavior, you must examine the various elements that can affect consumers, including the effect of marketing and advertising, the perceptions that consumers have about themselves, and the impact of global economic trends on the choices consumers make. Consumer behavior is also influenced by a consumer's income, lifestyle, and values.

② Practice the Skill

By mastering the skill of analyzing consumer behavior, you will improve your study and test-taking skills, especially as they relate to social studies high school equivalency tests. Read the information and strategies below. Use this information to answer question 1.

> **A** Text in advertisements that tries to persuade customers to make a purchase immediately is known as a "call to action."
>
> **B** Words are sometimes capitalized in advertisements to add emphasis and to catch customers' attention.

> Do you want to read the best travel magazine money can buy? **A** Then subscribe to *Time to Travel Magazine* now and get 6 ISSUES for only $29.95! Each issue is full of unique articles and spectacular pictures of far-away destinations. You'll also find reviews of hotels and restaurants from around the world. Order NOW and receive a pair of designer sunglasses at NO EXTRA CHARGE! So what are you waiting for? Start seeing the world in style with *Time to Travel Magazine* TODAY!

MAKING ASSUMPTIONS

You can assume that many advertisements provide more than one reason to motivate a consumer to purchase goods or services. For example, an advertisement might highlight both the attractiveness of the product and make a special offer.

1 This advertisement attempts to sell subscriptions to *Time to Travel Magazine* by offering
   A extra issues.
   B a discounted price.
   C a free item.
   D special contests.

Directions: Questions 2 and 3 refer to the following advertisement.

> **You Strive For Success At Work.**
> **We Strive To Help You Succeed.**
>
> Let's Work Together.
>
> **McClellan Office Products, Inc.**

2 How does McClellan Office Products, Inc., try to present itself in this advertisement?

A as the consumer's friend

B as the consumer's employee

C as the consumer's boss

D as the consumer's partner

3 People who would respond favorably to this advertisement would most likely view themselves as

A being successful at their jobs.

B wanting to reduce their workloads.

C needing more assistance with their work.

D wanting less-expensive office products.

Directions: Questions 4 and 5 refer to the following information.

Opportunity costs often shape consumer behavior. An opportunity cost is something that one gives up in favor of something else. For example, suppose Shane has to choose between playing either basketball or softball after work on Tuesday evening. He cannot choose both because he has only enough time to play one. If he chooses softball, then not playing basketball is the opportunity cost of Shane's choice. Shane's time is limited, so he has to make a choice. In much the same way, consumer resources are limited, but their wants can be unlimited. Therefore, people often consider opportunity costs in deciding whether or not to purchase a good or service. If a shopper enters a store with $10 and is faced with three items that each cost $10, the shopper has to make the choice about what to buy. The two items the shopper does not purchase are opportunity costs.

4 Why is it important for consumers to consider opportunity costs?

A so they can select the best products

B so they can maintain a budget

C so they can purchase more items on credit

D so they can differentiate between wants and needs

5 Which of the following explains why consumer resources are limited?

A There are more consumers than there are goods and services.

B Consumer demand for goods and services varies.

C Consumers earn a finite amount of money.

D The wants of consumers have increased over the years.

Directions: Questions 6 and 7 refer to the following advertisement.

6 **This advertisement is aimed toward consumers with a specific**

   A type of lifestyle.

   B level of income.

   C level of education.

   D type of job.

7 **What is the most likely reason some consumers would respond favorably to the words "power" and "speed"?**

   A The words help describe the perfect motorboat.

   B The words create a sense of excitement.

   C The words are short and easy to understand.

   D The words suggest that the motorboat is a bargain.

Directions: Questions 8 and 9 refer to the following information.

There are four types of consumer purchasing behavior. The first behavior is known as "Routine Response." This describes frequent and relatively low-cost purchases that require little decision making by the consumer. Examples of "Routine Response" purchasing behavior include the purchasing of basic food items. "Limited Decision Making" describes occasional purchases that may require some research on behalf of the consumer. For example, a consumer may read reviews of specific movies before deciding which one to see.

The third type of consumer purchasing behavior is "Extensive Decision Making." This describes expensive and infrequent purchases that require a great amount of decision-making by the consumer because there is a high degree of financial risk. Examples include buying a house or car. Finally, there is "Impulse Buying," which describes an inexpensive purchase requiring little thought by the consumer. Buying a pack of gum while waiting in line at a store is an example of "Impulse Buying."

8 **Which of the following purchases would most likely be considered a "Limited Decision Making" purchase?**

   A the purchase of a plane ticket

   B the purchase of a new computer

   C the purchase of a gallon of milk

   D the purchase of a newspaper

9 **What is the main difference between "Routine Response" purchases and "Impulse Buying" purchases?**

   A Unlike "Routine Response" purchases, "Impulse Buying" purchases are low-cost.

   B Unlike "Routine Response" purchases, "Impulse Buying" purchases occur on a regular basis.

   C Unlike "Impulse Buying" purchases, "Routine Response" purchases are low-cost.

   D Unlike "Impulse Buying" purchases, "Routine Response" purchases occur on a regular basis.

10 **Which of the following consumers would be most likely to respond favorably to the advertisement?**

A repeat Cundiff customers

B dissatisfied customers of competing companies

C those wanting a high-quality clock

D those concerned with shipping costs

11 **How does the statement "It's Time To Make A Choice!" function in this advertisement?**

The statement

A emphasizes the need for consumers to make a decision to purchase.

B highlights the value of the product.

C reminds consumers of their options.

D indicates that the offer is for a limited-time only.

Certain consumers buy goods that visibly show, or flaunt, their wealth. This type of purchasing is known as "conspicuous consumption." According to some economists, there are two basic motives for the buying of conspicuous goods:

- Someone among the "higher" class buys conspicuous goods to differentiate themselves from the "lower" class.
- Someone among the "lower" class buys conspicuous goods so they will be viewed as being part of the "higher" class.

Conspicuous consumption is encouraged by companies selling products that are often very expensive and limited in availability. These companies understand that their customers want to pay more for a good, not less.

12 **Which of the following best describes a highly conspicuous good?**

A an affordable good

B a high-quality good

C a popular good

D an exclusive good

13 **What would most likely happen if a "high-end" store started lowering prices on conspicuous goods?**

A Purchases by repeat customers would stay the same.

B Purchases by repeat customers would decrease.

C Purchases by repeat customers would vary.

D Purchases by repeat customers would increase.

UNIT 5

Directions: Questions 14 and 15 refer to the following information.

Consumer confidence is a term used to describe how consumers view their financial health and the health of the overall economy. When consumer confidence is high, people are more willing to spend and borrow more money. When consumer confidence is low, people are less willing to spend and borrow money.

Economists determine the status of consumer confidence by analyzing consumer debt, spending, and savings. Information about consumer confidence can also be determined by surveys. One notable survey is the Index of Consumer Sentiment, or the ICS. This survey asks consumers several questions, including what they think the economy will be like during the next several years, and whether or not they feel that the present is a good time to purchase major items for their homes.

Several different factors can affect consumer confidence. These include global economic statistics, the stock market, the real estate market, high unemployment, and inflation. Furthermore, many economists believe that media coverage of these factors can make consumers more or less reluctant to purchase goods and services.

14 **Which of the following would most likely indicate low consumer confidence?**
   A   more people buying homes
   B   more people applying for bank loans
   C   more people placing money into savings accounts
   D   more people buying goods on credit

15 **Which newspaper headline would most likely have a positive impact on consumer confidence?**
   A   "Inflation Rate Falls"
   B   "Dow Drops in Wild Day of Trading"
   C   "Overseas Financial Policies Remain Uncertain"
   D   "Household Debt on the Rise"

Directions: Questions 16 and 17 are based on the following chart.

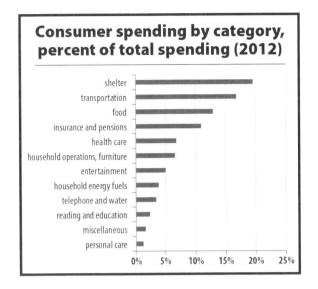

16 **How much more did consumers in 2012 spend on food than they did on reading and education?**
   A   about 3%
   B   about 5%
   C   about 10%
   D   about 13%

17 **Which of the following spending categories listed on the chart would be least likely to vary for the average consumer from month to month?**
   A   household operations, furniture
   B   entertainment
   C   personal care
   D   shelter

Interpret Flowcharts

① Learn the Skill

A flowchart is a graphic used to describe a sequence. It is a way to quickly communicate the steps of a process without using a lot of explanatory text. Learning to **interpret flowcharts** makes it easy to grasp the information they convey. Flowcharts are similar to sequence charts, but their main focus is to illustrate a process instead of providing only a sequence of events.

② Practice the Skill

By mastering the skill of interpreting flowcharts, you will improve your study and test-taking skills, especially as they relate to social studies high school equivalency tests. Examine the information and the flowchart below. Use this information to answer question 1.

The way in which businesses provide goods or services is called the production process.

A Flowcharts usually contain arrows to indicate the order of the sequence.

B Flowcharts are not always a simple line of boxes. A flowchart that demonstrates a cycle, for instance, might be circular.

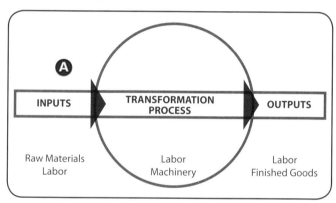

This flowchart is applicable to most businesses. For example, the input for a bakery is the labor, ovens, and ingredients needed to bake bread. After undergoing the transformation of mixing, baking, and packaging, the output is provided to the consumer.

⬛ MAKING ASSUMPTIONS

You can assume that labor is vital to almost all parts of the production process. Even if machines do a majority of the work, employees are necessary to operate and monitor the machines. Also, remember the labor involved in delivering, stocking, or selling a product.

1 **Which of the following best describes the transformation process for a candle-making business?**
   A purchasing string for wicks and blocks of wax, and hiring workers to run the melting machine
   B training workers to operate the melting machine
   C driving the trucks that deliver the candles
   D melting the wax, inserting the wicks, molding the wax, letting it cool

Directions: Questions 2 through 5 are based on the following flowchart and information.

PHASES OF A BUSINESS CYCLE

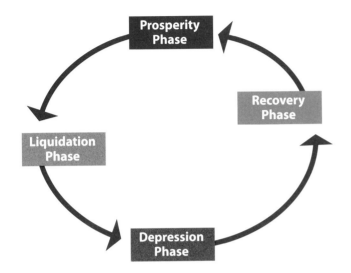

Economists use the term "business cycle" to describe recurring patterns of change in the economy. Although the specifics of a business cycle are not predictable, these four phases have been identified:

Prosperity phase: Businesses open and expand, production rises, profits increase, more money is invested, employment rate rises

Liquidation phase: Factors arise that make business less profitable, production drops, investment drops, employment drops

Depression phase: Businesses close, unemployment becomes widespread, little or no investment, demand rises for the government to reduce unemployment with legislation

Recovery phase: Factors arise that stimulate business, businesses open, investment resumes, employment rate rises

2 Where on the cycle would you expect to find the greatest number of families buying new homes?
   A   during the liquidation phase
   B   during the liquidation and depression phases
   C   during the depression phase
   D   during the recovery and prosperity phases

3 Which of the following is necessary to move from a depression phase to a recovery phase?
   A   a stimulation of the economy
   B   a drop in business profits
   C   a decrease in investment
   D   a slowdown in new business starts

4 The length of a prosperity phase is most associated with which of the following?
   A   an extended decrease in production
   B   a leveling-off in investment
   C   a decline in new business starts
   D   continued economic growth

5 Which factors were the main causes for the recovery phase during the Great Depression?
   A   the election of Franklin Roosevelt to four consecutive terms as president
   B   New Deal legislation and World War II
   C   the founding of the WPA and high unemployment
   D   the repeal of Prohibition and a reduction in lending

UNIT 5

Directions: Questions 6 through 9 are based on the following information and flowchart.

Prior to the production and distribution of a product or a good, three simple questions must be answered:

1) **What is to be produced?**
2) **How is it to be produced?**
3) **How is it to be distributed?**

The answers to the above questions drive the decisions that are made before, during, and after the development of any product or good. Such questions can be answered by examining the factors of production, which include all the raw materials, human resources, and money needed to make a given product. For example, an electrical fitting is a small, standardized part used in the electrical systems of homes and businesses. The flowchart below shows a portion of the production process of a single electrical fitting.

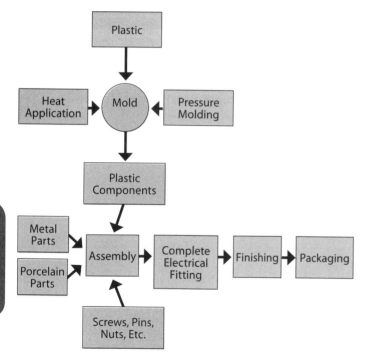

6   **The information and flowchart address which of the questions from the three factors of production?**
   A   question 1
   B   question 2
   C   question 3
   D   questions 1 and 2

7   **Which step occurs immediately before the parts of the electrical fitting are assembled?**
   A   The fitting is shipped to market.
   B   The screws and pins are packaged.
   C   The plastic components are molded.
   D   The complete electrical fitting is finished.

8   **The flowchart assumes that**
   A   the electrical fittings are already assembled.
   B   all raw materials, equipment, and human resources are available.
   C   the design of the product has yet to be determined.
   D   the fittings will be sold exclusively online.

9   **Based on the information and flowchart, which of the following statements is true?**
   A   Electrical fittings are very expensive for consumers.
   B   Electrical fittings are made entirely by hand.
   C   Electrical fittings require thousands of individual parts.
   D   Electrical fittings are mass-produced.

UNIT 5

Directions: Questions 10 through 12 are based on the information below.

In a free market economy, individuals own both the means of production and the means of distribution. In fact, many companies own and control their product distribution using their own transportation and employees to transport products to the marketplace.

Other companies, however, use distribution services. These distribution services are both international in scope and highly profitable. The cost of this additional service is passed along to customers. For example, one shipping service reported more than $1.5 billion in profits in 2013, simply from providing delivery and distribution services for companies that manufacture products.

As with companies that produce goods, businesses that provide services standardize and streamline their procedures to maximize profit. The flowchart below describes delivery patterns for a pesticide company. It displays a typical pattern of product distribution.

ACME PESTICIDE COMPANY

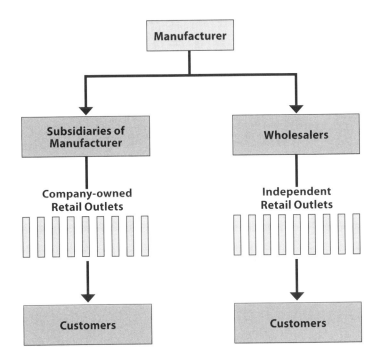

10 Based on the information and flowchart, the pesticide company distributes its product to independent retail outlets
   A directly, using its own trucks
   B indirectly, through its subsidiaries
   C indirectly, through wholesalers
   D directly, through its company-owned retail outlets

11 The flowchart assumes
   A that the pesticide already has been manufactured and packaged.
   B that the company produces many varieties of pesticide.
   C that customers buy pesticides directly from the manufacturer.
   D that the company ships directly to retail outlets.

12 Which retail outlets would likely sell the pesticide at the most cost-effective price, and why?
   A independent outlets, because they deal in volume sales
   B independent outlets, because they better understand the needs of the consumers
   C company-owned outlets, because they have a better understanding of the product
   D company-owned outlets, because they receive products through manufacturer's subsidiaries, not wholesalers

Directions: Questions 13 through 17 are based on the organizational flowchart, which illustrates the structure of a charitable foundation.

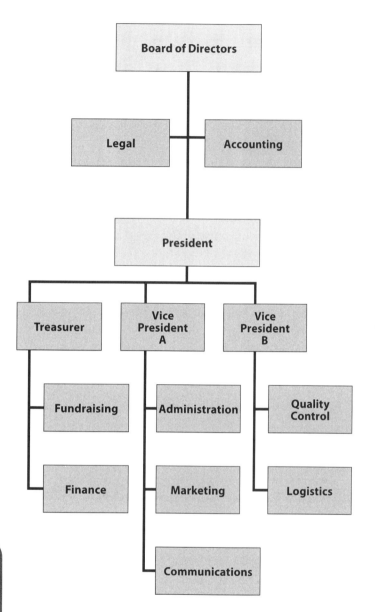

14 What additional information is included in the flowchart?
A   the length of time the foundation has existed
B   the number of people in each department
C   the pay scale for each position
D   each position's areas of responsibility

15 Which of the following two positions appear most equal in authority?
A   President and Vice President A
B   President and Vice President B
C   Vice President B and Treasurer
D   Board of Directors and President

16 A position that does not appear on the chart but can be assumed to exist is
A   Fundraising.
B   Chairman of the Board of Directors.
C   Vice President of Legal Affairs.
D   Vice President of Quality Control.

17 An important issue has arisen in Finance that could harm the foundation if it is not properly resolved. In what order should those on the chart become involved until the problem is resolved?
A   Board of Directors, Fundraising, President
B   Board of Directors, President, Vice President
C   Fundraising, Treasurer, Board of Directors
D   Treasurer, President, Board of Directors

13 The flowchart shows which of the following?
A   levels of annual salaries
B   levels of productivity
C   levels of authority
D   levels of efficiency

UNIT 5

Multiple Causes and Effects

1 Learn the Skill

Not every cause-and-effect relationship is simple. Many causes can contribute to a single result, and a single event or situation may result in multiple effects. Knowing how to identify **multiple causes and effects** will help you form a complete understanding of the subject you are studying. It will also help you be more aware of historical trends.

2 Practice the Skill

By learning to identify multiple causes and effects, you will improve your study and test-taking skills, especially as they relate to social studies high school equivalency tests. Examine the information and the bar graph below. Use this information to answer question 1.

A Inflation causes a chain reaction of events, such as rising prices and fewer purchases.

B Inflation is the cause. Wars, problems with the food supply, and political unrest are some of the effects.

One important area of macroeconomic study is inflation. **A** Inflation occurs when the supply of money exceeds the goods and services available. This causes the value of the money to fall and prices to rise. This, in turn, discourages people from making purchases. The effects are felt in all sectors of the economy and all segments of society.

Inflation and the economic instability it spawns have been known to cause wars, problems in the food supply, and political unrest. Developing nations are in the most danger from inflation.

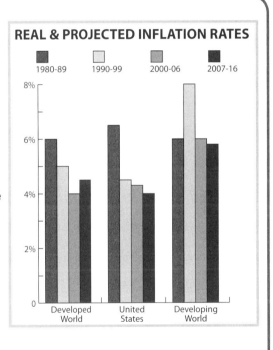

REAL & PROJECTED INFLATION RATES

■ 1980-89   □ 1990-99   ▨ 2000-06   ■ 2007-16

UNIT 5

MAKING ASSUMPTIONS

You might assume that having more money than can be spent is good for an economy. The information on this page explains why that is not true.

1 **Which part of the world is most affected by inflation?**

   A The United States is most affected.

   B The developing world is most affected.

   C The developed world is most affected.

   D All parts of the world economy are affected equally.

③ Apply the Skill

Directions: Questions 2 through 5 are based on the information below.

The cause-and-effect relationship between supply and demand is a strong determing factor of prices.

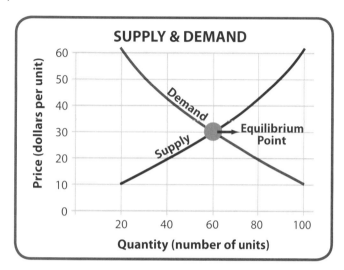

SUPPLY & DEMAND

According to the economic laws of supply and demand, people will pay more for something they want when less of it is available. On the other hand, if there is more of a supply of a good or service than people demand, the supplier will lower the price to coax people into buying more of it.

The point at which the price of an item and the amount of demand are the same is called the equilibrium point. At prices above the equilibrium point, demand drops. If the price becomes too high, demand may disappear completely. However, if the price becomes too low, the seller will be unable to make a profit and will stop producing the item.

Supply and demand are themselves the effects of other causes. For example, the effects of inflation can decrease demand and force down an item's price. Inflation can also raise the cost of producing an item, resulting in a higher price, which can also lead to a decrease in demand.

2 Which of the following statements is true?
  A Supply, demand, and inflation are each basic causes of economic activity.
  B Supply, demand, and inflation operate independently of one another.
  C Supply, demand, and inflation do not influence the economy.
  D Supply, demand, and inflation are each influenced by many causes.

3 Based on the information, what needs to exist for the law of supply and demand to function freely?
  A competition
  B government regulation of prices
  C inflation
  D a growing economy

4 What happens to the price and supply of an item once it is above the equilibrium point on the graph?
  A Price goes up; supply goes down.
  B Price goes up; supply goes up.
  C Price goes down; supply goes down.
  D Price goes down; supply goes up.

5 What is one disadvantage of price regulation?
  A Demand for items decreases.
  B Costs of items increase greatly.
  C When potential profit is limited, there is less incentive to produce goods.
  D When potential profit is limited, there is more incentive to produce goods.

Directions: Questions 6 through 8 are based on the information below.

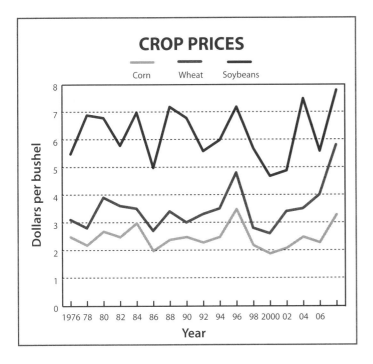

CROP PRICES

Corn   Wheat   Soybeans

Dollars per bushel

8
7
6
5
4
3
2
1
0

1976 78 80 82 84 86 88 90 92 94 96 98 2000 02 04 06

Year

In the United States, prices are set by the economic concept of supply and demand. When a product's supply is higher than its demand, the result is a surplus. When demand is higher than supply, the result is a shortage. Surpluses and shortages help determine prices. For example, a surplus of corn may result in lower prices to help encourage sales. When a shortage occurs, sellers raise prices because people are willing to pay more for the good or product.

Corn prices rose again in 2007. Increased sales of corn to overseas nations, combined with a 30 percent increase in the amount of corn used to produce the fuel called ethanol, resulted in a national shortage and a higher price per bushel. Higher corn prices also resulted in higher prices for foods that use corn as an ingredient. A third effect resulted from farmers using more of their land to grow corn. This meant that fewer acres were devoted to crops such as wheat and soybeans. The dip in wheat and soybean production led prices for those crops to rise also.

6 How does an increase in the price of corn lead to an increase in the price of food products containing corn?
  A Food manufacturers must use more expensive substitutes for corn.
  B Corn must be imported from other nations, which can be costly to consumers.
  C Food manufacturers pass along corn-related price increases to consumers.
  D The supply of corn outweighs the demand for corn-related products.

7 Which of the following is a by-product of increased ethanol production?
  A a drop in the price of soybean and wheat products
  B a rise in the prices of soybean and wheat products
  C a decrease in overall corn production
  D an increase in the price of ethanol

8 Based on supply and demand, if a sharp and sudden increase occurred in the price of corn, then
  A consumers would buy more corn and corn products, forcing the price of corn to decrease.
  B consumers would buy less corn and corn products, forcing the price to decrease.
  C farmers would grow less corn and more wheat and soybeans.
  D farmers would grow more corn and sell it cheaply to decrease market prices.

Directions: Questions 9 through 11 are based on the information below.

Supply and demand are major factors in the rise and fall of gasoline prices. Shortages and fears of shortages can cause these prices to fluctuate in a short period of time. As developing countries grow more industrialized, global demand for gasoline increases. From the beginning of 2005 through the middle of 2008, overall U.S. gasoline prices rose steadily. At that time, the average price of a gallon of gasoline in the United States was $1.78. By the middle of 2008, the price had reached a national average of nearly $4 per gallon. However, by the end of 2008, reduced demand sent prices back down to around $1.60 per gallon.

These changes occurred because of increases and decreases in crude oil prices. From 2005 to mid-2008, the price per barrel of crude oil rose from $42 to more than $100 per barrel. By the end of 2008, the price fell to less than $50 per barrel. In addition to free market effects, a number of other factors can and do play a role in gasoline prices. Developments in world politics sometimes disturb market forces. Oil prices are also subject to manipulation. The Organization of Petroleum Exporting Countries (OPEC) accounts for 40 percent of the world's crude oil production. This group routinely limits the amount of oil its members export. This results in higher gasoline and oil prices worldwide.

9 Why does an increase in the price of crude oil lead to a rise in the price of gasoline?

   A Both are sold at gas stations.
   B Crude oil is made from gasoline.
   C OPEC exports both gasoline and oil.
   D Gasoline is made from crude oil.

10 Why do OPEC's limits on oil exports lead to increased global gasoline prices?

   A Limits on exports increase the supply of oil.
   B Limits cause people to buy more gasoline.
   C Limits force people to drive more.
   D Limits on oil create a shortage.

11 Over which of the following factors in the price of gasoline could small U.S. businesses exercise control?

   A a global increase in the use of solar power
   B competition between neighboring gas stations
   C the discovery of new oil reserves in Saudi Arabia
   D a disruption in North American oil pipelines

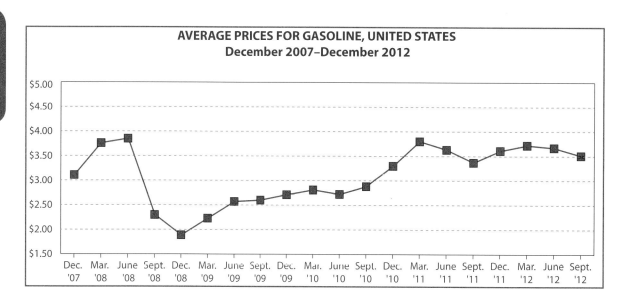

AVERAGE PRICES FOR GASOLINE, UNITED STATES
December 2007–December 2012

Lesson 4 | Multiple Causes and Effects

Directions: Questions 12 through 16 refer to the following information.

Economists make frequent use of economic indicators. An economic indicator is a statistic that often, but not always, predicts in which direction the U.S. economy is heading.

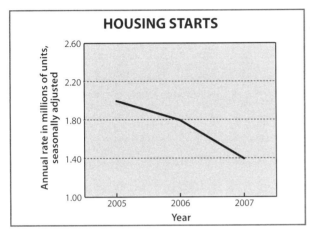

HOUSING STARTS

The above graph shows housing starts for a recent period. Housing starts are the number of new homes being built nationally. The number is considered a leading economic indicator. Beginning in 2006, U.S. housing starts began to decline. In addition, many people who had borrowed money to pay for their homes could no longer make their loan payments. Lenders took possession of the homes, resulting in an increase of empty houses for sale.

In many cases, the problems were caused by the type of loans taken out by homebuyers. These adjustable-rate loans offered affordable payments in the beginning, but the amount owed each month was connected to economic conditions. As economic expansion slowed, home payments grew. Many could no longer afford them. Lenders foreclosed on loans, taking ownership of the houses.

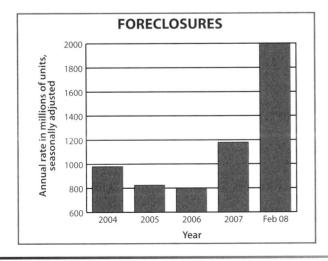

FORECLOSURES

12 Why is a large number of housing starts considered a positive economic indicator?
  A It indicates positive economic activity.
  B It indicates relocation.
  C It indicates widespread foreclosures.
  D It indicates negative economic activity.

13 How might a decrease in housing starts affect the construction and carpentry industries?
  A Their profits will increase.
  B Their profits will decline.
  C Their profits will remain steady.
  D They will generate new jobs.

14 What can you conclude about the effects of a slowing economy?
  A They are minor and short-term.
  B They lead to prosperity.
  C They do not matter at all.
  D They are many and widespread.

15 Why might housing starts decrease if foreclosures increase?
  A There are fewer homes available.
  B Construction companies will build more homes hoping the market will turn.
  C Fewer homes will be built because there are more existing homes on the market.
  D An increase in foreclosures makes many buyers fearful of taking loans to purchase new homes.

16 What factors caused the increase in foreclosures?
  A the number of housing starts and home prices
  B poor economic conditions and the number of lenders
  C adjustable-rate mortgages and generally poor economic conditions
  D the decrease in housing starts and adjustable-rate mortgages

Compare and Contrast Visuals

① Learn the Skill

When you **compare** two or more **visual elements**, you consider the similarities between them. Details about each item are used to gain insight into the other items.

After you have compared the items, you can **contrast** them. To contrast is to focus only on the differences. As you contrast items, you prepare yourself to analyze why the differences exist.

② Practice the Skill

By mastering the skill of comparing and contrasting, you will improve your study and test-taking skills, especially as they relate to social studies high school equivalency tests. Examine the graphs below. Then answer the question that follows.

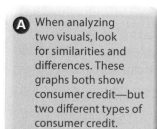

A When analyzing two visuals, look for similarities and differences. These graphs both show consumer credit—but two different types of consumer credit.

B Look for ways to connect the information in order to answer the question. In this case, study the trends beginning in 2009 and decide what they both support.

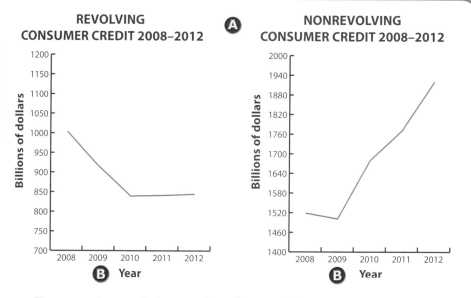

A REVOLVING CONSUMER CREDIT 2008–2012

A NONREVOLVING CONSUMER CREDIT 2008–2012

There are two main types of credit—revolving and nonrevolving. Revolving credit is a line of credit with a pre-approved limit, such as a credit card. As you make charges, less credit is available to you. You can pay the balance off at any time, or over time, but you also must pay finance charges on any unpaid balance. Nonrevolving credit is a loan paid back on a schedule with interest, such as a car loan or a home loan.

☑ TEST-TAKING TIPS

Examine graphics in testing materials thoroughly. Be sure you understand the information shown before trying to answer the questions.

1 **Which of the following does the shift in each graph most likely indicate?**
   A an upswing in the economy
   B increased fear of an economic downturn
   C the beginning of a recession
   D a decrease in the amount of credit available

UNIT 5

Directions: Questions 2 through 5 are based on the table and graph below.

AVERAGE ANNUAL EARNINGS BY EDUCATION: 2012	
EDUCATION LEVEL	**AVG. ANNUAL EARNINGS**
No High School Diploma	$22,900
High School Diploma or Equivalent	$30,000
Bachelor's Degree	$46,900
Advanced Degree	$59,600

Source: nces.ed.gov, accessed 2014

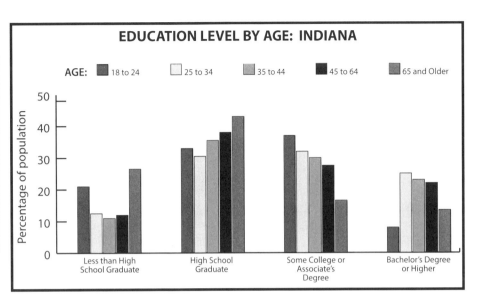

EDUCATION LEVEL BY AGE: INDIANA

2 **What can you infer by comparing and contrasting information on the two graphics?**
A Younger people have the best-paying jobs.
B Most people retire at age 65.
C People do not need a higher education to be successful.
D There is a connection between level of education and degree of economic success.

3 **Based on the graphics, which of the following is possible?**
A Twenty-five percent of Indiana residents aged 25 to 34 earn on average more than $46,000 per year.
B Most Indiana residents aged 65 and older only make, on average, around $23,000 per year.
C Indiana residents aged 18 to 24 have the highest average annual salaries.
D Most Indiana residents aged 35 to 44 have a Bachelor's Degree or higher.

4 **What cannot be determined by the graphics?**
A the average annual earnings for people with high school equivalency certificates
B which percentage of 30-year-old Hoosiers graduated from high school
C the percentage of Indiana residents with an earning potential of more than $60,000 per year
D the earnings limitations for people without a high school diploma or equivalent

5 **Braden, a 20-year-old Indiana resident, has just earned his high school equivalency certificate. What is his average annual earnings potential?**
A around $20,000
B around $30,000
C around $40,000
D around $50,000

UNIT 5

Directions: Questions 6 through 9 are based on the graphs below.

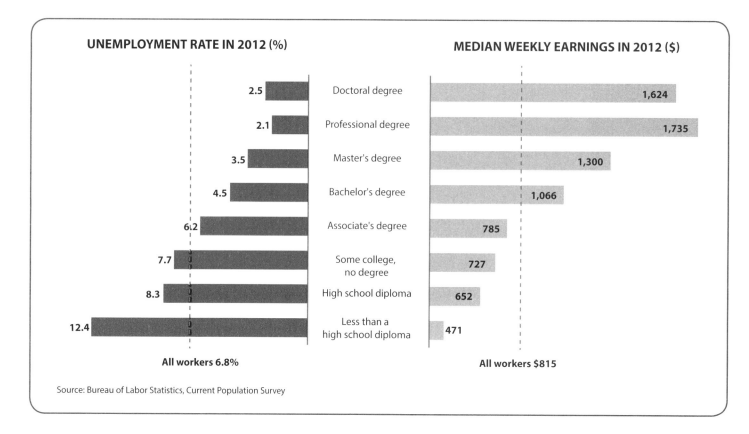

UNEMPLOYMENT RATE IN 2012 (%)

	Degree	
2.5	Doctoral degree	
2.1	Professional degree	
3.5	Master's degree	
4.5	Bachelor's degree	
6.2	Associate's degree	
7.7	Some college, no degree	
8.3	High school diploma	
12.4	Less than a high school diploma	

All workers 6.8%

MEDIAN WEEKLY EARNINGS IN 2012 ($)

Doctoral degree	1,624
Professional degree	1,735
Master's degree	1,300
Bachelor's degree	1,066
Associate's degree	785
Some college, no degree	727
High school diploma	652
Less than a high school diploma	471

All workers $815

Source: Bureau of Labor Statistics, Current Population Survey

6 In which of the following ways are median weekly earnings and unemployment related to each other?

A The higher the median weekly earnings, the lower the rate of unemployment.

B The lower the rate of unemployment, the lower the median weekly earnings.

C The higher the median weekly earnings, the higher the rate of unemployment.

D The higher the degree level, the lower both the unemployment rate and median weekly income.

7 Based on the graphs, which of the following is most likely true of a person with a bachelor's degree (4-year degree)?

A The person is unlikely to find a job and earn less than $1,300 per week.

B The person is likely to find a job and earn about $1,700 per week.

C The person is unlikely to find a job and will not earn more than $750 per week.

D The person is likely to find a job and earn about $1,000 per week.

8 Which of the following occupations would fall into both of these categories: second-lowest rate of unemployment and second-highest median weekly earnings?

A fast-food worker

B college professor

C teacher

D licensed electrician

9 A woman makes the individual choice not to complete college, and instead to begin working. What can you conclude about this woman?

A Her chances of finding a well-paying job are much better than the chances of a person with a bachelor's degree.

B She will be unable to find a job easily where she makes a median weekly income of more than $500.

C She will make more money and more easily find a job than a person who has not completed high school.

D Her income is more likely to be above average than the income of a person with a professional degree.

Directions: Questions 10 through 13 are based on the graphs below.

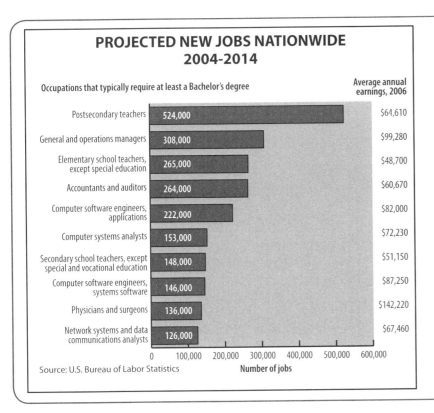

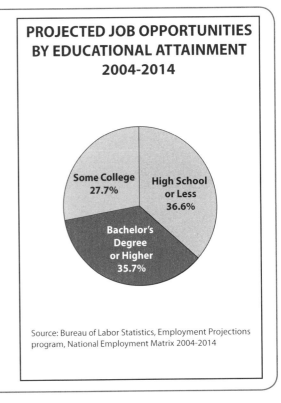

10 Which conclusion can be drawn by comparing and contrasting the bar and circle graphs?

A   College degrees are not cost-effective.

B   More jobs will be available to those with a Bachelor's Degree than those with some college.

C   Higher-paying jobs will be available to those with a high school diploma.

D   There are few openings in well-paid fields.

11 Based on the graphs, which of the following statements is correct?

A   The average annual income of accountants and auditors is more than that of computer software engineers.

B   More than twice as many elementary school teachers than physicians will be needed in the next ten years.

C   Most of the projected job opportunities will require some college or a Bachelor's Degree or higher.

D   36.6% of the jobs listed in the first graph require a high school diploma or less.

12 Which two career fields provide the greatest number of high-paying jobs?

A   education and computer technology

B   education and medicine

C   accounting and medicine

D   medicine and computer technology

13 Based on the data in the circle graph, why is it logical that the highest number of projected new jobs in the bar graph is in the field of postsecondary teaching?

A   because postsecondary teachers have the highest average annual income

B   because improvements in health care will mean fewer doctors are needed

C   because only 36.6% of people will have a high school diploma

D   more people will seek postsecondary education because most jobs in the future will require at least some college

GROSS PAY	AMOUNT OF PAY BEFORE DEDUCTIONS
Pre-tax Deductions	Deductions taken out before taxes. They are not themselves taxed.
After-tax Deductions	Deductions taken out after taxes. They are taxed at the same percentage as the gross pay.
Federal Withholding Deduction	Deduction put toward federal income tax obligation
State Tax	Deduction put toward state income tax obligation
Local Tax	Deduction put toward local income tax obligation
FICA	Social Security taxes
401(k)	Voluntary deduction requested by worker to go into retirement fund
Net Pay	Amount given to worker after deductions

Gross	$2,000.00
Federal Witholding	$ 500.00
FICA	$ 150.00
State	$ 100.00
Local	$ 24.00
Net	$1,226.00

14 **What is the difference between gross and net pay?**

A Gross pay is the same amount as net pay.

B Net pay is always more than gross pay.

C Gross pay is before deductions, while net pay is after deductions.

D Net pay is before deductions, while gross pay is after deductions.

15 **What can you infer about a 401(k)?**

A 401(k) monies never come out of a person's paycheck.

B Not everyone has 401(k) monies removed from his or her paycheck.

C The government randomly removes 401(k) monies from an individual's paycheck.

D 401(k) monies are a part of Federal Withholdings.

16 **Which conclusion can be drawn from comparing and contrasting the pay stub and table?**

A Net pay is the smallest amount that will appear on your pay stub.

B Gross pay is the largest amount that will appear on your pay stub.

C The table provides information to the employee, while the pay stub provides information to the employer.

D Paying taxes is optional.

17 **How much is taken from the sample pay stub for Social Security taxes?**

A $2,000

B $ 500

C $ 150

D $ 100

UNIT 5

Draw Conclusions from Multiple Sources

① Learn the Skill

In Unit 2, you learned that an **inference** is an educated guess based on available facts and evidence. Later, in Unit 3, you learned that a **conclusion** is a judgment you make by putting together two or more inferences. When learning about social studies, you will often be asked to make inferences and use them to **draw conclusions from multiple sources** of information.

② Practice the Skill

By mastering the skill of drawing conclusions from multiple sources, you will improve your study and test-taking skills, especially as they relate to social studies high school equivalency tests. Examine the circle graphs below. Then answer the question that follows.

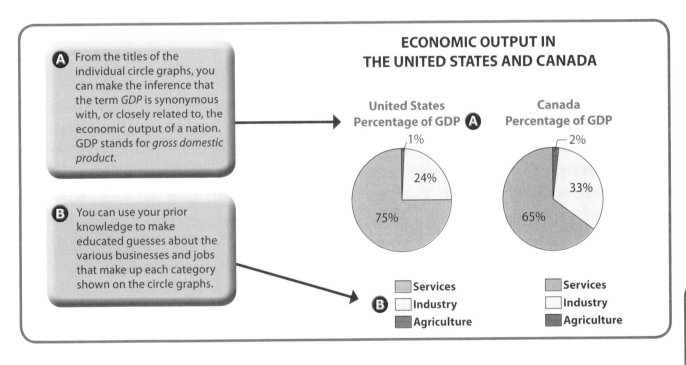

A From the titles of the individual circle graphs, you can make the inference that the term *GDP* is synonymous with, or closely related to, the economic output of a nation. GDP stands for *gross domestic product*.

B You can use your prior knowledge to make educated guesses about the various businesses and jobs that make up each category shown on the circle graphs.

ECONOMIC OUTPUT IN THE UNITED STATES AND CANADA

United States Percentage of GDP **A**
1%
24%
75%

Canada Percentage of GDP
2%
33%
65%

B
☐ Services
☐ Industry
☐ Agriculture

☐ Services
☐ Industry
☐ Agriculture

UNIT 5

USING LOGIC

Consider whether the information contained in the sources is similar to or different from one another. Also think about whether the information presented in one graph gives you new insight on the information in the other graph.

1 Based on these circle graphs, which of the following conclusions can be drawn?
  A Farming is more important to the economy of the United States than to that of Canada.
  B The United States and Canada have similar economies.
  C The United States is more industrialized than Canada.
  D Canada relies more on the service industry than the United States.

Directions: Questions 2 and 3 are based on the graph below.

The term *unemployment* refers to the state in which a person who is willing and able to work cannot find a job. For industrial nations, unemployment typically occurs during periods of depression and recession.

U.S. EMPLOYMENT RATE, 2002–2012

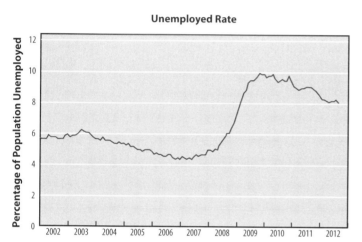

Source: Bureau of Labor Statistics

2 **Which of the following statements accurately describes unemployment in the United States?**
  A   The nation's unemployment rate has risen steadily since 2002.
  B   The unemployment rate rose to the highest levels in a decade during 2009–2010.
  C   The rate of employed people in the nation has never dropped to less than 90 percent.
  D   The nation experienced continuous improvement in unemployment rate after 2007.

3 **In which period on the graph did the United States likely experience its most severe recession?**
  A   From 2002–2004
  B   From 2004–2006
  C   From 2008–2010
  D   From 2010–2012

Directions: Questions 4 and 5 are based on the information below.

The Dow Jones Industrial Average is a set of indicators that measures changes in the performances of different groupings of stocks. Today, the industrial average includes 30 stocks. The number and selection of stocks have changed over time in order to reflect changes in the U.S. economy. Many people use the Dow Jones Industrial Average as an indicator for both the growth of the stock market and the strength of the economy.

DOW JONES INDUSTRIAL AVERAGE, 1985–2010			
YEAR	DOW AT START OF YEAR	DOW AT CLOSE OF YEAR	CHANGE
1985	1198.87	1546.67	+27.6%
1990	2810.15	2633.66	−4.34%
1995	3838.48	5117.12	+33.45
2000	11357.51	10786.85	−6.18%
2005	10729.43	10717.50	−0.61%
2010	10,428.05	11,577.51	+9.25%

4 **Which of the following most likely occurred between 1995 and 2000?**
  A   The U.S. economy grew significantly stronger.
  B   Unemployment skyrocketed.
  C   Many new businesses went bankrupt.
  D   The United States entered a period of recession.

5 **Why might the year 2000 be seen as a better economic year than 1990?**
  A   The percentage of increase during the year 2000 was higher than that of 1990.
  B   The year 2000 was a presidential election year.
  C   The Dow had more stocks listed in 2000 than in 1990.
  D   Despite a decrease over the course of the year, the Dow started significantly higher in 2000 than 1990.

Directions: Questions 6 through 9 are based on the information below.

For a nation such as the United States, international trade represents a crucial part of the national economy. Many governments impose policies or restrictions to protect their interests in international trade. A nation's balance of trade is the relationship between its exports and imports. A positive balance of trade results when the nation exports more than it imports.

For many years, the United States stood as one of the world's strongest nations in international trade. However, beginning in the 1960s, the nation's position began to diminish. In most years since 1970, the United States has reported a negative trade balance. This means that the nation has imported more than it has exported.

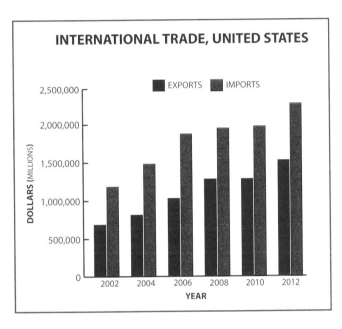

INTERNATIONAL TRADE, UNITED STATES

6   **When does a nation achieve a positive balance of trade?**
   A   when it exports to more countries than it imports from
   B   when it imports and exports the same value of products
   C   when the value of its exports is more than the value of its imports
   D   when the value of its imports is more than the value of its exports

7   **Approximately when did the balance of trade in the United States begin to reflect its diminishing strength in international trade?**
   A   1960
   B   1980
   C   2000
   D   2012

8   **In which of the following years did the United States experience its largest international trade deficit?**
   A   2002
   B   2006
   C   2010
   D   2012

9   **What conclusion can you draw about the balance of trade in the United States based on these sources?**
   A   The U.S. balance of trade frequently fluctuates between positive and negative.
   B   The U.S. economy has grown stronger over time due to the positive effects of international trade.
   C   Government policies and restrictions have not prevented the trade balance from remaining negative.
   D   The U.S. has improved its balance of trade by dramatically increasing production.

Directions: Questions 10 through 13 are based on the information below.

A housing start is a new home for which construction has already begun. New homes for which construction permits have been issued, but construction has not commenced, do not qualify as housing starts. Many people view the number of housing starts as an important economic indicator.

10 Construction began on approximately how many new homes in 1971?

A 2,000

B 1,500,000

C 2,000,000

D 2,500,000

11 Which of the following would you expect to coincide with a significant increase in housing starts?

A rising unemployment

B an increasing Gross Domestic Product

C a negative trade balance

D high levels of immigration

12 Between which two years did the number of housing starts experience the largest decrease?

A 1969 and 1970

B 1973 and 1974

C 2005 and 2006

D 2006 and 2007

13 What can you conclude about housing starts in the United States based on these sources?

A The number of U.S. housing starts is directly related to the health of the U.S. economy.

B The number of U.S. housing starts has increased significantly over the past 40 years.

C The number of housing starts in the United States is highly volatile.

D The United States economy expanded rapidly from 1971–1975 and 2005–2007.

Individual investment options vary greatly according to the potential risks and rewards associated with them. Some investments offer minimized risks through insurance or guarantees of repayment, while others offer no promises of protection to investors. The yield of an investment is a figure, given as a percentage, which measures the return that an investor receives on his or her investment. The FDIC protects savings account investments, which minimizes the risk involved. Because of this security, savings accounts tend to offer low interest rates to investors.

Like savings accounts, certificates of deposit, or CDs, are FDIC insured. However, because money cannot be withdrawn from a CD until it reaches maturity, CDs often offer higher interest rates to investors. U.S. government bonds are guaranteed by the government, ensuring little risk for investors. As a result, they also feature low interest rates.

The volatility of the stock market, and the lack of protection offered to investors, makes both significant returns and losses possible. Because of the high risks and high rewards associated with it, the stock market is best suited for long-term investing. A long-term investor can ride out turbulent times.

14 An individual wishing to pursue an aggressive short-term investment strategy, with little regard for risk, would be best advised to do what?

A purchase large quantities of government bonds

B purchase shares of stock on the stock market

C make the minimum possible investment in numerous different holdings

D open multiple savings accounts to secure a variety of interest rates

15 What can be concluded about investing?

A All investors should have savings accounts.

B All investments are high-risk.

C Everyone should invest in the stock market.

D All investors should make decisions based on their short- and long-term needs.

16 Which investment would be best for an individual seeking to invest $50 with little risk?

A a savings account

B a CD

C a government bond

D the stock market

17 Based on the information, which of the following is accurate?

An individual investing $10,000 in stock of the online search engine in January 2008 would have

A experienced a yield of more than 30% over the next year.

B faced little risk in his or her investment.

C lost more than $5,000 by January 2009.

D gained a higher yield than if he or she had invested in government bonds.

INDIVIDUAL INVESTMENT OPTIONS			
INVESTMENT TYPE	**YIELD**	**MINIMUM INVESTMENT**	**RISK LEVEL**
Savings Account	3.08%	$1	Low
CD	4.26%	$500	Low
Government Bond	3.99%	$100	Low
Share of stock in online search engine (Jan. '07–Jan. '08)	34.85%	None	High
Share of stock in online search engine (Jan. '08–Jan. '09)	-51.09%	None	High

UNIT 5

Interpret Pictographs

① Learn the Skill

Pictographs are visuals that use symbols to illustrate data in chart form. Pictographs are versatile because their symbols can represent any type of item. These symbols can also represent any quantity of the featured item. A single symbol could represent one dollar of income or one million members of a population group.

② Practice the Skill

By mastering the skill of interpreting pictographs, you will improve your study and test-taking skills, especially as they relate to social studies high school equivalency tests. Examine the pictograph below. Then answer the question that follows.

A The key plays a crucial role in your interpretation of a pictograph. It identifies the symbol used in the pictograph, and also gives its value so you can then calculate the values represented on the chart itself.

B At times, the symbol will appear in partial or incomplete form. In these instances, the incomplete symbols represent some portion of the full quantity indicated by the full symbol.

Countries and economies are interdependent, meaning that they rely on each other for goods and services. The amount of trade between two countries can be a measure of their interdependence.

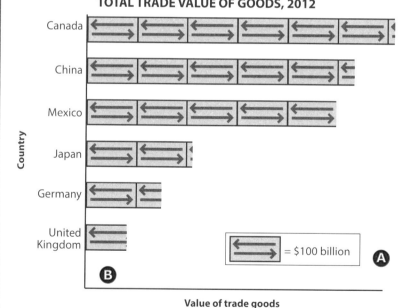

TOP U.S. TRADE PARTNERS: TOTAL TRADE VALUE OF GOODS, 2012

MAKING ASSUMPTIONS

You can assume that when interpreting a pictograph, you will be asked to estimate the values represented by the symbols on the chart.

1 **Which of the following is the approximate total value of goods traded between the United States and Japan?**
   A $100 billion
   B $150 billion
   C $200 billion
   D $250 billion

Directions: Questions 2 and 3 are based on the pictograph below.

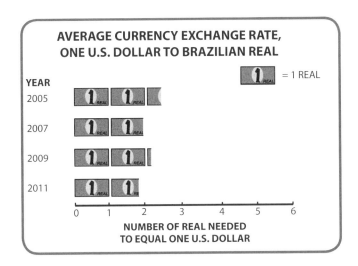

AVERAGE CURRENCY EXCHANGE RATE,
ONE U.S. DOLLAR TO BRAZILIAN REAL

2 **Which of the following was the approximate value of the U.S. dollar in 2007?**
   A 1 real
   B 1.5 real
   C 2 real
   D 2.5 real

3 **Based on the information in the pictograph, which of the following conclusions can you draw?**
   A The value of the real changes dramatically from year to year.
   B The value of the dollar decreased between 2007 and 2011.
   C The value of the real decreased between 2007 and 2011.
   D The exchange rate for these currencies would have increased in 2013.

Directions: Questions 4 and 5 are based on the pictograph below.

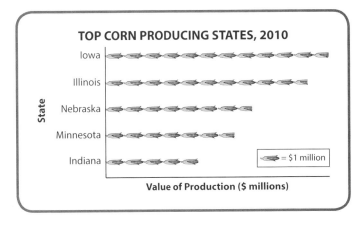

TOP CORN PRODUCING STATES, 2010

4 **Which of the following statements is true based on the information in the pictograph?**
   A The value of corn production in Iowa exceeded $11 million.
   B Illinois produced about $2 million worth of corn less than Iowa.
   C The value of corn production in Nebraska remained below $5 million.
   D Minnesota ranked third in the nation in the value of corn production.

5 **What can be inferred from the information in the pictograph?**
   A Corn is the crop most grown in Illinois.
   B Ohio does not produce corn.
   C Iowa produces more than twice as much corn as Nebraska.
   D The Midwest grows most of the corn produced in the United States.

UNIT 5

Directions: Questions 6 through 8 are based on the pictograph below.

U.S. EMPLOYEES BY ECONOMIC SECTOR, 2010

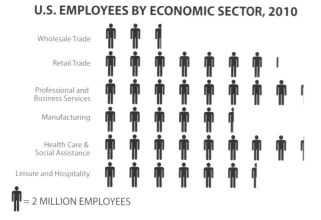

= 2 MILLION EMPLOYEES

6 **Based on the pictograph, which of the following statements is correct?**

   A   About 20 million people work in Wholesale Trade and Retail Trade combined.

   B   The Health Care and Social Assistance sector employs about twice as many people as Manufacturing.

   C   The Leisure and Hospitality sector employs the largest number of people.

   D   Fewer than 5 million people work in Wholesale Trade.

7 **In 2010, there were 19,513,100 people working in state and local government. If you were to add this sector to the pictograph, which of the following number of symbols would appear next to this sector?**

   A   8 ½
   B   9 ¾
   C   10 ¾
   D   19 ½

8 **Also in 2010, there were 64,000 people working for the legislative and judicial branches of the federal government. If you were to add this sector to the pictograph, which of the following would first need to be changed for the pictograph to be effective?**

   A   The economic sectors would need to be listed alphabetically.

   B   The icon of the person would need to change.

   C   The title would need to change.

   D   The key would need to change.

Directions: Questions 9 through 11 are based on the pictograph below.

U.S. FEDERAL BUDGET DEFICIT OR SURPLUS, 2000–2010

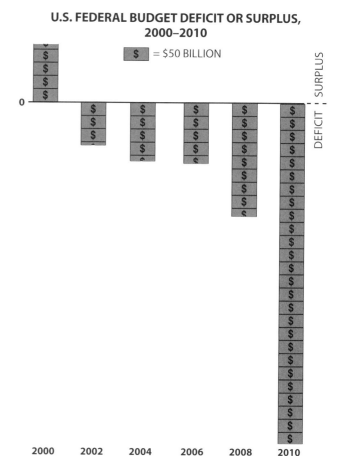

$ = $50 BILLION

9 **Based on the pictograph, which of the following describes the U.S. government's budget in 2004?**

   A   It broke even.
   B   It spent about $250 billion less than it made.
   C   It spent about $350 billion more than it made.
   D   It ran a larger deficit than it did in 2002.

10 **Which of the following could help explain the budgetary changes that occurred between 2000 and 2004?**

   A   higher taxes
   B   a reduction of federal aid programs
   C   funding for the war in Iraq
   D   an influx of new taxpayers

11 **Which years did the deficit increase the most?**

   A   between 2002 and 2004
   B   between 2004 and 2006
   C   between 2006 and 2008
   D   between 2008 and 2010

Directions: Questions 12 and 13 are based on the following information.

PRICE PER BUSHEL OF U.S. SOYBEANS, 2007–2011

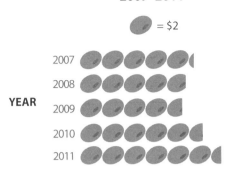

The United States has a mixed economy. It does not depend solely on supply and demand as does a market economy. Instead, some aspects are controlled by the government.

An example of this is subsidies. A subsidy is a benefit, typically in the form of cash, given by the government to groups or individuals. The purpose is to remove some type of burden. Subsidies are generally provided in certain industries for the best interest of the public. For example, agricultural subsidies, such as soybean subsidies, may be given to farmers. They receive subsidies so that they can sell at a low market price, but still make enough money to be profitable.

12 Which of the following could have caused the change in price per bushel for soybeans from 2009 to 2010?
  A   deflation in the U.S. economy
  B   a shortened growing season due to inclement weather
  C   decreased demand for soybeans and soy products
  D   an increase in the supply of soybeans

13 Subsidies often guarantee a minimum price for a product or good. If the market price is below this price, farmers will receive a subsidy. In which of the following years would farmers have received a subsidy if the minimum guaranteed price had been $9.65 per bushel?
  A   2007
  B   2008
  C   2009
  D   2010

Directions: Questions 14 through 16 are based on the following information.

U.S. UNEMPLOYMENT RATE
For Persons (16 Years & Older)

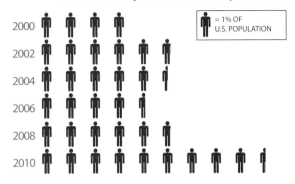

The unemployment rate is a commonly used economic indicator. The percent reported as the unemployment rate is the percent of people who are available and looking for work who do not have jobs. A person may be either employed, unemployed, or not in the labor force. Those who are not in the labor force are not calculated in the unemployment rate.

14 In which of the following ways would you describe the U.S. unemployment rate in the 10-year period represented by the pictograph?
  A   It experienced one sharp increase.
  B   It experienced several sharp increases.
  C   It increased steadily.
  D   It decreased steadily.

15 Between which of the following two years can you conclude that the U.S. economy experienced a sharp downturn based on the unemployment rate?
  A   between 2002 and 2004
  B   between 2004 and 2006
  C   between 2006 and 2008
  D   between 2008 and 2010

16 Between which of the following two years can you conclude that the U.S. economy experienced an upturn based on the unemployment rate?
  A   between 2002 and 2004
  B   between 2004 and 2006
  C   between 2006 and 2008
  D   between 2008 and 2010

Directions: Questions 17 through 20 are based on the information below.

The concept of interdependence is visible in exports and imports among countries. Countries may be dependent on other countries for the products they either cannot produce themselves, or cannot produce as efficiently as other countries. Countries will tend to export goods they produce efficiently to other countries and import the goods they produce less efficiently from other countries.

In these pictographs, the exports describe U.S. goods sent to Japan, and the imports describe Japanese goods sent to the United States.

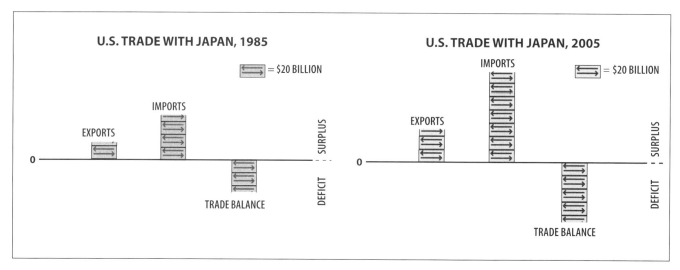

17 **Based on these pictographs, which of the following statements is correct?**

   A The United States imported about $40 billion from Japan in 1985.

   B The United States nearly achieved a trade balance with Japan in 1985.

   C The value of U.S. exports to Japan doubled between 1985 and 2005.

   D The value of U.S. imports from Japan changed only slightly during the period between 1985 and 2005.

18 **Which of the following describes U.S. trade with Japan in 2005?**

   A Exports totaled about $75 billion.

   B Imports totaled about $200 billion.

   C The trade surplus was about $25 billion.

   D The trade deficit was more than $80 billion.

19 **How did trade between the United States and Japan change from 1985 to 2005?**

   A The U.S. trade deficit grew by about $40 billion.

   B The value of exports increased by more than the value of imports.

   C The U.S. trade balance moved from a small surplus to a large deficit.

   D The value of imports increased by about $20 billion.

20 **In which of the following ways might the U.S. government seek to change its 2005 trade balance with Japan?**

   A lower taxes on imports

   B impose strict tariffs on exports to Japan

   C remove all trade restrictions between the two nations

   D provide tax relief to U.S. companies manufacturing technology products

UNIT 5

Interpret Multi-Bar and Line Graphs

① Learn the Skill

When studying economics, you will often encounter data presented in **multi-bar and line graphs**. Like single-bar and line graphs, these visuals can be used to compare values and to show changes over time. However, because they use more than one bar or line, they also allow for the comparison of varied, but connected, data over time.

② Practice the Skill

By mastering the skill of interpreting multi-bar and line graphs, you will improve your study and test-taking skills, especially as they relate to social studies high school equivalency tests. Examine the double-bar graph below. Then answer the question that follows.

A By studying the bars of a double-bar graph, you can compare two quantities at a given time, as well as the ways in which these quantities change over time.

B The key of a double-bar graph will typically use color or shading to identify what each bar represents. In this graph, one bar represents the average annual mortgage rate, while the other represents the average annual prime interest rate.

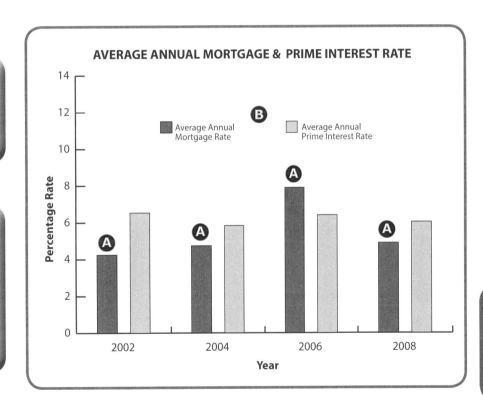

MAKING ASSUMPTIONS

You can typically assume that an author includes information in a multi–bar or line graph to convey a relationship, such as to compare and contrast data or to show cause and effect.

1 **Based on the double-bar graph above, which of the following statements is true?**

   A In 2002 the average mortgage rate was higher than the average prime interest rate.

   B The average prime interest rate in 2008 was about 6 percent.

   C The average mortgage rate in 2006 was about 10 percent.

   D The average mortgage rate dropped by about 2 percent between 2004 and 2006.

UNIT 5

③ Apply the Skill

Directions: Questions 2 through 4 are based on the information below.

The Federal Reserve, or "The Fed," as it is popularly known, is the central bank of both the United States government and the nation's banking system. The Fed regulates banks, in addition to issuing currency and carrying out monetary policy for the nation. One of the Fed's most notable functions is its control of the nation's money supply. To increase the nation's money supply, the Fed can buy U.S. Treasury securities from banks and the American public, injecting new cash into the economy. It also can increase the money supply by lowering the interest rate at which it lends to commercial banks. This will encourage banks to borrow more money from the Fed, thereby raising the money supply.

In the United States, money supply is evaluated in different categories, or measures. Items are placed into these categories according to their liquidity, or how easily they can be turned into cash. The first category, M1, includes the coins and paper money held by the public and checking deposits at public banks. The second category, M2, includes all of M1 plus savings deposits, interest-earning deposits less than $100,000, and money market deposits and mutual funds.

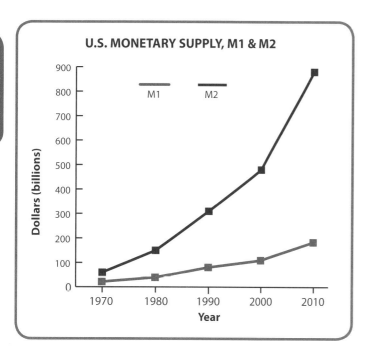

U.S. MONETARY SUPPLY, M1 & M2

2 Which of the following statements will always be true?
- **A** The value of M1 exceeds $300 billion.
- **B** The value of M2 is increasing steadily.
- **C** The value of M2 is greater than that of M1.
- **D** The value of M1 is approximately one-half the value of M2.

3 Which of the following was the approximate value of M1 in 2010?
- **A** about $100 billion
- **B** about $200 billion
- **C** about $300 billion
- **D** about $400 billion

4 Based on the information, in which of the following years did the economy probably have the most liquidity in total dollars?
- **A** 1980
- **B** 1990
- **C** 2000
- **D** 2010

Directions: Question 5 is based on the graph below.

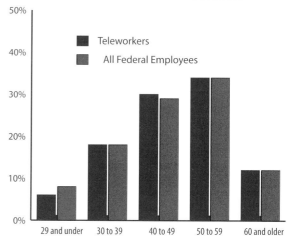

AGE DISTRIBUTION OF RESPONDENT TELEWORKERS

5 Which of the following is true of the federal labor force?
- **A** Older employees are less likely to telecommute than younger employees.
- **B** Age is not a factor in whether federal employees telecommute.
- **C** More younger employees than older employees telecommute.
- **D** The percentage of employees that telecommute decreases with age.

UNIT 5

Directions: Questions 6 through 9 are based on the information below.

One important aspect of U.S. fiscal policy is the preparation and approval of an annual budget for the federal government. A budget is a complex plan for collecting and spending the money required to carry out the government's operations. A budget surplus occurs when the amount of money received, or revenue, is greater than the amount of money spent, or expenditures. When expenditures exceed revenue, the result is a budget deficit.

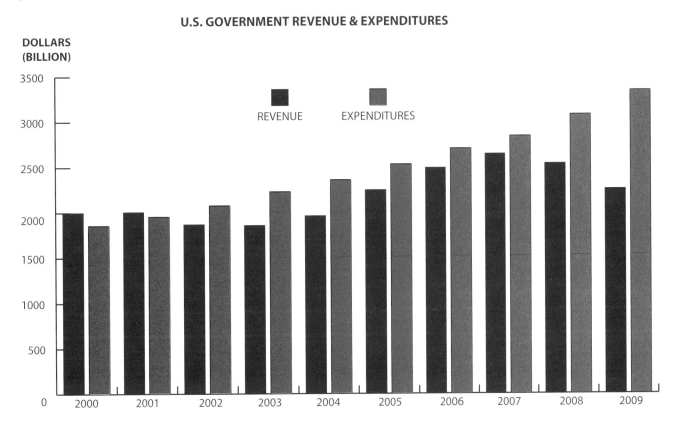

U.S. GOVERNMENT REVENUE & EXPENDITURES

6 Approximately how much money did the U.S. government receive in 2006?
  A $1,750 billion
  B $2,000 billion
  C $2,250 billion
  D $2,500 billion

7 Which of the following likely occurred in order to produce the trend in government spending shown on the graph?
  A the elimination of government aid programs such as welfare
  B tax increases on those making more than $250,000
  C the addition of many new government programs
  D a decrease in populations in the lower tax brackets

8 In which of the following years did the federal budget exhibit the largest budget deficit?
  A 2009
  B 2008
  C 2000
  D 2001

9 Using the double-bar graph, which of the following statements can you determine to be correct?
  A The U.S. government achieved a surplus in three different years during the period shown on the graph.
  B The smallest deficit shown on the graph appeared in 2005.
  C Government revenues exceeded $2,000 billion for the first time in 2005.
  D Government expenditures decreased during each year shown on the graph.

Directions: Questions 10 through 13 are based on the information below.

Just as the Federal Reserve sets the discount rate at which it lends money to commercial banks, these banks establish interest rates at which they lend money to their customers. The prime rate is the lowest rate of interest that commercial banks charge. Banks will typically only offer the prime rate to their customers who have the strongest credit. The prime rate is also usually available only on specific types of loans. The interest rates of other types of loans are often expressed as a certain percentage over time. The graph shows the prime rate used by banks during two different 10-year periods.

BANK PRIME INTEREST RATES

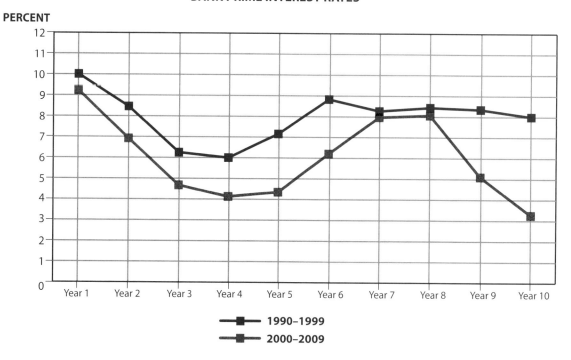

1990–1999
2000–2009

10 At the beginning of which of the following years did the prime rate reach its lowest point between 1990 and 1999?

A Year 3 (1992)

B Year 4 (1993)

C Year 5 (1994)

D Year 6 (1995)

11 Which of the following statements is correct, based on the double-line graph?

A The prime rate decreased dramatically between 2000 and 2003.

B The prime rate in 2007 was lower than the prime rate in 1994.

C The prime rate increased in three consecutive years from 1996 to 1998.

D The highest prime rate recorded between 2000 and 2009 occurred in 2006.

12 At the end of which of the following years would a preferred borrower have received the best prime rate?

A 1990

B 1993

C 2003

D 2009

13 Which of the following generalizations can you make, based on the information contained in this multi-line graph?

A The prime rate generally decreased throughout each 10-year period.

B The prime rate generally changed by about one percentage point each year.

C The changes in prime rate generally followed a bell-shaped curve in each decade.

D The prime rate generally remained higher in the 1990s than in the 2000s.

Directions: Questions 14 through 16 are based on the information below.

One important way to evaluate whether the government's monetary policy is benefiting the nation's economy is to examine the Gross Domestic Product, or GDP. As you have already learned, GDP is the total value of all goods and services produced in a nation during a specified time period. Many nations regard this value as the best indicator of a nation's economic activities. The multi-bar graph shows how the various components of the GDP changed in the United States between 2010 and 2012.

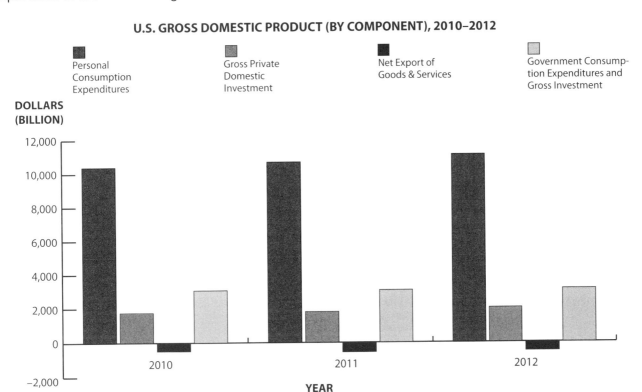

U.S. GROSS DOMESTIC PRODUCT (BY COMPONENT), 2010–2012

14 **Which of the following was the approximate value of gross private domestic investment in 2010?**
   A $1,500 billion
   B $1,750 billion
   C $2,000 billion
   D $2,250 billion

15 **Which of the following is most likely to account for the negative values shown on the graph?**
   A   large increases in government spending on community programs
   B   the growth of high-technology industries in the United States
   C   a negative balance of trade between the United States and other nations
   D   a seasonal increase in domestic consumer spending

16 **Based on the information in the graph, which of the following statements is false?**
   A   The value of personal consumption expenditures decreased each year shown on the graph.
   B   In 2012, the value of gross private domestic investment was less than that of government consumption expenditures and gross investment.
   C   The net export of goods and services had a less negative effect on GDP in 2010 than in 2011.
   D   The value of government consumption expenditures and gross investment stayed about the same each year.

Predict Outcomes

① *Learn the Skill*

Often in the study of economics, you will want to make a **prediction**, or a suggestion about what might happen next, after drawing conclusions. To **predict outcomes**, you must access your prior knowledge and experiences about a subject. Then, by applying this information to existing patterns that you recognize, you can make a prediction.

② *Practice the Skill*

By mastering the skill of predicting outcomes, you will improve your study and test-taking skills, especially as they relate to social studies high school equivalency tests. Examine the bar graphs below. Then answer the question that follows.

Ⓐ Consider how supply and demand might influence where a company decides to look for new employees. Companies want to have a large supply of qualified candidates, but also need to keep salary costs down in order to increase profits.

Ⓑ Together, these graphs reveal a pattern that can help you answer the question. Identify the nation that ranks high in the ratio of engineering degrees to bachelor degrees, yet low in annual salary.

MAKING ASSUMPTIONS

For the purposes of answering this question, you can assume that the company in question is motivated solely by the desire to make a profit. In reality, companies may consider other factors, such as government policies or public opinion, before deciding to outsource jobs to another country.

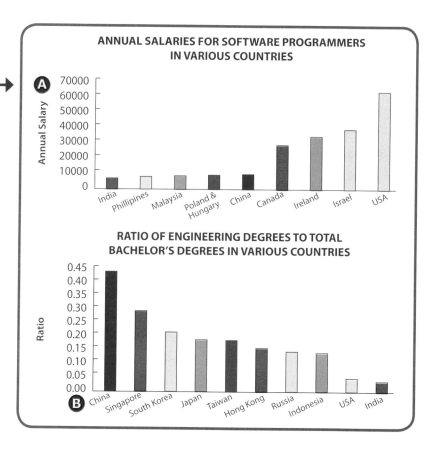

ANNUAL SALARIES FOR SOFTWARE PROGRAMMERS IN VARIOUS COUNTRIES

RATIO OF ENGINEERING DEGREES TO TOTAL BACHELOR'S DEGREES IN VARIOUS COUNTRIES

1 **Where would you predict that a U.S. corporation could find the best combination of highly trained, yet affordable prospective engineers?**

A United States

B Israel

C China

D Russia

UNIT 5

Directions: Questions 2 and 3 refer to the following information and bar graph.

Telecommuting is a system in which employees work from home, or some other location, instead of at an employer's office. These employees maintain close communication with their employers through the use of telephones, e-mail, the Internet, and other technologies. As technology improved during the 1990s, telecommuting became increasingly popular in the United States. By 1997, approximately 10 million U.S. workers regularly telecommuted. Proponents of telecommuting argue that it increases productivity, saves gasoline, and decreases pollution and congestion caused by traffic. Telecommuting can also allow companies to retain highly regarded employees who are unable or unwilling to work in the office. On the other hand, critics suggest that telecommuting can make it difficult for managerial workers to supervise their telecommuting employees.

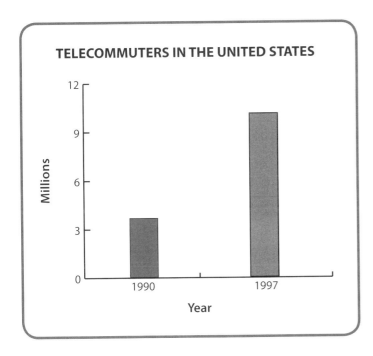

TELECOMMUTERS IN THE UNITED STATES

2 **Which of the following tasks would be the most difficult for a telecommuting employee?**
   A   sending and receiving e-mail
   B   participating in team building exercises
   C   maintaining schedules and deadlines
   D   taking part in company conference calls

3 **Consider the ways in which technology in the United States has changed since 1997.**

Based on your prior knowledge and the pattern shown in this graph, which of the following predictions would you make?
   A   The number of telecommuters returned to its 1990 level.
   B   The number of telecommuters decreased gradually in the years after 1997.
   C   The number of telecommuters continued to increase in the years after 1997.
   D   The number of telecommuters decreased sharply in the years after 1997.

Directions: Question 4 refers to the following information.

In November 2008, leaders of the "Big Three" automakers (Ford, Chrysler, General Motors) asked members of the U.S. House and Senate for billions of dollars in loans or a financial bailout.

4 **Assume that the legislature did not provide the money. What might be a potential outcome from that decision?**
   A   Taxes will increase.
   B   Many U.S. banks will fail.
   C   There will be a negative impact on U.S. exports.
   D   The mayor of Detroit will be impeached.

UNIT 5

Directions: Questions 5 and 6 refer to the following table.

WORK-AT-HOME WORKERS, 2010	
OCCUPATION	**NUMBER (IN THOUSANDS)**
Management, business, and financial	1,450
Computer, engineering, and science	432
Education, legal, community service, arts, and media	770
Healthcare practitioners and technicians	100
Service	956
Sales and related	849
Office and administrative support	595
Farming, fishing, and forestry	55
Construction and extraction	197
Installation, maintenance, and repair	116
Production, transportation, and material moving	296

Source: www.census.gov, accessed 2014

5 From which of the following occupational groups did approximately 600,000 people receive pay for their work at home?

A   sales occupations

B   office and administrative support occupations

C   service occupations

D   installation, maintenance, and repair occupations

6 According to the Bureau of Labor Statistics, two occupations that are expected to grow rapidly by 2022 are brickmasons and information security analysts. Which of the following work-at-home categories would you predict to be most affected by this growth?

A   Construction and extraction

B   Sales and related

C   Management, business, and financial

D   Computer, engineering, and science

Directions: Questions 7 and 8 refer to the following information and table.

Eddie is 35 years old and lives in North Dakota. He is taking classes at night to become a certified auto mechanic. As part of his income, he receives his mother's Social Security benefits. For years he has made a personal monthly budget to help him track both his income and expenses.

EDDIE'S MONTHLY BUDGET			
DESCRIPTION	**INCOME**	**EXPENSE**	**BUDGET BALANCE**
Wages	$1,000		$1,000
Social Security Benefits	$350		$1,350
Rent		$550	$800
Car Payment		$250	$550
Utilities/ Groceries		$150	$400
Car Insurance		$100	$300
Other Expenses		$100	$200
Savings		$100	$100
		MONTHLY BUDGET SURPLUS	**$100**

7 What element of Eddie's budget can you predict would be most likely to increase next year?

A   car payment

B   Social Security Benefits

C   savings

D   wages

8 Which of the following can you predict would cause the greatest disruption to Eddie's existing monthly budget?

A   Eddie decides to save $125 each month.

B   North Dakota experiences its longest and coldest winter in decades.

C   The price of bread increases by 1 percent.

D   Eddie gets a traffic ticket for going 10 mph over the speed limit.

Directions: Questions 9 and 10 refer to the following information.

… The American economy is failing to adapt to fundamental changes and to growing competition in the global economy. We are not just losing jobs—we may be losing critical parts of our innovation infrastructure, and with them, our competitive edge in the global marketplace. The offshore outsourcing of jobs is just the tip of the iceberg that America is sailing towards … .

We know that manufacturing jobs have been shifting overseas for some time. But now the services sector is being hit hard by offshore outsourcing—and that hurts. The services sector provides 83% of America's jobs, employing 86 million people. It dominates our economy. Customer call centers and data entry facilities are being relocated to places where capable labor can be found at lower wage levels. High-speed digital technologies make a connection between Boston and Bangalore as fast as between Boston and Baltimore.

Senator Joseph Lieberman, "Meeting the Offshore Outsourcing Challenge," May 11, 2004

9 **Based on the example of the U.S. manufacturing sector, which of the following does Senator Lieberman predict will happen?**
   A The United States will build new call centers.
   B The service industry will lose many jobs to offshore outsourcing.
   C Many new service jobs will be created in America.
   D India and the United States will work together at research and development.

10 **What solution might Senator Lieberman advocate for the problem he discusses?**
   A American companies should lower wages to become more competitive with other countries.
   B America should invest more money in high-speed digital technologies.
   C American businesses must become better at adapting to changes in the global economy to become more competitive.
   D American businesses should be prevented from moving jobs offshore.

Directions: Questions 11 and 12 refer to the following information.

The economic crisis of 2008–2009 affected almost all aspects of American life. Professional sports also fell victim. Because some sports, such as golf, tennis, and auto racing, rely on corporate sponsorships, they implemented cost-saving programs and held fewer events. NBA and NFL teams were also affected. Fewer people could afford the high ticket prices and companies filled fewer luxury boxes. Faced with the choice of spending over $200.00 dollars for two people to attend a high-profile Major League baseball game (and purchase food and a souvenir), many families instead chose to stay home and watch the game on television.

11 **Which of the following is a logically predicted outcome based on the effect of the economy on professional sports?**
   A NFL teams will raise ticket prices.
   B Major League teams will build more new stadiums.
   C NASCAR drivers will take a voluntary pay cut.
   D Leagues will lay off office and administrative employees.

12 **Based on this information, which of the following areas can you predict may be affected in the same way that professional sports organizations are affected?**
   A local libraries
   B automobile dealerships
   C city music and theater groups (i.e. a performing arts organization or symphony)
   D cable television providers

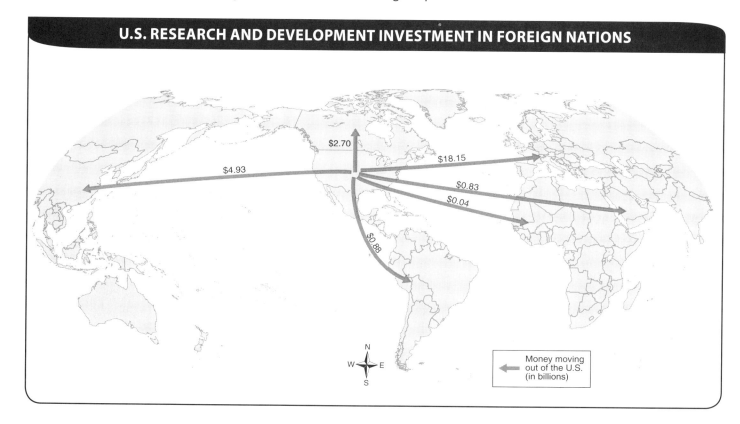

U.S. RESEARCH AND DEVELOPMENT INVESTMENT IN FOREIGN NATIONS

$2.70
$18.15
$4.93
$0.83
$0.04
$0.88

Money moving out of the U.S. (in billions)

13 **In which region did U.S. corporations invest nearly $5 billion for research and development?**
   A   Asia
   B   Canada
   C   South America
   D   the Middle East

14 **Which of the following predictions could you make based on the information contained in the map?**
   A   U.S. corporations' investments in research development in Africa will increase rapidly.
   B   South American nations will decrease their investment in U.S. research and development.
   C   U.S. corporations will continue to seek out diverse global sources of research and development.
   D   Research and development investment by U.S. corporations in the Middle East will be exceeded by Middle Eastern investment in American research and development.

15 **If the subject of this map was changed to show U.S. corporations' investment in service industries around the world, where would you predict expenditures to increase significantly?**
   A   Africa
   B   Europe
   C   Asia
   D   South America

16 **Where did U.S. corporations make their largest investment in foreign research and development?**

   U.S. corporations made their largest investment in
   A   Canada.
   B   Africa.
   C   Australia.
   D   Europe.

UNIT 5

Unit 5 Review

The Unit Review is structured to resemble social studies high school equivalency tests. Be sure to read each question and all possible answers very carefully before choosing your answer.

To record your answers, fill in the circle that corresponds to the answer you select for each question in the Unit Review.

Do not rest your pencil on the answer area while considering your answer. Make no stray or unnecessary marks. If you change an answer, erase your first mark completely.

Mark only one answer space for each question; multiple answers will be scored as incorrect.

Directions: Questions 1 through 3 refer to the following information.

A mixed economy is an economic system that operates partially as a free market capitalist economy. However, other parts of a mixed economy are operated by the government, as in a socialist economy.

India represents one notable example of a mixed economy. From the time of the nation's independence from Britain, the Indian government worked to control industry in the nation. Beginning in the late 1970s, the government slowly began to relinquish control of some elements of the economy. However, by 1991 the state still controlled important parts of India's economy, including the mining, banking, transportation, communications, and manufacturing industries.

Following a major financial crisis in 1991, the Indian government began to pursue more effective economic reforms. The goals of these reforms included deregulating industries and privatizing public sector industries such as aviation, power, and telecommunications. Today, some industries remain under government control. These include India's nuclear power, defense, and railway industries.

1 **Which of the following caused India to institute significant economic reforms?**
   A independence from Britain
   B the deregulation of the nation's industries
   C a major economic crisis
   D the privatization of India's public sector

2 **Which U.S. sector has a similar level of government control as India's railway industry?**
   A public primary and secondary education
   B transportation
   C communications
   D defense equipment

3 **Which part of India's economy represents socialism?**
   A the power industry
   B telecommunications
   C nuclear power
   D aviation

UNIT 5

Directions: Questions 4 and 5 refer to the following pictograph.

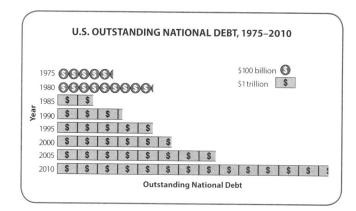

U.S. OUTSTANDING NATIONAL DEBT, 1975–2010

$100 billion ⑤
$1 trillion $

Year: 1975, 1980, 1985, 1990, 1995, 2000, 2005, 2010

Outstanding National Debt

Directions: Question 6 refers to the following two graphs.

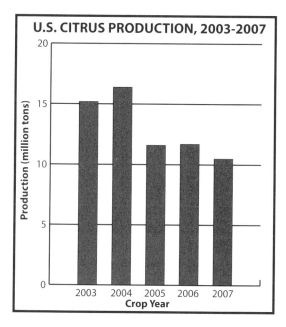

U.S. CITRUS PRODUCTION, 2003-2007

Production (million tons)

2003 2004 2005 2006 2007
Crop Year

4 **Which of the following actions would guarantee a reduction in the level of the U.S. national debt?**

  A the approval of a federal budget that produces a surplus dedicated to paying money owed to other nations

  B the continuation of many government programs

  C an increase in tax benefits given to large corporations

  D the passage of new legislation to stimulate economic growth in the nation

                       Ⓐ Ⓑ Ⓒ Ⓓ

5 **Which of the following statements can you determine to be true based on the pictograph?**

  A The U.S. national debt had exceeded $600 billion by 1975.

  B The U.S. national debt decreased between 1980 and 1985.

  C The U.S. national debt expanded more between 1995 and 2000 than it did between 2000 and 2005.

  D The national debt level has continued to rise since 1975.

                       Ⓐ Ⓑ Ⓒ Ⓓ

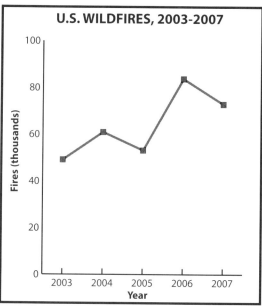

U.S. WILDFIRES, 2003-2007

Fires (thousands)

2003 2004 2005 2006 2007
Year

6 **On both graphs, examine the changes that took place between 2005 and 2007. These changes could be multiple effects of which common cause?**

  A an increased budget for forestry agencies

  B a nationwide drought

  C a greater demand for agricultural products

  D increased efforts to reduce the effects of natural disasters

                       Ⓐ Ⓑ Ⓒ Ⓓ

UNIT 5

Directions: Questions 7 through 9 refer to the following information.

An economic depression is a crisis period in which unemployment rises, prices drop, and credit is restricted. These periods are further characterized by reduced economic investment and output, as well as large numbers of bankruptcies.

Depressions usually begin through a combination of decreases in demand and overproduction. These factors lead to decreased production, workforce reductions, and diminished wages for employees. As these changes weaken consumers' purchasing power, a depression can worsen and become more widespread. Recovery from a depression typically requires either the existing overstock of goods to be depleted or the emergence of new markets. At times, government intervention may be necessary to stimulate an economic recovery. Due to today's global economy, present-day depressions often spread around the world.

REAL U.S. GROSS DOMESTIC PRODUCT, 1929–1939 (YEAR-2005 DOLLARS)	
YEAR	REAL GDP IN BILLIONS
1929	976.1
1930	892.0
1931	834.2
1932	725.2
1933	715.8
1934	793.7
1935	864.2
1936	977.0
1937	1,027.1
1938	991.8
1939	1,071.9

7 Which of the following conclusions can be drawn based on the information?

It can be concluded that
A the United States had been in a period of recession throughout the 1920s.
B the production of war supplies for World War II led to a depression in the United States.
C the purchasing power of U.S. consumers grew increasingly weak during the early 1930s.
D government intervention in the U.S. economy in the 1920s created a depression during the 1930s.

Ⓐ Ⓑ Ⓒ Ⓓ

8 Which of the following predictions could you make about the years following 1939?
A The United States would experience a growing number of bankruptcies.
B Decreases in demand would continue to drive prices down.
C Depression conditions would become more severe throughout the nation.
D Unemployment in the United States would gradually decrease.

Ⓐ Ⓑ Ⓒ Ⓓ

9 Which of the following explains why the table shows the U.S. GDP in year-2005 dollars?
A inflation
B overproduction
C unemployment
D supply and demand

Ⓐ Ⓑ Ⓒ Ⓓ

UNIT 5

Directions: Questions 10 through 13 refer to the following information and flowchart.

Factors of production are the items used to complete a production process. These factors typically fall into three main categories—land, labor, and capital. At times, a fourth category, defined as entrepreneurship or management, also appears alongside these. In order for a business to achieve success, it must maintain a healthy balance of these factors of production.

The flowchart below shows the flow of money, as well as goods and services, throughout the U.S. economy. In this flowchart, households own all of the factors of production. The people in these households sell their labor, land, and capital to firms. In exchange for these factors of production, the people receive wages, rent, and profits.

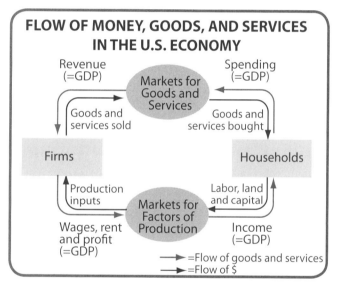

FLOW OF MONEY, GOODS, AND SERVICES IN THE U.S. ECONOMY

10 **Suppose you own a company that manufactures lawnmowers. Which of the following factors of production would fall under the category of labor?**

A money contributed by shareholders in your company

B the property on which your company is located

C the work of your employees

D your ability to effectively manage your employees

Ⓐ Ⓑ Ⓒ Ⓓ

11 **Which of the following factors of production is your willingness to start your own business and manufacture products?**

The willingness to start one's own business and manufacture products is an example of

A labor.

B capital.

C profit.

D entrepreneurship.

Ⓐ Ⓑ Ⓒ Ⓓ

12 **Which of the following actions generates revenue for firms?**

A buying goods and services from people in households

B selling goods and services to people in households

C buying factors of production from households

D avoiding the markets for goods and services and factors of production

Ⓐ Ⓑ Ⓒ Ⓓ

13 **Based on the information and flowchart, which of the following statements can you determine to be true?**

A Firms control all of the production inputs in this economic system.

B All transactions between firms and households contribute to the nation's GDP.

C After receiving wages, rent, and profit, firms use these items to purchase factors of production.

D Money and goods and services move in the same direction throughout this economic system.

Ⓐ Ⓑ Ⓒ Ⓓ

UNIT 5

Directions: Questions 14 through 16 are based on the following multi-bar and multi-line graphs.

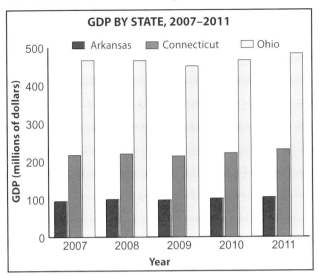

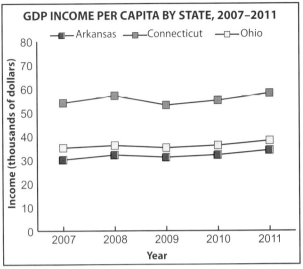

14 Which of the following statements is true based on the two graphs?

A The GDP and per capita income of Arkansas remained at about 50% of those of Ohio for the period shown.

B For each state, the GDP and per capita income increased at similar rates.

C The period from 2011 to 2015 would likely feature little change in GDP and per capita income for each state.

D GDP and per capita income are not related.

Ⓐ Ⓑ Ⓒ Ⓓ

15 Which conclusion are you able to reasonably draw based on a comparison of GDP and income by state as shown in the two graphs?

A Imports to Ohio have decreased each year since 2003.

B The population of Arkansas is expanding at a higher rate than that at which its wages are increasing.

C The GDP of Arkansas and Connecticut will eventually reach the same level.

D Connecticut has a smaller population than Ohio.

Ⓐ Ⓑ Ⓒ Ⓓ

16 Unlike the multi-line graph, the multi-bar graph does not take into account which of the following items when measuring the data?

A the population of each state

B the number of businesses in each state

C the variety of industries found in each state

D the national standard for its subject

Ⓐ Ⓑ Ⓒ Ⓓ

Directions: Question 17 refers to the following information.

Economic incentives are used to encourage people to make certain choices. Most often, economic incentives involve money, but they may also involve goods or services. An economic incentive can be positive or negative. A positive incentive rewards you for making a certain choice or behaving in a certain way. A negative incentive does the opposite—it punishes you for making a certain choice or behaving in a certain way.

17 Which of the following is an example of a positive economic incentive?

A interest charged on your credit card for nonpayment of the entire debt

B fines for returning library books late

C a $50.00 refund for opening a new checking account

D an extra ten-cent charge per minute on your monthly cell phone statement

Ⓐ Ⓑ Ⓒ Ⓓ

Glossary

A

absolute location: the position of a place on Earth according to coordinates of longitude and latitude

adjustable rate loan: a mortgage loan in which the interest rate paid by the borrower varies according to an index based on the underlying rate paid by the lender

administration: the officials in the executive branch of a government or organization

altitude: the height of a point in relation to sea level or ground level

Age of Discovery: the historical period lasting from the early 15th century to the 17th century during which European explorers explored the world by sea in search of trade routes, new goods, and new lands

ambassador: a person sent by a country to serve as the official representative to a foreign country

amendment: an official change to the words and meaning of a law or other document

ancestor worship: a religious custom of worshipping dead family members whose spirits are believed to have the power to intervene in the lives of the living

apartheid: a social system once practiced in South Africa in which non-white people did not have the same rights as white people and were forced to live separately

appellate: the aspect of the court system that deals with applications (appeals) for decisions to be reversed

article: a separate part of a legal document

Articles of Confederation: the agreement among the 13 founding states that established the United States of America as a confederation and served as its first constitution

assumption: an idea that is taken for granted as true

B

bar graph: a display that uses bars of different heights to represent quantities

bias: prejudice for or against something

Bill of Rights: the first ten amendments of the U.S. Constitution

Black Death: an outbreak of bubonic plague in the 1300s that killed about one third of the population of Europe

business cycle: patterns of increase and decrease in economic factors such as employment, income, production, and sales

C

candidate: a person who is seeking to be elected to office or chosen for a position

capital city: the city that is the administrative center and seat of governance in a country or region

capitalism: a system in which individuals and corporations own the land, factories, and resources used to make and transport products and provide services

caricature: an illustration that exaggerates a person's characteristics for comic effect

categorize: to describe a group of items by a common characteristic

caucus: a group of people convened within a political party to choose a candidate or set a policy

cause: an event or factor that produces an outcome

CD (certificate of deposit): a savings account for which the owner earns interest in return for leaving an amount of money in the bank for a specified period of time

centralized economy: an economic system in which the government plans and controls what is produced

chart: a visual presentation of information in which the organization of the data shows the relationship between ideas

charter: a document that officially creates and defines a group

checks and balances: the system within government in which different parts have powers that affect and control other parts so that no part becomes too powerful

circle graph: a visual representation that compares quantities as wedges (parts) in a circle (whole)

civil rights movement: the social movement in the U.S. from the mid-1950s to late-1960s aimed at ending racial discrimination against African Americans

Civilian Conservation Corps: a New Deal program created to put young men to work during the height of the Great Depression

civilization: the organized and developed condition of human society

climate: the prevailing weather patterns in an area over a long period

colonial: relating to the original 13 colonies forming the United States of America

colonization: the act of setting up a colony away from a people's country of origin

colony: an area that is apart from but controlled by a distant country

compare: to note a characteristic that two items have in common

compass rose: a symbol on a globe or a map used to indicate north, south, east, and west

competition: the act of trying to win something, such as when businesses compete for consumers to choose and purchase their goods or services

conclusion: a reasoned judgment following consideration of information

Confederacy: the group of Southern states that separated from the United States during the Civil War

congressional district: one of 435 areas in the U.S. in which the population selects one member of congress

conspicuous consumption: the purchase of goods or services for the purpose of displaying one's wealth

constitution: the documented beliefs and laws by which a country, state, or organization is governed

Constitutional Convention: the 1787 meeting of delegates in Philadelphia to revise the Articles of Confederation and frame the federal Constitution

consul: an official appointed to live in a foreign country to protect the home country's interests there

consumer behavior: the composite of decision making trends that influence what people buy

consumer: a person who buys and uses goods and services

context clue: hints about the meaning of an unknown word that a reader can derive from the text around it

continent: the world's main continuous expanses of land (Africa, Antarctica, Asia, Australia, Europe, North America, South America)

contrast: to note a characteristic that differentiates two items

county: a territorial and local administrative division within a state; sometimes called a parish

county seat: the town or city that is the government center of a county within a state

Crusades: a series of military campaigns by the Roman Catholic Church during the Middle Ages for the purposes of spreading Christianity into the region that is generally now referred to as the Middle East

cultural geography: the study of the patterns and interactions of people in relation to the place where they live

culture: the beliefs, customs, arts, and habits of the people in a particular group or society

currency: the accepted money that is used in a country to buy goods and services

D

D-Day: June 6, 1944, the day on which Allied forces invaded Normandy during World War II

deficit: an amount of money that is less than what is needed to meet an obligation

demand: the condition of being desired or having a market for purchase, such as the *demand* for oil to meet energy needs

democracy: a form of government in which citizens choose leaders by voting and in which the importance of each individual's vote is the same

Department of Homeland Security: a department of the U.S. government with the mission to protect the country from terrorist attacks and large-scale emergencies

depression: a severe form of economic recession which is characterized by a significant downturn in the economy, low production, business failures, and high unemployment

diagram: a simplified drawing that clarifies a concept or shows how a thing works

dissent: disagreement with official opinion

distribution: the process of delivering goods from the point where they are made to sellers and on to consumers

domestic policy: laws and programs that apply within a nation's borders

Dow Jones Industrial Average: an index that quantifies the volume of trading that occurs in the exchange of stock shares in a given day

E

economic indicators: statistics, such as consumer spending and employment rates, that provide a means to measure the health of the economy

economics: the study of the system of production and consumption of goods and services

editorial: an opinion piece written by senior level staff at a news agency

effect: a change or outcome that results from a cause

Electoral College: the process in which electors are selected and convened to officially cast votes to seat the president and vice president

electoral vote: a vote cast by an elector in the electoral college system that is determined by the popular vote of the people in the elector's congressional district

elevation: the height above sea level of a point on land

Emancipation Proclamation: the 1863 presidential proclamation issued by Abraham Lincoln declaring freedom for people enslaved in the states in rebellion during the Civil War

enslave: to make someone a slave

equator: an imaginary line that runs around the middle of Earth, separating it into the Northern and Southern Hemispheres

equilibrium point: the point at which the available supply of a product and the demand for it are equal

European Union: an economic and political partnership between 28 countries in Europe

exchange rate: the difference between the values of currency of two countries

executive branch: the part of government responsible for daily administration and carrying out laws

expenditure the amount of money spent on something

F

fact: a true detail that is not subject to differing interpretation

fascism: a centralized form of government that values nationalism and in which a dictator controls the lives of citizens, who are not permitted to disagree with the government or the leader

faulty logic or reasoning: the use of an invalid thought process to relate cause and effect or draw a conclusion

Federal Reserve System: the central bank of the U.S., which regulates the nation's financial system

federal: referring to a government structure in which power is shared between the central, national government and states or provinces

Federalists: supporters of the newly written constitution who became identified as a political party that favored a strong central government

feudalism: a social system in which vassals, subservient residents, work for landowners who give them use of the land for subsistence

fixed-rate loan: a loan for which the interest rate remains the same during the repayment period

flowchart: a diagram that represents the steps in a process

foreclosure: the process through which a bank seizes property, commonly a home, from a borrower who fails to repay a mortgage loan

foreign policy: laws and programs that apply to how a nation conducts itself outside of its borders

free trade: a policy wherein governments do not restrict the import or export of goods to and from other countries

free-market economy: a capitalist system in which competition, supply, and demand determine prices without government control

G

generalize: to make a broad statement that applies to entire groups of people, places, or events

geography: the study of the physical features of Earth

glasnost: a Soviet policy begun in the mid-1980s that permitted more open discussion of political and social issues

globe: a spherical model of Earth

Golden Age: a time in which the quality of life and the conditions that affect it are overwhelmingly positive

goods: tangible property that people buy and sell

Gothic: relating to a style of architecture popular in Europe from roughly the 1100s to the 1500s and characterized by the frequent use of pointed arches

government bond: a debt investment in which a person loans money to the government in return for a predetermined amount of interest after a specified time

graph: a diagram that shows the relationship between variables, one of which is frequently time

Great Society: an agenda of social programs launched by President Lyndon B. Johnson in 1964 and characterized as a "war on poverty"

gross domestic product (GDP): the total value of all the goods and services produced by a country in a year

gulf: a portion of the sea or ocean that is surrounded by land

H

hasty generalization: a claim that is applied too broadly or based on too little evidence

hemisphere: half of Earth, as divided north-to-south by the equator or west-to-east by an imaginary plane passing through the poles

hieroglyphics: a system of writing using mainly pictorial characters

housing starts: an economic indicator, based on the number of new residential units for which construction begins, typically in a month

I

immigrant: a person who moves to live permanently in a foreign country

impeach: to charge a holder of public office with misconduct

imperialist: referring to a nation with a policy of extending its power through colonization or gaining control over more territory

implied: expressed indirectly without being plainly stated

impulse buying: a purchase made quickly and without a prior plan as the result of a sudden impulse

inaugural: marking the beginning of a period in office

Industrial Revolution: the period ending the 18th and into the 19th centuries during which agriculture, manufacturing, transportation, and mining were all advanced dramatically by technology, changing almost every aspect of daily life for people in modernizing society

inference: an educated guess based on facts or evidence

inflation: a general increase in the prices of goods and services, while the amount that can be purchased for a given sum of money decreases

interest: an amount of money paid, usually as a percentage, for money borrowed in a loan

interstate: something that exists between states

J

Jim Crow laws: racial segregation laws enacted in the U.S. from the late 1870s to the 1960s

John Maynard Keynes (1883-1946): an English economist who was among the first to theorize about the effects of total spending on outputs and inflation in an economy; advocated for government intervention in the economy during times of recession

judicial: referring to the system of courts that interprets and applies laws

jurisdiction: the power to govern an area or apply laws

K

key: an area on a globe or a map that explains the meanings of colors and symbols

L

laissez-faire: the policy of allowing businesses to operate generally without government involvement or interference

landform: a natural feature on Earth's surface such as a mountain or plateau

League of Nations: an international organization formed after World War II for the purpose of promoting cooperation and peace among nations

legislator: a person who writes and passes laws

legislature: the branch of government that enacts and revises laws

levy: to impose an involuntary tax or fee on citizens

limited decision making: a process in which a consumer spends a moderate amount of time comparing options to evaluate a prospective purchase

lines of latitude: imaginary, horizontal lines on Earth that run parallel to the equator and indicate north-south position between the poles

lines of longitude: imaginary lines on Earth running north-south in equal distances from one another and indicating east-west position

liquidation phase: the phase during which a business dissolves and its assets are sold

lunar calendar: a calendar that bases the divisions of a year on the cycles of the moon

M

macroeconomics: the study of factors, such as employment and inflation, that affect the economy on its largest scale

magistrate: a local official with administrative and sometimes judicial functions

Magna Carta: Latin for "Great Charter"; a 1215 document guaranteeing English political liberties signed by King John under pressure from English barons

main idea: the topic of a piece of writing

map: a visual representation of a place, usually shown on a flat surface

medieval: relating to the period of European history from about AD 500 to about 1500

microeconomics: the study of small-scale interactions within an economy, such as the supply, demand, and consumer decision making in an individual market for one type of product

migrate: to move from one country or place in order to live or work in another place

monopoly: complete ownership or control, without competition, of an entire supply of something within a market

mortgage rate: the percentage of interest charged by a lender to a borrower taking a loan to buy property

multicultural: including aspects from different cultures

N

narrative: a story or explanation told or written in a series of connected statements

NATO: the North Atlantic Treaty Organization, a military alliance of 28 nations situated primarily in the northern part of the Western Hemisphere

natural border: a boundary between two locations that is formed by a natural feature such as a river, mountain range, or desert

Nazi: a member of the National Socialist German Workers' Party; under Adolf Hitler, the Nazi Party was characterized by fascist, racist, and atheist beliefs

net pay: the amount of wages an earner keeps after deductions such as taxes are taken out

O

oligarchy: a country, organization, or business that is controlled by a small number of people

opinion: a person's belief about something, which may be accurate but is formed without fidelity to facts

oppression: unjust application of control upon a person or people

output: something produced by a person, machine, or industry

P

pardon: to exempt someone from punishment

Peloponnesian War: a lengthy war between Athens and Sparta in Ancient Greece, from 431 to 404 BC

penal colony: a settlement used to isolate prisoners in a remote location away from the general population

peninsula: a piece of land that protrudes from a larger land area and is almost entirely surrounded by water

perspective: the point of view from which one considers something

persuade: to convince another person to agree with something or take an action

physical map: a map that shows land and water features of an area, such as mountains, plains, rivers, gulfs, and oceans, as well as climate and elevation

pictograph: a diagram that uses simple pictures to represent data

planned economy: an economic system in which the government plans and controls what is produced; also referred to as a centralized economy

plateau: an elevated, flat area of land surrounded by land of lower elevation

platform: the statement of the principles of a political party

point of view: the position, or attitude, from which something is observed

political border: an imaginary line separating places with different governing bodies

political cartoon: an illustration or comic strip that is intended to make a political or social statement

political map: a map that shows how people have divided Earth's area into identified regions, countries, states, counties, cities, and towns

political party: a group of people with shared values about governance who seek to have their members elected to positions of power

popular vote: the total of the votes made by the electorate, the collection of individual qualified voters

population density: a measurement of population per unit area, such as the number of people per square mile

population: the number of people living in a particular geographic place, such as a city or country

preamble: an introductory statement at the beginning of a document that usually explains the reason for the information that follows

precipitation: rain, snow, sleet, or hail that falls to the ground

primary election: a preliminary election that narrows the numbers of candidates running for political office

primary source: an original document or other material that consists only of that information provided by its creator and has not been altered in any way

problem: an unwanted situation that is difficult to deal with

profit: the amount of money earned for a sale of something that exceeds what it cost to produce that thing

prohibition: the act of forbidding something, such as a law prohibiting the sale and manufacture of alcohol

proportional representation: a system in which the power a political party has in a legislature is related to the number of votes its candidates receive in an election

province: an administrative area of territory of a country or region

R

Radical Republicans: a faction of the Republican Party during and after the Civil War committed to the emancipation of enslaved people and the their equal treatment during Reconstruction

ratification: to make a document official by a vote and/or authorizing signature

recession: a period in which the buying and production within an economy are decreased or slowed down

Reconstruction: the period in United States history immediately following the Civil War, during which the federal government imposed conditions of transformation on Southern states before they were permitted to rejoin the union

refugee: a person who escapes a country due to conditions of war, political persecution, or natural disaster

regime: a particular government, often associated with the rule of a dictator

relative location: the position of a point in relation to another point

Renaissance: the period of European cultural history following the Middle Ages and characterized by a surge in learning and discovery

Representative: a congressman or congresswoman elected to represent the people of a specific congressional district

revenue: money collected by a person or business

Roman Empire: the period of ancient Roman civilization, following the Roman Republic, during which a singular Emperor headed a vast territory that spanned most of Europe and into Asia and Africa

Roman Republic: the ancient state, centered around the city of Rome, during which a Senate and magistrates governed, as opposed to a monarchy or the rule of an emperor

S

scale: a map component that shows the ratio of distance on the map to the corresponding distance on Earth

secession: the formal withdrawal from a union or organization

secondary source: a document or record that discusses information originally presented elsewhere

sequence: the order in which things occur

Shang Dynasty: the first period in China to produce recorded history and in which bronze work became common in that civilization

sharecropping: a system in which a landowner permits a tenant to use land for agriculture in return for a predetermined share of the crops

socialism: an economic system in which the government, as opposed to individuals and corporations, owns the property and resources used to produce and distribute goods and services

solution: the remedy to a problem

special-purpose map: a map—such a tourist map, battle site map, product map, or congressional district map—used to convey information other than physical features or political borders

stock market: the collective system of buyers and sellers who exchange money for ownership shares of companies

suffrage: the right to vote in an election

summarize: to briefly restate the main points of a story or set of information

supply: the available amount of something

supporting detail: a fact, description, or example that clarifies a main idea

Supreme Court: the court of highest authority in the U.S., consisting of the Chief Justice and eight associate justices

surplus: the amount of something that is left over after the demand for it has been met

symbols: dots, stars, lines, arrows, or icons explained in a key and shown on a globe or map to indicate cities, capitals, movement, battles, or other data

T

table: a presentation of data in rows and columns

tariff: a tax on goods imported to or exported from a country

tax: an amount of money that is required to be paid to a government by an individual or corporation

telecommuting: a work arrangement in which employees do their jobs from home or remotely through the use of phone, e-mail, and the Internet

term: the period for which an official is elected to serve in office

timeline: a display of events in chronological order

tomb: a vault, typically underground, for burying the dead

topic sentence: the sentence that conveys the main idea of a paragraph

trade route: a series of land or sea pathways used for the commercial transport of goods by merchants

treaty: an official agreement between countries or groups

tributary: a smaller stream or river that flows into a larger stream, river, or lake

U

UN Security Council: a group within the United Nations organization that is responsible for maintaining international peace and security

unalienable: something that cannot be taken or given away; also *inalienable*

unemployment rate: the measure, by percentage, of people who are seeking paid jobs but are not part of the labor force

United States Constitution: the legal document that framed the U.S. government at its formation and continues to serve as the supreme body of laws for the nation

V

vassal: a person who receives protection and use of land from a feudal lord in exchange for the pledge of service

vested: fully guaranteed as a legal right or benefit

W

wages: the amount of money a worker is paid

welfare: a government program intended to provide financial support to poor or unemployed people

withholding: a deduction from wages of taxes and other expenses that an employee is required to pay

Answer Key

UNIT 1 Geography

LESSON 1, *pp. 2–6*

1. A, Brazil is in South America and is the only choice that is on the equator.

2. C, Ecuador's climate is different in the mountains, along the coast, and in the Amazon.

3. C, People moved to the Costa region because of increased banana production in the 1950s.

4. D, The Sierra region features the Andes Mountains.

5. B, The map shows the Costa region is coastal, and the text indicates that the Galápagos Islands are west of the mainland. From this you should infer that the islands are in the Pacific Ocean, and thus have an ocean border.

6. C, Egypt is located in North Africa on the Mediterranean Sea. It is therefore north of the Equator.

7. A, Argentina is one of the southernmost countries in South America. Therefore, it is in the Southern Hemisphere.

8. A, Kruger National Park is located in the Limpopo and Mpumalanga regions, which are in the northeast area of South Africa.

9. D, European imperialists wanted control over areas that would help them economically. Gold in South Africa would have most attracted the Europeans to the area.

10. D, The Pacific Ocean and the Rocky Mountains are the only natural features listed in the western United States.

11. C, North Carolina was logically the first state settled because it is located along the Atlantic coast. It is also the only answer choice that was one of the original Thirteen Colonies.

12. C, As a rule, waterways aid in settlement and mountains are barriers to settlement. Therefore, the Ohio River most logically aided settlement of the Midwest region.

13. B, The Rocky Mountains run north south, effectively forming a barrier between the Midwest and the West Coast.

14. B, Saudi Arabia is the only country listed that is in the Middle East. The information in the paragraph explains that the Middle East is located in central and southwest Asia. China and Japan are in the east. Russia is in the north.

15. A, China is the farthest away from Europe, so Europeans probably considered it to be in the Far East.

16. D, Asia is unlikely to have a shared culture, does not border the Atlantic or Indian Ocean, and does not include Africa. Therefore, the only logical answer is that Asia has a diverse climate.

LESSON 2, *pp. 7–11*

1. D, The maps shows six major cities in northeastern New Jersey, more than in any other area.

2. C, Sydney is east of 150°E longitude.

3. C, Looking at the map, it is easy to see that most of the cities are located south of 30°N latitude.

4. B, The star symbol indicates that Atlanta is the capital. Interstate 75 goes through Atlanta.

5. D, Highways 280 and 16 merge in Savannah.

6. D, Savannah is the city closest to those coordinates.

7. A, The two cities in the southeast with elevation ranges from 0 to 1,600 feet are Miami and Atlanta. Using the scale, you can determine that the distance between these two cities is approximately 625 miles.

8. B, Of the states listed as answer choices, only Colorado has elevations of over 6,561 feet.

9. C, Of the places listed as answer choices, only Atlanta falls between those coordinates.

10. A, Relative location does not include latitude or longitude. Therefore, the relative location of Detroit is north of Columbus.

11. B, The star symbol indicates that Olympia is the capital of Washington state. Using the scale, you can determine that Mt. Rainier National Park is the closest park to the capital.

12. C, I-5 connects Bellingham, Seattle, Tacoma, and Olympia.

13. A, Most of Washington's major cities are in the west. Therefore, you can assume that most of Washington's population is in the west.

14. D, Puget Sound connects several major cities to the Pacific Ocean. This facilitates economics and trade.

15. D, The P-in-a-square symbol represent parking lots. Most of the parking lots are near the Smithsonian museums.

16. B, The M-in-a-square symbol represents Metro stations. Of those shown on this map, the Metro station closest to the White House is Federal Triangle.

17. A, The most logical route would be the one with no backtracking. The first option is the only one that meets that criterion.

LESSON 3, *pp. 12–16*

1. A, The shading on the map indicates that the elevation of California is varied and has low land, hills, and mountains.

2. D, There are five Great Lakes, and Michigan borders four of them.

3. C, Silver Lake State Park is on the east coast of Lake Michigan.

4. C, The coastal areas receive more than 60 inches of rain a year, making them the wettest areas.

5. B, The shading on the map indicates that the lowest amount of precipitation along the Florida border is between 52 and 56 inches.

6. B, Virginia has average temperature ranges in July from 60° to 90°. In January, the temperature ranges are between 30° and 45°. The only answer option that fits these ranges is 30 degrees in January and 80 degrees in July.

7. D, Maine is the north-easternmost state in the United States. The temperature ranges in January are between 0° and 30°. Maine is by far the coldest of all states listed as answer choices.

8. C, Of the states listed, only Tennessee has average January temperatures that include temperatures below freezing.

9. A, The vast difference in temperature ranges shows that across the United States there is a wide range of temperatures.

10. A, The climate of the southeastern United States is affected by its proximity to the equator. Vegetation is a product of climate, not a cause. Also, there are not numerous mountain ranges in the southeast.

11. D, Farming is problematic in parts of South Asia because the area receives much of its yearly rainfall during the monsoon, or rainy, season from June through October.

UNIT 1 (continued)

12. D, All continents except Antarctica have a wide variety of average precipitation amounts.

13. A, Pakistan's urban population is concentrated along the coast and in the east-central plains.

14. D, By looking at the map, you can see that about half of Pakistan is covered with mountains or hills. Therefore, the best answer is 50%.

15. C, While the Indus River does separate the mountains from the desert and may have a large delta, it is probably most important because it runs the entire length of Pakistan. Remember how important rivers can be for transportation, trade, and irrigation.

16. D, The Pakistanis used irrigation (which is redirecting water to other areas) in order to create arable (or farmable) land.

LESSON 4, *pp. 17–21*

1. C, This map shows the counties in Wyoming and Wyoming's bordering states.

2. D, The shading on the map indicates that population density is greatest near the major cities.

3. A, You can logically assume that Madrid has the highest population because it has the largest area with more than 965 people per square mile.

4. B, The most logical option is that Tucson is both a large city and the county seat.

5. B, There are no large or small cities shown in the far northern part of the state.

6. A, Even though Coconino County has a larger area, most of the large cities are in Maricopa County. Therefore, it can be assumed that Maricopa County has the largest population.

7. B, While no cities are marked, you can assume that areas with the largest population density contain Brazil's major cities. The largest population density occurs along the east coast.

8. B, The growth of Brazil's population centers was probably most affected by the Amazon rainforest and the Atlantic Ocean. Most people do NOT live in the rainforest areas. European settlers arrived and built cities along the Atlantic coast.

9. A, Modern Brazil, like historic Brazil, has a low population in the Amazon area.

10. D, Brazil won its independence in 1822. Slavery was not abolished until 1888, a difference of 66 years.

11. A, The information mentions indigenous peoples, Portuguese colonizers, and Africans. Therefore, you can logically assume that Brazil's population is a mixture of people of different ethnicities.

12. A, Given the number of dots and the size of the Asian continent, it is logical to identify Asia as the continent with the largest population.

13. C, While parts of Europe have little population, overall, it is much more densely populated than North America.

14. B, Areas with a high population density logically produce the most pollution.

15. D, Based on the map, Europe is the most densely populated continent. While Asia may have more people, this map shows population density, so total geographic area must be taken into account.

16. C, The only county listed that has access to the sea is Dublin County.

17. B, By reading the map closely, you can determine that many county capitals share the same name as their county.

18. C, By reading the map closely, you can determine that Clonmel is the county seat of County Tipperary.

19. D, The map shows that Wisconsin is in the Midwest region. The information states that Illinois has the highest population among Midwest states only. You can use your knowledge of geography to make the judgment that the Midwest region does not feature the largest state.

20. B, While none of these cities are shown on the map, use your knowledge about geography to determine that Chicago is in Illinois. Therefore, it is the only city in the Midwest that is listed.

LESSON 5, *pp. 22–26*

1. D, After the founding of Jamestown, slave traders began taking slaves to North America.

2. D, The passage states that both trade goods and ideas were exchanged among countries along the Silk Road.

3. B, The best route from Alexandria to Kabul is through Seleucia and Bactra.

4. C, These four cities are all centrally located on the Silk Road.

5. D, According to the dotted lines, traders from Rome had to cross the Mediterranean, which would have been done by boat.

6. A, The best description of the map is that it shows the acquisition of land by the United States. Beginning with the first area ceded by Britain in 1783, each acquisition and the date of the acquisition is shown.

7. B, Except for the coastal portion of the Louisiana Purchase made from France, all of the land along the Gulf of Mexico was ceded by Spain.

8. B, The Louisiana Purchase opened much of the land west of the Mississippi River to settlement. The purchase was made in 1803.

9. D, California was included in the Mexican Cession of 1848.

10. B, While some of the explorers sailed south around South America, they all began by sailing west.

11. D, Use the map key to determine that the light-gray dotted line represents the Vikings. Follow that line to discover that they made their voyage to North America circa 1000, which was earlier than any of the other explorers listed.

12. B, Use your historical knowledge to correctly assume that European exploration of North America affected the continent through colonization, increased trade, and indigenous people's loss of land.

13. D, The trade routes on the map illustrate that the Romans traded both inside and outside their empire.

14. B, The Romans traded for several items from Spain. The only item listed as an answer option is grain.

15. B, By analyzing the map, you can determine that the Roman Empire existed and traded over three continents. The empire included much of Europe, the northern part of Africa, and part of western Asia.

UNIT 1 (continued)

16. C, You can logically assume that trading over a number of geographic areas allowed for an exchange of cultural knowledge throughout the empire. You know that Europe, Africa, and the Middle East had different cultures, even in ancient times.

LESSON 6, pp. 27–31

1. B, Use your historical knowledge to understand that the French and Indian War ended in 1763. The war was the cause of the change in territories. As a result of that war, the British gained territory in North America.

2. C, The Confederacy launched an attack over open ground. Their troops were stretched thin, while the Union had a more compact battle line.

3. A, Austria-Hungary and Serbia no longer existed in 1919 (after World War I). Their lands were divided into several new countries.

4. A, While Anglicanism existed in both England and Ireland during this period, it most logically originated in England.

5. D, Of the countries listed, Lutheranism was only prominent in Denmark, where the entire country was Lutheran.

6. B, Based on the number of different religions practiced within the Holy Roman Empire versus the other countries, that is logically the area in which religious conflicts would most likely occur.

7. C, While no present-day countries are named on the map, you can use your knowledge of geography and the cities listed to discover that both Turkey (the location of Istanbul) and Iran (the location of Tehran) were a part of Alexander's empire.

8. A, By analyzing the distance over which Alexander's empire stretched, the lack of rapid communication was an obvious difficulty.

9. D, Based on the size of the empire that Alexander established in this time period, it is logical to assume that he was an accomplished military commander.

10. D, The map indicates that the French had fortified their border with Germany.

11. D, By following the Schlieffen Plan and invading Belgium in order to gain access to France, Germany violated Belgian neutrality. This action forced Britain to enter the war in defense of Belgium.

12. A, By looking at the maps, you will notice that there were three airfields on Iwo Jima. They were most logically what made Iwo Jima so significant to the U.S. military.

13. C, By analyzing the small locator map, you can judge that Iwo Jima was a closer base than the Mariana Islands to launch an aerial invasion of Japan.

UNIT 1 REVIEW, pp. 32–36

1. A, This general description best explains Beijing's relative location.

2. C, Latitude and longitude are used to find absolute location.

3. D, All of the states that border the Gulf of Mexico are in the southern region.

4. D, Tennessee shares a border with Mississippi, Alabama, Georgia, North Carolina, Georgia, Kentucky, and Arkansas.

5. B, Nashville is in Tennessee. It is the only answer choice in a southern region state.

6. C, Using the scale, you can measure the distance at around 700 miles.

7. C, The majority of the population lives in the southeast, near Ottawa.

8. D, Because Alberta has the highest population of the provinces listed, it most likely has the highest total income.

9. B, Because the majority of the population lives along or near the Atlantic coast or the Great Lakes, you can logically assume that fishing and shipping are important industries.

10. A, Follow the lines of latitude and longitude to determine that Yellowknife is the closest city to those coordinates.

11. D, The routes on the map show that African Americans from Georgia most likely migrated to an east coast state such as New York.

12. C, World War I was happening in Europe in 1916. This led to an increase in manufacturing jobs. Jim Crow laws promoted discrimination in the South. These two factors most contributed to the Great Migration.

13. D, The Harlem Renaissance was a result of the migration of African American artists, authors, and musicians to New York during this period.

14. A, The United States saw an increase in its urban (city) workforce during the Great Migration.

15. A, The map shows that the French had more troops and cannons.

16. B, With their back against the Alle River, the Russians became trapped as the French advanced.

17. C, All of the early settlements were built along waterways.

18. A, The American Revolution ended in 1783. The settlements on the map were all founded soon after that date.

UNIT 2 U.S. HISTORY

LESSON 1, pp. 40–44

1. B, Using the columns and rows in the table, you can determine that the New England colonies included Connecticut and New Hampshire.

2. B, The data in the table supports only the fact that New York had a larger population than Delaware. Rhode Island is the smallest state, but in 1750, it did not have the smallest population.

3. D, This question requires you to use both logic and your knowledge of history. The smallest colonies did not have the smallest populations (Georgia and Connecticut disprove this). Neither Massachusetts (second largest population) nor Maryland (third largest population) was a Southern Colony. Both the New England and Middle Colonies had more than one populous colony. The only correct choice is that the earliest colonies (Virginia, Massachusetts, Pennsylvania, and Maryland) had larger populations that colonies established closer to 1750 (Georgia). This is also the logical choice. If a colony was founded shortly before 1750, its population would logically be much smaller than colonies established in the 1600s.

UNIT 2 *(continued)*

4. D, The details in the table clearly show that the population of Virginia increased dramatically between 1700 and 1750. Therefore, you need to find the answer choice that would logically and reasonably support this trend. The first two choices would indicate a decrease in population not an increase. Choice C is not logical. Choice D is correct. A diversified agricultural economy is a positive change and would encourage more people to move to Virginia because they would be able to support themselves and make a profit.

5. D, Connecticut's population grew by 4,596, which shows the least amount of growth.

6. B, Virginia's population of enslaved people increased more than New York's, Maryland's, or South Carolina's during the years 1720 to 1750, as clearly shown in the table.

7. C, In 1720, Virginia had a little more than 26,000 enslaved people. By 1770, Virginia had more than 187,000 enslaved people. The difference is more than 150,000.

8. C, By analyzing the population figures on the table, you will discover that the only correct answer choice is that about 400,000 fewer people lived in the Middle Colonies than in the Southern Colonies.

9. A, Natural increase is defined by an increased birth rate coupled with a decreased death rate. Therefore, the best reason for the population growth in the colonies was natural increase.

10. A, The conflicts on the table are listed in chronological (or time) order. Therefore, the earliest conflict was the Pequot Revolt, which took place in the New England region.

11. B, There were conflicts in New England, the Middle Colonies, and the Southern Colonies. Therefore, conflicts occurred between colonists and Native Americans throughout all regions. Even though the last conflict listed on the table happened in 1756, you know from your knowledge of history that conflict between settlers and Native Americans occurred for many years after.

12. D, This question requires you to use logic. The most logical reason for most of the conflicts between colonists and Native Americans was disputes over land.

13. C, By using logic and reasoning, you can determine that an increase in colonial population would lead to an increased need for land. This need for land would cause more conflict.

14. A, Agriculture is the only economic activity that occurred in all three regions in the table.

15. C, The middle column on the table is titled Economy. Therefore, it contains information about the economic activities of each region.

16. B, By closely reading the text, you can determine that it included specific examples of large cities in the Middle Colonies.

17. C, This question requires you to use logic. Think logically about which location would receive news the fastest—a location with mostly towns, small farms, and some large cities, or large plantations and small farms. Obviously, people in towns and cities would receive news faster than people on farms. This eliminates any Southern Colonies. Now consider which industries might be more helpful in spreading news, such as trade and shipping. Both of these enterprises occurred in New England. Therefore, the most logical choice is Massachusetts. Although New Hampshire was also a New England colony, it did was more rural than Massachusetts.

18. A, Because the area covered by the colonies is vast, stretching all along the Atlantic Coast, it is logical to assume that the geography and climate would differ among the colonies located in the three separate regions.

LESSON 2, *pp. 45–49*

1. B, In his pamphlet, Thomas Paine clearly states that the bravest achievements are accomplished by young nations.

2. C, The challenge here is to identify the main idea. Most answer choices include details from the Declaration of Independence, but only choice C clearly explains the main idea that people have the right to end destructive governments and form new ones. Details such as unalienable rights support this main idea.

3. C, The correct answer is that the colonists cautiously approached independence only after the British continued to violently oppress them. This is clear through the details in the paragraph. The fact that the Declaration of Independence was written over a year after war broke out between Britain and the colonies is a detail that supports this main idea. Despite having to fight the British army, the colonists' first option was not declaring independence.

4. A, Because Pennsylvania and Virginia had the largest number of signers of the Declaration of Independence, it is logical to assume that they were large and important colonies.

5. B, The last sentence of the passage states the main idea. The colonies were in agreement with Great Britain and Spain regarding Canada and Florida. The disputed land was east of the Mississippi.

6. C, The large size of the disputed territory emphasizes the importance of the conflict. The map shows the extensive unoccupied territory between the colonies and the Mississippi River.

7. B, When determining the main idea and purpose, you must always think about the big picture. Here, the purpose of the Declaration of Independence was to end political loyalty to Britain. The Declaration was intended to dissolve the political connection between Great Britain and the united colonies.

8. A, The Declaration of Independence claims the "authority of the good people of the these colonies" as its governing principle. This detail supports the main idea of self-government by the people of the colonies.

9. C, Because the paragraph mainly discusses the Articles of Confederation, the best choice for the main idea of the paragraph is The First Plan of Government.

10. B, The only choice that would have been possible under the Articles of Confederation would be that the state of Virginia collects taxes. The details about the Articles that appear in the table make this clear.

11. B, Because the American leaders had just fought the strong British national government, they wanted most of the power to rest with individual states.

12. D, Because the Articles of Confederation did not allow the federal government to levy taxes, it was difficult to collect money in order to pay the country's debts.

UNIT 2 (continued)

13. A, Proportional representation means that larger states receive more representatives than smaller states. Rhode Island is the smallest state in the country. Therefore, Rhode Island might have been most concerned about proportional representation in Congress.

14. B, This question requires you to use logic. When you review some of the main reasons states had for not ratifying the Constitution, the most important point was the lack of protection for individual rights. Britain brutally oppressed the rights of many people in colonial Massachusetts, especially in Boston. Therefore, because Boston was the birthplace of the American Revolution, people in Boston and colonial Massachusetts were more likely to not support a document that failed to protect individual rights.

15. D, The passage mentions checks and balances, the Constitutional Convention, and protecting personal freedoms, but these are details that support the larger main idea regarding the road from the Convention to the ratification of the Constitution. The table deals with the ratification by states. Taken together, the best title for all of the information is "From Convention to Ratification."

16. B, The details in the paragraph and in the table clearly show that the states had various concerns about ratifying the Constitution. The details also show that the states had different timetables for ratification.

LESSON 3, pp. 50–54

1. C, The Anti-Federalists believed that the government should favor agriculture over commerce and industry. Therefore, you can categorize "the future of the nation depends upon the work of farmers throughout the nation" as expressing an Anti-Federalist viewpoint.

2. B, John Jay categorizes those who want America united under a strong government and those who want states to have more power. Therefore, the correct answer is B: people who believe in a strong central government and people who believe in a number of strong state governments.

3. D, The Anti-Federalist sentiment in the second excerpt categorizes citizens as people who want a limited government. This is referenced throughout the excerpt and clearly stated in the last sentence.

4. B, Since this dispute occurred between Georgia and Spain, it is best categorized as international political history.

5. D, Georgia was the southernmost colony and bordered Florida, which was held by Spain. They had withstood a previous attack from the Spanish over land claims.

6. B, Washington is warning the country about the dangers of political parties. Therefore, his tone is best categorized as cautionary.

7. D, Bribery of an elected official by another government can be categorized as foreign influence and corruption.

8. C, The map shows 7 Federalist states, 6 Democratic-Republican states, 3 states with divided votes, and 4 territories. Therefore, most of the places on the map can be categorized as Federalist states.

9. D, The only state listed with ten or more electoral votes is Pennsylvania. You must add the 8 Democratic-Republican votes and the 7 Federalist votes to determine that Pennsylvania had 15 electoral votes in 1800.

10. C, The map shows that Vermont voted for John Adams. It can be categorized as a Federalist state based on the election results.

11. C, Bonaparte sold the land due to a conflicted political relationship with Great Britain. The sale prevented the British from occupying the territory.

12. D, Jefferson wanted land for both westward expansion and complete control over the Mississippi, a major trade route. These factors mean that his decision is best categorized as a geographic and economic decision.

13. A, The Mississippi River was a major trade route. It allowed people and goods to be transported easily. Therefore, the desire to control the Mississippi River falls into the category of economics.

14. D, Jefferson's main goal for The Corps of Discovery was to discover a northern water route between the Atlantic and Pacific oceans. This was for commercial and trade purposes.

15. B, While the journey did not achieve its main goal, it was not considered a failure. It succeeded in gaining knowledge about the American west.

16. B, *The Northwest Ordinance* prohibited slavery in any states created in the Northwest Territory, all of which were considered Northern states. Therefore, they can be categorized as free states.

17. D, The second column in the table indicates the year in which each state joined the Union. The only state that joined after 1840 was Wisconsin.

18. C, Jefferson's message describes the two categories of benefits as safe passage through the area and financial gain from the area's resources.

19. B, With the purchase of the Louisiana Territory, Jefferson's message is full of promise about the future of the United States. Therefore, his message can be categorized as hopeful.

LESSON 4, pp. 55–59

1. B, The information states "After taking office in 1829, Jackson spurred Congress to pass the Indian Removal Act of 1830." Therefore, the correct answer is B.

2. D, The Battle of Tippecanoe took place in 1811, so it preceded the War of 1812.

3. D, This question requires you to make an assumption. Choice A is not true (the United States never controlled Canada); choice B is not true (while the Battle of New Orleans did take place after the Treaty of Ghent was signed, Andrew Jackson defeated the British); choice C is not logical (the United States was less than 30 years old – it is not logical that the U.S. was the most powerful nation in the world). The correct assumption is choice D: After defeating the British in the War of 1812, nationalism, or national pride, began to grow in the United States.

4. B, Texas gained its independence in 1821. The Texas Revolution was in 1835, which was more than 10 years after Texas gained its independence.

5. C, The American Revolution occurred before all of the subsequent events. None of the other events would have been possible if the colonists had lost the Revolution.

UNIT 2 (continued)

6. C, The war that Monroe is referring to is the War of 1812.

7. C, President Monroe is referring to the Declaration of Independence. The Declaration essentially stated that the government was "in the hands of the people."

8. B, The incident that happened after British and American forces arrived at New Orleans included a number of small skirmishes that broke out between the two forces. Even though this event is not immediately after the arrival of the troops on the sequence chart, it is the next thing that happened in New Orleans.

9. C, This question requires you to make an assumption. The Treaty of Ghent was signed in late December in Belgium. Communications could only be conducted by sending information overseas on ships. The likelihood that the British and American forces in New Orleans in early January knew that a peace treaty had been signed is very small. Therefore, it is logical to assume that the Battle of New Orleans took place after the Treaty of Ghent was signed because the troops in New Orleans did not know about the signing.

10. A, Jackson states that the government's policy "is approaching to a happy consummation." Consummation means end. For this to be true, most Native American groups must have been gone from the eastern United States. Also, the date is 1830. Using your historical knowledge, you know that most Native Americans were gone from the eastern United States due to colonial and early American expansion.

11. B, Jackson states, "the present policy of the Government is but a continuation of the same progressive change by a milder process." He is essentially saying that the policy has become less harsh and confrontational toward Native Americans. He also states that Native Americans are now compensated for their lands and given land in the west.

12. D, Monroe was elected in 1816. He proposed the Monroe Doctrine in 1823, for a difference of seven years.

13. D, Monroe could use his accomplishments during his first term as a reason for voters to reelect him in 1820. In his first term, he settled many disputes with European countries.

14. D, The Monroe Doctrine stated that the United States would not tolerate European interference with countries the United States had acknowledged as independent states. The paragraph explains that this includes European colonies in America. Therefore, is it most logical that the doctrine was issued after Spain asked other European nations to help stop revolts in Spanish-American colonies.

15. B, The Mexican War, during which the United States fought with Mexico after acknowledging Texas's independence, is a case in which the United States acted on the threat stated in the Monroe Doctrine.

16. C, The sequence chart states that Louisiana became the first U.S. state located west of the Mississippi River in 1812. The chart states that Missouri joined the United States, therefore becoming a state, in 1821.

17. C, If American settlers in Texas fought the Texas Revolution in 1835, then it is logical to assume that Texas became a state sometime after 1835.

LESSON 5, pp. 60–64

1. C, The information states that the Northern economy featured commercial and industrial sectors as well as agriculture. Therefore, one effect of sectional differences between the North and the South was that the Northern economy became increasingly diverse.

2. C, The table shows that the population of enslaved African Americans in South Carolina grew dramatically over the years. Most enslaved people worked on farms or plantations, especially in South Carolina. Therefore, the most likely cause of the population increase was that agriculture remained the most common way of making a living in the South.

3. B, This question requires you to use logic. By examining the table, you can clearly see that over time, the growth of the enslaved African American population in South Carolina outpaced that of whites. The most logical effect of this large difference was that whites would become increasingly nervous about possible violence from the enslaved African American population. As a consequence, South Carolina had some of the harshest laws for slaves.

4. D, The last sentence in the paragraph tells you that Turner and his followers received harsh punishments for leading the revolt. It is logical to believe that whites would be afraid of similar action, so Turner's revolt most likely caused Southern officials to develop more restrictive policies towards enslaved people.

5. A, The most likely cause of Turner's actions was his (and others) anger over the harsh conditions under which they lived.

6. A, Lincoln's election affected the United States, which is shown by the fact that seven Southern states seceded from the Union afterward.

7. B, Limit this answer to the information presented in the paragraph. Lincoln's election resulted in seven states seceding from the Union and forming the Confederacy. The formation of the Confederacy caused Lincoln and other Union leaders to claim federal forts and other property located in the South. Therefore, the formation of the Confederacy was an effect of Lincoln's election and a cause of Lincoln's claim of forts located in the South.

8. C, If this map had been drawn by the South after the Southern states seceded, it would have labeled the Confederate states a separate nation.

9. B, Examine the territories on the map closely. More territories were open to slavery than were not. Therefore, this probably led to conflict over slavery in the territories.

10. D, It can be assumed from the information in the paragraph that the Confederates fired on Fort Sumter because Union Major Robert Anderson refused to surrender the fort.

11. A, This question asks you to make a judgment about the most significant effect of the attack on Fort Sumter. While all of the choices are factually true, the most significant effect was Lincoln's decision to call for volunteers to battle the Confederacy. This action meant war was inevitable.

12. A, Lincoln stated that the United States was founded on the proposition that all men are created equal. He said that the Civil War was testing whether a nation conceived with that notion could survive. Therefore, he is suggesting that one cause of the Civil War was that the Confederacy limited the rights of enslaved African Americans.

13. B, Lincoln stated, "those… here gave their lives that that nation might live." He hoped the effect of the battle would be that the soldiers' sacrifice would preserve the ideals of the founders.

14. B, Be sure to read the excerpt carefully. The Emancipation Proclamation only affected enslaved persons living in Southern states fighting against the Union. It did not free all enslaved people (in fact, it freed very few as Southern states ignored the proclamation).

15. C, The Proclamation explains that states represented in Congress on the first day of January 1864 will be considered non-rebellious.

16. D, Lincoln's Emancipation Proclamation only affected states currently in rebellion. He did not want to upset loyal states that allowed slavery. Therefore, Lincoln wanted to preserve the United States at all costs.

17. C, The Emancipation Proclamation officially made slavery an issue in the Civil War. The war became about freeing enslaved people. This gave Britain and other nations who already outlawed slavery pause. Because of its dependence on Southern cotton, Britain was considering supporting the Southern cause, but it would not officially support slavery. Therefore, one effect of the Emancipation Proclamation was that it generated support from other nations for the Union.

LESSON 6, pp. 65–69

1. B, In this case, you should contrast (or find differences) between Lincoln's plan and that of the Radical Republicans. Their plans featured different objectives for the process of Reconstruction.

2. B, Although they went about it in different ways, both Lincoln and the Radical Republicans wanted to successfully rebuild the United States.

3. A, Compared to the plans of the Radical Republicans, Lincoln's Reconstruction plans can be described as peacemaking.

4. D, This question requires you to make an assumption. If Sherman set out to demoralize the South, Lee's actions were kind. Therefore, it is logical to assume that Lee believed that by being kind to Northerners the Confederacy might win their support.

5. D, The ultimate goal for both Sherman and Lee was to find a way to win the war.

6. C, Read the information carefully to determine the similarities and differences between slavery and sharecropping. One difference was that in sharecropping, the workers could receive payment for their work on a plantation.

7. D, Slavery and sharecropping were similar in that, just as during the era of slavery, many sharecroppers worked at agricultural tasks under difficult conditions. The other answer choices each include a level of freedom that formerly enslaved people did not possess.

8. C, Read the details of each amendment carefully. Section 2 of each is identical. Therefore, both the Thirteenth and Fifteenth Amendments grant Congress the authority to enforce their provisions.

9. A, The Fifteenth Amendment prohibits denying or abridging voting rights of any citizen on account of race, color, or previous condition of servitude. The Thirteenth Amendment prohibits slavery. Therefore, it would be illegal under the Fifteenth Amendment (but not addressed in the Thirteenth Amendment) to establish poll taxes (a tax that must be paid in order to vote) for certain ethnic groups.

10. A, The information in the paragraph and in the table show that both the House and Senate experienced lengthy periods in the 1900s with no African American members. No African American served in the Senate between 1881 and 1967, and none served in the House of Representatives between 1901 and 1929.

11. D, While Hiram Revels was the first African American member of the U.S. Senate, he was elected by the Mississippi State Legislature, not the public. However, Joseph Hayne Rainey was the first African American to be popularly elected to serve in Congress.

12. C, This question requires you to use subject area knowledge. Jim Crow laws were popular in the South. They established poll taxes, literacy tests, and other measures designed to limit African American votes. The Fugitive Slave Acts were federal laws enacted by Congress to ensure the return of enslaved people who had escaped to the North. While both types of laws oppressed African Americans, Jim Crow laws were state and local acts, while the Fugitive Slave Acts were federal laws.

13. B, Blanche K. Bruce completed her term in office in 1867. No other African American served in the Senate until 1967. George Henry White completed his term in 1901. No other African American served in the House until 1928.

14. C, You know that Lincoln preferred a conciliatory Reconstruction plan designed to easily welcome the Southern states back into the Union, but the Radical Republicans in Congress wished to punish Southern states with harsh Reconstruction policies. By examining the actions of President Johnson in the information, you can determine that Johnson's policies were most similar to those of Abraham Lincoln.

15. B, The information says that while most states ratified the Thirteenth Amendment, the Fourteenth Amendment was rejected by most Southern states.

16. D, While Johnson's policies mostly mirrored those of Lincoln, one that did align with that of the Radical Republicans was his decision to take control of Reconstruction away from the Southern aristocracy.

17. A, The Fourteenth Amendment guaranteed citizenship to all people born in the United States, including formerly enslaved people, and the Fifteenth Amendment established voting rights for African American men.

LESSON 7, pp. 70–74

1. D, By interpreting the line graph, you can see that the number of manufacturing establishments in Illinois increased from 20,000 to almost 40,000 in the 1890s. This, compared to the growth between 1880 and 1890, was a dramatic increase.

2. C, By analyzing the bar graph, you can determine that the only correct statement is that Taft received nearly 3.5 million popular votes.

3. A, It is clear by the number of candidates that the 1912 presidential election was a multi-party race.

4. A, This question requires you to use logic and make an assumption. Germany is in western Europe. Russia is in eastern Europe. There were more than 3 million immigrants from western Europe and only about a half-million immigrants from eastern Europe. Therefore, it is logical to assume that in 1890, it is likely that more immigrants to the United States came from Germany than from Russia.

5. B, The most dramatic statistic in the second circle graph is the number of Irish immigrants to the United States. The likely reason for the large amount of Irish leaving their homeland was the continued eviction of poor Irish farmers.

6. B, Be sure to read the graph carefully and not be confused by the numbers. For example, the number of deaths in service was around 2,000, which is not the total number of U.S. troops who died. The correct answer is that U.S. troops suffered fewer than 500 deaths in battle.

7. D, Because more than 2,000 deaths were non-battle related, and less than 500 soldiers died in battle, it is logical to assume that in war, death by disease or accident was more likely than death in battle.

8. D, Only the first circle graph shows figures related to the popular vote. On that graph, Eugene Debs received the third largest percentage of the popular vote, with 2.83% (Taft: 51.59%; Bryan: 43.04%).

9. A, The second circle graph indicates that the electoral vote was split between Bryan and Taft. The first graph indicates that Hisgen, Chafin, and Debs received some percentage of the popular vote. By comparing the graphs, you can determine they indicate that three of the candidates received no electoral votes.

10. B, The graph shows the total manufacturing wages, so any changes must affect the total number. Therefore, if New York added many new manufacturing jobs during the 1880s, then that would help explain the increase in total manufacturing wages between 1880 and 1890.

11. C, The figures on the graph indicate that the total wages in 1880 were about 470 million dollars. In 1890, the total wages were a little more than 400 million dollars. Therefore, between 1880 and 1890, manufacturing wages decreased by about 70 million dollars.

12. C, The rural population of Alabama was much higher in both 1900 and 1910 than the urban population, so you can determine that the population was mostly rural.

13. A, By 1910, the urban population of Alabama had increased slightly, not dramatically.

14. B, When union membership increased, the lines on the graph go upward. When union membership decreased, the lines go downward. The only period on the graph where the line is going downward is between 1904 and 1906. Therefore, you can determine that union membership decreased in that period.

15. B, A dramatic increase or decrease is defined by a great change in the data. The period with the greatest change on the graph is between 1902 and 1904. Therefore, that is the time when union membership increased most dramatically.

16. A, While all of these historical themes took place during the late 1800s and early 1900s, the increase in labor union membership was a Progressive Era trend.

17. D, This question is asking you to identify a trend. To do so, look at the complete graph. Look for dramatic and slight changes. In the early years on the graph, membership grew rapidly, then increased more gradually in the later years.

LESSON 8, *pp. 75–79*

1. B, Because Wilson ran with the campaign slogan "He kept us out of war" and won, it is logical to infer that many Americans supported Wilson's policy of neutrality.

2. C, Because she served as a leader in the National Woman Suffrage Association, the most reasonable inference is that Susan B. Anthony traveled and lectured on the importance of women's suffrage.

3. D, By analyzing the arguments of the authors of *The Blue Book,* you can infer that they believed in using a logical, methodical approach to win an argument.

4. C, Because Pershing wanted the U.S. Army to fight as one unit, he would be able to lead the army himself and take credit for its victories. The U.S. Army would not simply be part of any French or British successes.

5. A, Since the French and British had been fighting Germany and its allies for four years, the commanders likely believed that their own troops were more skilled and experienced than the American Expeditionary Force. You can infer that the commanders did not believe the recently arrived U.S. troops were skilled enough to fight as a separate unit.

6. A, Anthony is referring to the Preamble to the U.S. Constitution when she says, "It was we, the people" and "who formed the Union." The Preamble begins, "We the People of the United States, in Order to form a more perfect Union."

7. C, Because Anthony claims "It was we, the people; not we, the white male citizens" that formed the United States, and that she says that women cannot enjoy the other things mentioned in the Constitution (the blessings of liberty) while they are denied the vote, you can assume that she believes that the Constitution already guarantees women the right to vote.

8. B, The text explains some reasons for Prohibition, but also outlines the difficulty in enforcement and the rise of criminal activity. Therefore, it is logical to infer that for many people, the problems caused by Prohibition outweighed the benefits.

9. D, The fact that some states had prohibition laws until 1966 indicates that some state legislatures believed that consumption of alcohol was dangerous and immoral.

10. B, Because Puerto Rico was an official U.S. territory from 1917, and the Constitution stated that Prohibition was law in all territories subject to the jurisdiction of the United States, you can infer that Puerto Rico was subject to the same prohibition policies as the states.

UNIT 2 (continued)

11. B, Because the text of the amendment states that the provisions would go into effect one year from ratification, and the amendment was ratified in 1919, you can infer that the amendment's measures took effect in 1920.

12. A, Because Congress opposed the United States joining the League of Nations, and the United States is not listed as a permanent member in the table, you can infer that the United States never joined the League of Nations.

13. B, Because the League of Nations was formed after World War I with the aim of preventing another world war, you can infer that it did not achieve its goal of preserving world peace.

14. D, Because of the numerous innovations and advances in society, you can infer that the 1920s was a time of exciting innovation.

15. C. Being allowed the right to vote in national elections was empowering for women. They gained the power to elect officials who created laws, and they could express their views in the ballot box. This was also the culmination of the Woman Suffrage movement in which many women served as leaders and organizers.

LESSON 9, pp. 80–84

1. B, The text in the cartoon indicates that the cartoonist has disdain for politicians. The character cutting down the tree appears to be a "strong man of the people." Therefore, you can assume that the cartoonist believes that the Prohibition Party is right in trying to outlaw alcohol.

2. B, The lines tying the hands of Uncle Sam (the United States) read "The League of Nations." This indicates that those pulling on the lines are trying to make the United States take their side, meaning that they are competing for their own best interests in the League of Nations.

3. C, The cartoon suggests that the United States had its hands tied by other groups in the League of Nations. Therefore, it is logical to assume that those parties have prevented the United States from taking any action of its own regarding the League of Nations.

4. B, Because Hoover is posting a detour sign to indicate the flow away from "Speculation Street" and onto "Business Boulevard," the cartoonist suggests that Hoover is guiding the country's economy back to stability.

5. C, The cartoon blames speculation. The cartoonist shows this by depicting President Hoover having placed a barrier over "Speculation Street." Hoover offers an alternative by guiding the nation down a "detour" that goes in a different direction.

6. C, The figure holding the cards has stars running along his cuff and a "U.S." cuff link. Therefore, you can infer that the figure represents the United States. He may be dressed like Uncle Sam.

7. A, The hand of cards the man is holding is very good. He has four aces and a king. It would be a winning hand in poker. Therefore, you can infer that the cartoonist is trying to convey a feeling of optimism.

8. A, By carefully reading the bandages on the patient (who represents the United States), you can identify depression, banking, national debt, budget, and taxes as being problems facing the United States.

9. C, The cartoonist states, "Trust in your doctor is half the battle." Here, the doctor represents President Franklin Roosevelt. Therefore, the cartoonist is trying to express the idea that Americans should trust Roosevelt to fix many of the nation's problems.

10. B, The artist shows the young man confidently holding the axe and smiling. You can infer that the young man is proud.

11. D, The young man is holding a tool. The poster states "for WORK" and advertises that applications will be taken by the Illinois Emergency Relief Commission. From this, you can infer that the CCC program was designed to combat unemployment.

12. A, The flag in the poster is torn and shows signs of having survived a battle. On December 7th, 1941, the Japanese bombed Pearl Harbor. This date was used to remind people why the United States entered World War II.

13. A, The text on the poster states, "we here highly resolve that these dead shall not have died in vain," which is quoted from President Lincoln's Gettysburg Address. It is designed to inspire loyalty and resolve among the American people.

14. D, The poster asks that American citizens do their part to ensure a military victory in World War II. According to the poster, a victory home is one that finds ways to support the war effort.

15. C, By walking and carrying packages, instead of driving and using other delivery methods, Americans could prevent shortages of gasoline needed for military vehicles.

16. C, Remember that a caricature is an exaggerated drawing of a person. The man eating the apples is wearing a top hat, along with spats on his shoes, and is carrying a cane. He looks like a character from a board game instead of a realistic drawing of a person. He is considered a caricature.

17. D, Because the man eating the apples is dressed as a wealthy man and appears to be starving, you can infer that the cartoonist is trying to convey the idea that the Great Depression affects the wealthy as well as the poor.

LESSON 10, pp. 85–89

1. B, Remember that a short summary does not include specific details. The best summary of the information is that the United States and the Soviet Union competed in a space race for scientific and political gains.

2. D, A summary is an overview, so a summary would likely include an overview of McCarthy's accusations and his eventual downfall.

3. C, The best summaries include all relevant information but do not offer opinions. Therefore, the best summary of the information is that McCarthy gained power through his hearings on Communism, but then lost it with a series of unfounded accusations.

4. C, This question is difficult, because the map does not provide information that relates specifically to the summary. The only correct summary of the information presented is that President Truman authorized various types of U.S. troops to aid South Korean forces.

UNIT 2 (continued)

5. D, The main point is not one detail. It should be an overview of the entire passage. Here, the main point of Kennedy's speech is that the United States will defend the principles of freedom upon which it was founded.

6. B, It is evident that Kennedy is announcing this statement to the world because he says, "Let every nation know . . ."

7. B, A summary should only include important information relevant to the subject of the passage. Therefore, the best thing to add to a potential summary would be the immediate impact of the Act on the nation.

8. C, The information is about the passage of the Civil Rights Act of 1964. Therefore, the main point is that the Act granted new rights and protections to people of all races, religions, and nationalities.

9. D, All of the programs listed in the table relate to domestic policy (policies for the United States, not for other countries, which is considered foreign policy). Therefore, the best summary of the information would be that the Great Society programs targeted many domestic issues facing the nation.

10. D, Affirmative action is a policy designed to ensure opportunities for people of all races. The program that best deals with opportunities such as these is education.

11. B, In his speech, Nixon basically declares that he is resigning because he does not have the support of Congress to carry out the duties of the president.

12. C, In this speech, Nixon does not seem sorry for his actions. His tone is regretful.

13. C, In this case, Reagan states his main purpose for delivering this speech at the beginning of this excerpt. He wants to encourage Soviet leadership to acknowledge the importance of freedom. The rest of the speech is Reagan's way of challenging the Soviets to make this happen.

14. A, Freedom is the main concept that Reagan wishes the Soviets to adopt.

15. D, Remember that in most cases, the main idea of a paragraph is presented in the thesis statement at or near the beginning. In this case, the writer states, "the Presidency of William J. (Bill) Clinton, from 1993 to 2001, was a period of significant economic growth and prosperity for the United States."

16. A, Because the writer states that President Clinton and Congress balanced the budget "for the first time in 30 years," you can determine that before Clinton other recent Presidents had not balanced the federal budget.

UNIT 2 REVIEW, pp. 90–95

1. D, Choice D is the only one that includes details about how the woman suffrage movement would have been divided.

2. B, By examining the information in the second column of the table, you can determine that Lyndon B. Johnson was president between 1963 and 1969.

3. D, Massachusetts, Texas, New York, Illinois, and California all have large populations. Only two of the ten presidents since 1961 have been from states with small populations (Georgia and Arkansas). Therefore, most presidents since 1960 have represented states with large populations.

4. A, Remember that the main idea is the entire point of the map, not a detail. All of the details on the map support the main idea that settlers followed several different trails to reach the western United States.

5. D, The only choice that illustrates a danger that may have occurred along the Oregon Trail is that many settlers along the trail died from diseases such as cholera.

6. D, Use both the x and y axes to determine that the population of Michigan in 1940 was approximately 5.25 million.

7. D, The population of Michigan grew by almost 2 million people between 1950 and 1960. Michigan experienced the greatest population growth in that decade.

8. C, This question requires you to make an assumption. Detroit, Michigan, was and is an important city to the automotive industry. The automotive industry grew dramatically between 1940 and 1960. During that time, Michigan experienced some of its largest population increases. Therefore, you can assume that Michigan's population was affected by the automotive industry.

9. D, Because one of the Anti-Federalists' main concerns with the original Constitution was that it lacked protection for individual rights, and James Monroe was an Anti-Federalist, it is logical to assume that Monroe supported the Virginia Declaration of Rights, which was the model for the U.S. Constitution's Bill of Rights. The fact that Madison also supported states' rights is also a clue that he probably supported the Virginia Declaration of Rights.

10. A, The information states that the Federalists favored industries and big business. Therefore, the correct choice is that the Federalists believed that support for industry and trade should come before support of small farmers.

11. B, By analyzing both Lincoln's and Douglas's arguments, you can determine that neither intended to interfere with slavery where it already existed.

12. D, Be sure to read the question carefully. You are being asked to decide with which of Douglas's assertions Lincoln would disagree. Lincoln clearly believes that all men have natural rights and does not think that states should be able to restrict those rights. Therefore, he would disagree with Douglas's assertion that each state has sovereign power.

13. C, Lyndon B. Johnson's policy was called the Great Society, so the figure on the left in this cartoon is Johnson. Lyndon Johnson is the only president listed who was in office during the Vietnam. The face of the man with the sword is a caricature of Johnson, with a large nose and ears.

14. D, In the cartoon, Johnson beheads a figure representing the Great Society with a sword called War Costs. This violent action illustrates that the costs of taking part in the Vietnam War would take away vital money from the Great Society programs. The action of the sword is more dramatic than accidental neglect.

15. C, The ultimate cause of the Missouri Compromise was fear of the spread of slavery. While it was important to some members of congress to have a balance, the balance needed to have been between free and slave states, not merely between Northern and Southern states.

UNIT 2 (continued)

16. A, Since the information states that the Missouri Compromise preserved the balance of free and slave states in the nation, and each state has two U.S. senators, then the fact that representation in the Senate would remain equal for free and slave states is an implied effect.

17. B, The first paragraph states that Bush's early foreign policy was dominated by the terrorist attacks on September 11, 2001. The document explaining the purpose of the Department of Homeland Security was dated June 2002. The details about the Department of Homeland Security in the document make it possible to infer that it was created in response to the terrorist attacks.

18. D, The only choice listed on the sequence chart as having happened before 1867 is that the Union Pacific crews reach the 100th Meridian line, which took place in October 1866.

19. D, The sequence chart indicates that the first event was the passing of the Pacific Railroad Bill.

20. A, This question requires that you make an assumption. It is logical to assume that since the railroad would bring both people and goods to new areas, significant economic growth would occur along the railroad lines.

UNIT 3 World History

LESSON 1, *pp. 98–102*

1. B, The second paragraph in the information states that Athens established a democracy in which every freeborn man older than 18 received an equal vote. The situation described in the question is a democracy.

2. D, The first paragraph states that Ancient Egypt was an agrarian society. Agrarian is another word for agriculture. Both paragraphs discuss daily life. Therefore, the concepts which are most important in the text are agriculture and daily life.

3. B, While women in Ancient Egypt did all of the things listed as answer choices, the best way to categorize women in Ancient Egypt is to say that they had many rights.

4. B, By examining the map, you can see that Athens had control of much of the coastline of the Aegean Sea. As you know, in ancient times, travel by water was faster than travel over land. The information also mentions that both Athens and Sparta had sea trade routes. Combine all of this information to categorize Athens as a naval power.

5. D, Because both Athens and Sparta were Greek city-states, a conflict between the two, such as the Peloponnesian War, would be considered a civil war. Remember that the American Civil War was fought between two groups of American states.

6. A, To the ancient Egyptians, the *ka* was a life force that left the body after death. Therefore, *ka* can be categorized as a spiritual force.

7. D, The only correct pairing is Egyptian burial practices—preservation of the body. The ancient Egyptians practiced mummification.

8. D, Do not be confused by the table headings. In some cases, the age, structural components, and uses overlap. The only differentiating category for the pyramids is geographic location.

9. C, The only possible category that would include pyramids from the Americas is pyramids built after 1000 AD.

10. B, Because the information describes the workings of the government in the Roman Republic, it is best categorized as political history.

11. C, Because citizens had a vote (although not all citizens had an equal vote), the government of the Roman Republic is best categorized as representational democratic.

12. D, The system giving one vote to each block is similar to the system outlined in the Articles of Confederation in which each U.S. state was given one vote.

13. B, Because both civilizations surround major rivers, they can be categorized as river civilizations.

14. D, Of the answer choices, only Egypt was settled along a river. Egyptians lived along the Nile River.

15. D, In early civilizations, writing was an important breakthrough in communications.

16. B, Because both paragraphs present general information about life and society, the information is best categorized as social history.

17. B, Plays are considered part of literature. Choice D is really a contribution to art because it is a painting of a scene from a Greek myth.

18. D, Cultural history is the category that deals with art, literature, and music.

LESSON 2, *pp. 103–107*

1. D, When examining a Venn diagram, such as the one on this page, be sure to note what each section of the diagram describes. In this diagram, you need to identify something that France did but England did not. Unlike England, France claimed new territories for the nation.

2. C, The diagram shows that flying buttresses were used in Gothic architecture, not in Romanesque architecture.

3. D, The diagram shows that Gothic architecture featured pointed arches instead of round. This gave Gothic structures a soaring look. The information also states that Gothic buildings were taller than Romanesque buildings. Therefore, Gothic churches were taller and appeared to be soaring.

4. B, According to the diagram, medieval tournaments featured jousts on horseback and hand-to-hand melees. Therefore, medieval tournaments were similar to present-day sporting events.

5. D, The diagram classifies knights as being members of the Court.

6. C, If most medieval towns only had several thousand residents, it would be unlikely to find towers in which thousands of people lived. The diagram also states that most people lived on the second story above their businesses.

7. B, Because most medieval towns were surrounded by walls for protection, the population of the towns was most likely limited by the available space within the city walls.

8. C, Italy (the location of Naples) was a major trading power in the 1300s. The ships from the Black Sea most likely carried trade goods. Trading ships also sailed to England. Therefore, you can infer that the Black Death was spread through trade.

UNIT 3 (continued)

9. B, Because children were not exposed to the disease in the 1340s (because they were not yet born), they were more likely to catch the disease when it reappeared in 1361. Children had not developed immunity from the earlier outbreak.

10. A, While all of the men listed as answer choices played important roles during the Crusades, it is logical that Pope Urban II was the most important figure. He called for the First Crusade, and all other Crusades happened as a result of this first act of aggression.

11. B, Thousands of western (European) men went to the Middle East to fight in the Crusades. As a result, they were exposed to Middle Eastern culture.

12. C, It is unlikely that so many European leaders would have participated in the Crusades if it were not for the chance to gain territory and power.

13. D, The Renaissance – or rebirth – was a period of cultural growth and exchange. The cultural exchanges between East and West during the Crusades (including food, trade goods, philosophy, medical knowledge, and art) helped start this trend.

14. D, The box under "The right to hold land" in the diagram explains that vassals gained land and the right to govern that land in a feudal system.

15. B, The advances in communication and the development of centralized governments explained in the diagram suggest that feudalism gave way to more regularized and firmly established systems of government.

16. A, The pyramid in the diagram explains the feudal power structure. In the pyramid, squires have the least amount of power.

17. B, Because vassals received their land, and therefore their authority, from the lord, the lord could expect to receive loyalty from the vassals. The vassals could show their loyalty by supplying troops to the lord.

LESSON 3, *pp. 108–112*

1. B, While the text of the *Magna Carta* does discuss the church and archbishops, the main purpose of the document was to establish basic rights of Englishmen.

2. B, In the first paragraph, Locke states that men are in "a state of perfect freedom." Therefore, you can infer that his point of view is that people are naturally free.

3. D, In the second paragraph, Locke states that "unless the lord and master of them all [God] should, by any manifest declaration of his will, set one above another, and confer on him, by an evident and clear appointment, an undoubted right to dominion and sovereignty." He therefore believes that government should promote equality and only be led by a divinely-appointed sovereign.

4. C, Thomas Jefferson rejected monarchy and the belief that some men were born to rule over others. However, he and Locke both believed that man has natural rights.

5. A, In the quotation, Michelangelo is saying that an uncarved block of marble is the blank slate for an artist's ideas. Therefore, Michelangelo's point of view is that each new sculpture offers an opportunity for greatness.

6. B, When Machiavelli states, "appear to all who see and hear him to be completely pious, completely faithful," etc., and that "the masses always follow appearances," it is clear his point of view is that appearance of belief is more important than actual belief.

7. D, Because Machiavelli discusses projecting power and staying popular with the masses [the people], his purpose is best described as highlighting the ways in which rulers maintain power.

8. B, In the law, the poor are described as "wretched," "miserable," "beggars," and "idle." It is most likely that the King views poor people in England with scorn. The wording of the law suggests that the king believes that the poor are lazy and unwilling to work.

9. D, The tone of the poor law is fairly strict. Therefore, it is unlikely that people would be given aid unless their need was dire. It is more likely that poor children would be provided with apprenticeships [job training].

10. C, The last sentence in the excerpt summarizes Descartes' point of view that over time he realized that the certain knowledge he once sought did not exist.

11. B, While Descartes probably studied many subjects in his journey to acquire knowledge, his overall tone shows that he would most likely be interested in the study of philosophy.

12. A, The author provides several details about the court in Africa. Therefore, you can determine that the author's purpose in writing this excerpt was to offer an accurate description of court life in Timbuktu.

13. D, Each edict first gives an instruction, or piece of advice. Then the edict provides an explanation of why it is important. For example, instruction: "Work hard in your professions"; explanation: "in order to quiet your ambitions." Therefore, the second part of each edict can be characterized as explanatory.

14. C, This list is most similar to an advice manual because it gives advice in many different areas.

15. B, Copernicus's tone indicates that his purpose in writing this was to persuade people that the universe is spherical.

16. A, Copernicus believes that the universe is spherical because Earth, the moon, and the sun are spherical.

LESSON 4, *pp. 113–117*

1. A, The information states that Britain had expanded its colonial interests in India and that was the reason for the Great Trigonometrical Survey. Add that information to the fact that Nepal and Tibet refused to allow British surveyors on their land and you can draw the conclusion that they were worried about British colonial ambitions.

2. C, Because explorers experienced great difficulty in crossing the continent, you can conclude that the British were anxious to explore Australia's rivers because they were searching for an easy way to explore the continent's interior.

3. B, Britain had a history of colonization and you know that they established colonies in Australia. Therefore, you can conclude that European explorers likely experienced conflict with Aboriginal (native) Australians because the Aborigines feared British imperial ambitions. The word *imperial* is related to the word *empire*.

4. D, Because each expedition experienced problems, and because the South Pole is extremely cold, you can conclude that the greatest obstacle to reaching the South Pole was most likely cold temperatures.

5. B, The map shows that Cook explored different places on each of his three voyages. Therefore, you can logically conclude that he hoped to keep exploring and acquiring new territories.

6. B, The map shows that Cook explored almost the entire Pacific area, from Alaska to Australia. His explorations included four continents. Therefore, you can conclude that Cook was interested in exploring many different areas of the world.

7. D, The information states that the English East India Company received a charter from Queen Elizabeth I. Therefore, you can conclude that the English East India Company received support from the national government.

8. C, The East India companies were primarily trading companies. Therefore, you can conclude that their primary goal was to profit through trade.

9. A, Livingstone was a Christian missionary, and his work eventually brought more Christian missionaries to Africa. Therefore, you can conclude that Livingstone may have wanted to open interior areas of Africa to western ideas in order to bring Christianity to the Africans.

10. B, European nations claimed lands in other countries primarily for economic reasons. Therefore, you can conclude that Livingstone's explorations encouraged European nations to claim land in Africa because these nations learned the value of the continent's resources.

11. D, The third column in the table hints that the most enduring legacy of the Silk Road was the exchange of cultural elements among traders.

12. A, Transporting heavy goods or a large quantity of any one type of good over the vast distances that made up the Silk Road would not have been cost effective for the traders. Fewer, more expensive items, like luxury items, would have been easier to transport over land.

13. C, By analyzing the key, you can determine that Great Britain and France controlled the most land in Africa in 1914.

14. C, Determine the answer to this question through a process of elimination. Nigeria is not near the Indian Ocean or the Nile River. It is not large compared to other territories. Nigeria does border the Atlantic Ocean, so you can conclude that ocean harbors would make Nigeria a valuable territory to possess.

15. D, Think carefully about the early North American colonies. They did not cover an entire continent and were not located in the Southern Hemisphere. There is no way to know whether the African territories were united against a common enemy (neither were the early North American colonies). The best answer is that they both were controlled by several different European nations. Britain, France, and Spain all had colonies in North America.

16. A, You have already determined that France and Great Britain controlled the most territory. Of the two countries' languages, only French is an answer choice here. Therefore, you can conclude that the European language spoken the most in Africa was probably French.

LESSON 5, *pp. 118–122*

1. C, Because the question asks what directly led to the Nazi Party receiving the most votes in the 1932 German elections, you should determine which event occurred right before the election on the timeline. In this case, it was because the Germans were unhappy with other politicians because of the economic crisis.

2. B, It is clear by the events on the timeline that Germany met with little resistance to its invasions of European countries. Therefore, the trend supported by the information on the timeline is that Germany showed its strength, and many European countries gave in.

3. D, Think of reasons why the European countries were reluctant to stop Hitler and the Germans. Remember that most western European nations suffered tremendous casualties and economic turmoil because of World War I. These memories were still fresh for most of their leaders. They were obviously reluctant to stop the Germans for fear of another war. Therefore, the prior event that most affected the actions shown on the timeline was World War I.

4. C, The only correct conclusion in the answer choices is C. You can determine this because Germany began attacking the British during the Battle of Britain. The last event on the timeline also states that Hitler called off a ground invasion of Britain. None of this would have been necessary if Britain had surrendered.

5. A, Based on the information in the timeline, you can conclude that because he easily forced the surrender of Belgian forces and reached an armistice with France, Hitler was confident of victory during the summer of 1940 when he began the Battle of Britain.

6. C, According to the timeline, the allied planning team first met to consider dates for the D-Day invasion in March 1943. The actual invasion took place in June 1944, for a difference of 15 months.

7. A, Use the other events listed on the timeline between March 1943 and June 1944 to determine that the reason the D-Day invasion was delayed was because the allies were focused elsewhere, such as in Africa, the Soviet Union, and the North Atlantic.

8. D, It is clear from the events on the timeline that the allies worked together in a coordinated manner. They planned new offensives and provided support for existing fronts.

9. B, Because the allies focused on the Soviet Union and Africa before the D-Day invasion, the timeline supports the trend that the allies garnered victories in the Soviet Union and in Africa before turning to France.

10. A, Be sure to read this timeline carefully. The top section shows events that occurred in Europe during World War II, and the bottom section shows events that occurred in the Pacific. This question asks you to find parallel [very similar] events that happened in Europe and in the Pacific during the dates listed. In May 1945 on the Europe timeline, Germany surrendered. In September 1945 on the Pacific timeline, Japan surrendered. While other events may have taken place during the dates listed as answer choices, those events were not parallel.

UNIT 3 (continued)

11. C, The event on the Pacific timeline that eventually led to the dropping of atomic bombs was the launch of the Manhattan Project. That project developed the atomic bomb. It would have been impossible to drop an atomic bomb if it were not developed.

12. C, The timeline headings here give you a clue. The top heading is "Europe," which signifies battles on land. The bottom heading is "Pacific," which signifies battles on the water. Therefore, the U.S. Navy was vital in the war against Japan.

13. B, The allies did not attack Germany or Japan directly until they had secured territory closer to those nations. In Europe, the allies defeated the Germans in North Africa, the Soviet Union, and France before advancing on Germany itself. In the Pacific, the United States sought to control Pacific islands gradually closer and closer to Japan. Therefore, the timeline supports the trend that the allied strategies for reaching Germany and Japan were similar.

14. D, Because Gandhi was involved in the Independence movement the longest, and he is the most recognizable figure, he was probably the most important leader for Indian independence.

15. B, According to the timeline, the British government took direct control of India because of the Sepoy Mutiny.

16. B, Because the Muslim League and Muslim leader Ali Jinnah were pushing for an independent Muslim state, the British supported partition.

17. C, Britain held on to India for almost 100 years, despite campaigns by Gandhi and others for them to leave. This supports the conclusion that India was a valuable part of the British Empire. Until the 1940s, the British seemed to do all they could to repress rebellion.

18. D, Gandhi's actions can be categorized as working for civil rights. While some answer choices were humanitarians, Gandhi's actions most closely resemble those of Martin Luther King, Jr., who worked for civil rights for African Americans.

LESSON 6, *pp. 123–127*

1. A, The text states that people attempting to cross from East Germany into West Berlin mostly lost their lives. This is a generalization. The author is saying that East Germans generally did not cross successfully from East Germany to West Berlin.

2. A, Answer choice A is the correct generalization because it is supported by details in each bullet point. Choice B is not correct (don't be fooled by the word 'generally'), choice C is a fact, not a generalization, and choice D cannot be proven true.

3. B, The generalization that best describes the full scope of the agreement is that it is primarily concerned with peace, recognition of nations, and human rights. There is no mention of war reparations, and the other answer options are too narrow in focus to provide a valid generalization.

4. D, The United Kingdom (UK) is part of the European Union, but is not listed as a country that uses the euro. The UK still uses the British pound as its currency.

5. A, Because the information deals primarily with economics, you can assume it is correct that countries generally joined the European Union for economic reasons.

6. A, The keywords *ending, division, solidarity,* and *within a single framework* let you know that all of these items are aimed at unifying the nations of Europe.

7. C, Those same keywords let you know that those who support this agreement would likely oppose diverse, separate European economies.

8. D, Because Gorbachev's policy of *glasnost* was generally aimed at changing existing Soviet policies, you can assume that communist leaders would have generally opposed *glasnost.*

9. C, In general, *glasnost* promoted freedom of speech and expression and the ability to criticize the government. In the United States, these freedoms are protected by the First Amendment to the Constitution.

10. D, The information states that conservative communist leaders tried to take back power from democratic reformers. Therefore, to refute the generalization that all Eastern Europeans supported democratic reforms during this time, you can cite that conservative leaders staged a coup against the Soviet government.

11. A, From the information, you can conclude that in general, the Soviet Union used military force to stop uprisings.

12. B, Based on the information in the passage, the dissolution of the Soviet Union happened very quickly. Democratic governments were formed in Eastern Europe in 1989, and the Soviet Union was dissolved only two years later in 1991.

13. C, The Soviet Union incorporated people from many different ethnic backgrounds (remember that it included former European countries as well as several Asian territories). With the break-up of the Soviet Union, many countries were formed based on the ethnic make-up of their populations. Many of these people identified themselves as Georgians, Ukrainians, Kazaks, and Armenians. Therefore, you can assume that the general factor that led to the formation of the countries in the Commonwealth of Independent States was ethnic nationalism.

14. C, This question may seem difficult, but only one country on the list was a former Communist country: Poland. Therefore, the changes taking place in Hungary during the late 1980s and early 1990s were similar to those in Poland.

15. B, The information states that the government reduced censorship, which would support the argument that Hungary allowed increased freedom of expression during that time.

16. D, The cartoonist shows Milosevic as a tank driving through all the lines without stopping. Therefore, you can generalize that Milosevic blatantly disregarded NATO's warnings.

17. B, A tank is generally seen as a representation of aggression.

UNIT 3 REVIEW, *pp. 128–133*

1. B, The timeline shows that China, Britain, and the Soviet Union were writing proposals for the U.N. Charter from August to October 1944. During that same time, World War II was taking place.

UNIT 3 (continued)

2. D, Because of what was happening in the world during the establishment of the United Nations, it is logical to assume that the nations were eager to form the organization because they wanted to help rebuild Europe after World War II and forestall another war.

3. D, Because James Cook studied the fertile land of Australia in 1770, it is logical to conclude that the British were interested in Australia because they hoped to farm the fertile soil. In fact, the information states that wheat became an important agricultural product in the early part of the 1800s.

4. B, You can conclude that, if the British went to the trouble of sending criminals all the way to Australia, the British penal system was under strain.

5. C, You can conclude that, because communities began supporting the arts, and artists began to merge their art with concepts of math and science, the arts generally became more supported and respected during the Renaissance.

6. A, It is clear by the description of new techniques and the combining of art with mathematics and science that the author views the Renaissance as a period of innovation.

7. C, Because the information states that the British expanded their power in India and that the British military officers commanded an army in India, you can conclude that India gained its independence from Britain.

8. C, The main ideas of this information are related to British trade and control in India. These ideas are best categorized as colonialism.

9. B, The diagram states that the Inca extended their influence over other groups between 1200 and 1440, or a period of more than 200 years.

10. B, This information comes after the fact that the Inca gradually expanded their influence and before the period of civil war. Therefore, it should be placed between the first and second boxes.

11. D, Because the Greeks told a wide variety of stories about Greek gods, Greek mythology could best be described as varied.

12. D, The second paragraph clearly states that Roman mythology was influenced by Greek mythology.

13. C, You can conclude that the majority of Eastern European countries did not join the European Union until 2004 because before then they had been part of the Soviet Union.

14. A, By reading the table carefully, you can determine that the only correct answer choice is that Ireland joined the organization more than 20 years before Hungary. Ireland joined in 1973, and Hungary joined in 2004—a difference of 31 years.

15. A, Hobbes discusses the peaceful nature of man, but also concludes that people should use whatever means necessary to defend themselves.

16. B, Because Hobbes believes that man should "seek and use all helps and advantages of war" if peace cannot be maintained, his writings would be best used to support the point of view of a monarch offering protection in exchange for reduced individual rights.

17. C, The information states that the Shang Dynasty was considered the first historical dynasty because the earliest written records from ancient China date from this period. In general, "historical record" is written record.

18. B, Because the writings and carvings of the kings made predictions about a variety of topics, they are best categorized as wide-ranging.

19. D, While all of the answer choices can be considered causes of World War I, the extensive alliances formed among nations was the cause that turned the conflict that started World War I into a world war. Those alliances brought countries not directly related to the initial conflict between Austria-Hungary and Serbia into the war.

20. C, Remember that during wartime, industries are needed to produce military items such as weapons and ammunition. You can also assume that most men who worked in those factories were needed to fight the war. Therefore, while women took over jobs left by men in many areas, the most logical answer is that women most likely worked as industrial workers.

21. C, The diagram indicates that Britain was anxious to keep its colonial territories and feared that Germany might win the war and dominate Western Europe. The arms race between Germany and Britain was very competitive. Therefore, you can conclude that rivalry between Britain and Germany became an important cause of World War I.

22. D, World War I led to the end of three European empires, killed millions of people, changed political landscapes, and had severe economic consequences for many of the countries involved. The effects of the war were felt not only in Europe, but throughout the world.

UNIT 4 U.S. Government/Civics

LESSON 1, pp. 136–140

1. B, The sentence discusses regulatory matters, which signals *regulations*. The most logical choice is that jurisdiction probably means the right to regulate, or make judgments.

2. C, The key terms in this question are *members at large,* meaning "from any part of the city," and *successor,* which means "a newly elected member." The sentence that restates the details in the charter is choice C.

3. B, Because the states are only empowered to call on their militias during local emergencies, it is logical to assume that keeping a peacetime army is a federal power.

4. C, Alimony and child support are types of *other income.* Mortgages and personal loans are types of debt. The sentence states that an applicant does not have to report other income if he or she does not want it considered as a basis for repaying *this obligation.* The *obligation* refers to the credit card debt incurred if the applicant is approved. Remember, this is a credit card application.

5. D, Because this is a credit application, and several of the questions deal with income, the creditor is probably most concerned with your ability to pay debt.

UNIT 4 (continued)

6. B, The second question on the form asks if the person will be 18 on or before election day and advises him or her not to register to vote if the answer is no. Therefore, you can determine that one requirement for voting in the United States is to be at least 18 years old.

7. B, In several places on the form, prospective voters are asked to refer to instructions from their state. Therefore, you can conclude that both the federal and state governments have voting regulations.

8. D, The second and third columns of the table tell you that the corporate department (corporate headquarters) is located in Detroit.

9. A, Because this company has departments in several large cities, you can determine that this is a large corporation.

10. A, A reference is someone who can speak to your good character or work ethic. Because the instruction states that the personal reference should not be a family member or former supervisor, you can eliminate those answer choices.

11. C, If you are applying for a *position,* you are applying for a specific job, such as sales associate, assistant manager, cashier, etc.

12. C, "Graduate or Degree" is asking whether you have graduated from the educational institution in the first column, and if graduating from a college or a business or technical school, which degree you earned. The only possible answers would be "graduate" or a specific degree, such as Associate of Applied Science.

13. D, A temporary job is a job that is only available for a specific period of time, such as a summer lifeguard at the community pool. Therefore, a short-term contract job would be an example of a temporary job.

14. C, Several times in his testimony, Powell states that the Iraqis were moving "things," meaning weapons and materials to make weapons, from place to place ahead of the UN inspectors. Therefore, you can determine that Powell believes that the inspectors are being deliberately misled.

15. B, If *they* are moving something so that it will not be discovered, then you can assume "they" are Iraqis who are hiding weapons.

16. C, Powell states that those who sent the message did not want the message seen because they were moving evidence of weapons of mass destruction. That way, they could claim nothing was there and allow the inspectors in. The only group that would have this authority would be high-ranking Iraqi officials.

17. D, Powell was speaking in 2003. Twelve years earlier would have been 1991, the year of the Persian Gulf War when President George H.W. Bush declared war on Iraq after it invaded its neighbor Kuwait.

18. B, It is clear that Powell believes the Iraqi government is misleading inspectors. Therefore, it is not logical to assume that he wants more inspectors. The United Nations cannot declare war, but can support the use of force in Iraq. While Powell does want the Security Council to believe that Iraq has weapons of mass destruction, his ultimate goal is to get them to support the use of force in Iraq. Remember that shortly after Powell's testimony, the United States under George W. Bush declared war on Iraq.

LESSON 2, pp. 141–145

1. D, The term *domestic* in this excerpt means "within the nation." Therefore, "insure domestic tranquility" means to maintain peace within the nation.

2. B, The terms "we the people" and "do ordain and establish" signify that the Preamble is a declaration.

3. D, The last sentence in Article I explains that Congress can override the president's veto through approval from two-thirds of both houses.

4. B, Article I states that "all bills for raising revenue shall originate in the House." Therefore, the Senate could not introduce a bill that institutes a higher tax on gasoline.

5. C, Amendment IX basically states that even though the Constitution describes certain rights, it does not mean that citizens do not have additional rights.

6. B, The amendment deals with the rights of the accused. It states that the accused has the right to a speedy and public trial, to an impartial jury, to be confronted by the witnesses against him, and to have the assistance of counsel.

7. C, The first paragraph of Section 2 states that the president "may require the opinion, in writing, of the principal officer in each of the executive departments." State militias fall under the president's command only "when called into the actual service of the United States," so not during times of peace. The other three answer choices are specifically prohibited in Section 2.

8. A, Substitute each answer choice for the word *concur* in the sentence to determine that "agree" is the best choice.

9. A, Article V clearly states that a proposed amendment becomes part of the Constitution "when ratified by the legislatures of three fourths of the several states, or by conventions in three fourths thereof."

10. D, The beginning of this excerpt states that only Congress or "legislatures of two thirds of the several states" can propose amendments to the U.S. Constitution.

11. C, While all of these rights are protected by the Constitution, only the right to publish criticisms of government policies ("Congress shall make no law . . . abridging the freedom of speech, or of the press") is protected by the First Amendment.

12. B, The Second Amendment protects the right of a well-regulated militia to bear arms (possess weapons). It has also been interpreted to protect the right of individuals to keep and bear arms.

13. B, In the case of an appeal (appellate jurisdiction), a higher court—in this case the Supreme Court— reviews the decision of a lower court and does not hold a trial itself.

14. D, The first sentence in Section 1 states that "Congress may from time to time ordain and establish" federal courts.

15. C, The boxes *The Supreme Court over Congress* and *The Supreme Court over the President* both state that the Supreme Court can declare actions of other government bodies unconstitutional.

16. B, The box *Congress over the Supreme Court* states that Congress must confirm judicial nominees.

UNIT 4 (continued)

17. A, The box *The President over Congress* states that the president has the power to veto laws created by Congress. Remember, though, that Congress can override that veto with the support of two-thirds of each house.

18. C, Because each branch checks one another, you can conclude that the system of checks and balances was designed to keep one branch of government from becoming too powerful.

LESSON 3, *pp. 146–150*

1. A, The text clearly shows that Kennedy supported service programs.

2. B, The *.gov* site states that the Department of Homeland Security was established in 2002, whereas the .com site declares that it was formed on September 11, 2001.

3. A, The first excerpt provides facts and presents them in an unemotional way. Therefore, the tone of the first excerpt can be described as scholarly.

4. C, The U.S. Bureau of the Census is a federal government agency.

5. B, Choice B is both biased and prejudiced. It is not supported by any information in the graph.

6. B, In the cartoon, an African American man is climbing a thorny rose bush in order to get equality. Because the bush is very thorny, and his clothes look tattered and torn, you can assume that reaching "equality" has taken a long time. Therefore, the text "What do you mean, 'not so fast'?" is a commentary on how the civil rights movement had to overcome many obstacles (thorns) determined to slow it down.

7. D, This cartoon was published in 1963. The civil rights movement began in the early 1950s and continued through the 1960s. Remember that Martin Luther King, Jr. was assassinated in 1968. Therefore, you can assume that this cartoon was published during the height of the civil rights movement.

8. C, Because this table includes only facts about a branch of government and not any comment about the justices, you can determine that this type of information is most likely from a government Web site.

9. B, The only fact that you can determine from the table is the president who appointed each justice. While the year in which the justice joined the court is listed, that was not necessarily the year in which he or she was nominated. Prospective Supreme Court Justices have to be confirmed through Senate hearings.

10. A, Both Gore and Bush offer statistics in an attempt to gain support for their arguments. Gore claims that "for every new dollar that I propose for spending on health care, Governor Bush spends $3 for a tax cut for the wealthiest 1%." Bush claims that Gore's middle class tax cut "excludes 50 million Americans."

11. C, Both Gore and Bush are trying to persuade voters. This shows their bias. Remember that all politicians are biased when trying to earn people's votes.

12. B, While both candidates do offer a few details about their tax proposals, they do not provide extensive details about their plans like you would see in primary source documentation of each candidate's tax proposals. This would more likely be a published plan from the candidate's election committee or party platform. Because both candidates show bias, they are by definition not impartial. Therefore, these excerpts would prove useful as historical summaries of presidential debates because they include direct quotes from each candidate and show how, during a timed debate, each candidate tries to earn the support of the voters.

13. C, Because both Gore and Bush accuse each other's tax plans of being bad for the American people, you can conclude that their tone is combative. Most debates are combative.

14. C, Sources such as encyclopedias present facts and possibly some established historical theories, but they are unlikely to contain opinions about the most successful types of local government.

15. A, Sometimes bias can be unfairly negative (or positive). In this case, only choice A is biased against local governments because it paints them as being sidelined by petty disputes among residents. Choice B can be seen as biased toward local governments, and choices C and D present facts.

16. C, The author of this letter's main goal is to secure funding for a community park, so he or she is biased towards community parks. While securing a park will require a tax increase, that is only a means of achieving the main goal of getting a park.

17. B, The author states, "studies have indicated that it will likely also spur additional development in the neighborhood." This statement may persuade others in the community to support the park. Citing studies helps the author support his or her argument.

LESSON 4, *pp. 151–155*

1. B, Paulson states in his opening sentence that "the underlying weakness in our financial system today is the illiquid mortgage assets."

2. D, The language of the act states that it was designed to combat the problem of loss of wilderness due to increasing growth and development.

3. B, The solution provided in the act is to establish protected wilderness areas.

4. D, This amendment addresses the lack of presidential term limits.

5. C, Only Franklin Delano Roosevelt served more than two terms as president. Also, the amendment was ratified in 1951, before Kennedy, Nixon, Ford, and Lyndon B. Johnson served as president.

6. A, From the opening sentence it is clear that in this excerpt, Obama is describing the problem of America's dependence on oil.

7. D, In the middle and end of the first paragraph, Obama discusses the energy policies of China, Japan, and Brazil. It is clear by the examples he uses of how these countries are dealing with their dependence on oil that he believes these solutions were highly successful.

8. C, In the last sentence, the Supreme Court looks to "legislative bodies nationwide" to solve the problem encountered in the 2000 presidential election.

UNIT 4 (continued)

9. C, You can use the context clues "the District" and "electors" to determine that this amendment addresses the problem of Washington, D.C.'s [the District's] participation in presidential elections.

10. B, Remember that the only groups who can propose Constitutional amendments are Congress or two thirds of the state legislatures acting together. Therefore, the only possible answer choice is Congress.

11. C, In this cartoon, police officers who are beating an African American man are shouting that they are "Free at last!" The cartoonist is trying to draw attention to the lack of punishment for police brutality.

12. B, In the cartoon, the little bird is stating that "The President would like you to remain calm" while the beating is going on. This suggests that the cartoonist's assessment of the president's response to this problem is insulting. Why should citizens remain calm while police are allowed to abuse people without punishment?

13. D, In his address, Roosevelt states that "on the spur of the moment it was, of course, impossible to sell perfectly sound assets of a bank and convert them into cash except at panic prices far below their real value . . . . It was then that I issued the proclamation providing for the nationwide bank holiday." Therefore, Roosevelt closed the banks because the rush would have caused banks to sell assets for below real value.

14. D, One step that Roosevelt took in this crisis was to convince Congress to broaden [expand or allow additional] his powers. Because the Constitution has a clearly defined balance of powers, it could be seen as dangerous for Congress to grant the president additional powers.

15. B, The information states that "nations around the world" signed the Montreal Protocol, designed to reduce CFCs. Therefore, you can determine that the problem of CFCs was solved through international cooperation.

16. D, The last sentence in this information lets you know that while the solution had some short-term effects, the long-term goal was that the ozone layer would, over time (50 years), heal itself.

LESSON 5, pp. 156–160

1. C, Texas is located in the 11th District. Dallas provides a clue for the location.

2. B, The population of each state is represented by the "person" icons in the map key. Each icon stands for 1 million people. If you count the icons in each state, you will see that Illinois has the most, and therefore, the largest population.

3. C, By counting the number of icons, you can determine that Ohio and Michigan had a combined population of more than 20 million in 2010.

4. D, The passage explains the basis for the number of districts in a state; you cannot find that information on the map. Only the map shows the number of large cities and the number of districts. Neither the passage nor the map gives the basis for the census in districts.

5. D, Each state is given (apportioned) a certain number of representatives (1 per district) based on the population of each state and the total number of U.S. representatives (435).

6. A, Population loss is shown in gray--the darker the gray, the greater the loss of population. Among the states listed here, North Dakota has the most significant areas of dark gray, indicating population loss.

7. C, To answer this question, you would look for the areas of the country with the largest areas shaded in dark gray, indicating population loss. The only area listed with a significant amount of dark gray is the Great Plains.

8. B, Areas with significant growth are shaded in dark red. Of the areas listed, the Southwest includes the most areas with dark red, particularly in parts of Texas and Arizona. From your knowledge of geography, you will know that these areas include some of the larger cities in both states.

9. D, Within the three states on the West Coast (California, Oregon, and Washington), eastern Oregon has a large area of population loss and only a few areas of light red indicating population gain. You can infer that this area has did not attract a high number of new residents during the time period shown on the map. While there are population losses shown in some areas of every state, the map does not provide information about yearly gains and losses. Therefore, you do not have enough information to know if choice C is correct.

10. A, On the map, determine what each picture represents. Then, locate Pueblo. The pictures nearest Pueblo represent vegetables, coal, and wheat. The only answer choice that matches is coal.

11. D, You should assume that it would be very difficult to grow crops or raise livestock in the mountains. Therefore, to determine the location of the mountains, you should look for an area that has the fewest pictures representing crops or livestock. On this map, that area is in the center-west of the state.

12. C, Determine in which states the Republican primary turnout increased more than the Democratic primary turnout. That occurred only in Alabama.

13. D, The question is basically asking which state had the highest increase in primary voter turnout for both Democrats and Republicans. In Florida, the Republican turnout increased by 175% and the Democratic turnout increased by 214%. While the Democratic turnout was higher in some states, Florida had the most consistent increases for both parties.

14. A, Examine the map to determine that the highest number of West Nile cases was found in Colorado. The postal abbreviation for Colorado is CO.

15. C, You must use context clues to determine what the CDC does. Because this map tracks a disease, it is most likely that the CDC would produce a similar map about cases of Type 2 diabetes in the United States. Diabetes is also a disease. CDC stands for the Centers for Disease Control and Prevention.

16. B, You can assume that the gray color represents animal West Nile cases, but not human cases (that is represented by states colored red). The only answer choice with no human cases in 2007 was Washington.

UNIT 4 (continued)

17. D, In this case, you need to make a generalization. Arizona reported 97 cases, Minnesota reported 101 cases, and Illinois reported 101 cases. Therefore, you can make the generalization that Arizona, Minnesota, and Illinois each reported about 100 cases.

LESSON 6, pp. 161–165

1. B, The statement that the U.S. should extend its freedom to the world is an opinion. Unlike the other answer choices, it cannot be proven true or untrue.

2. A, Defenders of the Electoral College can use the fact that in the long history of presidential elections, the Electoral College has only failed to select the winner of the popular vote three times.

3. C, One of the main opinions of the critics of the Electoral College is that it is no longer needed.

4. B, Campaign posters feature opinions in order to appeal to the emotions of the voters. This poster does not provide details about the candidates' platform.

5. A, The poster states "for lasting peace," but it is a fact that Roosevelt had taken the country into World War II.

6. D, The first three answer choices are opinions about primaries and caucuses. They would be difficult to prove true or untrue. However, choice D states a fact that would be easy to prove true. Most states now hold primary elections, rather than caucuses.

7. D, The only possible choice that clearly favors a primary election over a caucus is that many voters wish to become more involved in the nomination process. Caucuses are held at certain places at certain times. People attending a caucus need to commit to spending several hours there. However, a primary election is like a regular election. All people need to do is cast their vote at a polling place any time it is open on the polling day. This would allow more people to be involved in the nomination process.

8. B, The Library of Congress is a respected government library. It would be a reliable source of unbiased information. The key here is to choose the source with the least amount of bias in favor of a particular political party or issue.

9. B, The fact you are trying to confirm is the quote Reagan uses from Abraham Lincoln. The best source to use to confirm this quote would be a dictionary of quotations.

10. D, In this excerpt, Reagan is basically saying that even though Carter was a virtuous man, he caused harm to the American people during his time as president. Therefore, you can conclude that Reagan views the Carter administration as incompetent.

11. A, This passage features many facts and no opinions. All details can be proven true or untrue.

12. C, The information states that the Republican Party allows states to choose proportional representation or a winner-take-all plan. Under proportional representation, the total state vote would be split among candidates. That way the state could award some of its electoral votes to one candidate and some to another. Therefore, if a Republican candidate lost a closely contested primary election, he or she might be of the opinion that the state in which the primary was held should employ proportional representation.

13. A, Gore states that "this is a time to respect every voter and every vote," and that "we need a solution that is fair and final." Therefore, you can conclude that in Gore's opinion, first and foremost—the election should be decided fairly.

14. A, Remember that a fact must be able to be proven true or untrue. The only answer choice that can be proven is that "checking the machine count with a careful hand count is accepted . . . as the best way to know the true intentions of the voters."

15. D, The information describes a situation in which one candidate received a clear majority of the popular vote, yet did not become president because of a dispute among electors in the Electoral College. This information could be used to support the opinions of an opponent of the Electoral College.

16. C, Remember that university and government Web sites (.edu or .gov) can be relied upon to provide accurate factual information, much more so than a contemporary newspaper editorial from the time period of the election or a novel about Reconstruction.

17. C, All of the answer choices are opinions, so you have to carefully review the text to determine which one Clinton expresses. At the beginning of the excerpt, Clinton discusses "trickle-down economics" and states that it has "been tried for 12 years." Here, Clinton is specifically referring to the economic policies of Reagan and Bush and concluding—in his opinion—that they have failed.

18. B, Clinton gives a lot of opinions in his closing remarks, but does offer a fact, by supplying a statistic, in the area of health care. Clinton states, "100,000 people a month [are] losing their health insurance."

LESSON 7, pp. 166–170

1. C, A military defeat of a liberation movement in Asia would prove Castro's statement that nothing could stop a liberation movement in the contemporary world to be faulty reasoning.

2. D, Mussolini states that rising peoples are always imperialist. This type of statement is almost always an oversimplification, such as, *People from the Midwest **always** drive pick-up trucks.* In social studies, things are rarely that absolute.

3. B, Mussolini makes errors in logic and reasoning because he makes absolute and universal claims, such as, "Fascism is the doctrine best adapted to represent the tendencies and the aspirations of a people," and, "there are a thousand signs which point to Fascism as the characteristic doctrine of our time."

4. D, The oversimplification here is that all criticism of the government should be treated as a crime. Pasternak was being punished (like a criminal in the cartoon) for doing so.

5. A, Khrushchev begins this excerpt by declaring the unity of the Communist Party. While the goals in the rest of the excerpt depend on this unity, Khrushchev does not offer evidence to support that the Communist Party enjoys complete unity.

6. C, Khrushchev states that the cult of personality [the cult of the individual] is "alien to Marxism-Leninism [the basis of Soviet Communist philosophy]." Therefore, you can conclude that the greatest threat to the Soviet Union's system of government is the cult of personality.

UNIT 4 (continued)

7. B, In this cartoon, the artist is pointing out how even the behaviors of Santa Claus can be seen as suspicious if one is anxious about suspicious people. Therefore, you can conclude that Herb Block suggests the Dies Committee shows faulty logic and reasoning by suggesting that all people who exhibit suspicious behaviors are Communists.

8. C, When trying to determine faulty reasoning, look for a statement or belief that is unfounded in reality or exhibits an irrational fear. Racism is one example of faulty reasoning. Therefore, the statement that "equality will mean national suicide for the White race" is an example of faulty reasoning. The country will not cease to exist if native South Africans are granted equal rights.

9. B, The National Party of South Africa proposed the doctrine of apartheid, or separation, so that "the character and the future of every race will be protected and safeguarded with full opportunities for development and self-maintenance in their own ideas." This policy most resembles the doctrine of "separate but equal" practiced for many years in the United States, but struck down by the Supreme Court in the landmark *Brown v. Board of Education* decision.

10. A, Remember that a generalization includes a large number of people or things, or a long period of time. Therefore, Wallace is making a hasty generalization when he says, "never before in the history of this nation have so many human and property rights been destroyed in a single enactment of the Congress."

11. B, Wallace refused to support the civil rights bill. Therefore, he would likely support segregationist policies.

12. D, In this cartoon, the artist shows a Mississippi Grand Jury blaming an injured U.S. marshal for the riots. Therefore, the cartoonist is calling attention to the faulty reasoning of Mississippi authorities.

13. B, To answer this question, you have to determine the invalid cause-and-effect relationship. An invalid cause and effect is one in which one action did not cause another, yet is being blamed as the cause. For example, *I had a bad day so my car broke down*. The car broke down because the transmission failed, not because the driver had a bad day. In this cartoon, the artist suggests an invalid cause-and-effect relationship between the work of the federal marshals and the outbreak of violence. The Mississippi authorities blamed the marshals for causing the violence, even though the rioters became violent because they disagreed with the law the marshals were there to enforce.

14. B, Racial discrimination best illustrates the dangers of faulty logic and reasoning. It is faulty logic and reasoning to assume that one race of people is inferior to another. There are no facts to support this reasoning. Policies of racial discrimination are dangerous, as illustrated by the example provided in the information.

15. C, In the cartoon, the U.S. marshals are being blamed for the violence that broke out when they were doing their jobs. That situation is most similar to a firefighter being blamed for the actions of an arsonist. A firefighter is not at fault for the crimes of an arsonist.

LESSON 8, pp. 171–175

1. A, The first underlined section suggests that Johnson and Humphrey will be able to guide the nation's foreign policy because of their foreign policy experience.

2. D, In the second paragraph, the pamphlet states that both men "have made every possible effort to keep the nation fiscally strong," yet "the nation received a dollar's worth for every dollar spent." Therefore, the characteristic praised in the last paragraph is fiscal responsibility.

3. B, The positive details about America show that the purpose of the information in the excerpt was to foster a sense of well-being and encourage the reelection of Bill Clinton, the Democratic president in 1996.

4. D, The claim that the deficit is lower is the easiest to support with facts.

5. B, The author of the editorial cites the No Child Left Behind Act to support George W. Bush's domestic policy accomplishments.

6. D, Newspapers endorse candidates in editorials to explain why the editorial staff supports one candidate over the others. This editorial was designed to convince people to vote for George W. Bush.

7. C, In the second paragraph, Reagan states that his opponent's party "lives in the past, seeking to apply the old and failed policies to an era that has passed them by." Therefore, you can conclude that Reagan portrays his opponent's approach as outdated.

8. A, In the last line of the excerpt, Reagan claims that his plan is proven.

9. D, Because this article comes from a newspaper and does not simply report on a news story, you would expect to find it in the Opinion section. It expresses an opinion and does not relate newsworthy events, so it does not matter that the subject is politics or national news.

10. B, Because this opinion supports Kerry and urges others to do the same, it would be most useful to students tracking Kerry's supporters.

11. B, The platform describes several issues affecting the United States in 1968. Therefore, the best source to assess the validity [truth] of the list of problems would be an encyclopedia article about 1968. A biography might include facts about a certain time period, but remember that John F. Kennedy was assassinated in 1963, so a biography of his life would probably not include details about 1968.

12. D, At the beginning of this excerpt, the Republican Party seeks to remind voters that "twice before, our Party gave the people of America leadership at a time of crisis." Therefore, you can conclude that the Party seeks to highlight the effectiveness of its ideas by referring to its track record of providing leadership in times of crisis.

13. C, The format of this campaign brochure uses a quote from Carter, followed by an explanation of the quotation in an effort to effectively persuade readers.

14. D, The brochure mentions trust and dishonesty several times. Therefore you can conclude that this brochure is designed to address the public's bias that the government is dishonest. Remember that in 1976, Carter was running against Gerald Ford who became president on the resignation of Richard Nixon in 1974 over fallout from the Watergate break-in and cover-up.

15. D, Many general ideas for change are listed, but the list lacks specifics. The broad changes listed are likely to appeal to voters.

16. D, Choices A, B, and C can all be verified with the proper sources. D cannot, because it predicts a result in the future. Therefore, it would be the most difficult to verify.

17. B, President Obama asks people to compare his plan to his opponent's. Obama believes that people will be better able to evaluate his agenda by making this comparison between plans.

18. A, If President Obama has accomplishments that he is proud of from his first term in office, he can call attention to them in his speech. In his first campaign, he would not yet have a track record as president.

LESSON 9, *pp. 176–180*

1. C, McCain could have strengthened his argument by providing details from both his and his opponent's proposed federal budgets.

2. C, Fulbright uses his beliefs about the president's intent to support his argument when he says, "I think it would indicate that he [Johnson] would take reasonable means first to prevent any further aggression . . . "

3. A, Gruening argues that the resolution will lead to unchecked U.S. aggression in Southeast Asia when he says that the president may see fit to move troops into countries other than Vietnam.

4. D, Obama strengthens his argument by providing details about the economic improvements made during the last Democratic administration when he discusses progress during Bill Clinton's presidency.

5. D, Read the sentences in which Hamilton mentions each of these positions carefully. You'll see that Hamilton is saying that while an executive authority (in this case the U.S. president) *MAY* in some ways resemble the king of Great Britain, the khan of Tartary [the leader of China], the Man of the Seven Mountains, or the governor of New York, the president will have to be elected by the people for four-year terms. In that way, the president is *NOT* like a king or khan, but most like the governor of New York.

6. C, Hamilton declares that the president will be different from a king because he will have to be elected by the people of the United States for four-year terms and then only reelected if they see fit.

7. D, In the "Cato" letter, the author states, "if you adopt this government [outlined in the Constitution], you will incline to an arbitrary and odious aristocracy or monarchy."

8. A, The excerpt from the "Cato" letter ends by warning, "beware of the fallacious resemblance [an untrue resemblance] that is held out to you by the advocates of this new system between it and your own state governments." If the author wanted to strengthen his argument, he could have provided examples of the difference between the proposed government and state governments in order to prove that the comparisons were untrue.

9. C, In his statement, President George W. Bush highlights accomplishments of the war on terror abroad [in other countries] by mentioning "ridding the Taliban out of Afghanistan" and "we held to account a terrorist regime in Saddam Hussein."

10. B, During his argument, Kerry uses the statistic that "95 percent [of shipping containers] come in today uninspected" to strengthen his argument that the United States is still vulnerable to terrorists.

11. D, Bush states that in order for the nation to remain safe and secure from terrorist threats, it should help install free governments around the world ["we can be safe and secure if we stay on the offense against the terrorists and if we spread freedom and liberty around the world"].

12. B, Bush strengthens his argument by detailing achievements in the war on terror, such as "three-quarters of al-Qaeda leaders have been brought to justice" and "ridding the Taliban out of Afghanistan."

13. C, In the first paragraph of the majority decision, Justice Brennan states that "the government may not prohibit the expression of an idea simply because society finds the idea itself offensive or disagreeable."

14. D, In the second paragraph of the majority decision, Justice Brennan states that "nothing in our precedents suggest that a State may foster its own view of the flag by prohibiting expressive conduct relating to it." Most appellate courts, like the Supreme Court, often rely on legal precedents [previous legal decisions] when deciding cases. Here, Brennan is saying that there are no previous legal decisions [precedents] that support a state, in this case Texas, making laws prohibiting free expression when it comes to the American flag. Therefore, Brennan supports his argument with legal precedent, or in this case, the lack of a precedent.

15. D, The situation that is most similar to Brennan's opinion is the recording of a song that features curse words. Some people would find such a song offensive, but that does not prevent it from being protected free speech.

16. B, Rehnquist disagrees with the majority opinion. He uses examples of the symbolic value of the American flag; most notably that members of the Armed Forces fight and sometimes die for the flag and what it represents, to support his argument.

UNIT 4 REVIEW, *pp. 181–185*

1. B, While many believe that this was true, it obviously cannot be proven true that if Perot had not entered the election, Bush would have been reelected as president.

2. D, Only answer choice D is a primary source.

3. C, The second paragraph explains that affirmative action programs were established to address the harmful effects of past discrimination.

4. C, The root word of *inviolable* is *violate*. Therefore, *inviolable* means "safe from violation." The sentence includes the words *guarantee* and *remain*. These words provide clues that suggest that *inviolable* means something that won't be harmed or taken away.

UNIT 4 (continued)

5. B, The details in Section 3 show that the main focus of this section is the formation of new states.

6. A, Read the sentence to determine the context. The best substitution for be *convened* is *brought together*. The context suggests that the executive may act when the legislature is not able to come together to meet.

7. A, Bush opens and closes his remarks by discussing his presidential experience.

8. D, Bush claims that children no longer go to bed at night fearing a nuclear war. Bush uses this example to claim that he solved a foreign policy problem.

9. C, The second paragraph of Clinton's statement includes details about economic improvements in Arkansas during his tenure as governor. Clinton uses these statistics to strengthen his argument.

10. D, The only statement that can be proven is that there have been twice as many bankruptcies as new jobs created.

11. B, Because the cartoonist is showing a voter putting money in a ballot box, he is drawing attention to the increasing importance of campaign fundraising in the electoral process.

12. C, This source, like most political cartoons, can be best described as commentary.

13. A, California has more electoral votes (55) than any other state because it has the largest population of the states listed. California would have provided a greater electoral benefit for the winning candidate than New York, Georgia, or Texas.

14. D, Checking the map, you can see that states in New England largely supported the Democratic candidate, Barack Obama. The New England area has a high concentration of donkeys, indicating victory by Obama.

15. D, The figures in the cartoon seem to be in charge of giving a literacy test, yet they are not able to read the word *literacy*. These figures demonstrate faulty logic because an honest literacy test would prevent them from voting.

16. C, Literacy tests were just one way that Southern states tried to prevent African Americans from voting before the success of the civil rights movement. Often white voters were given very simple tests, while African Americans who attempted to vote would be given extremely difficult ones. By pointing out the unfairness of this, the cartoonist is making a statement about civil rights.

17. B, The only hard statistics quoted in the platform are related to the economy. Therefore, the claim best supported by the facts is that twenty years ago, the economy was in shambles.

18. B, The party platform is biased because it discusses the New Economy, but does not include the accomplishments of President Clinton's eight years in office.

UNIT 5 Economics

LESSON 1, *pp. 188–192*

1. B, The fact that a can of frozen orange juice costs $2.09 at the supermarket is an example of microeconomics. The example gives very specific information about the price of one can of frozen orange juice at the supermarket.

2. C, The information states that Smith believed that a country's economy works best when its government does not interfere with it. Therefore, he believed that the best economies are free-market economies.

3. A, Because Smith believed that the government should not interfere with business, it is logical to conclude that he thought that government should remove obstacles to business growth.

4. B, The first sentence in the excerpt tells you that Smith believes that a nation's wealth is produced by the labor of its workforce.

5. B, Except in times of economic turmoil, the type of economic system most often practiced in the United States is *laissez-faire* capitalism.

6. A, Because Keynes believed that the government should make investments in society and businesses to spur the economy, you can conclude that during the Great Depression Keynes believed that the United States government should create jobs to lower unemployment.

7. D, The information states that in a Communist economic system, the government owns all means of production and decides what goods are produced and how they are distributed. Remember that in a capitalist economic system, private businesses produce and distribute goods. Despite the differences in who controls the means of production, both communism and capitalism concern themselves with the distribution of goods and services.

8. D, The last sentence in paragraph 2 states, "In practice, Communist economies have tended to use resources for military development at the expense of consumer goods." Therefore, you can conclude that, in a Communist economy, production of consumer goods may suffer because of military advances.

9. C, When a tariff is added to an imported good, it raises the price above that of the domestic good. If the domestic good is less expensive than the imported good, people will tend to buy the domestic good instead of the imported good, resulting in greater profit for the domestic company.

10. B, A company's goods will be more expensive in a foreign country that attaches a tariff to their goods, but the company's profit will remain the same. This is because the tariff attached to the company's goods is paid to the country assessing the tariff, not to the company.

11. D, The second paragraph explains that "socialist systems place essential industries and services, such as health care, under government control." Therefore, you can determine that the best available description of a socialist economic system is a government-run distribution of essential goods and services.

12. C, Because countries with socialist economic systems rely on the government to provide essential services, they need to collect more taxes in order to pay for these services. Therefore, you can determine that the difference between the tax rates in the United States and those of European countries is due in part to the socialist nature of European economies.

13. B, In the United States, Social Security and welfare programs are provided by the government and paid for by taxes. Therefore, you can determine that these programs can be classified as socialism because they are government-administered programs funded by a free market economy.

14. D, Because the government decides what socialist programs to support, and those government officials are elected by the people, you can determine that the voters ultimately decide what is to be funded in a socialist economy.

15. A, Competition among sellers encourages prices to be held at about the same level in a market.

16. C, A monopoly can occur when one company sells a good that has no substitutes and other companies are blocked from entering the market.

17. D, An investor is most likely to invest in U.S.-based companies if the GDP of the United States is consistently increasing. This is a leading economic indicator and, therefore, a good predictor of the future economy.

18. B, Unemployment is a lagging indicator as employment may not increase for two or three quarters after an economic improvement.

LESSON 2, pp. 193–197

1. C, The advertisement offers a "pair of designer sunglasses at NO EXTRA CHARGE" to consumers who subscribe to the magazine today. The other answer choices are not mentioned or alluded to in the advertisement.

2. D, The advertisement states that McClellan Office Products, Inc., wants the customer and the company to "work together." In a business environment, a partner is more likely to work together with someone than a friend, an employee, or a boss.

3. A, The first line of text makes it clear that the advertisement is directed toward people who "strive for success at work." People who respond to this advertisement will likely view themselves as successful.

4. B, In order for consumers to maintain a budget, they have to decide which goods and services they will buy, and which goods and services they won't buy. If they were to buy all the goods and services they want, they wouldn't maintain a budget, and would therefore develop serious financial problems.

5. C, Consumers earn a finite, or limited, amount of money. Therefore, they have limited resources with which to purchase needs and wants.

6. A, Owning a motorboat often reflects a person's lifestyle, such as how the person likes to spend his or her free time. Owning a motorboat does not necessarily reflect a person's job or level of education. Furthermore, since the advertisement makes no mention of price, it is not necessarily aimed toward people who make a specific level of income.

7. B, Although the words "power" and "speed" are short and easy to understand, the way they are presented in the advertisement—larger than the rest of the text, and paired with an exclamation point—indicate that they are meant to create a sense of excitement. They do not necessarily describe a "perfect" motorboat, and they have no clear connection to the concept of a bargain.

8. A, Buying a plane ticket requires more thought and research than buying a gallon of milk or a newspaper. However, there is less financial risk in buying a plane ticket than there is in buying a new computer.

9. D, While both "Routine Response" and "Impulse Buying" purchases are low-cost, only "Routine Response" purchases occur on a regular basis.

10. D, The advertisement points out that shipping and handling costs are included with the price of the Cundiff clock, while they are not included with the price of competitors' clocks.

11. A, "It's Time To Make A Choice!" is a call to action, urging the consumer to purchase the clock now. The statement neither highlights the value of the clock, reminds customers of their options, nor suggests that the price of the clock is for a limited-time only.

12. D, Conspicuous goods are often expensive and limited in availability. Therefore, they are more likely to be considered exclusive than popular, and they are certainly not considered affordable. While the good might be high quality, the purchase is motivated more by exclusivity than quality.

13. B, Purchases by repeat customers would decrease because customers of conspicuous goods often want to pay more for goods in order to differentiate themselves from others who cannot afford the goods.

14. C, When consumer confidence is high, people spend and borrow money. Buying homes, applying for bank loans, and buying goods on credit involve spending or borrowing money. When consumer confidence is low, people tend to save money.

15. A, High inflation rates have a negative impact on consumer confidence. Conversely, a falling inflation rate would logically have a positive impact on consumer confidence.

16. C, In 2012, about 13% of consumer spending went toward food purchases, and about 3% of consumer spending went toward reading and education. Therefore, consumers spent about 10% more on food in 2012 than they did on reading and education.

17. D, The cost of shelter is most likely to be fixed in a given month for a consumer. In most cases, this cost would be equal to the cost of rent or a mortgage payment. The other spending categories would likely fluctuate more from month to month based on a consumer's spending choices.

LESSON 3, pp. 198–202

1. D, The transformation process implies that something transforms, or changes, into something else. In a candle-making business, melting the wax, inserting the wicks, molding the wax, and letting it cool would transform wax and string into candles.

2. D, According to the business cycle, investment (home buying) would be the highest during the recovery and prosperity phases.

3. A, An economic stimulation of some type is required to move from the depression phase to the recovery phase.

4. D, The prosperity phase is most associated with continued economic growth.

5. B, New Deal legislation created jobs and a social safety net for retirees and those without health care. The outbreak of World War II stimulated the economy with a huge increase in manufactured goods necessary to fight the war.

UNIT 5 (continued)

6. B, The flowchart shows the process of producing an electrical fitting. Therefore, it answers question 2 of the three factors of production: How is it to be produced?

7. C, In the flowchart, before the "assembly" step, each part to be assembled is listed: plastic components; metal parts; porcelain parts; screws, pins, nuts, etc. Before the assembly, the plastic components are molded.

8. B, The flowchart shows the assembly and packaging processes, so it does not assume that the fittings are already assembled or packaged. The product design has to have been determined if assembly is to begin. The flowchart mentions nothing about delivery. Therefore, the logical choice is that the flowchart assumes that all raw materials, equipment, and human resources are available to do the work.

9. D, The information states that electrical fittings are small, standardized parts used in electrical systems of homes and businesses, so they must be very common. Therefore, it is unlikely that they are expensive or made entirely by hand. The flowchart lists several parts, but does not imply that "thousands of individual parts" are needed for their assembly. The logical choice is that the electrical fittings are mass-produced.

10. C, Examine the flowchart to determine that the pesticide goes from the pesticide company, to wholesalers, and then to independent retail outlets.

11. A, Because the flowchart only shows the delivery and sales process, it has to assume that the pesticide has already been manufactured and packaged.

12. D, If a manufacturer controls distribution and sales, they can have more control over costs and price. Therefore, the retail outlets that would most likely sell the pesticide at the most cost-effective price would be company-owned outlets, because they receive products though manufacturer's subsidiaries, not wholesalers.

13. C, This flowchart shows a hierarchy, or levels of authority. For example, the head of Fundraising reports to the Treasurer, who reports to the President, who reports to the Board of Directors.

14. D, The only answer choice that is shown on the flowchart is each position's areas of responsibility. This is best determined by analyzing which areas have specific responsibilities (such as Finance or Marketing) and to whom those people report.

15. C, Vice President B and the Treasurer are on the same line/ level, have positions that directly report to them, and report to the President. Therefore, you can determine that those positions appear most equal in authority.

16. B, Fundraising, Quality Control, Legal, and Communications are already listed on the flowchart. The Chairman of the Board of Directors is not listed, but this foundation does have a Board of Directors. Therefore, it is logical to assume that the position of Chairman of the Board of Directors does exist.

17. D, In this foundation's structure, it is logical to assume that an issue with one position would be taken up through the hierarchy (or levels of authority) until it reaches the very top. Therefore, you can follow the flowchart from Finance, up to the Treasurer [Finance does not report to Fundraising; they both report to the Treasurer], then up to the President, and finally to the Board of Directors.

LESSON 4, *pp. 203–207*

1. B, Except for in the 1980s, the developing world has always had a higher real and projected inflation rate. Therefore, the developing world is most affected by inflation.

2. D, According to the information, supply, demand, and inflation are each influenced by many causes.

3. A, Supply and demand require competition to function freely. Competition helps regulate prices and the supply of goods. Also, if demand is higher, more companies will start producing an item, which can help drive prices down to the equilibrium point.

4. C, If both price and supply are above the equilibrium point, then both price and supply will go down. If there is too much of an item on the market, producers will stop making as much of the item (reducing supply) and cut the price so that more consumers will buy the item (reducing price).

5. C, Price regulation interferes with the free market philosophy. Price is no longer based on supply, demand, and competition. Therefore, if potential profit is limited by a price regulation, fewer companies will have the incentive to produce the goods.

6. C, It is logical to conclude that if the price of corn increases, then manufacturers who use corn to make other products would have to pay a higher price for corn. It then follows that those manufacturers would pass along corn-related price increases to consumers because the products cost more to produce, and the manufacturers need to maintain profit levels.

7. B, The second paragraph in the information states that because farmers can make more money by growing and selling corn, "fewer acres were devoted to crops such as wheat and soybeans." The laws of supply and demand state that if a product is scarce, then the price of the product will go up. Therefore, you can determine that a by-product of increased ethanol production (which is the same as an increase in corn production) is a rise in the prices of soybean and wheat products.

8. B, The laws of supply and demand state that if the price of a product gets too high, people will stop buying it, and producers will have to lower the price. Therefore, it is reasonable that if a sharp and sudden increase occurred in the price of corn, then consumers would buy less corn and corn products, forcing the price to decrease.

9. D, While it is not directly stated in the information, you can infer by the context clues that gasoline is made from crude oil, so logically an increase in the price of crude oil would lead to an increase in the price of gasoline.

10. D, The laws of supply and demand state that if there is less of a needed product, then people will pay more for it, and producers can charge more. Therefore, if OPEC limits the supply of oil exports, then gas prices will increase because of the oil shortage.

11. B, A small U.S. business could not have any control over a global increase in the use of solar power, the discovery of new oil reserves in Saudi Arabia, or a disruption in North American oil pipelines. However, if the business in question was a gas station, it could have some control over competition between neighboring gas stations.

12. A, The information states that the number of housing starts is an accepted economic indicator. It is logical to assume that if people are building more new homes, the economy is doing well (it indicates positive economic activity).

13. B, If housing starts decrease, fewer people are building new homes. Therefore, profits for the construction and carpentry industries (which are important to home builders) will decline.

14. D, The second paragraph hints that the effects of a slowing economy are many and widespread by discussing the link between economic conditions and the struggles of homeowners.

15. C, Use logic to determine that an increase in foreclosures means that there are more houses on the market and that people cannot afford to buy or keep their homes. If there is already a glut of existing homes on the market, construction companies and others would not have any reason to build new homes because they may not be able to find buyers. Therefore, you can conclude that housing starts might decrease if foreclosures increase because fewer homes will be built due to there being more existing homes on the market.

16. C, The second paragraph in the information states that poor economic conditions caused homeowners with adjustable-rate mortgages to pay higher monthly mortgage payments. Many could not make their payments, so lenders foreclosed on their homes.

LESSON 5, *pp. 208–212*

1. A, An upswing in the economy is the most likely reason for the increase in nonrevolving consumer credit beginning in 2009. When people are optimistic about their financial future, they will make more substantial purchases, such as a car or a home, each of which usually involves nonrevolving credit. In addition, revolving consumer credit became fairly flat just after 2009.

2. D, By comparing the data in the table and the graph, the only logical choice is that there is a connection between level of education and degree of economic success.

3. A, Because around 25% of Indiana residents aged 25 to 34 have a Bachelor's degree or higher, it is possible that that group earns on average more than $46,000 per year.

4. C, Because the bar graph does not distinguish between percentages of Indiana residents with a Bachelor's Degree or an advanced degree, you cannot determine the percentage of Indiana residents with an earning potential of more than $60,000 per year.

5. B, Based on the data in the table, Braden's average annual earnings potential is around $30,000.

6. A, The higher the median weekly earnings, the lower the rate of unemployment. When you compare the two graphs, you can see that as the unemployment rate goes up, the median weekly earnings goes down. This implies that the more money a person makes, the less likely he or she is to be unemployed.

7. D, For a person with a bachelor's degree, the unemployment rate is less than average, so he or she is likely to find a job. The median weekly earnings for someone with a bachelor's degree is $1,066, so he or she is likely to find a job earning about $1,000 per week.

8. B, Of the occupations listed, college professor fits into both the category of second-lowest rate of unemployment and the category of second-highest median weekly earnings.

9. C, A woman who makes the individual choice to quit college and begin working will more easily find a job than a person who has not completed high school.

10. B, The circle graph shows that 35.7% of job opportunities between 2004 and 2014 will require a Bachelor's Degree or higher, and only 27.7% of those opportunities will require some college. Also, the jobs listed on the bar graph with the highest need require at least a Bachelor's Degree.

11. C, The only correct answer choice is that most of the projected job opportunities will require some college or a Bachelor's Degree or higher. You can determine this by scanning the types of jobs listed on the bar graph and adding the percentages of both of those categories on the circle graph.

12. A, The careers on the bar graph that provide the greatest number of high-paying jobs include postsecondary and elementary school teachers, and computer software engineers and computer systems analysts. Those belong in the career fields of education and computer technology.

13. D, Because most of the job opportunities between 2004 and 2014 will require at least some college, it is logical to assume that the greatest need will be postsecondary teachers (such as college professors and technical school instructors).

14. C, You can determine by examining the pay stub that gross pay is before taxes and other deductions are taken out, and net pay is after those deductions.

15. B, The table states that a 401(k) is a "voluntary deduction requested by the worker." The pay stub shows no deduction for a 401(k). Therefore, you can determine that not everyone has 401(k) monies removed from his or her paycheck.

16. B, The table states that taxes are an "obligation" or are required, so they are not optional. Both the table and the pay stub provide information for the employee (the worker). While net pay is smaller than gross pay, the deductions are all smaller than net pay. What you can conclude is that gross pay is the largest amount on your pay stub. While some pay stubs show year-to-date information (showing the total amounts of gross and net pay and deductions), the total gross pay amount would still be the largest.

17. C, Use the table to determine that FICA stands for Social Security taxes. Then examine the pay stub to determine that the amount taken from the pay stub for Social Security taxes was $150.

LESSON 6, *pp. 213–217*

1. B, Even though the data in the two circle graphs is not the exact same, the figures are very similar. Therefore, you can conclude that the United States and Canada have similar economies. No GDP figures are provided, only percentages of an unknown total GDP.

UNIT 5 (continued)

2. B, By studying the upward trend of the line, you can determine that unemployment was highest in 2009–2010.

3. C, Because the unemployment rate is often linked to recession, and the years of highest unemployment on the graph were between 2008 and 2010, you can assume that the period in which the United States likely experienced a severe recession was from 2008 to 2010.

4. A, Because the Dow increased dramatically between 1995 and 2000, it is most likely that the U.S. economy grew significantly stronger during that period.

5. D, Despite the fact that the Dow decreased by a larger percentage in 2000 than in 1990, the average at the start of 2000 was significantly larger than that of 1990, indicating that the economy was stronger overall that year.

6. D, The information states that "a nation's balance of trade is the relationship between its exports and imports. A positive balance of trade results when the nation exports more than it imports." The information is referring to the dollar value of the exports and imports, not the number of countries. Therefore, you can determine that a nation achieves a positive balance of trade when the value of its exports is more than the value of its imports.

7. A, According to the information, "beginning in the 1960s, the nation's position began to diminish," meaning that was when the balance of trade in the United States began to reflect its diminishing strength in international trade.

8. B, Remember that a trade deficit occurs when the value of a country's imports is more than its exports. According to the bar graph, the year in which the deficit was the largest was in 2006.

9. C, The information states that "many governments impose policies or restrictions to protect their interests in international trade." However, the bar graph clearly shows that over the last several years, the United States has had an consistently negative balance of trade. Therefore, you can conclude that government policies and restrictions have not prevented the negative trade balance.

10. C, The first bar graph shows data from 1971. According to that graph, the number of housing starts in 1971 was approximately 2,000,000 homes. Remember that the data on the graph is listed in thousands, so 2,000 thousands would be 2,000,000.

11. B, If housing starts are considered an important economic indicator, it is logical to conclude that an increase in housing starts would be a positive sign. Therefore, you can conclude that a significant increase in housing starts would coincide with an increase in Gross Domestic Product.

12. B, By examining the data on both bar graphs, you can determine that the number of housing starts decreased by the greatest amount between 1973 and 1974 (a decrease of approximately 700,000).

13. A, The information makes it clear that the number of housing starts is an important economic indicator. By examining both graphs, you can determine that housing starts have changed over time. There has to be a reason for these changes. Therefore, you can conclude that the number of U.S. housing starts is directly related to the health of the U.S. economy.

14. B, The information and the table explain that investing in the stock market can provide significant returns on an investment, but carries a high risk. Therefore, an individual wishing to pursue an aggressive short-term investment strategy, with little regard for risk, would be best advised to purchase shares of stock on the stock market.

15. D, Investors must consider their level of risk, the amount of money they have to invest, and what sort of return they need in a given time period. Therefore, you can conclude that all investors should make decisions based on their short-and long-term needs.

16. A, According to the table, a person who can only invest $50 is limited to either putting the money in a savings account or investing in the stock market. However, because the person wants to invest with little risk, his or her best option would be a savings account.

17. C, The information reminds you that the stock market can be volatile (or change dramatically over a short period of time, either up or down). The last two rows on the table show what happened to a share of stock in an online search engine. The last row explains that if an individual invested $10,000 in that stock in January 2008, they would have lost more than $5,000 by January 2009. The table shows that the stock increased 34.85% from 2007 to 2008, but lost 51.09% from 2008 to 2009.

LESSON 7, pp. 218-222

1. C, According to the pictograph, the value of trade between the United States and Japan is just over two symbols' worth. Each symbol is worth $100 billion, so the value of trade between the United States and Japan is about $200 billion.

2. C, The approximate value of the U.S. dollar in 2007 was 2 real. The key shows 1 bill as being equal to 1 real. The symbols for 2007 show almost 2 bills, or 2 real. One real and 1.5 real are too few, and 2.5 real is too many.

3. B, The value of the dollar decreased between 2007 and 2011 because fewer real were needed to equal one dollar. The value of the real did not change dramatically from year to year. The value of the real increased between 2007 and 2011 based on the fact that fewer real were needed to equal one dollar.

4. A, The corn symbols each represent $1 million, and Iowa has eleven solid corn symbols and part of another one. Therefore, you can determine that the value of corn production in Iowa in 2010 exceeded $11 million.

5. D, Look closely at the states listed on the pictograph. These are the top corn producing states in the United States. All of the states are in the Midwest. Therefore, you can conclude that the Midwest grows most of the corn produced in the United States.

6. A, About 20 million people work in Wholesale Trade and Retail Trade combined.

7. B, 9 3/4 symbols would appear next to state and local government. Each symbol on the pictograph represents 2 million employees. 19.5 million employees divided by 2 million per symbol is 9 3/4 symbols.

8. D, The key for the pictograph would need to change to reflect thousands of employees, rather than 2 million employees, since the number of federal employees does not nearly reach 2 million. For a pictograph to be effective, its key needs to accurately depict what is portrayed.

9. D, In 2004, the U.S. government ran a larger deficit than it did in 2002. In 2004, there was a deficit of about $250 billion; in 2002, there was a deficit of just over $150 billion. The government spent about $250 billion more than it made in 2004.

10. C, Funding for the war in Iraq could help explain the budgetary changes between 2000 and 2004. There was a budget surplus in 2000 and a budget deficit in 2004, so the government began spending more money than it had

11. D, The deficit increased the most between 2008 and 2010, by about $835 billion.

12. B, The price increased from 2009 to 2010. An increase in price is due to an increase in demand, which correlates to a decrease in supply. A shortened growing season leads to decreased supply, increased demand, and higher prices.

13. C, Farmers would have received a subsidy in 2009 if the minimum guaranteed price had been $9.65. Only in 2009 was the market price below $9.65. In every other year, it was higher than $9.65.

14. A, The U.S. unemployment rate experienced one sharp increase in this 10-year period. Between 2000 and 2006, it fluctuated around 5%. In 2008, it increased slightly, but by 2010, it was significantly higher.

15. D, The U.S. economy experienced a downturn between 2008 and 2010 based on the unemployment rate. When the unemployment rate jumps significantly higher, this is an indication that the economy is experiencing a downturn. A lower unemployment rate indicates a stronger economy.

16. B, The U.S. economy experienced an upturn between 2004 and 2006 based on the slight decrease in the unemployment rate. A lower unemployment rate indicates a stronger economy.

17. C, The value of U.S. exports to Japan doubled between 1985 and 2005. In 1985, the value of exports was about $25 billion. In 2005, the value of exports was about $50 billion.

18. D, Using the key, you can determine that in 2005, the trade deficit was more than $80 billion.

19. A, Using the key, you can determine that the U.S. trade deficit grew by about $40 billion. The trade deficit was about $50 billion in 1985 and about $90 billion in 2005.

20. D, The government could change the nation's trade balance with Japan by providing tax relief to U.S. companies that manufacture technology products. This would enable these companies to more easily produce technology products on par with Japan and offer them at lower prices. Americans would be more likely to purchase American-made technology products if they cost less than those from Japan.

LESSON 8, *pp. 223–227*

1. B, Based on the bar graphs, the only correct statement among the answer options is B: The average prime interest rate in 2008 was about 6 percent.

2. C, The value of M2 will always be greater than that of M1 because M2 includes all of M1, in addition to other items.

3. B, The approximate value of M1 in 2010 was $200 billion. The point on the graph is higher than $100 billion and lower than both $300 billion and $400 billion.

4. D, Liquidity is measured in how easily items can be turned into cash. The M1 value contains the most liquid assets, so the economy had the most liquidity when the M1 value was the highest. It was the highest in 2010.

5. B, According to the graph, in nearly every age group, the percentage of employees telecommuting is about the same as the percentage of all federal employees in that age group.

6. D, Locate the black bar for 2006 and follow across to the left to determine that the U.S. government received about $2,500 billion in 2006.

7. C, The budgetary results show that the government was spending more money than it was bringing in.

8. A, The U.S. government showed the largest budget deficit in 2009, when expenditures topped revenue by $1,088 billion.

9. C, 2005 is the first year shown on the graph that the United States' revenue exceeded $2,000 billion.

10. B, The prime rate reached its lowest point between 1990 and 1999 at the beginning of Year 4, or 1993.

11. A, The prime rate decreased dramatically between 2000 and 2003. It was more than 9% in 2000 and dropped to just over 4% by 2003.

12. D, A preferred borrower would have received the best prime rate in 2009. At that time, the prime rate for banks was the lowest. Banks will offer the lowest prime rates to their customers when their prime rates are also low.

13. D, In the 1990s, the prime rate was often above 8%, whereas in the 2000s, it dipped below 5% in several years.

14. B, The height of the bar indicates that the approximate value of gross private domestic investment in 2010 was $1,750 billion.

15. C, A negative balance of trade between the United States and other nations most likely accounts for the value of net export of goods and services shown on the graph. The negative values are all in the category Net Export of Goods and Services, which is the category under which a negative trade balance between the United States and other nations falls.

16. A, As shown on the graph, the value of personal consumption expenditures increased each year, not decreased.

LESSON 9, *pp. 228–232*

1. C, For this question, you must decide which country produced the greatest number of people with engineering degrees, yet had the lowest annual salaries. According to the graphs, you can predict that a U.S. corporation could find the best combination of highly trained yet affordable prospective employees in China.

2. B, Because telecommuters would be working separately from other employees, they would have the most difficulty participating in team building exercises.

3. C, Because the number of telecommuters increased dramatically between 1990 and 1997, you can predict that the number of telecommuters continued to increase in the years after 1997.

UNIT 5 (continued)

4. C, If the U.S. automakers had been allowed to fail, then fewer cars would be made in the U.S. and more cars would have to be imported, which would have a negative impact on U.S exports.

5. B, The first column on the table describes occupational groups, and the second column lists the number of work-at-home workers in each of those occupational groups, in thousands. Therefore, the occupational group with approximately 600,000 people receiving pay for work done at home was the office and administrative support group (595,000).

6. D, Drawing upon your knowledge of careers, you can assume that a brickmason would be grouped within the category of construction and extraction. An information security analyst works with securing technological information and would be grouped with computer, engineering, and science occupations. While both occupational categories are expected to grow, a brickmason is much less likely to be able to work from home because the work requires going to a specific construction or building site. An information security analyst is more likely to be able to work from home using a computer and other technology.

7. D, The information states that Eddie is taking night classes to become a certified auto mechanic. Therefore, you can predict that if Eddie were to gain his certification, he might be able to get a higher paying job, so his wages would be most likely to increase next year.

8. B, While each answer option would affect Eddie's budget, if a state like North Dakota had an extremely long and harsh winter, then Eddie's utility bills would increase dramatically, thus causing the greatest disruption to his existing budget.

9. B, The second underlined sentence explains that Lieberman predicts the service industry will lose many jobs to offshore outsourcing.

10. C, Lieberman believes that American businesses must become better at adapting to changes in the global economy to become more competitive. He points to a loss of innovation and failure to address competition from other countries.

11. D, To determine the correct answer, you need to determine an answer choice that would cut costs and be logical. While NFL teams could earn more revenue by raising ticket prices, an increase may cause more fans to stay home and watch the games on television. The most logical choice is that the leagues will lay off office and administrative employees.

12. C, Professional sports are affected by economic conditions because they are seen as entertainment, a luxury that people could do without if they had to. Also, they rely heavily on corporate sponsorships. To answer this question, you must determine which of the answer choices can also be seen as a luxury and relies on corporate sponsorships. The best choice is city music or theater groups, such as a performing arts organization or a symphony.

13. A, The dollar amounts above the arrows on the map show how much money U.S. corporations invest in foreign nations.

According to the data, U.S. corporations invested nearly $5 billion dollars for research and development in Asia.

14. C, The map shows that U.S. corporations invest in research and development all around the world. Therefore, you can predict that they will continue to seek out global sources of research and development.

15. C, U.S. corporations are more likely to invest in service industries (such as call centers and customer service) in places where people speak English but earn less money than workers in the United States. European wages are probably similar to American wages. The best prediction is Asia. Because of British imperialism, many Asians, especially in India, speak fluent English. That continent best fits the criteria for service industry investment.

16. D, According to the data on the map, U.S. corporations made their largest investment in Europe, spending $18.15 billion dollars.

UNIT 5 REVIEW, pp. 233–237

1. C, The economic crisis in 1991 caused India to institute significant economic reforms.

2. A, India's railway industry is controlled by the government. In the United States, the government controls primary and secondary education through local school districts.

3. C, Socialism is an economic system in which the government controls some aspects of the economy deemed vital to the nation. In India, socialism is represented by the government's control of nuclear power.

4. A, Only choice A would guarantee a reduction because it would produce a surplus specifically for reducing debt. Although new legislation aimed at economic stimulation might help the overall economy, this would not directly address national debt.

5. D, This pictograph can be tricky. The gray circles represent $100 billion whereas the red blocks represent $1 trillion. By analyzing the pictograph carefully, you can determine that the national debt level has continued to rise since 1970.

6. B, An increase in the number of wildfires and a decrease in citrus production can both be linked to a nationwide drought.

7. C, The information states that if the people's purchasing power is weakened, an economic depression can get worse. When a depression increases, the Gross Domestic Product (GDP) can decrease. When examining the Real GDP in the table, you can see that it decreases in the early years of the 1930s. Therefore, you can conclude that the purchasing power of U.S. consumers grew increasingly weak during the early 1930s.

8. D, Remember that World War II began in Europe in 1939 and the U.S. supplied European allies with goods, therefore increasing demand. This would only increase when the United States entered the war. An increased demand for industrial goods would lead to a decrease in unemployment.

9. A, To make an accurate comparison, historians and economists often list economic figures in current value. They are adjusting for inflation.

10. C, Labor is another word for work, so the work of the lawnmower company's employees would be considered labor.

11. D, An entrepreneur is someone who displays the willingness to start one's own business.

12. B, According to the flowchart, firms generate revenue (earn money) by selling goods and services to people in households.

13. B, All four corners of the flowchart show examples of how all transactions between firms and households contribute to the nation's GDP.

14. C, The period from 2011 to 2015 would likely feature little change in GDP and per capita income for each state based on the charts.

15. D, You can conclude that Connecticut has a smaller population than Ohio. *Per capita* means "per person," so the second graph takes the entire income of each state and divides it by the population of the state. The first graph shows that Ohio has a much higher GDP than Connecticut, but in the second graph, Connecticut has a much higher per capita income. Therefore, you can conclude that Connecticut has a smaller population than Ohio.

16. A, The multi-line graph takes the population of each state into account when measuring data. That is why it is called "per capita income by state." The multi-bar graph does not take the state's population into account.

17. C, A $50.00 check to open a new checking account is a positive incentive. The bank rewards you with $50.00 for bringing your business to it.

Index

Note: Page numbers in **boldface** indicate definitions or main discussion with examples. Page numbers in *italic* indicate a visual representation. Page ranges indicate practice.

INDEX

INDEX

F

Fact and opinion, **161**, *162–165*
Factors of production, **236**
Family life in ancient Egypt, 99
Fascism, **135**, 167
Faulty logic or reasoning, **165**
FDIC, 217
Federal budget, **225**
Federal employees, age distribution, *224*
Federal government, **135**, *137*
Federal Republic of Yugoslavia, 124
Federal reserve districts, *156*
Federal Reserve System, **187**
Federal Reserve ("The Fed"), 224, 226
Federal withholding deduction, *212*
The Federalist Papers: No. 2 (Jay), 51
The Federalist Papers: No. 69 (Hamilton), 178
Federalists, 39, *50*, 92
Ferdinand, Archduke, *133*
Feudalism, 97, *106*
FICA, *212*
Fifteenth Amendment to U.S. Constitution, 67, *69*
Financial system, 151
First Amendment, 180
Flappers, *79*
Flinders, Matthew, 114
Florida's secession, *62*
Flowcharts, 198, *236*
Ford, Gerald R., *91*
Ford Motor Company, 229
Foreclosures, *207*
Foreign policy, **135**, 171
Fort Sumter, 63
401(k), *212*
Fourteenth Amendment, *69*
France
  African colonies of, *117*
  fall to Germany, *121*
  in League of Nations, *79*
  taxes in, *191*
  World War II, *119*
Franklin, Benjamin, 46
Free and slave states, *62*, 94
Free-market economy, **187**, 191, 192, 201
Free trade, **187**, 190
Friedland, Battle of, *36*
Fulbright, William, 177

G

Gadsden Purchase, *24*
Galápagos Islands, 3

Gandhi, Mohandas K., *122*
Gasoline prices, *206*
GDP (gross domestic product), **187**, 213, *227, 235*
General Motors, 229
Generalization, **123**, *124–127*
Generalizing, **165**
Geography, 1
  defined, **2**
  history related to, **27**, *28–31*
  importance of, xviii
  understanding, **2**, *3–6*
  See also **Topics in Unit 1 on pages xviii-36**
Georgia, *8*, 62
Georgia colony, *41, 49,* 51
German imperialism, 4
German-Soviet nonaggression pact, *119*
Germany
  African colonies of, *117*
  alliance with Italy, *119*
  attacks on Britain and France, *119*
  German-Soviet nonaggression pact, *119*
  Hitler's rise to power, *118*
  invasions prior to World War II, *119*
  in League of Nations, *79*
  reunification of, 123
  taxes in, *191*
  Treaty of Versailles, 133
  World War II, *121*
Gettysburg Address (Lincoln), 63
Gettysburg, Battle of, *28*
Ghent, Treaty of, *56*
Ginsburg, Ruth Bader, *148*
Glasnost, **97**, 125
Global economic statistics, 197
Globe, 1, 2
Goods, 187
  communists' view of, 190
  conspicuous goods, 196
  consumption of, 193, 196, 197
  effect of inflation on, 203
  flow through economy, *236*
  importing and exporting of, 222, 227
  as incentives, 237
  interdependence of countries for, 218
  production of, 192, 198, 201
  See also **Gross domestic product (GDP)**
Goods and services, *236*
Gorbachev, Mikhail, 89, 125, 126
Gore, Al, 149, 164
Gothic architecture, **97**, *104*
Government
  of Alexandria, Virginia, 137
  fascism, **135**, 167

  federal and state powers, *137*
  government of Greek city-states, 98
  importance of, 134
  local government, 150
  oligarchy, 98
  of Roman Republic, 101
  of South Africa, 169
  in South America and Africa, 161
  of state government, *137*
  transition from communism to democracy, 126, 127
  of the United States, *48, 49,* **135**, *137, 145*
  See also **Topic in Unit 4 on pages 134-185**
Government bonds, *217*
Graphs
  circle graphs, *213*
  interpreting, **70**, 234
  interpreting multi-bar and line graphs, **223**, *224–227, 234, 237*
  interpreting pictographs, **218**, *219–222*
Great Britain
  American Revolution, 46, 60
  conflict in India, 122
  East India Company, 115, 130
  exploration from, *114, 115,* 129
  Great Trigonometrical Survey of India, 113
  immigration to U.S. from, *71*
  imperialism in Africa, 4, 116, *117*, 133
  in League of Nations, *79*
  Magna Carta, 108
  taxes in, *191*
  War of 1812, *56*
  war with Spain, 51
  World War II, *119, 121*
  See also **British colonies in North America; Colonies**
Great Depression, *82, 83, 84,* 155, 189
Great Lakes, *13*
Great Lakes states, *157*
Great Migration, *35*
Great Recession (2008-2009), 189, 231
Great Society, **39**, *88,* 93
Great Trigonometrical Survey of India (1700s), 113
Greece
  arts and crafts in ancient times, 102
  culture of, 131
  government of city-states, 98
  Peloponnesian War, 99
Greek mythology, 131
Gross domestic product (GDP), **187**, 213, *227, 235, 237*
Gross pay, *212*
Gruening, Ernest, 177
Guadalcanal, Battle of, *121*

INDEX

INDEX

Y